Enterprise OSGi in Action

Enterprise OSGi
in Action

WITH EXAMPLES USING APACHE ARIES

HOLLY CUMMINS
TIMOTHY WARD

MANNING
SHELTER ISLAND

For online information and ordering of this and other Manning books, please visit
www.manning.com. The publisher offers discounts on this book when ordered in quantity.
For more information, please contact

    Special Sales Department
    Manning Publications Co.
    20 Baldwin Road
    PO Box 261
    Shelter Island, NY 11964
    Email: orders@manning.com

Manning Publications Co.
20 Baldwin Road
PO Box 261
Shelter Island, NY 11964

Development editors: Sebastian Stirling, Frank Pohlmann
Technical proofreader: Mark Nuttall
Copyeditor: Benjamin Berg
Proofreader: Katie Tennant
Typesetter: Gordan Salinovic
Cover designer: Marija Tudor

ISBN 9781617290138
Printed in the United States of America
1 2 3 4 5 6 7 8 9 10 – MAL – 18 17 16 15 14 13

brief contents

contents

CONTENTS

PART 3 INTEGRATING ENTERPRISE OSGi WITH EVERYTHING ELSE 239

10 *Hooking up remote systems with distributed OSGi 241*

10.1 The principles of remoting 242

The benefits of remoting 242 ▪ The drawbacks of remoting 246 Good practices and the fallacies of remoting 249

10.2 The Remote Services Specification 249

Exposing endpoints 250 ▪ Discovering endpoints 251

10.3 Writing a remotable service 251

Coding a special offer service 252

10.4 Adding in your remote service using Apache CXF 254

Making your service available 254 ▪ Discovering remote services from your superstore 256

10.5 Using your remote application 259

Setting up your remote database connections 260

10.6 Using SCA for remoting 263

Apache Tuscany 263 ▪ Importing a remote service 264 Exporting remote services 267 ▪ Interfaces and services 267

10.7 Summary 268

11 *Migration and integration 270*

11.1 Managing heterogeneous applications 271

Using SCA to integrate heterogeneous systems 271 ▪ Integrating using an ESB 274

11.2 Migrating from Java EE 276

Moving from WARs to WABs 276 ▪ Using persistence bundles 280 EJBs in OSGi 283 ▪ Moving to Blueprint from the Spring Framework 286

11.3 Summary 289

12 *Coping with the non-OSGi world 291*

12.1 Turning normal JARs into OSGi bundles 292

Finding bundled libraries 292 ▪ Building your own bundles 294 ▪ Generating bundles automatically 296

preface

I first used Java EE many years ago, in 2002. (Yes, Stateless Session Beans and Passivated Entity Beans, stop hiding at the back—I'm talking to you.) I can't remember when I started using OSGi, but it was also a long time ago. Nonetheless, until recently, I'd never used the two technologies at the same time. If I was writing a desktop application or an application server (as one does), I used OSGi. If I was writing a web application, I used Java EE.

But OSGi seemed the most natural way to develop a working system. When I was writing Java EE applications, the thought of leaving my dependencies to chance or exposing all the internals of my JARs made me pretty uneasy. It felt downright icky. What if classes I needed weren't on the classpath when my application was deployed? What if the classes I needed were there, but the version was incompatible with the one I used when I was developing? What if a colleague coded against one of my internal classes, and then I refactored and deleted it? What if I accidentally coded against the internals of a library I was using? And wasn't there a cleaner way to get hold of interface implementations than the reflective factory pattern? Applications might work in the short term, but it felt like an accident waiting to happen.

For a long time, Java EE developers didn't have much choice except to close their eyes, hold tight, and wait for the accident. It's not that they didn't want to use OSGi—they couldn't. OSGi didn't play well with the Java EE programming model. OSGi's tightly modularized classpath wasn't compatible with the discovery mechanism for Java EE services, which assumed global visibility. Similarly, many of the Java EE implementations relied on classloading tricks to do their work, and these tricks failed miserably in the more controlled OSGi environment.

In 2009, I heard Zoe Slattery give a talk on a new Apache incubator, Apache Aries. Aries promised to allow Java EE technologies to work in an OSGi environment. It wasn't reinventing the Java EE wheel, just allowing Java EE developers to take advantage of OSGi. I thought it was cool—and desperately needed. A few months later, I was signed up to help develop Aries and the IBM WebSphere feature pack built on top of it.

As well as developing Aries itself, I was speaking at conferences about enterprise OSGi. Manning contacted me and asked me if I'd be interested in writing a book on the subject. I was excited by the idea, but scared—after all, there were lots of people who'd been working with enterprise OSGi for much longer than I had. What I did have was insight into what people learning enterprise OSGi needed to know. After all, I'd had lots of the same questions and made lots of the same mistakes myself pretty recently.

But it was clear that reinforcements would be required. This is where Tim Ward came in. Tim is one of the brightest guys I know, and I was delighted when he said he was interested in the book. Tim was one of the first developers to prototype the early implementations of the OSGi Enterprise Specifications, and he's been working with enterprise OSGi ever since. Even better, he's coauthored some of the specifications. There isn't much about enterprise OSGi that Tim doesn't know. Although my name is first on the cover (thank you, alphabet!) this book is authored by both of us equally.

Writing this book has been a great adventure. We hope you enjoy it and find it useful, and we'd love to hear from you on the Manning Author Online forum.

HOLLY CUMMINS

acknowledgments

Where do we even start in thanking all the people who made this book possible? You fed us, encouraged us, and taught us. Going back to the beginning, this project wouldn't even have gotten off the ground without the good folks at Manning. Thanks to Marjan Bace, our publisher, Michael Stephens, our editor, and Sebastian Stirling and Frank Pohlmann, our development editors. You helped us figure out what makes a good book and guided, coaxed, and nudged us in the right direction. Thanks also to Christina Rudloff and Nick Chase.

The quality of this book has been hugely improved by the detailed comments we received from our reviewers. We really appreciate you taking the time to read our efforts and tell us what we got right and wrong. Thanks to Alasdair Nottingham, Andrew Johnson, Charles Moulliard, David Bosschaert, Felix Meschberger, John W. Ross, Kevin Sheehan, Kin Chuen, Tang, Marcel Offermans, Mirko Jahn, Paul Flory, Pierre De Rop, Teemu Kanstrén, and Tim Diekmann.

Thanks also to everyone who participated in the Manning Early Access Program. Special thanks to our technical proofer, Mark Nuttall, who went over the book several times with an eagle eye, and was patient with silly mistakes and last-minute improvements.

We couldn't have written this book without the help of our colleagues at IBM. Thank you, Ian Robinson. Without your vision and commitment, it's likely that neither of us would have had the opportunity to work so closely with enterprise OSGi. Thanks to Andy Gatford and Nickie Hills for supporting us. We'd like to thank Jeremy Hughes, Alasdair Nottingham, Graham Charters, Zoe Slattery, Valentin Mahrwald, Emily Jiang, Tim Mitchell, Chris Wilkinson, Richard Ellis, Duane Appleby, and Erin Schnabel for the many valuable discussions we shared with them.

We borrowed the phrase "bundle flake" from Alex Mulholland, who deserves credit for bringing the fun back into debugging OSGi fragments. We'd also like to give special mention to Sarah Burwood, who possibly didn't realize what she'd signed up for when she offered to review the book as an OSGi beginner! We've learned loads from all of you, so thank you.

In addition to our IBM colleagues, we thank the members of the OSGi Alliance Expert Groups and Apache Aries. You put up with our ideas and questions and built the enterprise OSGi programming model with us, many of you donating your time to do so. There are too many names to even begin to list here, but particular thanks are deserved by Peter Kriens and David Bosschaert, both for direct help with the book and for their years of support building the OSGi Enterprise Specifications.

On a personal level, we're indebted to our partners, Paul and Ruth, who picked up a great deal of domestic slack, as well as provided apparently limitless encouragement and support. At the times when this book didn't seem possible, you persuaded us it was (and then fed us a snack). Holly would like to apologize to Paul for the six application servers and four IDEs now installed on his laptop; everyone knows not to let software engineers touch one's computer! Tim would like to apologize to Ruth for all the times that "I just need to finish this paragraph" took rather longer than the implied five minutes; it turns out that writing prose is more like writing code than you might think...

Tim would like to thank the rest of his immediate family, Pauline, Gareth, Ron, Eve, Sarah, and Maurice, for their interest and their unwavering belief that not only would the book eventually be finished, but that it would also be worth reading. He also thanks them for helping him "remember to bring the funny." He's sure many of the readers will want to thank them for that, too.

Holly would also like to thank her mom, dad, John, Ioana, Heather, and Phil for helping her find the time and space for writing. Acknowledgment is also owed to Laurie Hodkinson, who has spent many hours helping write this book, and occasionally throwing up on the keyboard. Holly has every expectation that his first word will be "OSGi."

As with many books, some of the people and things that helped make it possible probably aren't even aware of their contribution. The writing of this book was fueled by coffee—lots of coffee—and cheese. Holly would like to thank the makers of her Beco Gemini baby carrier, which is essentially a concurrency framework for infants. Tim would like to thank the makers of his Vi-Spring mattress, which is essentially the cure to hunching over a laptop all day.

Finally, our thanks wouldn't be complete without thanking you, the readers, for buying our book. We hope that you enjoy it, and that maybe you'll end up liking OSGi just as much as we do.

about this book

This is a book about the enterprise OSGi programming model, and it's also a book about using OSGi in the enterprise. It shows you how to combine OSGi's elegant, modular, service-oriented approach with Java EE's well-established persistence, transaction, and web technologies. It guides you through the cases when your project has lots of bits spread all over the network, some new, some old, some that you don't even recognize, and many that you didn't write yourself. It's packed with tips on how to use OSGi in the messy real world, with guidance on tools, building, testing, and integrating with non-OSGi systems and libraries.

Audience

Three groups of developers should find this book interesting. The first is developers who know Java EE, but who want to bring more modularity to their applications by learning OSGi. The second is those who know OSGi, but want to learn how to take advantage of some of Java EE's higher-level programming models. The last is developers who are familiar with both Java EE and OSGi, but who never knew the two could be combined! We don't assume knowledge of either Java EE or OSGi, but familiarity with at least one of them will help.

Roadmap

This book is divided into three parts. Part 1 introduces the most important enterprise OSGi technologies: web applications, JNDI lookups of OSGi services, Blueprint dependency injection, JPA persistence, declarative transactions, and application packaging.

Part 2 explains how to use these building blocks most effectively with best practices, tools, and a deeper understanding of some subtle areas. Part 3 considers how enterprise OSGi fits in with your existing applications and systems. It covers distribution technologies, migration tips and traps, and server options.

The appendixes provide important OSGi background. If you're new to OSGi, you may want to skip to the appendixes after reading chapter 1.

Chapter 1 explains what OSGi is, why it's such an exciting technology, and why it's so relevant to the enterprise.

Chapter 2 lets you get your hands dirty with real code. It introduces the OSGi sandbox you'll use to run the samples. You'll write an OSGi web application and hook it up to backend OSGi services. You'll use JNDI to connect OSGi services to legacy code, and Blueprint dependency injection to wire together the services.

Chapter 3 introduces JPA persistence and JTA transactions, and shows how to use them in an OSGi environment.

Chapter 4 shows how to group OSGi bundles together into coarser-grained applications.

In part 2, chapter 5 steps back from new technologies and discusses best practices for writing enterprise OSGi applications. It explains how to structure your applications, introduces some new OSGi-centric patterns, and discusses which familiar patterns may not be such a great idea in an OSGi environment.

Chapter 6 investigates OSGi dynamism and Blueprint dependency injection in more depth.

Chapter 7 discusses how to use OBR to dynamically provision application dependencies.

Chapter 8 introduces a range of command-line tools for generating OSGi manifests and building bundles. It also considers how to test OSGi bundles.

Chapter 9 continues the discussion of useful tools by comparing several IDEs that support OSGi.

In part 3, chapter 10 explains how to use distributed OSGi to allow OSGi services to be published and consumed across remote systems.

Chapter 11 discusses your options for migrating non-OSGi legacy code to OSGi. It also discusses technologies for integrating OSGi applications with the non-OSGi legacy code you haven't yet migrated!

Chapter 12 sets out strategies for handling non-OSGi libraries. It shows how to turn ordinary JARs into bundles and explains how to deal with common problems, such as classloading and logging issues.

Finally, chapter 13 compares the various commercial and open source OSGi runtimes and gives guidance on how you should choose a stack that's right for you.

Appendix A covers the basics of OSGi. It explains why OSGi is such a necessary technology, and provides grounding in versioning, bundles, bundle lifecycles, and OSGi services. It includes some practical hints on OSGi frameworks and consoles.

Appendix B describes the broader OSGi ecosystem. It explains how the OSGi alliance works and what's in the various OSGi specifications.

Code downloads

You can download the sample code for this book via a link found on the book's homepage on the Manning website, www.manning.com/EnterpriseOSGiinAction. The SourceCodeEnterpriseOSGiinAction.zip archive includes source code for an application with a web frontend and a JPA backend, as well as distributed variations. There's a Maven build that produces bundles and a .eba application that can be installed into an OSGi framework. See section 2.1.2 for instructions on how to assemble a runtime environment in which to run the application.

Author Online

The purchase of *Enterprise OSGi in Action* includes free access to a forum run by Manning Publications where you can make comments about the book, ask technical questions, and receive help from the authors and other users. You can access and subscribe to the forum at www.manning.com/EnterpriseOSGiinAction. This page provides information on how to get on the forum once you've registered, what kind of help is available, and the rules of conduct in the forum.

Manning's commitment to our readers is to provide a venue where a meaningful dialog between individual readers, and between readers and the authors, can take place. It isn't a commitment to any specific amount of participation on the part of the authors, whose contributions to the book's forum remain voluntary (and unpaid). We suggest you try asking the authors some challenging questions, lest their interest stray!

The Author Online forum and the archives of previous discussions will be accessible from the publisher's website as long as the book is in print.

about the authors

HOLLY CUMMINS has been developing Java applications for a decade. She is an advisory software engineer with IBM, where she has worked on the development of the WebSphere Application Server and on Java performance. She is also a committer on the Apache Aries project and speaks widely at conferences.

TIM WARD is a senior software engineer at Zühlke Engineering. Previously, he was a design and development lead for IBM's OSGi Applications support in WebSphere. He's on the OSGi Alliance Core Platform and Enterprise Expert Groups and is a member of the Project Management Committee for the Apache Aries project.

about the cover illustration

The figure on the cover of *Enterprise OSGi in Action* is captioned a "Man from Slovania." This illustration is taken from a recent reprint of Balthasar Hacquet's *Images and Descriptions of Southwestern and Eastern Wenda, Illyrians, and Slavs*, published by the Ethnographic Museum in Split, Croatia, in 2008. Hacquet (1739–1815) was an Austrian physician and scientist who spent many years studying the botany, geology, and ethnography of many parts of the Austrian Empire, as well as the Veneto, the Julian Alps, and the western Balkans, inhabited in the past by peoples of many different tribes and nationalities. Hand-drawn illustrations accompany the many scientific papers and books that Hacquet published.

Slavonia is a historical region in eastern Croatia. Part of the Roman Empire until the fifth century, then part of Pannonian Croatia, subsequently ruled by Hungary, the Ottomans, and the Hapsburgs, Slavonia was briefly an independent entity until it became a part of Yugoslavia after World War II. Today Slavonia encompasses five counties in inland Croatia with a population of almost one million inhabitants.

The rich diversity of the drawings in Hacquet's publications speaks vividly of the uniqueness and individuality of Alpine and Balkan regions just 200 years ago. This was a time when the dress codes of two villages separated by a few miles identified people uniquely as belonging to one or the other, and when members of an ethnic tribe, social class, or trade could be easily distinguished by what they were wearing. Dress codes have changed since then and the diversity by region, so rich at the time, has faded away. It is now often hard to tell the inhabitant of one continent from another and the residents of the picturesque towns and villages in the Balkans are not readily distinguishable from people who live in other parts of the world.

We at Manning celebrate the inventiveness, the initiative, and the fun of the computer business with book covers based on costumes from two centuries ago brought back to life by illustrations such as this one.

Part 1

Programming beyond Hello World

Welcome to enterprise OSGi! In this first part, you'll get a feel for the modularity of OSGi bundles, programming web applications, accessing data in a database, controlling the flow of transactions, and packaging bundles into a single unit.

Chapter 1 starts off gently by introducing OSGi and explaining why modularity—which is what OSGi provides—is so important.

If you're itching to get coding, don't worry. Chapter 2 shows you how to develop your first enterprise OSGi application. You'll write a modular web application and connect it to OSGi services using JNDI and Blueprint dependency injection.

Having mastered the frontend, what about the backend? Chapter 3 shows you how to use JPA persistence and JTA transactions in an OSGi environment.

Chapter 4 discusses how to package OSGi bundles together into OSGi applications.

By the time you've finished reading this part, you'll be able to write your own enterprise OSGi application, with a web frontend and a transactional database backend. It will be loosely coupled and nicely modularized. And best of all—writing it will be easy!

OSGi and the enterprise—why now?

This chapter covers

- Why modularity is important, and how Java stacks up
- How OSGi enforces some simple rules to make Java better at modularity
- Why enterprise Java and OSGi traditionally don't play well together
- How enterprise OSGi fixes this, and what the enterprise OSGi programming model looks like

Enterprise OSGi combines two of Java's most enduringly popular programming models: enterprise Java and OSGi. Enterprise Java is a loosely defined set of libraries, APIs, and frameworks built on top of core Java that turn it into a powerful platform for distributed, transactional, interactive, and persistent applications. Enterprise Java has been hugely successful, but as the scale and complexity of enterprise Java applications have grown, they've started to look creaky, bloated, and monolithic. OSGi applications, on the other hand, tend to be compact, modular,

3

and maintainable. But the OSGi programming model is pretty low-level. It doesn't have much to say about transactions, persistence, or web pages, all of which are essential underpinnings for many modern Java programs. What about a combination, something with the best features of both enterprise Java and OSGi? Such a programming model would enable applications that are modular, maintainable, and take advantage of industry standard enterprise Java libraries. Until recently, this combination was almost impossible, because enterprise Java and OSGi didn't work together. Now they do, and we hope you'll agree with us that the merger is pretty exciting.

We'll start by taking a look at what modularity is, and why it's so important in software engineering.

1.1   Java's missing modularity

When it was first introduced, in 1995, Java technology represented an enormous leap forward in software engineering. Compared to what had gone before, Java allowed more encapsulation, more abstraction, more modularity, and more dynamism.

A decade later, some gaps were beginning to show. In particular, the development community was desperate for more encapsulation, more abstraction, more modularity, and more dynamism. Java's *flat classpath* structure wasn't scaling well for the massive applications it was now being used for. Developers found that, when deployed, their applications picked up a bunch of classes from the classpath that they didn't want, but were missing some classes that they needed. In figure 1.1, you can see an example of a typical Java classpath.

It was impossible to keep component internals private, which led to constant arguments between developers (angry that the function they relied on had been changed) and their counterparts, who were annoyed that developers had been coding against things that were intended to be private. After 10 years of continuous development, there was an urgent need to be able to label the many iterations of Java code that were out there with some sort of versioning scheme. Core Java was starting to feel pretty tightly coupled and undynamic.

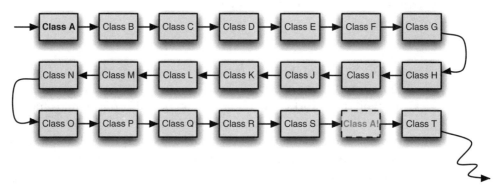

Figure 1.1   Conventional Java has a flat classpath which is searched in a linear order. For large applications, this classpath can be long, and searches can be time consuming. If a class occurs more than once on the classpath, only the first instance is used—even if the second copy is better.

Doesn't Java's object orientation enable modularity? Well, yes and no. Java does a great job of providing modularity at the class and package level. Methods and class variables can be declared public, or access can be restricted to the owning class, its descendants, or members of its package. Beyond this, there's little facility for modularity. Classes may be packaged together in a Java Archive (JAR), but the JAR provides no encapsulation. Every class inside the JAR is externally accessible, no matter how internal its intended use.

One of the reasons modularity has become increasingly necessary is the scale of modern computer programs. They're developed by globally dispersed teams and can occupy several gigabytes of disk space. In this kind of environment, it's critical that code can be grouped into distinct modules, with clearly delineated areas of responsibility and well-defined interfaces between modules.

Another significant change to software engineering within the last decade is the emergence of *open source*. Almost every software need can now be satisfied by open source. There are large-scale products, such as application servers, IDEs, databases, and messaging engines. A bewildering range of open source projects that address particular development needs, from Java bytecode generation to web presentation layers, is also available. Because the projects are open source, they can easily be reused by other software. As a result, most programs now rely on some open source libraries. Even commercial software often uses open source componentry; numerous GUI applications, for example, are based on the Eclipse Rich Client Platform, and many application servers incorporate the Apache Web Server.

The increasing scale of software engineering projects and the increasing availability of tempting open source libraries have made modularization essential. Stepping back, what exactly do we mean by modularity, and what problems does it fix?

1.1.1 Thinking about modularity

Modularity is one of the most important design goals in modern software engineering. It reduces effort spent duplicating function and improves the stability of software over time.

SPAGHETTI CODE

We've all heard code that's too coupled and interdependent described as *spaghetti code* (figure 1.2).

This sort of code is unfortunately common—both in open and closed source projects—and is universally despised. Not only is code like this hard to read and even harder to maintain, it's also difficult to make even slight changes to its structure or move it to a new system. Even a slight breeze can be enough to cause problems! Given how strongly people dislike this sort of code, it should be a lot less common than it is, but, sadly, in a world where nothing stops you from calling any other function, it's easy to write spaghetti by accident. The other problem with spaghetti is that, as soon as you have some, it tends to generate more quickly. . .

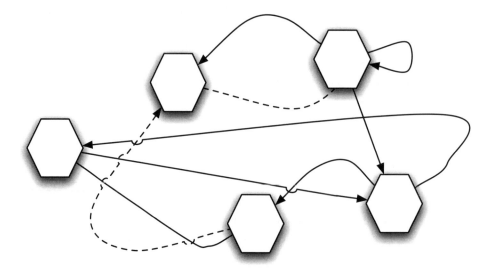

Figure 1.2   A highly interconnected spaghetti application with little structure. The solid lines represent dependencies that are identifiable at both compile-time and runtime, whereas the dotted lines are runtime-only dependencies. This sort of dependency graph is typical of procedural languages.

Object orientation marked a big shift in the development of programming languages, providing a strong level of encapsulation in them. Objects were responsible for maintaining their internal, private state, and could have internal, private methods. It was believed that this would mark the end of spaghetti code, and to an extent it did.

Extending the spaghetti metaphor, conventional Java programs (or any other object-oriented language, for that matter) can be thought of as *object minestrone* (figure 1.3)—

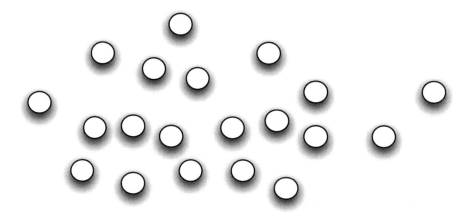

Figure 1.3   An application with no structure beyond individual well-encapsulated objects (connections between objects aren't shown). This sort of structure is typical of object-oriented languages. Although the objects themselves are highly modular, there's no more granular modularity.

although there's a distinct object structure (the chunks of vegetable and pasta), there's no structure beyond the individual objects. The objects are thrown together in a soup and every vegetable can see every other vegetable.

CLASSPATH HELL

Insufficient encapsulation isn't the only problem with Java's existing modularity. Few Java JARs are entirely freestanding; most will have dependencies on some other libraries or frameworks. Unfortunately, determining what these dependencies are is often a matter of trial and error. Inevitably, some dependencies may get left off the classpath when it's run. In the best case, this omission will be discovered early when a `ClassNot-FoundException` is thrown. In the worst case, the code path will be rarely traveled and the problem won't be discovered until weeks later when a `ClassNotFoundException` interrupts some particularly business-critical operation. Good documentation of dependencies can help here, but the only reliable way of ensuring every dependency is present is to package them all up in a single archive with the original JAR. This is inefficient and it's extra frustrating to have to do it for common dependencies.

What's worse, even packaging JARs with all the other JARs they depend on isn't guaranteed to make running an application a happy experience. What if a dependency is one of the common ones—so common that other applications running in the same JVM (Java Virtual Machine) depend on it? This is fine, as long as the required versions are the same. One copy will come first on the classpath and be loaded, and the other copy will be ignored. What happens when the required versions are different? One copy will still be loaded, and the other will still be ignored. One application will run with the version it expects, and the other won't. In some cases, the "losing" application may terminate with a `NoSuchMethodError` because it invokes methods that no longer exist. In other, worse cases, there will be no obvious exceptions but the application won't behave correctly. These issues are incredibly unpleasant and in Java have been given the rather self-explanatory name *classpath hell*.

Although classpath hell is a bad problem in core Java, it's even more pernicious in the enterprise Java domain.

1.1.2 *Enterprise Java and modularity—even worse!*

Enterprise Java and the Java EE programming model are used by a large number of developers; however, there are many Java developers who have no experience with either. Before we can explain why enterprise Java suffers even more greatly than standard Java, we need to make sure that we have a common understanding of what the enterprise is.

WHAT DISTINGUISHES ENTERPRISE JAVA FROM NORMAL EVERYDAY JAVA?

Part of the distinction is the involvement of the enterprise—enterprise Java is used to produce applications used by businesses. But then businesses use many other applications, like word processors and spreadsheets. You certainly wouldn't say that a word processor, no matter how business-oriented, had been produced to an enterprise programming model. Similarly, many "enterprise programmers" don't work for particularly large corporations.

What's different about enterprise applications? In general, they're designed to support multiple simultaneous users. With multiple users, some sort of remote access is usually required—having 50 users crammed into a single room isn't going to make anyone happy! Nowadays, remote access almost always means a web frontend.

To store the information associated with these users, enterprise applications usually persist data. Writing database access code isn't much fun, so persistence providers supply a nicer set of interfaces to manage the interaction between the application code and the database.

This is a business application, and so transactions are usually involved—either buying and selling of goods and services, or some other business agreements. To ensure these "real" transactions proceed smoothly and consistently, even in the event of a communications problem, software transactions are used.

With all this going on, these enterprise applications are starting to get pretty complex. They're not going to fit into a single Java class, or a single JAR file. It may not even be practical to run every part on a single server. Distribution allows the code, and therefore the work, to be spread across multiple servers on a network. Some people argue that distribution is *the* key feature of what's known as enterprise computing, and the other elements, like transactions and the web, are merely there to facilitate distribution (like the web) or to handle some of the consequences of distribution on networks which aren't necessarily reliable (such as transactions).

Java EE provides a fairly comprehensive set of standards designed to fit the scaling and distribution requirements of these enterprise applications, and is widely used throughout enterprise application development.

MODULAR JAVA EE—BIGGER ISN'T BETTER
Our enterprise application is now running across multiple servers, with a web frontend, a persistence component, and a transaction component. How all the pieces fit together may not be known by individual developers when they're writing their code. Which persistence provider will be used? What about the transaction provider? What if they change vendors next year? Java EE needs modularity for its applications even more than base Java does. Running on different servers means that the classpath, available dependencies, and technology implementations are likely to diverge. This becomes even more likely as the application is spread over more and more systems.

With these interconnected applications, it's much better for developers to avoid specifying where all their dependencies come from and how they're constructed. Otherwise the parts of the application become so closely coupled to one another that changing any of them becomes difficult. In the case of a little program, this close coupling would be called spaghetti code (see figure 1.2 again). In large applications, it's sometimes known as the *big ball of mud*. In any case, the pattern is equally awkward and the consequences can be just as severe.

Unfortunately for Java EE, there's no basic Java modularity to fall back on; the modules within a Java application often spaghettify between one another, and inevitably their open source library dependencies have to be packaged within the applications. To improve cost effectiveness, each server in a Java EE environment typically hosts multiple applications, each of which packages its own dependencies, and potentially requires a different implementation of a particular enterprise service. This is a clear recipe for classpath hell, but the situation is even worse than it first appears. The Java EE application servers themselves are large, complicated pieces of software, and even the best of them contain a little spaghetti. To reliably provide basic functions at low development cost, they also depend on open source libraries, many of the same libraries used by the applications that run on the application server! This is a serious problem, because now developers and systems administrators have no way to avoid the conflict. Even if all applications are written to use the same version of an open source library, they can still be broken by the different version (typically undocumented) in the underlying application server.

1.2 OSGi to the rescue

It turned out that a number of core Java's modularity problems had already quietly been solved by a nonprofit industry consortium known as the OSGi Alliance. The OSGi Alliance's original mission was to allow Java to be used in embedded and networked devices. It used core Java constructs such as classloaders and manifests to create a system with far more modularity than the core Java it's built on.

OSGi is a big subject. Entire books are dedicated to it—including this one! This section reviews the basics of OSGi at a high level, showing how OSGi solves some of the fundamental modularity problems in Java. We also delve into greater detail into some aspects of OSGi which may not be familiar to most readers, but which will be important to understand when we start writing enterprise OSGi applications. We explain the syntax we use for the diagrams later in the book. This section covers all the important facts for writing enterprise OSGi applications, but if you're new to OSGi, or if after reading it you're bursting to know even more about the core OSGi platform, you should read appendixes A and B. We can't cover all of OSGi in two appendixes, so we'd also definitely recommend you get hold of *OSGi in Action* by Richard Hall, Karl Pauls, Stuart McCulloch, and David Savage (Manning Publications, 2011).

In a sense, OSGi takes the Java programming model closer to an "ideal" programming model—one that's robust, powerful, and elegant. The way it does this is by encouraging good software engineering practice through higher levels of modularity. These, along with versioning, are the driving *principles* behind OSGi. OSGi enables abstraction, encapsulation, decomposition, loose coupling, and reuse.

1.2.1 Modularity, versioning, and compatibility

OSGi solves the problems of sections and in one fell swoop using an incredibly simple, but equally powerful, approach centered around declarative dependency management and strict versioning.

OSGI BUNDLES—MODULAR BUILDING BLOCKS

Bundles are *Java modules*. On one level, a bundle is an ordinary JAR file, with some extra headers and metadata in its JAR manifest. The OSGi runtime is usually referred to as the "OSGi framework," or sometimes "the framework," and is a container that manages the lifecycle and operation of OSGi bundles. Outside of an OSGi framework, a bundle behaves like any other JAR, with all the same disadvantages and no improvement to modularity. Inside an OSGi framework, a bundle behaves differently. The classes inside an OSGi bundle are able to use one another like any other JAR in standard Java, but the OSGi framework prevents classes inside a bundle from being able to access classes inside any other bundle unless they're explicitly allowed to do so. One way of thinking about this is that it acts like a new visibility modifier for classes, with a scope between protected and public, allowing the classes to be accessed only by other code packaged in the same JAR file.

Obviously, if JAR files weren't able to load any classes from one another they would be fairly useless, which is why in OSGi a bundle has the ability to deliberately expose packages outside itself for use by other bundles. The other half of the modularity statement is that, in order to make use of an "exported" package, a bundle must define an "import" for it. In combination, these imports and exports provide a strict definition of the classes that can be shared between OSGi bundles, but express it in an extremely simple way.

Listing 1.1   A simple bundle manifest that imports and exports packages

```
Manifest-Version: 1.0
Bundle-ManifestVersion: 2
Bundle-SymbolicName: fancyfoods.example
Bundle-Version: 1.0.0
Bundle-Name: Fancy Foods example manifest
Import-Package: fancyfoods.api.pkg;version="[1.0.0,2.0.0)"
Export-Package: fancyfoods.example.pkg;version="1.0.0"
```

Many more possible headers can be used in OSGi, a number of which are described in later chapters.

By strictly describing the links between modules, OSGi allows Java programs to be less like minestrone and more like a tray of cupcakes (figure 1.4). Each cupcake has an internal structure (cake, paper case, icing, and perhaps decorations), but is completely separate from the other cupcakes. Importantly, a chocolate cupcake can be removed and replaced with a lemon cupcake without affecting the whole tray. As you build relationships between OSGi bundles, this becomes like stacking the cupcakes on top of one another. Exporting a package provides a platform onto which an *import* can be added. As you build up a stack of cupcakes, the cupcakes in the higher layers will be resting on other cupcakes in lower levels, but these dependencies can be easily identified. This prevents you from accidentally removing the cupcake on the bottom and causing an avalanche!

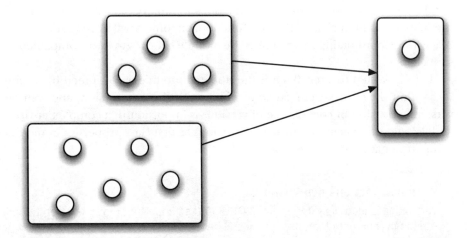

Figure 1.4   A well-structured application with objects grouped inside modules. Dependencies between modules are clearly identified. This is typical of the application structure that can be achieved with OSGi.

By enforcing a higher level granular structure on Java application code, OSGi bundles strongly encourage good software engineering practice. Rather than spaghetti code being easy to produce accidentally, it's only possible to load and use other classes that are explicitly intended for you to use. The only way to write spaghetti in OSGi is to deliberately expose the guts of your OSGi bundle to the world, and even then the other bundles still have to choose to use your packages. In addition to making it harder to write spaghetti, OSGi also makes it easier to spot spaghetti. A bundle that exports a hundred packages and imports a thousand is obviously not cohesive or modular!

In addition to defining the API that they expose, OSGi bundles also completely define the packages that are needed for them to be used. By enforcing this constraint, OSGi makes it abundantly clear what dependencies are needed for a given bundle to run, and also transparent as to which bundles can supply those dependencies. Importing and exporting packages goes a long way to solving the issues described in this section, because you no longer have to guess which JAR file is missing from your classpath. In order to completely eradicate classpath hell, OSGi has another trick up its sleeve—versioning.

VERSIONING IN OSGI

Versioning is a necessary complement to modularity. It doesn't sound as enticing as modularity—if we're being perfectly honest, it sounds dull—but it's essential if modularity is to work at all in anything but the simplest scenarios. Why?

Let's imagine you've achieved perfect modularity in your software project. All your components are broken out into modules, which are being developed by different teams, perhaps even different organizations. They're being widely reused in different contexts. What happens when a module implements a new piece of functionality that breaks existing behavior, either by design or as an unhappy accident? Some consuming modules will want to pick up the new function, but others will need to stick with the old behaviors. Coordinating this requires the module changes to be accompanied by a version change.

Let's go a step further. What if the updated module is consumed by several modules within the same system, some of which want the new version, and some the old version? This kind of coexistence of versions is important in a complex environment, and it can only be achieved by having versions as first-class properties of modules and compartmentalizing the class space.

> **Versions, versions everywhere!**
> Versioning is incredibly important in OSGi. It's so important that if you don't supply a version in your metadata, then you'll still have version 0.0.0! Another important point is that versioning doesn't only apply to packages; OSGi bundles are also versioned. This means that in a running framework you might have not only multiple versions of the same package, but multiple versions of the same bundle as well!

The semantic versioning scheme

Versioning is a way of communicating about what's changing (or not changing) in software, and so it's essential that the language used be shared. How should modules and packages be versioned? When should the version number change? What's most important is being able to distinguish between changes that will break consumers of a class by changing an API, and changes that are internal only.

The OSGi alliance recommends a scheme called *semantic versioning*. The details are available at http://www.osgi.org/wiki/uploads/Links/SemanticVersioning.pdf. Semantic versioning is a simple scheme, but it conveys much more meaning about what's changing than normal versions do. Every version consists of four parts: major, minor, micro, and qualifier. A change to the major part of a version number (for example, changing 2.0.0 to 3.0.0) indicates that the code change isn't backwards compatible. Removing a method or changing its argument types is an example of this kind of breaking change. A change to the minor part indicates a change that is backwards compatible for consumers of an API, but not for implementation providers. For example, the minor version should be incremented if a method is added to an interface in the API, because this will require changes to implementations. If a change doesn't affect the externals at all, it should be indicated by a change to the micro version. Such a change could be a bug fix, or a performance improvement, or even some internal changes that remove a private method from an API class. Having a strong division between bundle internals and bundle externals means the internals can be changed dramatically without anything other than the micro version of the bundle needing to change. Finally, the qualifier is used to add extra information, such as a build date.

Although our explanation focuses on the API, it isn't only packages that should be semantically versioned. The versions of bundles also represent a promise of functional and API compatibility. It's particularly important to remember that semantic versions are different from *marketing versions*. Even if a great deal of work has gone into a new release of a product, if it's backwards compatible the version would only change from, for example, 2.3 to 2.4, rather than from version 5 to version 6. This can be depressing for the release team, but it's helpful for users of the product who need to understand the nature of the changes. Also, think of it this way—a low major version number means you don't make a habit of breaking your customers!

Guarantees of compatibility

One of the benefits provided by the semantic versioning scheme is a guarantee of compatibility. A module will be bytecode compatible with any versions of its dependencies where the major version is the same, and the minor version is the same or higher. One warning about importing packages is that modules should not try to import and run with dependencies with lower minor versions than the ones they were compiled against.

> ## Forward compatibility
>
> Version ranges are important when importing packages in OSGi because they define what the expected future compatibility of your bundle is. If you don't specify a range, then your import runs to infinity, meaning that your bundle expects to be able to use any version of the package, regardless of how it changes! It's good practice to *always* specify a range, using square brackets for inclusive or parentheses for exclusive versions. For example, [1.1,2) for an API client compiled against a package at version 1.1 would be compatible up to, but not including, version 2.

Coexistence of implementations

The most significant benefit provided by versioning is that it allows different versions of the same module or package to coexist in the same system. If the modules weren't versioned, there would be no way of knowing that they're different and should be isolated from one another. With versioned modules (and some classloading magic courtesy of OSGi), each module can use the version of its dependencies that's most appropriate (figure 1.5).

As you can see, being explicit about dependencies, API, and versioning allows OSGi to completely obliterate classpath hell, but OSGi on its own doesn't guarantee well-structured applications. What it does do is give developers the tools they need to define a proper application structure. It also makes it easier to identify when application structures have slid in the direction of highly coupled soupishness. This is a pretty big improvement over standard Java, and OSGi is worth considering on the basis of these functions alone. OSGi has a few more tricks up its sleeve. Curiously enough, modularity was only one of the aims when creating OSGi: another focus was dynamic runtimes.

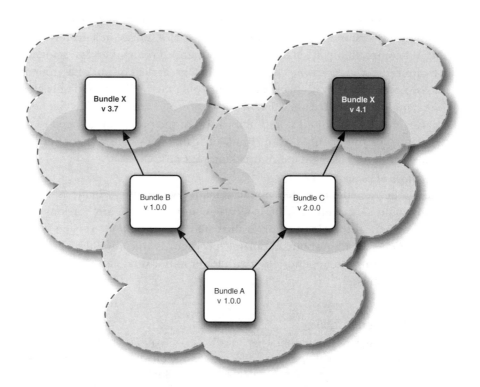

Figure 1.5 **The transitive dependencies of a module (the dependencies of its dependencies) may have incompatible versions. In a flat classpath, this can be disastrous, but OSGi allows the implementations to coexist by isolating them.**

1.2.2   *Dynamism and lifecycle management*

Dynamism isn't new to software engineering, but it's fundamental to OSGi. Just as versioning is part of OSGi to support proper modularity, modularity is arguably an OSGi feature because it's required to support full dynamism. Many people are unaware that OSGi was originally designed to operate in small, embedded systems where the systems could physically change. A static classpath wasn't good enough in this kind of environment!

Why did OSGi need a new model for dynamism? After all, in some ways, Java is pretty dynamic. For example, *reflection* allows fields to be accessed and methods to be invoked on any class by name. A related feature, *proxies*, allows classes to be generated on the fly that implement a set of interfaces. These can be used to stub out classes, or to create wrappers dynamically. Arguably another even more powerful dynamic feature of Java is *URL classloaders*. Classes may be loaded from a given URL at any point in time, rather than all being loaded at JVM initialization from a static classpath. Furthermore, anyone can write a classloader.

Java's ability to write custom classloaders and add classes dynamically to a running system isn't to be sniffed at. It's this feature that makes much of OSGi possible. But Java's classloading APIs are too low-level to be widely useful on their own. What OSGi provides is a layer that harnesses this dynamism and makes it generally available to developers who aren't interested in writing their own classloaders or hand-loading all the classes they need.

BUNDLE LIFECYCLES

Unlike most JAR files on the standard Java classpath, OSGi bundles aren't static entities that live on the classpath indefinitely. Dividing classloading responsibility among multiple classloaders enables the entire system to be highly dynamic. Bundles can be stopped and started on demand, with their classloaders and classes appearing and disappearing from the system as required. Bundles that have been started are guaranteed to have their requirements met; if a bundle's dependencies can't be satisfied, it won't be able to start. The complete state machine for bundle lifecycles is sufficiently simple to display in a single picture (see figure 1.6).

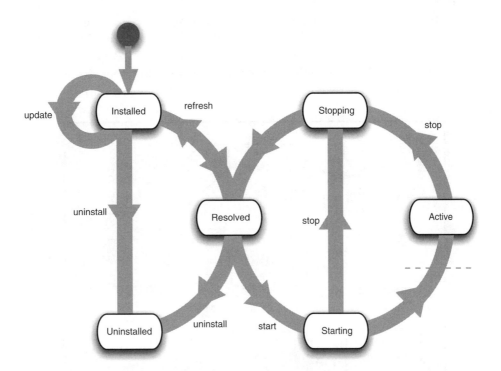

Figure 1.6   Bundles may move between the installed, resolved, starting, active, and stopping states. A starting bundle can be lazily activated, and if so it won't move to the active state (crossing the dashed line) until it's needed by another bundle. A bundle is resolved if it's installed and all its dependencies are also resolved or started. When a bundle is uninstalled, it's no longer able to start, nor can it provide packages to any new bundles.

The most interesting states are installed, resolved, and active. An installed bundle doesn't expose any classes until it's resolved. After it's resolved by having its dependencies satisfied, it can provide classes to other bundles. An active bundle can interact directly with the OSGi framework and change the behavior of the system by automatically executing nominated code.

Giving bundles a lifecycle has a few implications. The ability to execute code on bundle activation allows the system to dynamically update its behavior. Classes need not be loaded until required, reducing the memory footprint of the system. Because classes have the possibility of *not* being loaded, the system is able to ensure loaded classes have their dependencies satisfied. Overall, the system is both flexible and robust, which we think is pretty appealing!

CLASSLOADING

OSGi's classloading is at the heart of what makes it different from standard Java. It's an elegant and scalable system. Unfortunately, it's also one of the greatest sources of problems when adapting applications that weren't designed with modularity in mind to run in an OSGi environment.

Instead of every class in the virtual machine being loaded by a single monolithic classloader, classloading responsibilities are divided among a number of classloaders (see figure 1.7). Each bundle has an associated classloader, which loads classes contained within the bundle itself. If a bundle has a package import wired to a second bundle by the framework resolver, then its classloader will delegate to the other bundle's classloader

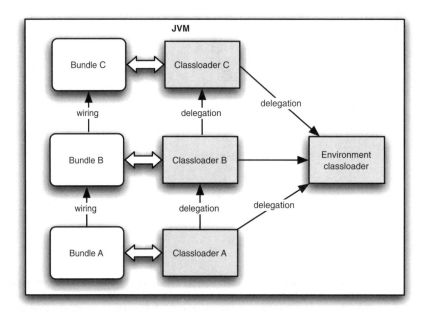

Figure 1.7   **The JVM contains many active classloaders in an OSGi environment. Each bundle has its own classloader. These classloaders delegate to the classloaders of other bundles for imported packages, and to the environment's classloader for core classes.**

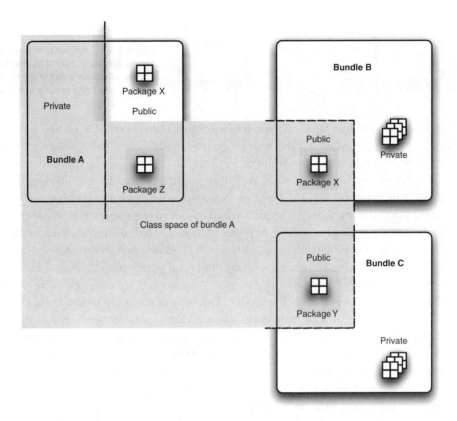

Figure 1.8 **The class space for a bundle includes all of its private classes, and the public classes of any bundle it's wired to. It doesn't necessarily include all the bundle's public classes, because some might be imported from other bundles instead.**

when attempting to load any class or resource in that package. In addition to the bundle classloaders, there are environment classloaders which handle core JVM classes.

Each classloader has well-defined responsibilities. If a classload request isn't delegated to another bundle, then the request is passed up the normal classloader delegation chain. Somewhat surprisingly, this means that being included in a bundle doesn't guarantee that a package will be loaded by that bundle. If that bundle also has an import for the package that's wired by the framework resolver, then all class loads for that package will be delegated elsewhere! This is a principle known as *substitutability*. It allows bundles to maintain a consistent class space between them by standardizing on one variant of a package, even when multiple variants are exported. Figure 1.8 shows the class space for a bundle that exports a substitutable package.

SERVICES AND THE SERVICE REGISTRY

Bundles and bundle lifecycles are as far as many OSGi developers go with OSGi. Enterprise OSGi makes heavy use of another fundamental OSGi feature—services. OSGi services are much more dynamic than their Java Enterprise Edition (Java EE) alternatives.

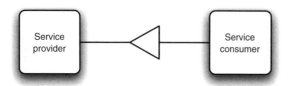

Figure 1.9   A service that's provided by one bundle and used by another bundle. The narrow end of the triangle points toward the service provider.

OSGi services are like META-INF services without all the messy files, or like Java Naming and Directory Interface (JNDI) with more power and less … JNDI. Although OSGi services fill the same basic requirement as these two technologies, they have important extra features such as dynamism, versioning, and property-based filtering. They're a simple and powerful way for bundles to transparently share object instances without having to expose any internal implementation—even the name of the class implementing the API. By hiding the service implementation and promoting truly decoupled modules, OSGi services effectively enable a single-JVM service-oriented architecture. Services also enable a number of other useful architectural patterns.

Figure 1.9 shows a simple OSGi service, represented by a triangle. The pointy end faces toward the provider of the service. One way of thinking of this is that the arrow points in the direction of invocation when a client calls the service. Another way to think of it is that the provider of a particular service is unique, whereas there may be many clients for it; as a result, the triangle must point at the only "special" bundle. Alternatively, if you squint really hard the service might look to you like the spout of an old-fashioned watering can, spreading water—or a service—out from a single source to many potential recipients.

Providing services

Services are registered by a bundle using one or more class names that mark the API of the service, and the service object itself. Optional properties can provide extra information about the service and can be used by clients to filter which services get returned when they're looking for one. Service properties aren't intended for use by the service itself.

```
Dictionary<String, String> props = new Hashtable<String, String>();
props.put("check.type", "slow");
ctx.registerService(InventoryLister.class.getName(), props);
```

Properties can be used to refine lookups.

As you can see, providing a service is easy. Of course providing a service isn't useful unless people have a way of finding and using it.

Accessing services

Services can be looked up using a simple API. Enterprise OSGi also allows services to be accessed declaratively and injected as a dependency. We'll make use of service dependency injection throughout this book, starting in section 2.3.8. Before we get there, let's have a peek at what a service lookup looks like without dependency injection:

```
String interfaceName = InventoryLister.class.getName();
ServiceReference ref = ctx.getServiceReference(interfaceName);
InventoryLister lister = (InventoryLister) ctx.getService(ref);
```

What happens when multiple providers of the service have been registered? Service consumers have a choice between getting one, or a list containing all of them. If the service is something like a credit card processing service, it's only necessary to take a payment once. In this situation one service provider is sufficient, and it probably doesn't matter too much which provider is chosen. In the case of a logging service, on the other hand, logged messages should probably be sent to all the available loggers, rather than one of them. Fortunately, OSGi also allows you to find all of the services that match a particular request:

```
ServiceReference[] refs = ctx.getServiceReferences(Logger.class
        .getName());
if (refs != null) {
    for (ServiceReference ref : refs) {
        Logger logger = (Logger) ctx.getService(ref);
        logger.doSomeLogging();
    }
}
```

As you can see, in addition to its modular, versioned runtime and flexible lifecycle management, OSGi provides an elegant services infrastructure and a lightweight dynamic framework. All of these encourage good engineering practice, but, as with most things, using OSGi doesn't guarantee that your application will be well structured. What OSGi does is give developers the tools they need to be able to define a proper application structure. It also makes it easier to identify when application structures have slid in the direction of highly coupled soupishness. Given its obvious advantages, why isn't everyone using OSGi already?

1.2.3 Why isn't everyone using OSGi?

As we've mentioned previously, OSGi isn't a new technology; the ideas have been around for more than a decade now. But OSGi adoption within the Java community isn't as ubiquitous as you would expect, given its obvious advantages. There are several reasons for this.

THE ORIGINS OF OSGI

The OSGi Alliance's original mission was to allow Java to be used in embedded and networked devices. In addition to Sun, IBM, and Oracle, its original members were, for the most part, mobile phone manufacturers like Motorola and Ericsson, and networking companies like Lucent and Nortel. There were also energy companies involved, such as Électricité de France and the late Enron Communications. Within a few years, OSGi was being used inside set-top boxes, Siemens medical devices, Bombardier locomotives, and the entertainment system of the BMW 5 Series. The main reason for this is that the advantages of OSGi are particularly useful in constrained devices, or in applications where the system must remain running for long periods, including through maintenance updates.

The next wave of OSGi adoption happened in large-scale software projects, particularly IDEs, application servers, and other middleware. It's initially surprising that a

> **The meaning of OSGi**
>
> Because of its embedded origins, the acronym *OSGi* used to stand for *Open Services Gateway initiative*. Now, if you didn't already know what OSGi was about, the phrase "Open Services Gateway initiative" doesn't shout "dynamic module system for Java." The name is so divorced from what OSGi is used for today that the original expansion of the acronym has been abandoned, and OSGi now stands for, well, OSGi.

technology designed for the tiniest Java installations should be such a good fit for the largest ones. Do the software running a car stereo and the software in an enterprise application server have much in common? As it happens, yes. What embedded devices needed was modularity and dynamism; software with large codebases has the same requirements. Despite the huge increase in processing power and memory available to modern devices, OSGi is, if anything, even more useful in these big systems. The increasing complexity of software projects is a key driver for OSGi adoption in Java applications.

Until recently, desktop applications suffered from neither the level of constraint of embedded systems nor the complexity of hefty middleware systems. In these environments the advantages of OSGi are sometimes viewed as insufficient when compared to its perceived drawbacks.

OSGI—BAD PRESS AND POOR UNDERSTANDING

During its lifetime, OSGi has suffered from some misconceptions and rather poor press. One of the big hurdles initially for OSGi was the perception that it was purely a technology for the embedded market, and that it was not needed, not useful, and, worst of all, a hindrance in the desktop and server space. This perception is clearly wrong, and was proved so when the Eclipse runtime chose to use an OSGi framework as its basis. It should be noted that Eclipse initially didn't believe an OSGi platform would be suitable, but were later convinced by the huge increases in startup speed, reduced footprint, and complexity management offered by OSGi.

Despite OSGi's success in Eclipse, OSGi is still perceived by many as being "too complex" for use in normal Java applications. Although OSGi metadata is simple, it isn't part of base Java. This means that even experts in Java are usually novices in the use of OSGi. Further, the OSGi classloading model is significantly different from base Java and requires developers to understand the dependencies that their code has. This is, in general, good practice but it's also something that developers aren't used to. Particularly with established projects, retro-fitting modularity by unpicking entangled dependency graphs can be pretty daunting. The change of mindset in OSGi doesn't always come easily, with the result that many people write OSGi off as too hard to be useful. While this may seem a little short-sighted, there are real reasons why OSGi feels excessively complex, particularly when applications try to make use of existing open source libraries.

UTILITY LIBRARIES AND OSGI

One of the big successes for Java has been that a large open source community has grown around it, providing a cornucopia of libraries, frameworks, and utilities. These libraries are so commonly used that there are almost no applications that don't use any and most applications use several. Some libraries are so commonly used that many developers consider them to be part of the Java API.

Many of these Java libraries were not originally written with OSGi in mind. This means that they have to be manually converted into OSGi bundles by the developers using them. The developers have to guess which packages are API and which package dependencies exist, making the conversion process time consuming and error prone. We think this is a key reason why OSGi is often perceived as difficult.

Unfortunately for developers new to OSGi, the problems with open source libraries don't end with packaging. Many libraries require users to provide some configuration, and sometimes implementations of classes. In standard Java, with its flat classpath, these resources and classes can be loaded easily using the same classloader that loaded the library class. In OSGi, these resources and classes are private to the application bundle, and can't be loaded by the library at all! Problems like this are widespread in libraries that weren't written with OSGi in mind and can't usually be solved without re-engineering the library significantly.

Fortunately for OSGi, open source libraries are increasingly available with OSGi-friendly packaging and API, meaning that OSGi is becoming easier to use than ever before. This effort is being made not only by the open source community, but also in new OSGi specifications, where the OSGi alliance is providing new, OSGi-aware mechanisms to make use of existing technologies.

1.2.4 Why OSGi and Java EE don't work together

Unfortunately, utility libraries aren't the only barrier to OSGi adoption. Many Java applications run on application servers, and use some form of enterprise Java, even if it's only servlets or dependency injection. Sadly, the Java EE programming model has historically been incompatible with OSGi. Enterprise Java exists because the Java community recognized common needs and practices across a variety of business applications. Java EE provides a common way to make use of enterprise services. Unfortunately, Java EE aggravates the modularity problems present in standard Java, and is more resistant to OSGi solutions.

FRAMEWORKS AND CLASS LOADING

Enterprise Java application servers are large beasts, and typically host multiple applications, each of which may contain many modules. In order to provide some level of isolation between these applications, there's a strict classloading hierarchy, one which separates the applications and modules from each other, and from the application server. This hierarchy is strongly based on the hierarchy of the classloaders in standard Java. Classes from the application server are shared between the applications through a common parent classloader; this means that application classes can't easily be loaded from the application server classes. This may not seem like a big problem, but Java EE contains an awful lot of containers and frameworks that provide hook and plug points to application code. In order to load these classes, the frameworks, which are part of the base application server runtime, have to have access to the application.

This problem is bypassed in enterprise Java using the concept of the *thread context classloader*. This classloader has visibility to the classes inside the application module and is attached to the thread whenever a managed object (like a servlet or EJB) is executing. This classloader can then be retrieved and used by the framework code to access classes and resources in the application module that called into it. This solution works, but it means that many useful frameworks rely heavily on the thread context classloader being set appropriately. In OSGi, the thread context classloader is rarely set, and furthermore it completely violates the modularity of your system. There's no guarantee that classes loaded by the thread context classloader will match your class space; in particular, there's no assurance that you'll share a common view of the interface that needs to be implemented. This causes a big problem for Java EE technologies in OSGi.

META-INF SERVICES AND THE FACTORY PATTERN

Although reflection, dynamic classloading, and the thread context classloader are useful, they're of limited practical use in writing loosely coupled systems. For example, reflection doesn't allow an implementation of an interface to be discovered, unless the implementation's class name is already known. Having to specify implementation names in advance pretty much defeats the point of using interfaces. This problem crops up again and again in Java EE and, unsurprisingly, there's a common pattern for solving it.

For many years, the best solution to the problem of obtaining interface implementations was to isolate the problem to one area of code, known as a *factory*. The system wasn't loosely coupled, but at least only one area was tightly coupled. The factory would use reflection to instantiate a class whose name had been hardcoded into the factory. This didn't do much to eliminate the logical dependency between the factory and the implementation, but at least the compile-time dependency went away.

A better pattern was to externalize the implementation's class name out to a file on disk or in a JAR, which was then read in by the factory. The implementation still had to be specified, but at least it could be changed without recompiling the factory. This pattern was formalized into what's known as META-INF services. Any JAR can register an implementation for any interface by providing the implementation name in a file named after the interface it implements, found in the META-INF/services folder of the JAR. Factories can look up interface implementations using a `ServiceLoader` and all registered implementations will be returned.

This mechanism sounds similar to OSGi services. Why isn't this good enough for OSGi? One practical reason is that the service registry for META-INF services wasn't available when OSGi was being put together. The other, more relevant issues are that, although META-INF services avoids tight coupling in code, it doesn't give any dynamism beyond that, and it still relies on one JAR being able to load the internal implementation class of another. Furthermore, META-INF services can't be registered programmatically, and they certainly can't be unregistered.

1.3   *Programming with enterprise OSGi*

From what you've read so far, it probably sounds like OSGi is a lost cause for enterprise programming. Sure, it has some cool ideas and lets you do some things that you couldn't easily do before, but who could give up the smorgasbord of enterprise services that don't work in OSGi? Obviously this isn't the case, or this would be a short book! Recently the gap between Java EE and OSGi has grown much smaller, with the introduction of *enterprise OSGi*.

One of the fascinating things about OSGi's development from a platform for home gateways, to a platform for trains and cars, to a platform for IDEs and application servers is that OSGi itself hasn't had to change that much. Even though the domains are totally different, the capabilities provided by OSGi solved problems in all of them. Enterprise OSGi is different because basic OSGi by itself isn't enough. To address the needs of the enterprise, the OSGi Alliance has branched out and produced an Enterprise Specification with enterprise-specific extensions to core OSGi.

1.3.1   *Enterprise OSGi and OSGi in the enterprise*

Like the term *enterprise Java*, *enterprise OSGi* can mean different things to different people. Some people refer to the use of core OSGi concepts, or an OSGi framework, to provide business value for one or more applications. This definition is a little looser than is normally accepted; many people feel that merely using an OSGi framework to host business applications isn't enough to justify the description "enterprise OSGi." A parallel can be drawn to enterprise Java programming, a term which is linked to the use of the Java Enterprise Edition programming model, and usually an application server or servlet container. Using a Java Virtual Machine (JVM) and the Java Standard Edition (Java SE) APIs to write a business application would not normally be considered an "enterprise Java application." Similarly, when business applications are merely using an OSGi framework and features from the core OSGi specifications, it's not *enterprise OSGi*, although it might be *OSGi in the enterprise*.

Enterprise OSGi sometimes refers strictly to the set of specifications defined by the OSGi Enterprise Expert Group in the OSGi Enterprise Specification 4.2 and 5 releases. This narrow definition would exclude some open source technologies which aren't in the enterprise OSGi specification but which clearly have an enterprise OSGi "feel." Probably the most common and accurate definition of enterprise OSGi is a blend of what's in the specification with the more general usage of OSGi in the enterprise we discussed. What we mean by *enterprise OSGi* in this book is an OSGi-based application that makes use of one or more enterprise services, as described in the OSGi Enterprise Specification, to provide business value. This links both the use of OSGi concepts and an OSGi framework with the OSGi Enterprise Specification, which defines how enterprise services can be used from inside an OSGi framework. What does this enterprise OSGi programming model look like?

1.3.2   *Dependency injection*

Dependency injection, sometimes called *inversion of control*, defines both an enterprise technology and an architectural model. Dependency injection has only recently become part of the official Java EE standard, but it has been a *de facto* part of enterprise programming for many years through the use of frameworks like Spring. Dependency injection is, if anything, even more valuable in an OSGi environment. Because the OSGi Service Registry is such a dynamic environment, it's difficult to correctly write a bundle that makes use of a service in a safe way, monitoring its lifecycle, and finding an appropriate replacement.

Using and providing services becomes even more difficult when an implementation depends upon more than one service, with a user having to write some complex thread-safe code. Using dependency injection eliminates this complexity by managing the lifecycle of both the services exposed, and consumed, by a bundle.

Because of its ability to dramatically simplify programming in OSGi, dependency injection is at the heart of the enterprise OSGi programming model. Without it, business logic is difficult to separate from dependency management logic, and development is slow. The other key advantage of dependency injection is that it allows application code to avoid dependencies on core OSGi APIs, dramatically reducing the amount that developers need to learn before they can start making use of OSGi and making applications easier to unit test.

1.3.3   *Java EE integration*

As we mentioned previously, enterprise OSGi wouldn't be useful if it didn't provide at least some of the functions available in Java EE. Furthermore, Java EE already has a lot of experienced developers, and it wouldn't be helpful if the OSGi way of doing things was completely different from the Java EE way. These two requirements are fundamental drivers of the OSGi Enterprise Specification, which aims to provide core enterprise services, reusing Java EE idioms and structure where possible.

The OSGi Enterprise Specification is large, and covers many of the Java EE services that developers know and love. For example, it includes an OSGi-friendly version of a Web Archive (WAR), declarative Java Persistence API (JPA) database access, and access to Java Transaction API (JTA) transactions. It also includes, not one, but two dependency injection systems, Java Management Extensions (JMX) management, and a way of distributing work across multiple JVMs. The OSGi Enterprise Specification Releases 5 even includes support for dynamically exposing META-INF services as OSGi services. If you're not familiar with JPA, JTA, and the other Java EE technologies we've mentioned, don't worry—we'll introduce them in later chapters with worked examples.

1.4 *Summary*

As we're sure you've noticed by now, this chapter doesn't contain a Hello World sample. We hope that, rather than rushing to get your money back, you understand the reason for this. The enterprise is a huge place, containing lots of platforms, technologies, and some extremely difficult problems. In the enterprise, Hello World doesn't cut the mustard. There will be plenty of sample code throughout the rest of the book, and we promise that in the next chapter our first sample will be rather more than five lines of code and a call to `System.out`!

What this chapter does contain is a discussion of the problems with the current enterprise technologies. For some of you with years of OSGi experience, this information probably confirms what you already know. For others, we hope you now have a sense of how easily applications can become complex, particularly when they're enterprise-scale.

With its long history and the breadth of support now offered by OSGi for enterprise technologies, it should be clear that OSGi is ready for the enterprise. It should also be clear that, whether you're an OSGi developer whose application needs are getting too big, or you're a Java EE developer tired of object minestrone and debugging your application's classpath for the thousandth time, you're ready for enterprise OSGi.

Developing a simple
OSGi-based web application

2

This chapter covers

- Setting up an enterprise OSGi container
- Developing a simple OSGi-based web application
- Wiring components together with Blueprint
- Using JNDI to integrate enterprise OSGi and Java EE code

The web is one of the most fundamental parts of enterprise Java programming, providing a frontend for almost every enterprise application. At the end of the chapter 1, we mentioned that a trivial Hello World application didn't make much sense when we were talking about enterprise OSGi, because enterprise applications are by definition *nontrivial*. But that doesn't mean that writing them has to be complicated or difficult! In this chapter, we'll get you going with a simple web application, and then we'll move on to discuss the essential glue of enterprise OSGi: Blueprint dependency injection. Think of it as *Hello World Wide Web*.

We're sure you're eager to get going playing with real code, so we'll begin by introducing our sample application and letting you get your hands dirty with a handy development sandbox.

2.1 The development sandbox

In the succeeding chapters, we'll build up a small sample enterprise application, the Fancy Foods web store. By the end of the book, the Fancy Foods application will have a web frontend, a database backend, and transactional purchasing. Its modules will be wired to one another using dependency injection, and packaged together as an installable archive.

Before you get started writing this application, you'll need a way to run it. Enterprise OSGi is a programming model, not a product, so there are lots of ways of running an enterprise OSGi application. Several open source and commercial application servers support enterprise OSGi, and we'll discuss some of the available platforms in chapter 13. As a starting point, the Apache Aries project provides a simple runtime with their samples. We think this is one of the best ways of getting going with enterprise OSGi.

2.1.1 Introducing Apache Aries

The open source community has been quick to respond to the OSGi Enterprise Specification with implementations. (At least some of these implementations were in place before the Enterprise Specification was released, and the implementation experience guided the final shape of the specification.) Open source enterprise OSGi implementations are available from both the Eclipse Foundation and the Apache Source Foundation, and many other implementations are available elsewhere. The primary enterprise OSGi project in Eclipse is called Eclipse Gemini, and in Apache the project is known as Apache Aries. These projects have the express aim of providing a set of reusable OSGi components that can be used as the basis of an enterprise OSGi programming model.

ARIES AND THE OSGI ENTERPRISE SPECIFICATION

Apache Aries (see figure 2.1) also provides some extensions to what's included in the OSGi Enterprise Specification, and at least some of these extensions have been wrapped back into release 5. For example, Aries provides fuller container management of persistence and transactions. It also provides a new application-level (rather than bundle-level) granularity that wasn't available in the first release of the enterprise OSGi specification.

These extensions are tremendously useful and make what's provided by enterprise OSGi map more closely to what's in JEE. Apache Aries also has a number of other benefits that make it a nice place to start learning enterprise OSGi. It has a helpful users' mailing list and an active development community. It can be consumed in a number of forms. The JARs can be downloaded as-is and dropped into any OSGi framework. Aries is also integrated into several existing application servers. Both Apache Geronimo and IBM's WebSphere Application Server provide an OSGi programming model based on Aries.

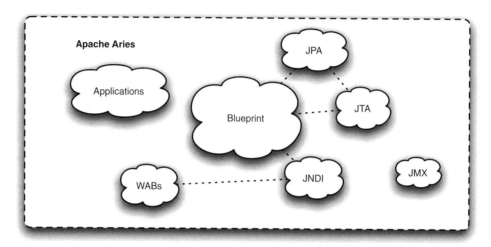

Figure 2.1   The elements of Apache Aries. Aries includes a Blueprint implementation, OSGi integrations for JPA, JTA, and the web, application packaging, and JMX management. Blueprint is at the heart of a lot of the Aries function.

We'll focus on Apache Aries and a number of its sibling Apache projects in our examples in this book. It's not necessary to use an Apache stack to use enterprise OSGi. You can replace parts of the stack with other implementations, or you can use an entirely Eclipse stack, or you can opt for one of the commercial products, such as the WebSphere Application Server.

2.1.2   *My first enterprise OSGi runtime*

Apache Aries by itself isn't enough to run enterprise applications; there's no web container, database implementation, or OSGi framework. But it's fairly straightforward to add these things to Aries, and the result is a handy little sandbox environment. Aries has already done this, providing an assembly for the Aries samples, and this runtime can be reused for your own applications.

Begin by downloading the source zip for the latest release of the Aries samples from http://aries.apache.org/downloads/currentrelease.html. The samples are listed at the top of the page, and you want the main samples download, a zip that contains the source for all the samples. Unzip and navigate down one level in the directory structure. You'll find the source code and build files for all the Aries samples. Navigate to blog/blog-assembly. Finally, use Maven to build the assembly:

```
mvn install
```

This build isn't building any samples, just preparing a runtime environment for the samples to run in. It downloads the binaries for the latest Aries release and all their dependencies. It also includes Pax Web for running OSGi web applications. When the build has completed, have a look in the target directory. You should see lots of Aries JARs, and also a few Derby, OpenJPA, and Geronimo JARs. Perhaps most importantly, there's a single JAR containing an OSGi container. See figure 2.2.

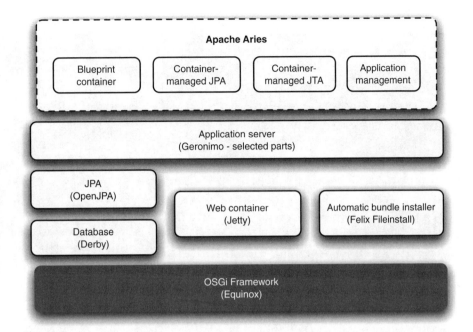

Figure 2.2 As well as Apache Aries components, the Aries sandbox stack includes an OSGi framework, a database, web container, JPA and JTA implementations, and a few pieces of the Geronimo application server.

What do all those JARs do?

If you count the JARs in the target directory, you may be surprised by how many there are. Does it take 35 JARs to run an OSGi web application? No. You could get away with a handful of bundles, but then you'd need to download a few more to get the Blueprint dependency injection going, and then a few more once you start playing with persistence in chapter 3. We thought it was probably easier to download everything at once!

If you're the sort of person who likes to take everything apart and then put it back together again, we've got a detailed guide to what's what in the Aries sandbox in appendix B.

Launch the OSGi framework using the OSGi JAR:

```
cd target
java -jar org.eclipse.osgi-3.7.0.v20110613.jar -console
```

(Depending on which release you're using, the version of the OSGi JAR may be different.) The -console argument is important, because it brings up the OSGi console that allows you to see what OSGi bundles are active and start, stop, and install new bundles.

Type ss to see a list of all the bundles in the framework (see figure 2.3). The ss stands for "short status" and provides a high-level view of the bundles available in the

Figure 2.3   The output of the `ss` **command, showing all the bundles in the OSGi framework**

framework. Each bundle should be in `ACTIVE` state. That's it! Your new enterprise OSGi container is now ready to run applications.

It's probably obvious that this runtime isn't suitable for use in production. Support for administering applications is limited, and there's no support at all for security, load balancing, or failover. Don't worry, we'll cover a variety of production-worthy

OSGi consoles

The OSGi console you're using now is a standard Equinox OSGi console. There's nothing specific to Apache Aries in the user interface. The command line environment of an OSGi console can feel intimidating at first, but you won't need to know many commands other than `ss` to show the bundles.

options in chapter 13. In the meantime, the sandbox is a good environment for play-ing with various bits of enterprise OSGi. We'll start with the public face of almost any enterprise application, the web frontend.

2.2 *Writing an OSGi web application*

In Java EE the servlet and JavaServer Pages models have provided the basic building blocks for Java web applications for many years. OSGi web applications are a standard-ized OSGi version of Java EE web applications. An OSGi web bundle is similar to a Java EE WAR, except that it also gets the benefits of operating in an OSGi framework. Enter-prise OSGi web bundles are known as WABs. (In contrast to WARs, which are *Web Archives*, WABs are *Web Application Bundles*.)

2.2.1 *Building a simple OSGi web application bundle*

Let's give WABs a try. You can use your favorite OSGi or Java EE development tools. All you need for now is the ability to compile Java code and build JARs. (We'll cover spe-cialist enterprise OSGi development tools in chapter 8. Feel free to peek ahead now if you're struggling to make OSGi JARs.)

WAB LAYOUTS

The simplest WAB contains three files. These are a Java servlet class, a JAR manifest, and a web deployment descriptor. Figure 2.4 shows how they're laid out in the WAB. Like WARs, WABs are a special kind of JAR. Unlike WARs, the enterprise OSGi specifica-tion doesn't require a particular file extension. As a result, WAB files may have any

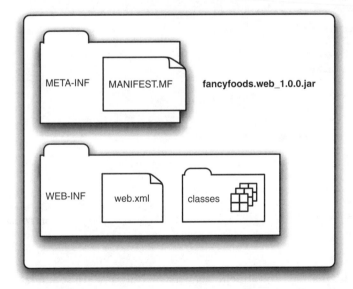

Figure 2.4 The layout of the `fancyfoods.web` JAR. All code lives in WEB-INF/classes. The web container looks at WEB-INF/web.xml to find out what servlets are provided by the bundle. Finally, the standard JAR manifest, META-INF/MANIFEST.MF includes important extra metadata for the OSGi container.

extension, but typically use .jar or .war to avoid confusion. We'll call our WAB fancy-foods.web_1.0.0.jar.

WEB DEPLOYMENT DESCRIPTORS

Let's start with the deployment descriptor. Listing 2.1 shows the web.xml file for the web application. It's a typical web.xml file whose syntax will be reassuringly familiar to everyone who has developed Java EE web applications. The web application has one servlet, whose class is `fancyfoods.web.SayHello`.

Listing 2.1   The WEB-INF/web.xml file

```
<web-app>
    <servlet>                                               A servlet with backing
        <servlet-name>SayHello</servlet-name>          ◁──┘ class SayHello
        <servlet-class>fancyfoods.web.SayHello</servlet-class>
    </servlet>
    <servlet-mapping>
        <servlet-name>SayHello</servlet-name>
        <url-pattern>/SayHello</url-pattern>              ◁──┐ URL is
    </servlet-mapping>                                        │ SayHello
</web-app>
```

A SIMPLE SERVLET

The servlet class `SayHello` is also exactly the same as it would be in a WAR. Listing 2.2 shows the source. There's one method, which—unsurprisingly—issues a greeting to a user.

Listing 2.2   The SayHello.java file

```
package fancyfoods.web;

import java.io.IOException;
import java.io.PrintWriter;

import javax.servlet.ServletException;
import javax.servlet.http.*;

public class SayHello extends HttpServlet {

    protected void doGet(HttpServletRequest request,
                    HttpServletResponse response)
                    throws ServletException, IOException {
        PrintWriter writer = response.getWriter();          ◁──┐ Write to response's
        writer.append("Hello valued customer!");               │ PrintWriter
    }

}
```

So far, so familiar. It's perhaps a bit anticlimactic that writing a WAB is so similar to writing a WAR in some respects, but this is one of the strengths of the enterprise OSGi programming model—it's like existing programming models, only better. The differences between WABs and WARs start to become obvious when you look at the manifest file.

A WAB MANIFEST

The final file needed in your WAB is the bundle manifest. Every JAR has a MANI-FEST.MF file, but an OSGi bundle's manifest has extra headers, such as the symbolic name of the bundle and the bundle's version.

Listing 2.3   The MANIFEST.MF file

```
Manifest-Version: 1.0
Bundle-ManifestVersion: 2
Bundle-SymbolicName: fancyfoods.web
Bundle-Version: 1.0.0
Bundle-ClassPath: WEB-INF/classes
Web-ContextPath: /fancyfoods.web
Import-Package: javax.servlet.http;version="[2.5,3.0)",
 javax.servlet;version="[2.5,3.0)"
```

To be consistent with the layout of a WAR, the class files for `fancyfoods.web` have been packaged in the WEB-INF/classes folder. But there's no need for this. Classes can live anywhere in an OSGi bundle, or even be spread across multiple locations. If the class files aren't directly in the root directory, the classpath needs to be specified in the manifest:

```
Bundle-ClassPath: WEB-INF/classes
```

Packages used by the servlet that aren't in the servlet's own bundle must be explicitly imported in the manifest. Otherwise, they won't be visible. The exception is that there's no need to import the core Java language classes, `java.*`, which are implicitly imported. Bundle wiring rules are a bit different for the `java.*` packages, which *must* come from the core Java runtime for security and for compatibility with the virtual machine. Imagine if someone could replace the implementation of String or Integer!

In the case of the web bundle, this means the `javax.servlet` and `javax.servlet.http` packages are imported. The servlet is expected to work with any version of `javax.servlet` with version 2.5 or higher, up to but not including version 3.0.

```
Import-Package: javax.servlet.http;version="[2.5,3.0)",
 javax.servlet;version="[2.5,3.0)"
```

> **WARNING: WHAT ABOUT SERVLET 3.0?** The meaning of the version range `"[2.5, 3.0)"` isn't entirely straightforward. You're mostly right if you assume that the *2.5* part implies version 2.5 of the servlet specification. But *3.0* definitely *doesn't* mean version 3.0 of the servlet specification! Remember, OSGi versions are semantic package versions, not marketing or specification versions. Servlet 3.0 is backwards compatible with servlet 2.5, and so the package versions for servlet 3.0 won't be versioned at 3.0. Version 3.0 of the servlet packages would be some change to the servlet specification so radical that the interfaces were no longer backwards compatible. The reason the bottom range starts at 2.5 and not 1.0 is that when the WAB specification was written, the current version was 2.5, and so 2.5 seemed like a logical starting point. Unfortunately, some application servers have deviated from the semantic version and use the package version 3.0 for the servlet 3.0 specification, which doesn't help!

The manifest includes one final header that's specific to WABs and defines the web context root. This header is required for a bundle to be recognized as a WAB. Many enterprise OSGi implementations also allow the context root to be changed after deployment:

```
Web-ContextPath: /fancyfoods.web
```

Build these three files into a JAR, and the web application is ready to try out!

2.2.2   Deploying and testing

Because OSGi is so dynamic, testing OSGi bundles is pretty easy. The same bundle can be loaded repeatedly without having to stop or start anything else. If you're as prone to typos as the authors, you'll find this extremely handy.

THE LOAD DIRECTORY

The Apache Aries runtime you assembled earlier includes Felix File Install, which provides a simple mechanism for discovering and starting new applications. The target directory includes a folder called load (if the load directory isn't there, you can add it yourself). Any OSGi bundles copied into this directory will automatically be started.

To try this out, start the Aries runtime using

```
java -jar org.eclipse.osgi-3.7.0.v20110613.jar -console -clean
```

Type ss to see the list of installed bundles. Now copy the web bundle you've built into the load directory. You'll see a bunch of output scroll by in the OSGi console. Type ss again. You'll see a new bundle is listed, the `fancyfoods.web` bundle you copied into the load directory. This new bundle should be in ACTIVE state.

All that remains now is to try it out. Point a browser at http://localhost:8080/fancyfoods.web/SayHello. You'll see more debug output scroll by in the OSGi console, and the browser should display a response like the one shown in figure 2.5.

What if nothing happens?

Our sandbox uses Apache Felix's File Install bundle to install bundles that we drop into the load directory. This is quick and easy, but it's also quiet when there's a failure. It's quite common for nothing to be output at all. If you don't see anything happen when you drop your bundle into the load directory, don't panic. You can use one of the other Equinox console commands to find out what's gone wrong.

The install command allows users to install a bundle from a particular URL. In your case, you want to point at the `fancyfoods.web_1.0.0.jar`, and need to run the following command:

```
install file://<path_to_file>/fancyfoods.web_1.0.0.jar
```

This command will almost certainly generate a useful error. Typically the error will indicate that the bundle's manifest is malformed, often because there aren't any " characters around a version range. Whatever the error is, it should provide enough information to help you fix the problem and continue on with the example.

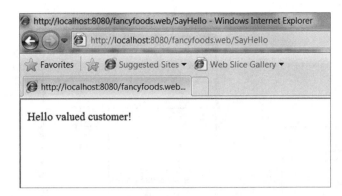

Figure 2.5   The web
application in action

2.2.3   *A familiar feeling—and important differences*

Even with the extra headers in the manifest, the web bundle you've written looks a lot like a conventional Java EE WAR. In fact, it's so similar that you could probably deploy it as a WAR in a Java EE application. What's different about it, then? A WAB is *a bundle*, and not just a normal JAR, which means it has some new behaviors.

> ### WAR to WAB conversion
>
> The structure of WARs and WABs is similar enough that the OSGi Enterprise Specification supports automatic conversion of WARs to WABs at deploy time. A bundle symbolic name and package imports are automatically generated. This can be convenient when doing an initial migration from Java EE to enterprise OSGi, but in general it's better to write web applications as WABs. This ensures the bundle has a proper, well-known, symbolic name, and it also allows package imports to be versioned. Versioning package imports is always a good idea. The WAB format also provides a convenient mechanism for setting the web context root.

PACKAGE PRIVACY

What are the implications of being an OSGi bundle? The biggest implication is what can't be seen—nothing outside the `fancyfoods.web` bundle (see figure 2.6) can see the `SayHello` class, because it's not exported. This cozy privacy is exactly what you want, because there's no reason for any code outside your bundle (except for perhaps the web container, which can use the OSGi API) to be messing around directly with your servlet class. If you did want to make the `SayHello` class externally accessible for some reason, all that would be required is to add a package export of the `fancyfoods.web` package. But you'd probably want to consider your design carefully before doing this. Could the shared code be externalized to a utility bundle instead?

Although package privacy is a good thing, not all Java code can cope with it. Some existing libraries, particularly ones that use reflection to load classes, may not work properly. We'll discuss strategies for handling awkward existing libraries in chapter 12.

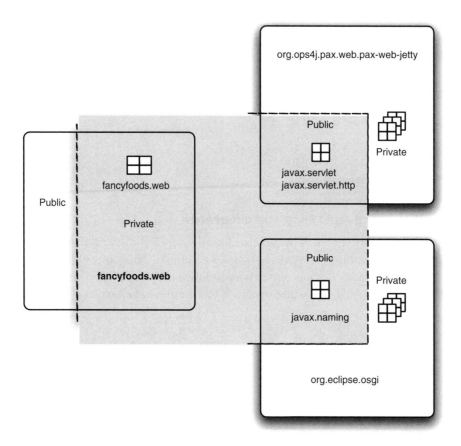

Figure 2.6   **The class space of the** `fancyfoods.web` **bundle. It doesn't have any public packages. To confirm which bundle exports the** `javax.servlet` **package, type** `packages javax.servlet` **in your OSGi console, or** `bundle fancyfoods.web` **to see where all of the packages used by** `fancyfoods.web` **come from.**

EXPLICIT DEPENDENCIES

Being a bundle has a second implication, which is that all the packages required by `SayHello` must be explicitly imported in the manifest. If you're just getting used to OSGi, this can seem like an unnecessary—and annoying—extra step.

Let's step back and think about how Java handles package imports for classes. If you were writing a Java class, you'd always import the packages you were using, rather than expecting the compiler to choose a class with the right name from a random package. Some class names are unique, and you'd probably end up with the right one, but other class names are not at all unique. Imagine how horrible it would be if your class could end up running against any class called `Constants`, for example.

You might also end up with the opposite problem—instead of a class name that was too common, you could be trying to use a class that didn't exist at all. If the package you needed didn't exist at all, you'd expect an error at compile time. You certainly wouldn't want the compilation to limp along, claim success, and produce a class that half-worked.

Luckily, the Java compiler doesn't do this. If your declared dependencies aren't present, the compilation will fail quickly. At runtime, on the other hand, you're in a situation which is similar to the undeclared dependencies. You have to wait until your class is invoked to discover its dependencies are missing. You won't ever end up running against a class from a totally different package to the one you expected, but you could end up running with a class of a different version, with totally different methods and behaviors.

Explicitly declaring the dependency on the `javax.servlet` and `javax.servlet` `.http` packages ensures the `fancyfoods.web` bundle won't run in a container that doesn't support servlets. Better yet, it won't even run in a container that supports an obsolete version of the servlet specification. To try this out, go to the OSGi console for the Aries runtime. At the prompt, use the `packages` command to see which bundles import and export the `javax.servlet` package:

```
osgi> packages javax.servlet
```

The response should be something like that shown in figure 2.7.

The output shows that the org.apache.geronimo.specs.geronimo-servlet_2.5_spec bundle exports the `javax.servlet` package, and five bundles import it, including `fancyfoods.web`.

Does it matter who provides the servlet package?

Depending on which version of the Aries sample assembly you're using, your console output may be different from what's shown in figure 2.7. In particular, it may be a different bundle that provides the `javax.servlet` package. Declaring dependencies on packages, rather than bundles, allows more deployment flexibility. In this case, the Aries team has taken advantage of that flexibility by swapping the web container implementation.

What would happen if the Aries assembly hadn't included the Geronimo servlet API JAR? Quit the OSGi console, and move the Geronimo servlet bundle (geronimo-servlet*jar) out of the target directory. (Don't lose it though!) Restart the OSGi console, and type

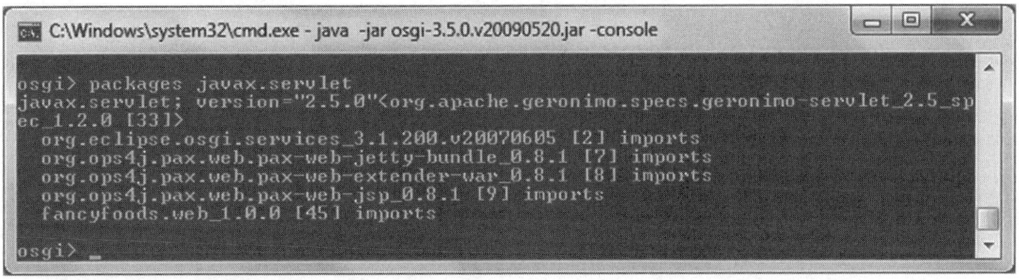

Figure 2.7 The OSGi console can provide the list of bundles providing and consuming the `javax.servlet` **package.**

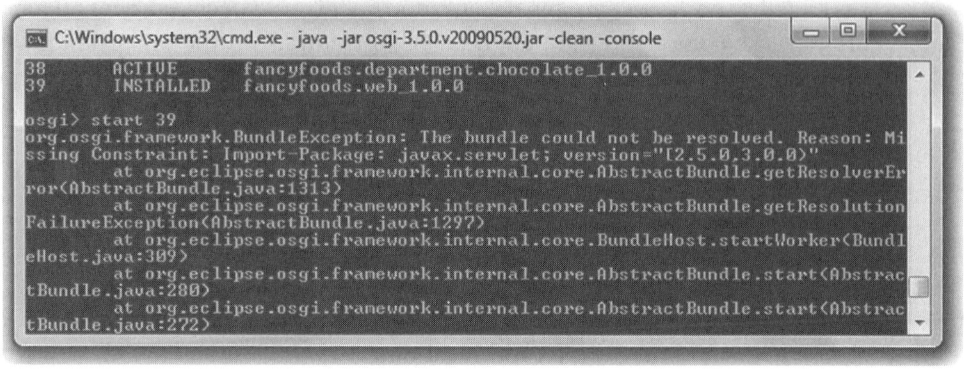

Figure 2.8 If the Geronimo servlet bundle is removed from the runtime, the `fancyfoods.web` bundle can't be started, because no servlet API is present.

ss to see the list of bundles. You'll see a number of bundles, including `fancyfoods.web`, are in the `INSTALLED` state instead of the `ACTIVE` state. This means the bundles couldn't be resolved or started because some dependencies were missing. Make a note of the bundle identifier to the left of `fancyfoods.web` in the bundle list. Try starting the bundle to see what happens. See figure 2.8.

Because your assembly no longer has servlet support, `fancyfoods.web` won't start. The bundle definitely wouldn't work properly if the code inside it was to run, so not starting is the right behavior. Don't forget to put the Geronimo servlet bundle back into the target directory before you try to use the web application again. (The authors forgot to do this on several occasions, and were confused each time.)

FRAGMENTS

OSGi bundles have a third advantage over normal WARs. OSGi is all about modularity, and so OSGi bundles can themselves have modular extensions, known as *fragments*. Fragments are extensions to bundles that attach to a host bundle and act in almost every way as if they were part of the host. They allow bundles to be customized depending on their environment. For example, translated resource files can be packaged up by themselves into a fragment and only shipped if needed. Fragments can also be used to add platform-specific code to a generic host.

2.2.4 *Spicing things up with fragments*

How would a fragment work with your little application? The first version of the `fancyfoods.web` application is only intended to work in English, but if the business takes off, it will expand into other markets. The first step in internationalizing `fancyfoods.web` is to externalize the strings in `SayHello.java`. Write a properties file called fancyfoods/web/messages.properties with the following content:

```
SayHello.hello=Hello valued customer!
```

The new `doGet` method looks like the following.

Listing 2.4 The `doGet` method with message translation

```
protected void doGet(HttpServletRequest request,
                     HttpServletResponse response)
                     throws ServletException, IOException {
    PrintWriter writer = response.getWriter();
    Locale locale = request.getLocale();                          Where
    String bundleName = "fancyfoods.web.messages";                are we?
    ResourceBundle resources = ResourceBundle.                    Get right
        getBundle(bundleName, locale);                            resource
    String greeting = resources.getString("SayHello.hello");      bundle.
    writer.append(greeting);
}                                                  Get translated message.
```

Bundles, bundles, or bundles?

You've got a few different kinds of bundles floating around at the moment, but the resource bundles here have nothing to do with OSGi bundles—they're ordinary Java resource bundles.

If you build the bundle and test the web page, it will work exactly as it did before. This is reassuring if you're browsing in English, but not ideal if you're browsing in French. To try it out: change your web browser's preferred language to French. (If you don't want to do that, you can hardcode the locale in the `getString()` call in `SayHello`.java.) Most pages you browse to, like Google, for example, will show French text. But if you reload the Fancy Foods web page, the greeting is disappointingly English. To get the Fancy Foods page to display in French, you need to provide some French translations—obviously.

To be accessible to the `SayHello` class, the properties files need to be loaded by the same classloader—which (mostly) means they need to be in the same bundle. But rebuilding JARs is no fun, and you definitely don't want to be repackaging your existing code every time you have a new translation. You want to be able to easily drop in support for other languages in the future.

Resource loading between bundles

We've simplified our discussion of resource loading slightly. It's possible to load resources from other bundles, but it's ugly. The package containing the resource must be exported by the providing bundle and imported by the consuming bundle. To avoid clashes with packages in the consuming bundle, the consuming bundle shouldn't export the package it's attempting to import. Having trouble following? You won't be the only one! We've seen this pattern used, but we definitely don't recommend it.

Luckily, this is the sort of job for which OSGi fragments are perfect. OSGi fragments are a bit like OSGi bundles. But instead of having their own lifecycle and classloader, they attach to a host bundle. They share the host's classloader and behave in almost every way as if they're part of the parent (see figure 2.9). But they can be installed and uninstalled independently of the host.

In this case, a translation fragment can be built and attached to `fancyfoods.web`. To provide the translations, you'll need a new fragment JAR. All it needs inside it is a manifest and a properties file (see figure 2.10).

The French language properties file, messages_fr.properties, might read like this:

```
SayHello.hello=Bienvenue aux Aliments de Fantaisie!
```

The MANIFEST.MF is similar to a bundle manifest, but it has an extra header that identifies the host of the fragment—`fancyfoods.web` in this case. It's a good idea to also specify a minimum version of the host bundle, to ensure compatibility:

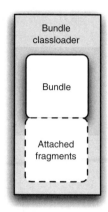

Figure 2.9   OSGi fragments attach to a parent bundle and share its classloader.

```
Manifest-Version: 1.0
Bundle-ManifestVersion: 2
Bundle-Name: French language resources
Bundle-SymbolicName: fancyfoods.web.nls.fr
Bundle-Version: 1.0.0
Fragment-Host: fancyfoods.web;bundle-version="[1.0.0,2.0.0)"
```

Build the fragment into a JAR, `fancyfoods.web.nls.fr_1.0.0.jar`. After the fragment is built, you can drop it into the load directory of your running framework. Type `ss` and you'll see your new fragment included in the list of bundles. Fragments can't

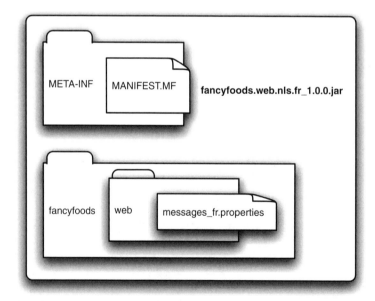

Figure 2.10   The layout of the `fancyfoods.web.nls.fr` fragment

Figure 2.11 The Fancy Foods web page, before and after deleting the French-language translations from the load directory

be started and stopped like bundles, so the fragment will be shown as INSTALLED. Refresh the web bundle with `refresh [web bundle number]` and the fragment will attach to the bundle and move to the RESOLVED state.

Check the web page again, and the greeting should be shown in French. Delete the `fancyfoods.web.nls.fr` fragment JAR from the load directory, and try the web page again—back to English (figure 2.11)!

Although internationalization is the most popular use for fragments, it's not the only one. Anything can be put into a fragment, including Java classes. But including classes in fragments for pluggability isn't the best implementation. OSGi provides higher-level ways of achieving pluggability through services.

2.3 *Decoupling with dependency injection*

Despite working in two languages, the web application you've written is pretty limited so far. Not only does it not do anything beyond issuing a greeting, it doesn't even say hello in a particularly dynamic way. What if you wanted to change the greeting depending on the time of day, or take the opportunity to highlight items which were on special offer?

All of this logic could be coded into `SayHello.java`, but that's not a flexible or dynamic architecture. (Remember—recompiling is no fun.) What you'd like is the ability to publish, or register, extra content providers that are made available to the web page without it having to hardcode lookups.

As you've seen, code can be separated out into fragments that are installed independently. This is slightly more modular and dynamic than lumping everything into one JAR. But a fragment's host must be specified at build time, which isn't modular. As you've seen, they also aren't that dynamic, because the host bundle needs to be refreshed to attach and detach them. This makes them a useful mechanism for extending or modifying bundles, but not great for reuse or dynamic behavior changes.

If you're familiar with OSGi services, you might be thinking right now that OSGi services are an excellent way of providing chunks of function that can appear and disappear dynamically. A service can be used without ever specifying where the service comes from or who provides it, which means service-oriented code remains loosely coupled. But the code for looking up services can be a bit verbose. The code for managing services that might appear and disappear dynamically is even more long-winded.

If you're not coming from the world of OSGi, you're probably thinking of a different solution instead—dependency injection.

2.3.1 *Inversion of control*

Inversion of control is an elegant programming pattern where required services are supplied rather than looked up. This is often known as dependency injection, and occasionally as the *Hollywood principle* ("don't call us, we'll call you").

In general, dependency injection refers to a dependency injection container that wires together managed objects, injecting the dependencies into an object. The dependency injection container manages the lifecycle of objects, typically supporting callbacks for initialization and destruction. Figure 2.12 shows the differences between dependency lookup and dependency injection.

Dependency injection allows applications to be configured differently in different environments. For example, it's often useful to do unit testing with a lightweight version of a required component, possibly even a mocked implementation. Furthermore, as the business expands or requirements change, a different version of the component can be wired in, one that's more available, or scales better, or one that has better performance.

Dependency injection extends the loose coupling model to completely externalize the couplings from the code. Instructions for wiring components together are usually stored in XML metadata that can be changed relatively easily, without a recompile.

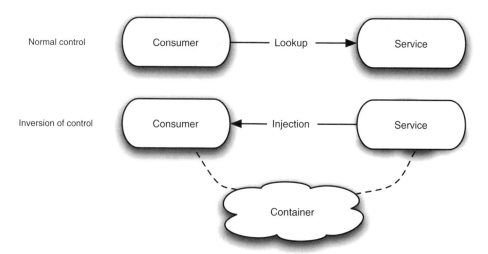

Figure 2.12 Normal control and inversion of control. In the normal case, the consumer looks up a service it requires. In the inversion of control model, also known as dependency injection, the consumer is automatically given the service. An application container manages passing the service to the consumer.

> **Who injects the dependency?**
>
> One of the nice things about dependency injection frameworks is how easy it is to *not* use them—when it suits you. When code constructs all its own dependencies, it can be difficult to bypass that code and run against stubs for testing. If dependencies are passed in, on the other hand, all that's required is for your test code to call a setter with a mock object of your choice.

2.3.2 *Introducing the Blueprint service*

Enterprise OSGi provides a simple way of accessing services declaratively, known as *Blueprint*. Blueprint supports inversion of control; a component's dependencies are injected into it rather than being looked up by it. Like almost everything in the enterprise OSGi programming model, Blueprint itself is implemented as a service. (It's a service for registering and injecting services.)

DEPENDENCY INJECTION AND OSGI

Dependency injection is useful everywhere, but has special benefits in an OSGi environment. Because the OSGi Service Registry is such a dynamic environment, it's difficult to correctly write a bundle that makes use of a service in a safe way, monitoring its lifecycle and finding an appropriate replacement. Using and providing services becomes even more difficult when an implementation depends upon more than one service, with a user having to write some complex thread-safe code. Using dependency injection eliminates this complexity by managing the lifecycle of the services exposed and consumed by a bundle.

In Apache Aries, Blueprint is used as a core part of the OSGi programming model. It's used not only to provide a dependency injection model, but it's also the integration point for many enterprise technologies and declarative qualities of service, such as managed JPA and container managed transactions. We'll explain more about JPA and JTA in the next chapter and discuss alternative OSGi dependency injection frameworks in section 6.2.

2.3.3 *Coupling two components with Blueprint*

One thing that would enhance the Fancy Foods web page is a listing of special offers. The Fancy Foods shop will have several departments, each with their own criteria for what goes on offer. For example, prices of fresh fruit and vegetables will vary a lot depending on the season and the weather. (In general, fruit prices and vegetable prices move in opposite directions. Summer is best for most fruits, whereas many vegetables are at their best in winter. This is partly why Brussels sprouts are so popular for Christmas dinner.) Other products don't have the same seasonal price fluctuations, but sell better at certain times of the year. For example, it makes sense to highlight premium chocolates on the front page around Valentine's Day, bulk candies for Halloween, and pickled onions and organic turkeys before Christmas. Clearly all this logic won't fit into `HelloWorld.java`, or even into a single other class.

Let's define an interface that can be implemented by everything that describes a special offer.

Listing 2.5   The `SpecialOffer` interface

```
package fancyfoods.offers;

import fancyfoods.food.Food;

public interface SpecialOffer {

    public Food getOfferFood();

    public String getDescription();
}
```

It relies on another interface for Food. (This is a food shop—you need food!)

Listing 2.6   The `Food` interface

```
package fancyfoods.food;

public interface Food {

    String getName();

    double getPrice();

    int getQuantityInStock();

}
```

To keep the application modular, these interfaces should go in their own bundle, `fancyfoods.api`. The `fancyfoods.api` bundle should export the `fancyfoods.offers` and `fancyfoods.food` packages. Keeping shared interfaces in an API bundle is a good OSGi practice; it ensures that only one copy of the interface is on the classpath, and that implementations can be swapped around without worrying about interbundle dependencies.

EXPOSING SERVICES WITH BLUEPRINT

What we'd like is a way of registering (or publishing) special offers for each department, without anyone having to maintain a central list of what offers are available. Enter Blueprint. Let's define a third bundle, `fancyfoods.department.chocolate`. The manifest for `fancyfoods.department.chocolate` should declare a dependency on the `fancyfoods.offers` package:

```
Manifest-Version: 1.0
Bundle-Blueprint: OSGI-INF/blueprint/*.xml
Bundle-SymbolicName: fancyfoods.department.chocolate
Bundle-Version: 1.0.0
Import-Package: fancyfoods.offers;version="[1.0, 2.0)",
 fancyfoods.food;version="[1.0, 2.0)"
Bundle-ManifestVersion: 2
```

Next, you need to provide a `SpecialOffer` implementation:

Listing 2.7   The `RomanticChocolateOffer` class

```
package fancyfoods.chocolate;

import java.util.Calendar;

import fancyfoods.food.Food;
import fancyfoods.offers.SpecialOffer;

public class RomanticChocolateOffer implements SpecialOffer {

    @Override
    public String getDescription() {
        return "A wonderful surprise for someone you want to impress.";
    }

    @Override
    public Food getOfferFood() {                        ⟵  What's on offer depends
        if (isNearValentinesDay()) {                         on time of year.
            return new HeartShapedChocolates();
        } else {
            return new SquareChocolates();
        }
    }

    private boolean isNearValentinesDay() {              ⟵  Is it early
        Calendar today = Calendar.getInstance();              February?
        return today.get(Calendar.MONTH) == Calendar.FEBRUARY
            && today.get(Calendar.DAY_OF_MONTH) <= 14;
    }
}
```

There's no need to export the `fancyfoods.department.chocolate.offers` package, because nothing else in the application should depend on it. It's not always possible, but a good goal in application design is to try to divide bundles into those with exported packages but no package dependencies (like `fancyfoods.api`) and those with imported packages but no externals (like `fancyfoods.department.chocolate`). A bundle that both exports a lot of packages and imports a lot of packages is highly coupled, and therefore fragile. The ideal dependency graph should look more like a fork than like spaghetti.

How will other code get hold of the `RomanticChocolateOffer` if the package isn't exported? To make the class available for dependency injection, you need to provide metadata for the Blueprint service.

Blueprint metadata should live in a folder called OSGI-INF/blueprint. (If for some reason you need to use a different folder, you can point Blueprint to your files by listing them in an optional `Bundle-Blueprint:` header.) The filename doesn't matter, but blueprint.xml is a popular choice.

Listing 2.8   A simple blueprint.xml file

```
<?xml version="1.0" encoding="UTF-8"?>
<blueprint                                         ⟵  Namespace is important!
    xmlns="http://www.osgi.org/xmlns/blueprint/v1.0.0">
```

```
<service
    interface="fancyfoods.offers.SpecialOffer"          ⟵── Declare OSGi service.
    ref="romanticOffer" />
<bean                                                   ⟵── Service implementation.
    id="romanticOffer"
    class="fancyfoods.chocolate.RomanticChocolateOffer" />
```

```
</blueprint>
```

The `service` element declares that a bean should be exposed as an OSGi service, suitable for injection into other Blueprint-managed beans or direct lookup. The `bean` element describes a managed bean. Blueprint will take care of instantiating the bean and initializing it with required properties. In this case, the `RomanticChocolateOffer` class doesn't need any external configuration.

CHECKING OUT THE SPECIAL OFFERS

Build the `api` and `chocolate` bundles and drop them into the load directory. They'll start automatically. When you query the chocolate department bundle, you'll see that it has registered an OSGi service implementing the `SpecialOffer` interface (figure 2.13).

Annotations and Blueprint

One of the questions we get asked most often about Blueprint is whether it supports annotations. Java 7 and Spring both support annotation-driven injection of dependencies, and an extension for Aries Blueprint does too. Because annotations aren't part of the Blueprint standard, we won't cover them; however, we do expect Blueprint annotations to appear in a future release of the enterprise OSGi specification.

WIRING BLUEPRINT BEANS TOGETHER

Who's going to use this service? Rather than hooking the service right up to our web bundle, let's make the dependency chain a bit more interesting by adding an `Offer-Aggregator` service. The `OfferAggregator` takes all the available special offers and works out which ones should be displayed to the user, and in what order. Separating interface from implementation is always a good idea, so the interface should live in the `api` bundle.

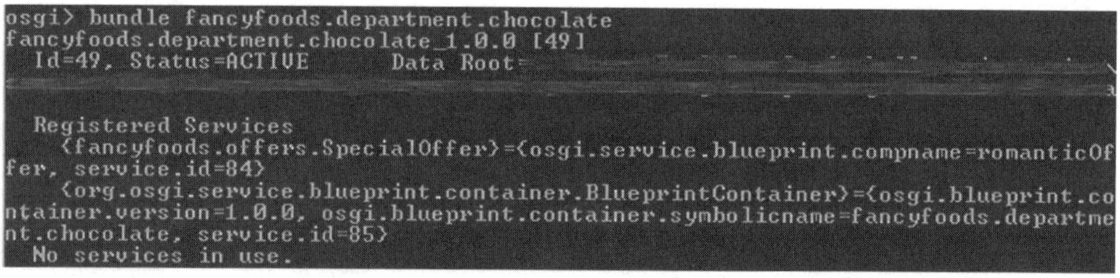

```
osgi> bundle fancyfoods.department.chocolate
fancyfoods.department.chocolate_1.0.0 [49]
  Id=49, Status=ACTIVE        Data Root=

  Registered Services
    {fancyfoods.offers.SpecialOffer}={osgi.service.blueprint.compname=romanticOf
fer, service.id=84}
    {org.osgi.service.blueprint.container.BlueprintContainer}={osgi.blueprint.co
ntainer.version=1.0.0, osgi.blueprint.container.symbolicname=fancyfoods.departme
nt.chocolate, service.id=85}
  No services in use.
```

Figure 2.13 The bundle details for the `chocolate` bundle show that it registers an OSGi service implementing the `SpecialOffer` interface. A Blueprint container for this bundle is also registered as a service by the Blueprint implementation.

```
package fancyfoods.offers;

import java.util.List;

public interface CurrentOffers {

    public List<SpecialOffer> getCurrentOffers();

}
```

Next, we'll need a new bundle, with another blueprint.xml file. We'll call this bundle fancyfoods.business and its manifest will need to look something like the following listing.

```
Manifest-Version: 1.0
Bundle-Name: Fancy Foods Business Logic
Bundle-Blueprint: OSGI-INF/blueprint/*.xml
Bundle-SymbolicName: fancyfoods.business
Bundle-Version: 1.0.0
Bundle-ManifestVersion: 2
Import-Package: fancyfoods.food;version="[1.0, 2.0)",
 fancyfoods.offers;version="[1.0, 2.0)"
```

Like the chocolate department bundle, our bundle will use Blueprint to publish a service. In this case, the bean we're exposing as a service also has dependencies injected into it.

Listing 2.10 Using Blueprint to inject dependencies

```
<?xml version="1.0" encoding="UTF-8"?>
<blueprint
    xmlns="http://www.osgi.org/xmlns/blueprint/v1.0.0">          Expose
    <service                                                     service
        interface="fancyfoods.offers.CurrentOffers"
        ref="offerAggregator" />
    <bean                                                        Inject property
        id="offerAggregator"                                     to setOffers()
        class="fancyfoods.offers.impl.OfferAggregator">          method
        <property
            name="offers"
            ref="specialOffers" />
    </bean>                                    Pass in all SpecialOffers
    <reference-list                            to setOffers()
        id="specialOffers"
        interface="fancyfoods.offers.SpecialOffer" />
</blueprint>
```

The implementation of the OfferAggregator doesn't need to instantiate the special offers it's going to be aggregating—the container injects them. A null check isn't needed, either, because the container won't instantiate the class unless its dependencies are available.

Listing 2.11   The `OfferAggregator` class

```
package fancyfoods.offers.impl;

import java.util.*;

import fancyfoods.offers.CurrentOffers;
import fancyfoods.offers.SpecialOffer;

public class OfferAggregator implements CurrentOffers {

    private static final int MAX_OFFERS = 4;
    private List<SpecialOffer> offers;

    public void setOffers(List<SpecialOffer> offers) {          List of offers
        this.offers = offers;                                   gets injected
    }

    @Override                                                   Format offers
    public List<SpecialOffer> getCurrentOffers() {              into a table
        List<SpecialOffer> sortedOffers =
            new ArrayList<SpecialOffer>(offers);                Sort offers
        Collections.sort(sortedOffers, new OfferComparator());  by price
        int offerCount = Math.min(MAX_OFFERS, sortedOffers.size());
        return sortedOffers.subList(0, offerCount);             Trim list
    }                                                           down

    private static class OfferComparator implements
        Comparator<SpecialOffer> {

        @Override
        public int compare(SpecialOffer offer1, SpecialOffer offer2) {
            return ((Double) offer2.getOfferFood().getPrice()).
                compareTo(offer1.getOfferFood().getPrice());
        }
    }
}
```

If you want to liven things up and make the OfferAggregator work a bit harder, you can register more SpecialOffer implementations. They will all magically appear in the list passed to the OfferAggregator. Figure 2.14 shows how the application architecture would look with an extra cheese department.

The offer aggregator applies the Fancy Foods business logic to the raw list of current offers. Flooding customers with a big long list of promotions will only confuse them, so the aggregator restricts the offer count to four. Customers will probably get more excited by offers for high-cost items, so the aggregator puts those at the top of the list.

References and reference lists

The offer aggregator assumed that multiple offers would be registered, and presenting a list of offers was the right thing to do. For some other types of service, only one is ever required. For example, it would be quite wrong to process credit card payments more than once just because multiple credit card payment processing providers were available! If you only want one implementation, use a <reference> element instead of a <reference-list>. If multiple services are available, the container will supply one

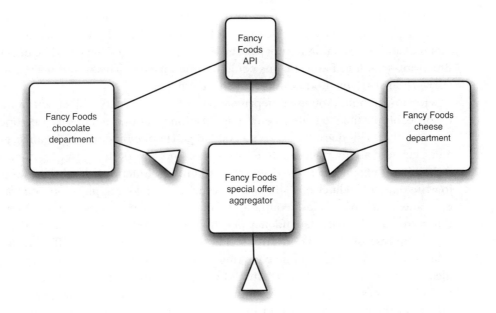

Figure 2.14 The backend of the Fancy Foods application. Triangles represent service dependencies, with the broad end of the triangle facing the consumers of the service. There isn't a direct dependency between the chocolate department and the offer aggregator, but the offer aggregator does consume a service provided by the chocolate department.

of them more or less at random. The order in which services get returned, and therefore the one you get, can be influenced by specifying a ranking in the Blueprint service definition. Finer control can also be achieved using service properties, but for now we're happy to accept every offer in whatever order it arrives.

Getting into the service-oriented frame of mind

Both of these operations take in a list of special offers and then return a modified list, which is then used as input to the next adjustment. If you're keen on abstraction, you may already be thinking that each adjustment could be represented as an instance of an `OfferListAdjuster` interface:

```
public interface OfferListAdjuster {
    public List<SpecialOffer> adjust(List<SpecialOffer> offers);
}
```

With this change, the offer aggregator no longer needs to include the code for individual adjustments to the offer list:

```
public List<SpecialOffer> getCurrentOffers() {
    OfferListAdjuster[] adjusters = new OfferListAdjuster[] {
        new OfferSorter(), new OfferTrimmer() };
    for (OfferListAdjuster adjuster : adjusters) {
        offers = adjuster.adjust(offers);
    }
    return offers;
}
```

The offer aggregator still has to know what adjustments to make, because the list of adjuster classes is hardcoded. We hope at least some of you have just had a lightbulb moment and realized that it's not just the list of special offers that could be injected by Blueprint—the list of adjustments could also be injected. This would make the `get-CurrentOffers()` method wonderfully short and generic.

How much should you use Blueprint and OSGi services? With a bit of determination, it's probably possible to code an entire application without ever constructing one class from another. This doesn't mean it's a good idea! Despite Blueprint's elegance, getting an instance of an interface via Blueprint is a bit more work than just constructing the darn thing. In many cases, the decoupling offered by Blueprint clearly justifies having to write one or two lines of XML, but for some parts of your application, the transparency and concision of close coupling is fine. We'll discuss architectural patterns for Blueprint and alternate dependency injection frameworks more in chapter 6.

In the case of Fancy Foods, using Blueprint to publish special offers feels right. The list of special offers will be changing regularly, so hardcoding them isn't a good idea. Each department will know what's best to offer when—pink chocolates at Valentine's Day, cheese when it's approaching its sell-by date. The logic for aggregating the offers, on the other hand, will probably always be centrally managed. You wouldn't want a chocolate maniac in the chocolate department to be able to publish a rule that always put chocolate offers first in the pile of promotions! Bearing this in mind, even though you *could* rewrite the offer aggregator to be even more service-oriented, it's probably not worth it—listing 2.11 is good as it is.

Blueprint beans can be wired together to get some pretty complex behavior. Blueprint isn't a substitute for good, old-fashioned Java code, but it sometimes can make it an awful lot shorter!

Spring and Blueprint

If you think this looks a lot like Spring Dynamic Modules, you're right. Blueprint is based on Spring DM. Blueprint does have some areas of technical difference from Spring DM, but the most significant difference is that Blueprint is an open standard.

We'll be coming back to Blueprint and some of its more advanced features in chapter 6. For now, we'll show you how to get the web frontend talking to the current offers service.

2.4   *Bridging JNDI and OSGi*

The final piece is to hook these special offers up to the servlet. There's a snag, though—most web container implementations aren't fully integrated with Blueprint (and at the moment, there's nothing in the specification that says they should be). The problem is that the Blueprint container takes a lot of control over the lifecycle of Blueprint beans—it identifies when the services they require are present, instantiates

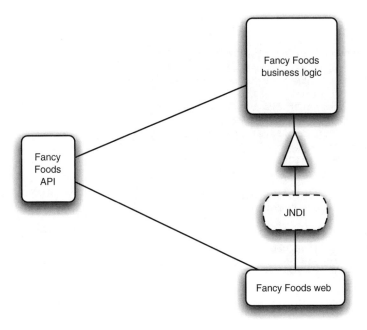

Figure 2.15 The Fancy Foods web bundle accesses the offer aggregator service using JNDI. It has no direct dependency on the chocolate or cheese department services.

the classes, and injects any references. Often, tens of classes will be bootstrapped by the Blueprint container in a big chain of managed dependencies. Unfortunately, the web container also takes a lot of control over servlet lifecycles, instantiating them in response to incoming web requests.

It's easy to see that if something is both a Blueprint bean and a servlet, the Blueprint container and the web container could have a messy tussle over what happens when to the poor servlet, which is caught in the middle. Getting the two to integrate neatly hasn't been done yet—especially not in a standards-based way.

Unless you're writing an enterprise OSGi application from scratch, the web container is unlikely to be the only place where the Blueprint injection model doesn't fit quite right. Luckily, Blueprint has a nice integration with JNDI. Services registered by Blueprint are all available in JNDI, and can be looked up using the interface name (see figure 2.15).

Let's have a look at how you can use JNDI to access your Blueprint service (figure 2.15) by writing another servlet called fancyfoods.web.SayHelloJNDI and putting it into our web bundle. You can see how the doGet method works in the following listing.

Listing 2.12   Adding special offers using JNDI to access OSGi Services

```
public class SayHelloJNDI extends HttpServlet {

    protected void doGet(HttpServletRequest request,
                    HttpServletResponse response)
                throws ServletException, IOException {
```

```
        PrintWriter html = response.getWriter();
        html.append("<html>");
        html.append("Hello valued customer!<br/>");
        try {
            InitialContext ctx = new InitialContext();
            String jndiName = "osgi:service/" +
                CurrentOffers.class.getName();
            CurrentOffers offers =
                (CurrentOffers) ctx.lookup(jndiName);
            html.append("<table>");
            List<SpecialOffer> currentOffers =
                offers.getCurrentOffers();

            for (SpecialOffer offer : currentOffers) {
                writeRowForOffer(html, offer);
            }
            html.append("</table>");
        } catch (NamingException e) {
            html.append("We have no special offers today. " +
                    "Try again tomorrow.");
        }
        html.append("</html>");
    }

    private void writeRowForOffer(PrintWriter html,
                                    SpecialOffer offer) {
        html.append("<tr>");
        String description = offer.getDescription();
        Food offerFood = offer.getOfferFood();
        html.append("<td>" + offerFood.getName() + "</td>");
        html.append("<td>" + offerFood.getPrice() + "</td>");
        html.append("<td>" + description + "</td>");
        html.append("</tr>");
    }
}
```

The osgi:service/ namespace provides access to services in the OSGi Service Registry. Services are registered under their interface name, which makes them easy to find. If no services implementing the SpecialOffer interface are registered, a NamingException will be thrown. In this case that's not a problem—special offers aren't compulsory! (The sharp-eyed among you will notice that we've abandoned internationalization again to keep the sample shorter.)

Implementing SayHelloJNDI has added some new dependencies, and that needs to be reflected in the manifest. The fancyfood.offers, fancyfoods.food, and javax .naming packages need to be imported:

```
Manifest-Version: 1.0
Bundle-ManifestVersion: 2
Bundle-SymbolicName: fancyfoods.web
Bundle-Version: 1.0.0
Bundle-ClassPath: WEB-INF/classes
Web-ContextPath: /fancyfoods.web
Import-Package: fancyfoods.offers;version="[1.0, 2.0)",
```

```
fancyfoods.food;version="[1.0, 2.0)", javax.naming,
javax.servlet;version="[2.5, 3.0)",
javax.servlet.http;version="[2.5, 3.0)"
```

Finally, you need to add a new entry into your web.xml to register our servlet:

```
<servlet>
    <servlet-name>SayHelloJNDI</servlet-name>
    <servlet-class>fancyfoods.web.SayHelloJNDI</servlet-class>
</servlet>
<servlet-mapping>
    <servlet-name>SayHelloJNDI</servlet-name>
    <url-pattern>/SayHelloJNDI</url-pattern>
</servlet-mapping>
```

Try adding the updated fancyfoods.web to the load directory before the fancy-foods.api bundle. There's no need to restart the OSGi container; file changes will be detected and the bundle will be automatically refreshed. When you list the bundles with ss, fancyfoods.web will only be INSTALLED instead of STARTED. This means some of its dependencies were missing. When you copy across the fancyfoods.api JAR into the load directory, the fancyfoods.web bundle will spontaneously leap into life and become STARTED.

When you load the SayHelloJNDI web page, you should see a helpful message explaining that there are no special offers (figure 2.16).

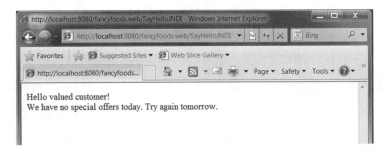

Figure 2.16 Before the aggregator bundle is started, the Fancy Foods welcome page won't be able to display any special offers.

After dropping your aggregator into the load directory, a CurrentOffers object will be available in JNDI, but there won't be any special offers available, so the web page will show an empty table. Adding the chocolate bundle to the load directory will cause the chocolate offer to be injected into the offer aggregator (see figure 2.17).

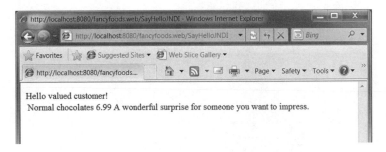

Figure 2.17 After the aggregator and chocolate bundle are loaded, the page will display a special offer for chocolate.

2.5   *Summary*

If you've been working through the Fancy Foods application with us, you've achieved a lot in this chapter. Take a moment to pat yourself on the back. You now have a simple enterprise OSGi container going. You've written a web application, hooked components together with dependency injection, and integrated Blueprint with legacy Java using JNDI. You have half the building blocks you'll need for a complete enterprise application. We'll cover the missing blocks in the next chapter—persistence and transactions.

Persistence pays off

This chapter covers

- The benefits of JDBC and JPA, and why they won't work in an OSGi environment without help
- How enterprise OSGi and the Apache Aries extensions restore a lovely programming model
- How to read and write from a database in your sample application
- How to use transactions for cleanup when things go wrong

Just as it needs a frontend, every enterprise application needs a backend. For many business applications the heart of the backend is persistence—either read-only access to a directory service, or a full read–write relational data mine, or something in between. This chapter explains how to use persistence and transactions in an enterprise OSGi environment.

Let's start with a reminder of the persistence options available in Java.

3.1   Java and persistence

Persistence has been a core part of the Java platform since its introduction. Although the designers of Java didn't envisage it being used in the kinds of enterprise environments where it's now common, databases have always been important.

3.1.1   Making persistence easy

One of the aims of the early Java persistence support was to provide solid abstractions for database access. Databases are notoriously idiosyncratic, and accessing them can be hard work, so it's an area that benefits from a little help from the platform.

JDBC

Java support for databases began with the *Java Database Connectivity (JDBC) API*, a part of the core Java platform. All of the classes in the `javax.sql` and `java.sql` packages are part of the JDBC API. JDBC abstracts away the vendor-specific details of connecting to databases. It also provides interfaces that represent SQL statements and the results of a query.

Although they're database-independent, these interfaces are thin wrappers for the raw database access. Developers assume complete responsibility for converting the result set into Java objects. Developers must also code all of the SQL statements for inserting and retrieving data. Developers need a fairly solid grasp of SQL and database administration to achieve much with JDBC. Because SQL support tends to vary between database vendors, developers also need to know a good deal about the intended deployment environment for their applications.

This programming model is clearly not ideal, and there have been a number of attempts over the years to provide more substantial abstractions between the developer and the database.

ENTITY BEANS

The first attempt to protect developers from databases was the *entity bean*. Entity beans were introduced in the Java Enterprise Edition as part of the Enterprise JavaBeans (EJB) specification. Entity beans moved to an object-oriented view of database access; each entity bean represented a collection of data that was persisted. The job of managing the persistence was handled by the container, leaving the programmer free to focus on the data structure and the business logic.

It all sounds nice, but after some initial uptake, EJBs were criticized and largely dropped from any serious business use. There was widespread agreement that the problem they were trying to solve was a real one, but the entity bean cure might be worse than JDBC disease. EJBs were heavyweight, difficult to use, and verbose. Developers were required to implement a dizzying assortment of interfaces and lifecycle methods.

The EJB 3.0 specification has gone some way to rehabilitate EJBs by replacing the creaking interface-driven beans with annotated Plain Old Java Objects (POJOs). But the original entity beans didn't even survive to EJB 3.0, having been replaced with their more popular competitor, JPA.

HIBERNATE

Despite their eventual unpopularity, entity beans did much to popularize *Object-Relational Mapping (ORM)*. The ORM ideas were picked up by a range of lightweight alternatives to EJBs. The dominant competitor was an open source product called *Hibernate*. Hibernate uses an XML file (or, in later versions, annotations) to define the mapping between data objects and database content. The Hibernate framework does all the JDBC work so that the application doesn't have to.

JPA

The *Java Persistence API (JPA)* is a Java EE 5 specification that's a natural evolution of Hibernate and another ORM technology known as JDO. Many Hibernate ideas were incorporated into JPA, and more recent versions of Hibernate implement the JPA specification (as do many other persistence providers such as EclipseLink and OpenJPA). The standardization of JPA allows different persistence providers to be used without rewriting applications.

Although JPA (and its precursors, like Hibernate) is now the persistence programming model of choice, JDBC hasn't gone away. JPA implementations are all built internally on JDBC (figure 3.1).

Although it's a Java EE specification, JPA also works well in a conventional Java environment. Unfortunately, until recently, neither JDBC nor JPA worked well in an OSGi environment. This was a shame, because these technologies had some limitations that could be fixed by OSGi. Although JPA gives good vendor-independence, because there's no support for dynamic replacement, JPA providers can't be swapped without restarts. Similarly, JDBC drivers can't be removed from a running system.

3.1.2 *The problems with traditional persistence in OSGi*

Why don't JDBC and JPA work well as designed in an OSGi environment? After all, OSGi is Java with a fancy classpath.

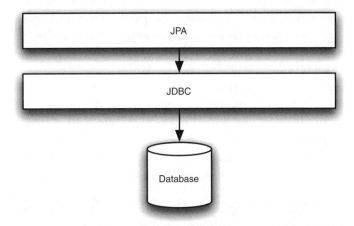

Figure 3.1   JDBC provides a useful Java-language access layer on top of a raw database. JPA and other ORM frameworks add support for transparently moving between database entries and Java objects.

It turns out that it's exactly the classpath that causes problems. JDBC driver implementations rely heavily on `Class.forName()` and META-INF services. This sort of reflection doesn't work in OSGi without an explicit package dependency on the driver implementation. The `DriverManager` only scans the META-INF/services folder once, on initialization, so it might not even find all of the available drivers. (Remember that in OSGi things appear on and disappear off the classpath.)

The general experience of using JDBC in an OSGi environment, therefore, is that often the `DriverManager` won't recognize your datasource drivers. Even when the `DriverManager` does find the drivers and tries to initialize them, the result is almost always a `ClassNotFoundException`.

JPA faces similar problems because it uses similar patterns. `EntityManagerFactories` are constructed reflectively from META-INF services by a static `Persistence` class. The consequence is that the `EntityManagerFactories` can't be found and can't be constructed if they *are* found.

Workarounds for both JPA and JDBC are possible, but they're not pretty. They generally involve strange little wrappers to bundle-ize JDBC and JPA providers and register them by hand with the static `DriverManager` or `Persistence` factory classes. Explicit dependencies on the exact JDBC and JPA provider in the manifest of the consuming code are unavoidable.

What the META-INF services pattern is trying to achieve is a loose, service-oriented coupling between the consuming code and the implementation. The ironic and unintended side effect of this pattern in core OSGi is tight coupling and explicit management of implementations.

Happily, enterprise OSGi offers a first-class services solution. It's natural to register both JDBC and JPA providers as OSGi services. These can then be looked up from the Service Registry or injected using Blueprint.

APPLICATION-MANAGED AND CONTAINER-MANAGED PERSISTENCE

With a JDBC provider that adheres to the enterprise OSGi JDBC service specification, an application is well positioned to access a database using JDBC in a clean, service-oriented way. But few developers use JDBC to access databases anymore, unless they're writing a JPA implementation!

The JPA service specification also allows clean, service-oriented database access, but it's not as complete a solution as the JDBC one. Conventional JPA can be used in both Java SE and Java EE environments. In Java SE environments, the application needs to do a reasonable amount of work to get hold of the right bits of the JPA implementation, define scopes, handle exceptions, and generally manage the lifecycle of the JPA resources. This is described as unmanaged or application-managed JPA. In a Java EE environment, the container can take over much of this work, significantly reducing the amount of boilerplate code.

What's offered by the JPA service specification is the equivalent of the Java SE level of support. Apache Aries provides extensions to this that bring the support up to the level of container-managed Java EE.

MANAGED JPA IN ENTERPRISE OSGI

The Aries JPA container makes use of the metadata required by the JPA service specification, but provides managed resources rather than unmanaged ones. By using dependency injection, an enterprise application can integrate with managed JPA using a single line of XML. The resulting code will automatically participate in JTA transactions and will have its lifecycle managed by the container.

How does this all look in action? Let's start by extending your Fancy Foods application with some persistent data.

3.2 Building a persistent application

The Fancy Foods application you've written is a nice application. It's got clean and elegant modularization and a fully dynamic architecture. New translations can be dropped in, and it has a nice push-based model for publishing special offers. Nonetheless, you may have a bothersome feeling that something is missing. The only Food instance in the entire system is one hardcoded box of chocolates. Not quite a superstore yet! We probably won't have to work hard to persuade you that a food shop needs more food, and that the most sensible way to manage ever-growing stock lists, variable prices, fluctuating inventory levels, and complex systems of categorization is with a database.

3.2.1 Setting up a datasource

Before you can do anything exciting with databases, you need to set up a datasource. The datasource is a mechanism for talking to the backend database from Java code. All that's required is a garden-variety datasource, but the pattern for setting it up may be new to you. Application servers usually support using an administrative console or series of configuration files for defining datasources. The platform you're using is a bare-bones runtime, so it doesn't have a user interface for datasources—or any graphical user interface at all, in fact.

Luckily, some of the generic wiring utilities provided by enterprise OSGi work well for configuring datasources. You'll use Blueprint to help out (figure 3.2). As you continue through the book, you'll see this is a common pattern.

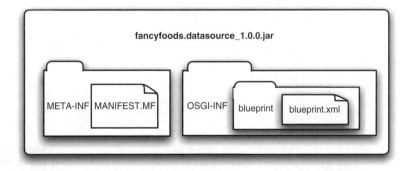

Figure 3.2 The datasource bundle is about as simple as a useful bundle could be. It has a manifest and a Blueprint file, but nothing else.

You've already seen how to add Blueprint metadata to an OSGi bundle in section 2.3.8. Set up a new bundle, `fancyfoods.datasource`, with a blueprint.xml file in OSGI-INF/ blueprint.

Do you really need a whole bundle?

Isn't a bundle with nothing inside it but a manifest and a Blueprint file a bit of a heavy-weight way of setting up a datasource? Well, if we're honest, perhaps! But the data-source configuration is closely tied to the database implementation. The Apache Aries sandbox that we're using comes with the Apache Derby database, but as you explore other stacks (chapter 13) you may wish to switch databases, or move to an application server with built-in admin support for configuring datasources. Isolating the datasource ensures you won't have to rewrite or rip out datasource configuration from another bundle as you update your stack.

Listing 3.1 shows the Blueprint for setting up the datasources. It defines two data-sources, one for transactional writes, and one for optimized nontransactional reads. A lot is going on in this Blueprint file, so we'll walk through the parts in detail.

Listing 3.1 An OSGI-INF/blueprint/blueprint.xml file that defines a Derby datasource

```
<blueprint
    xmlns="http://www.osgi.org/xmlns/blueprint/v1.0.0">         ❶ Use Blueprint to construct
    <bean                                                          datasource bean
        id="derbyDataSource"
        class="org.apache.derby.jdbc.EmbeddedDataSource">
        <property
            name="databaseName"
            value="memory:fancyfoodsDB" />                      ❷ Autocreate
        <property                                                  database
            name="createDatabase"
            value="create" />
                                                                ❸ Another bean for
    </bean>                                                        XA datasource
    <bean
        id="derbyXADataSource"
        class="org.apache.derby.jdbc.EmbeddedXADataSource">
        <property
            name="databaseName"                                 Properties are same
            value="memory:fancyfoodsDB" />                      as for non-XA bean
        <property
            name="createDatabase"
            value="create" />
    </bean>                                                     Expose bean as
    <service                                                    DataSource service
        ref="derbyDataSource"
        interface="javax.sql.DataSource">
        <service-properties>                                    Use nondefault
            <entry                                              JNDI name
                key="osgi.jndi.service.name"
                value="jdbc/fancyfoodsdb" />
```

```
        </service-properties>

    </service>

    <service
        ref="derbyXADataSource"
        interface="javax.sql.XADataSource">
        <service-properties>
            <entry
                key="osgi.jndi.service.name"
                value="jdbc/xafancyfoodsdb" />
        </service-properties>
    </service>

</blueprint>
```

Expose XA bean as
DataSource service

Use distinct
JNDI name

The first thing that's interesting about this Blueprint is that the classes that are being instantiated for the bean (❶ and ❸) aren't ones from the datasource bundle itself. This is different from what you were doing in chapter 2, where you were wiring together your own classes. It turns out the origin of the class doesn't matter at all. As long as the class can be loaded and has a public constructor, then Blueprint can create it and set properties on it. Even constructors that take arguments can be accommodated with Blueprint's <argument> element.

In this case, the essential property is the name of the physical database. You want to get up and going quickly, so you'll opt for an in-memory database by prefixing memory: to the database name. (It should be obvious that this is great for testing but not recommended for long-term business use!) For convenience, the datasource should automatically create the database, which can be achieved by setting the createDatabase property ❷.

With those properties set, you'll have good transactional and nontransactional datasources that come with free autocreated databases. The next step is to make these datasources available to be connected to.

SERVICES, SERVICE PROPERTIES, AND FILTERS

For this, you'll use another feature of Blueprint: the ability to set *service properties*. Service properties are a general OSGi concept. When it's registered in the Service Registry, any service can have arbitrary properties set on it. Unlike bean properties, the service properties aren't for the benefit of the service. In fact, the service doesn't even get to see them. Instead, the service properties tell the rest of the world a bit more about the service, so that they can decide between multiple possible matches. See figure 3.3.

Services can be looked up using the interface name, or extra criteria can be specified. These extra criteria are set using OSGi *service filters*. The filter syntax is based on LDAP syntax. It can take a bit of getting used to all the ampersands and parentheses, but filters are actually straightforward. If you'd like to brush up on the finer points of filters, we've got more examples in appendix A.

The most important thing to remember about filters is that they're directly related to service properties; if it can be set using a service property, it can be queried using a

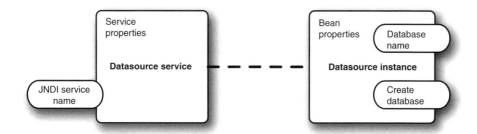

Figure 3.3 Properties can be set for both beans and services using Blueprint. Bean properties are used by the bean's business logic. Service properties are invisible to the object implementing the service, but they're visible to consumers of the service.

filter. This means service lookups can be general—"give me anything that implements this interface"—or very, very specific—"give me a service with this interface that also has this property set to that value but *also* doesn't have this other property set to some other value."

How does that relate to datasources? In section 2.4, we explained how our Aries stack helpfully publishes services to JNDI. Like a web container, most JPA implementations weren't originally written with enterprise OSGi in mind, and they rely on JNDI to find their datasources. Luckily, any Blueprint service can be looked up in JNDI. The lookup name is the interface implemented by the service, `javax.sql.DataSource` in this case. Anything can look up the datasource for your fancyfoodsdb database using the JNDI name `osgi:service/javax.sql.DataSource`.

This works nearly perfectly. JPA can be pointed to the JNDI name for the datasource, and it can look it up and use it as intended. The problems happen when the server has more than one datasource. Which one is returned from a service lookup of the `javax.sql.DataSource` interface? Well, it depends, but it's probably not the one you were hoping for. Because each datasource is closely associated with a particular database, a datasource isn't the sort of service where any arbitrary implementation will do!

This is where service properties and filters come to the rescue. Service properties can be added to the service, and then any JNDI lookup can filter on those properties. In listing 3.1 you specified a service property for the datasource:

```
<service-properties>
        <entry
            key="osgi.jndi.service.name"
            value="jdbc/fancyfoodsdb" />
    </service-properties>
```

This service can be looked up from JNDI using the following name:

```
osgi:service/javax.sql.DataSource/
 (osgi.jndi.service.name=jdbc/fancyfoodsdb)
```

Specify the `osgi:service` namespace, and then the interface name, and then you can add on any filters you like.

That's a slightly long-winded way of getting hold of a datasource from JNDI. It's too long to fit on a single line in this book, in fact! Enterprise OSGi gives you the tools to do better than that. The `osgi.jndi.service.name` property is a special property that tells the container to register the service in JNDI under that name. You can shorten the JNDI name to just the namespace and the name you provided:

```
osgi:service/jdbc/fancyfoodsdb
```

> **NOTE: APACHE ARIES LIMITATIONS** For Apache Aries transactions wrappers bundle versions 0.3 and below, the short-form JNDI lookup won't work, and the long-form lookup should be used instead.

The `osgi.jndi.service.name` property works in both directions. Objects registered in JNDI can be looked up as OSGi services using their interface name. As part of the conversion, the container will set the `osgi.jndi.service.name` to the object's original JNDI name.

THE DATASOURCE MANIFEST

Before the datasource can be deployed as an OSGi bundle, it will also need a manifest. The manifest defines the bundle symbolic name, and it will also need to import some packages. But wait—why does a bundle with no source code need to import packages?

Just because the bundle doesn't have any class files doesn't mean it's not doing anything. The datasource bundle does a great deal, but does it declaratively with Blueprint metadata. In this example, the Blueprint file refers to classes and interfaces in the `javax.sql` and `org.apache.derby.jdbc` packages. These classes will be instantiated by the Blueprint container on behalf of the bundle.

Think for a moment about what would happen if you tried to start the datasource bundle in an environment where nothing provided the `javax.sql` or `org.apache.derby.jdbc` packages. When the Blueprint container tried to instantiate the `EmbeddedDataSource` class it would fail horribly with a `ClassNotFoundException`. Not good. OSGi is all about avoiding these unpleasant runtime surprises by declaring dependencies up front.

With those dependencies, the manifest is as follows:

```
Manifest-Version: 1.0
Bundle-ManifestVersion: 2
Bundle-Name: Fancy Foods Datasource
Bundle-SymbolicName: fancyfoods.datasource
Bundle-Version: 1.0.0
Import-Package: javax.sql,
 org.apache.derby.jdbc
```

CONFIRMING YOU HAVE A DATASOURCE—OR THREE

Build your JAR and drop it into the load directory. When you list the bundles with `ss`, you should see your datasource bundle. If you get the bundle details with the `bundle` command, you'll see that your bundle is providing several datasource services (figure 3.4).

Not only do you have the two datasource services you registered, the container has helpfully provided you with a third. The third service implements the `DataSource`

```
osgi> bundle 36
fancyfoods.datasource_1.0.0 [36]
   Id=36, Status=ACTIVE          Data Root=

   Registered Services
      {javax.sql.XADataSource}={osgi.service.blueprint.compname=derbyXADataSource,
   osgi.jndi.service.name=jdbc/xafancyfoodsdb, service.id=67}
      {javax.sql.DataSource}={service.id=68, osgi.service.blueprint.compname=derby
   XADataSource, osgi.jndi.service.name=jdbc/xafancyfoodsdb, aries.xa.aware=true}
      {javax.sql.DataSource}={osgi.service.blueprint.compname=derbyDataSource, osg
   i.jndi.service.name=jdbc/fancyfoodsdb, service.id=69}
      {org.osgi.service.blueprint.container.BlueprintContainer}={osgi.blueprint.co
   ntainer.version=1.0.0, osgi.blueprint.container.symbolicname=fancyfoods.datasour
   ce, service.id=70}
```

Figure 3.4   The datasource bundle provides three datasource services. The first and third were explicitly configured in the blueprint.xml, but the second was automatically created by the container to provide support for implicit transactions.

interface, as expected by JPA, but it provides an extra function built around the XADataSource you registered, to provide full container-managed transaction support (figure 3.5).

This has perhaps been more work than you expected to have to do to set up a datasource. It's important to remember that the assembly shipped with the Apache Aries samples isn't a proper application server, or even half an application server. If you opt

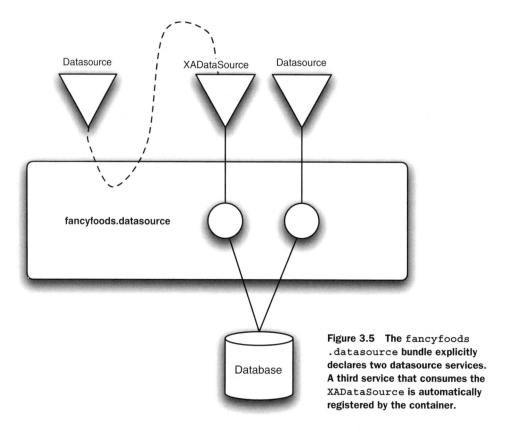

Figure 3.5   The fancyfoods .datasource **bundle explicitly declares two datasource services. A third service that consumes the** XADataSource **is automatically registered by the container.**

to use Apache Aries with one of the open or commercial application server integrations—which we heartily recommend—setting up the datasources will be much less verbose. In the interim, think of the process of setting up the datasources as a useful exercise in advanced Blueprint.

Now that you have a datasource service, what can you do with it?

3.2.2 Creating a persistence bundle

The datasource groundwork allows you to move on to the real meat of the Fancy Foods persistence. You set your datasources up to use in-memory databases, so you don't need to worry about creating physical databases or writing lots of SQL to set them up. It's still worth thinking, though, about what you're trying to model with the database and what kind of data you want to store.

THE FANCY FOODS SCHEMA

The schema for modeling the Fancy Foods shop is fairly straightforward—so straightforward, in fact, that it contains only one small table. Figure 3.6 shows the schema. You shouldn't infer anything from our tiny schema about the general scalability of JPA in enterprise OSGi. We'll play with quite a small database, but complicated databases can also be handled with ease.

Food
Name
Price
QuantityInStock

Figure 3.6 The schema for the Fancy Foods database. It's probably not the most complex schema you're likely to see in your career! The database only has one table, representing a food. Foods have a name, a price, and a stock level.

DEFINING A PERSISTENCE UNIT

You tell JPA about your schema in two ways. The first is in the persistence.xml file. This file is the heart of a JPA application, whether it's running in Java SE, Java EE, or enterprise OSGi. It sets up one or more persistence units. Each persistence unit defines a relationship between a datasource and Java classes that represent database tables (see figure 3.7).

We won't cover persistence units in too much detail, because an enterprise OSGi persistence.xml file is pretty much the same as a Java EE persistence unit or even a Java SE persistence unit. Listing 3.2 shows the persistence.xml for the Fancy Foods shop.

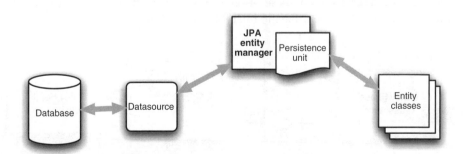

Figure 3.7 The connection between a database and Java objects is managed by a JPA entity manager. The persistence unit defines the relationship between the datasource and the classes.

Each table is represented by one Java POJO, known as an entity. In your case you only have one table, so you only declare one entity.

Listing 3.2   The META-INF/persistence.xml file

```
<persistence
    xmlns="http://java.sun.com/xml/ns/persistence"
    xmlns:xsi="http://www.w3.org/2001/XMLSchema-instance"
    xsi:schemaLocation="http://java.sun.com/xml/ns/persistence
    http://java.sun.com/xml/ns/persistence/persistence_2_0.xsd"
    version="2.0">

    <persistence-unit name="fancyfoods">                          Defines new
                                                                  persistence unit
        <jta-data-source>
            osgi:service/jdbc/xafancyfoodsdb                      Datasource
         </jta-data-source>                                       JNDI names
        <non-jta-data-source>
            osgi:service/jdbc/fancyfoodsdb
        </non-jta-data-source>                                    Entity
        <class>fancyfoods.persistence.FoodImpl</class>            implementation class
        <exclude-unlisted-classes>true</exclude-unlisted-classes>
        <properties>
            <property
                name="openjpa.jdbc.SynchronizeMappings"           Generates schema
                value="buildSchema(ForeignKeys=true)" />          from Java entities
        </properties>
    </persistence-unit>
</persistence>
```

The persistence unit must declare both a JTA and a non-JTA datasource (see figure 3.8). JPA-managed database access usually requires a transactional datasource, but transactions can be expensive, so in some cases the JPA container optimizes operations by using a nontransactional datasource. We'll come back to transactions in section 3.3. Use the JNDI names you configured in listing 3.1.

The persistence unit also declares one or more class files, each of which contains an entity that's mapped to a database table. Finally, you don't want to have to worry about SQL and table creation, so add an extra property that requests that the database tables are generated on the fly, based on the Java entities. The combination of this and the setting to create the database in section 3.3 means that you can now do database programming without ever having to create or configure a database.

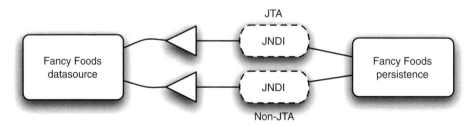

Figure 3.8   The persistence bundle uses the services exposed by the datasource bundle. It accesses them by JNDI lookup.

ENTITIES

For the moment, the persistence unit declares one entity, `fancyfoods.persistence`
`.FoodImpl`. `FoodImpl` is an implementation of the `Food` interface we defined in section 2.3.9. It allows `Food` objects to be persisted to, and read from, a database. The
nice thing about it, and the reason why so many people use JPA, is that it does all this
with one or two tiny little annotations; JPA does all the work for you, as shown in the
following listing.

Listing 3.3 The implementation of the `FoodImpl` entity class

```
@Entity(name = "FOOD")                              ⟵—— Entity annotation declares JPA entity
public class FoodImpl implements Food {

    @Id
    private String name;            ⟵—— Primary key
    private double price;
    private int quantity;
                                                    ┐ No-argument
    public FoodImpl() {                          ⟵—┘ constructor for JPA
    }

    public FoodImpl(String name, double price, int quantity) {   ⟵┐ With-argument
        this();                                                   │ constructor for
        this.name = name;                                         │ convenience
        this.price = price;
        this.quantity = quantity;
    }

    @Override
    public String getName() {                        ┐ Getter and setter
        return this.name;                         ⟵—┘ for name column
    }

    public void setName(String name) {
        this.name = name;
    }
                                                   ┐ More getters
    //...                                       ⟵—┘ and setters
```

Although it's too long to include in full here, the `FoodImpl` class is a thin data carrier.
It only contains getters and setters, without any business logic. It doesn't have responsibility for persisting itself.

Enhancing the entities

Before they can be used by most JPA providers, entity POJOs must be *enhanced*.
Enhancement adds extra bytecode to the classes. If you're running in a Java EE 5 (or
later) application server, JPA entities will be automatically enhanced. Usefully, recent
versions of Apache Aries are also able to perform this enhancement. If you aren't running in a system that provides automatic enhancement, then an Ant task (or similar)
can be used to enhance the entities when building, but it can also be done using an
Eclipse builder.

NOTE: APACHE ARIES LIMITATIONS   For versions of Apache Aries JPA below 1.0, or OSGi framework versions earlier than 4.3, entities aren't automatically enhanced. The OpenJPA documentation has instructions on build-time enhancement. If you're using one of the application servers discussed in chapter 13, rather than our little Aries assembly, the server may take care of enhancing the entities at runtime.

THE PERSISTENCE MANIFEST

To achieve full container management of your persistence, you need to let the container know that this is an OSGi persistence bundle by telling it about the persistence.xml file in the bundle manifest:

```
Manifest-Version: 1.0
Bundle-ManifestVersion: 2
Bundle-Name: Fancy Foods Persistence Bundle
Bundle-SymbolicName: fancyfoods.persistence
Bundle-Version: 1.0.0
Meta-Persistence:
Import-Package: fancyfoods.food;version="[1.0.0,2.0.0)",
 javax.persistence;version="[1.1,2.0)",
 org.apache.openjpa.util
```

The `Meta-Persistence:` header tells the JPA service where to look for the persistence.xml file (which therefore doesn't need to be called persistence.xml). The header must be specified for the bundle to be eligible for managed JPA, but the location is optional. If no location is specified, it defaults to META-INF/persistence.xml, the same as in the Java SE and Java EE cases.

As usual, the bundle also needs package imports, but not many. The persistence bundle will provide implementations of the Fancy Foods API, so it will need to import that package. It also needs the JPA API, but nothing else. Because of the OSGi services approach, it doesn't need any implementation-specific packages.

Notice that the `fancyfoods.persistence` package isn't exported. In fact, no packages are exported. Data is persisted using JPA, but consuming code shouldn't have to know these implementation details. In fact, consuming code shouldn't even have to know that there's a `fancyfoods.persistence` bundle. How does anything get hold of the persistence classes? Blueprint!

SETTING UP A PERSISTENCE SERVICE

Define a new interface, `fancyfoods.food.Inventory`, shown in the following listing. To keep the interface separate from implementation, it should be packaged in the `fancyfoods.api` bundle you wrote in chapter 2.

> **Listing 3.4   The interface for the food persistence service**

```
package fancyfoods.food;

import java.util.List;

public interface Inventory {
```

```
    Food getFood(String name);

    List<Food> getFoodsWhoseNameContains(String name, int maxResults);

    void createFood(String name, double price, int quantity);

    int removeStock(String name, int quantity);

    int getFoodCount();

}
```

The `Inventory` interface provides methods for adding and removing food from the database, searching for food in the database, and finding out how much food there is in the database. In a more complex application, you might want to expose more complex queries as well. You haven't exposed the fact that you're using JPA in your interface. This keeps things more flexible and decoupled, and it can be particularly handy when it comes to unit testing.

> ### Modularity, rebuilding, and split packages
>
> You may be wondering why you're rebuilding bundles you wrote earlier. After all, OSGi is all about modularity, and modularity definitely doesn't mean rebuilding existing bundles every time you add new function to your application. Our excuse is that you'd normally do a bit more up-front design work rather than build an application up one chapter at a time!
>
> But, if you don't like the idea of rebuilding the API bundle, feel free to add a new bundle instead. Our one caution is that you must choose a different package name for `Inventory`. Packages are closely associated with bundles in OSGi, and splitting a package across multiple bundles is best avoided. For one thing, it's not very modular! More seriously, by default OSGi will only wire importing bundles to *one* of the exporting bundles, leaving some of your interfaces inaccessible.

The Blueprint for the persistence service

In the cases where you're not unit testing, it's most convenient to allow the Blueprint and JPA containers to do most of the work to set up and manage the instances of `Inventory`.

You'll be relieved to see that the Blueprint for setting up the managed persistence is much shorter than the Blueprint for setting up the datasource, even though it's arguably achieving a great deal more, as shown in the following listing.

Listing 3.5 The blueprint.xml for the persistence bundle

```
<blueprint
    xmlns="http://www.osgi.org/xmlns/blueprint/v1.0.0"          ◁── Two new namespaces
    xmlns:jpa="http://aries.apache.org/xmlns/jpa/v1.0.0"             needed.
    xmlns:tx="http://aries.apache.org/xmlns/transactions/v1.0.0">

    <bean
        id="inventory"
```

```
    class="fancyfoods.persistence.InventoryImpl">
    <tx:transaction
        method="*"
        value="Required" />
    <jpa:context
        property="entityManager"
        unitname="fancyfoods" />
</bean>
<service
    ref="inventory"
    interface="fancyfoods.food.Inventory" />
```

❶ All method calls should have transactions.

❷ Inject persistence context.

Expose as InventoryService.

```
</blueprint>
```

This creates an instance of InventoryImpl, performs some magic with transactions ❶, and injects the InventoryImpl with a JPA EntityManager ❷. For application-managed persistence, an EntityManagerFactory could be injected instead with the following line:

```
<jpa:unit property="entityManagerFactory" unitname="fancyfoods" />
```

PROGRAMMING WITH JPA

The InventoryImpl class is where you get to see the JPA programming model in action. The reference to the EntityManager is injected, and so the InventoryImpl never needs to worry about creating it, closing it, or checking that it's associated with the right persistence context:

```
public class InventoryImpl implements Inventory {

    private EntityManager em;

    public void setEntityManager(EntityManager em) {
        this.em = em;
    }
```

Writing and retrieving data

Food can be retrieved from the database and persisted to the database easily using the JPA API:

```
@Override
public FoodImpl getFood(String name) {
    return em.find(FoodImpl.class, name);
}

@Override
public void createFood(String name, double price, int quantity) {
    FoodImpl food = new FoodImpl(name, price, quantity);
    em.persist(food);
}
```

The find() method retrieves a persisted FoodImpl by its primary key, and the persist method writes a new or modified FoodImpl to the database.

Using the Java Persistence Query Language

If you want to do anything more than find objects by their primary key, you'll need to use *Java Persistence Query Language (JPQL)*:

```
@Override
public List<Food> getFoodsWhoseNameContains(String foodName,
                                            int maxResults) {
    String query = "SELECT f FROM FOOD f WHERE f.name LIKE '%" +
            foodName + "%' ORDER BY f.quantity DESC";
    Query q = em.createQuery(query);

    q.setMaxResults(maxResults);
    List<Food> list = q.getResultList();

    return list;
}

@Override
public int getFoodCount() {
    Query query = em.createQuery("SELECT COUNT(f) FROM FOOD f");
    Number count = (Number) query.getSingleResult();
    return count.intValue();
}
```

JPQL may bring back unpleasant (or pleasant) memories of SQL for some of you. In terms of syntax, it's much like SQL, but avoids most vendor-compliance compatibility issues. It breaks the object-oriented abstraction provided by JPA and makes it clear that there is a database involved in all this.

INITIALIZING THE DATABASE

One slight disadvantage of allowing JPA to create all your database tables for you in memory is that the database will always be completely empty when you start the system. This is fine for some applications, but it's not ideal for a food shop that's supposed to have food. Use another Blueprint bean to initialize the database when the system starts:

```
<bean
    id="populator"
    class="fancyfoods.persistence.InventoryPopulater"
    init-method="populate"
    activation="eager"      >
        <property
            name="inventory"
            ref="inventory" />
</bean>
```

If you're familiar with OSGi bundle activators, you'll recognize that this bean plays a similar role. It's activated as soon as the bundle starts, rather than waiting to be looked up or injected into another bean. The advantage over a normal bundle activator is it can be injected with any other Blueprint reference.

Another advantage of the InventoryPopulater over a bundle activator is that an eager Blueprint bean isn't required to implement any special interface (see the following listing). It only needs to provide the declared initialization method and setters for any injected properties.

Listing 3.6 `InventoryPopulator` fills the database when the bundle starts

```
public class InventoryPopulater {

    private Inventory inventory;

    public void setInventory(Inventory inventory) {
        this.inventory = inventory;
    }

    public void populate() {
        boolean isInventoryPopulated = (inventory.getFoodCount() > 0);

        if (!isInventoryPopulated) {
            inventory.createFood("Blue cheese", 3.45, 10);
            inventory.createFood("Wensleydale cheese", 1.81, 15);
            inventory.createFood("Normal chocolates", 6.99, 8);
        }
    }
}
```

Check if there's food before making more ❶

The `populate` method adds two cheeses and a chocolate to the database. To avoid trying to persist the same blue cheese row six times, the populater is defensive and only creates new foods if the database is empty ❶.

> **WARNING: HOW MANY TIMES IS AN EAGER BLUEPRINT BEAN INITIALIZED?** The eager Blueprint runs once when its bundle is started. Be careful here—this feels a lot like constructing and initializing a Java singleton, but it's not the same. A singleton will be initialized once in the lifetime of a JVM. Bundles, on the other hand, can be stopped and started repeatedly without restarting the JVM. This means each eager Blueprint bean will be created the same number of times that the bundle is started during the lifetime of the virtual machine. Be careful using init methods to change the external state. We're patently using the init method as a simple way to change the external state here, so this is a case of "do as we say, not do as we do!"

3.2.3 *Making use of the data*

Now that Fancy Foods has a datasource and a JPA persistence bundle, all that's needed is something to take advantage of the persistence. The special offer in section 2.3.3 used the time of year to determine which chocolates should be on offer. Many other foods, on the other hand, aren't seasonal purchases. Instead, shops aim to promote foods that are selling poorly, so that they don't get left with piles of food that are past their sell-by dates. The container-managed persistence makes that kind of promotion simple.

Let's add a second department, in charge of cheese. The appeal of cheese doesn't vary seasonally, but cheese does have a limited lifespan, so it's important to keep the stock moving. Whichever cheese has the highest stock levels should be displayed prominently on the front page to try to spark interest. To work out the list of available cheeses and their stock levels, we use Blueprint to wire together a `SpecialOffer` service and the `Inventory` service, as shown in the following listing.

Listing 3.7   The Blueprint for registering a special offer with an `Inventory` dependency

```xml
<?xml version="1.0" encoding="UTF-8"?>
<blueprint xmlns="http://www.osgi.org/xmlns/blueprint/v1.0.0">
  <service interface="fancyfoods.offers.SpecialOffer">
    <bean
      class="fancyfoods.department.cheese.offers.DesperateCheeseOffer">
      <property    name="inventory" ref="inventory" />
    </bean>
  </service>

  <reference id="inventory" interface="fancyfoods.food.Inventory" />
</blueprint>
```

With this new bundle, our system has the architecture shown in figure 3.9.

The special offer implementation takes advantage of the injected `Inventory` service to work out which cheese has the highest stock levels, as shown here.

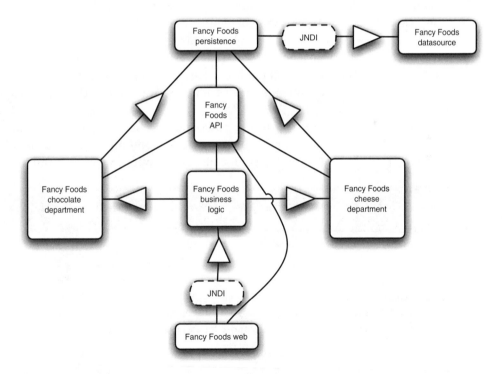

Figure 3.9   The architecture of the Fancy Foods application

Listing 3.8   The `DesperateCheeseOffer` class

```
public class DesperateCheeseOffer implements SpecialOffer {

    private Inventory inventory;                              Inventory gets
                                                             injected
    public void setInventory(Inventory inventory) {
        this.inventory = inventory;
    }

    @Override
    public String getDescription() {
        return "A wonderful surprise for someone cheesy.";
    }

    @Override
    public Food getOfferFood() {
        List<Food> cheeses =
            inventory.getFoodsWhoseNameContains("cheese", 1);
        Food leastPopularCheese = cheeses.get(0);            Food list already
        return leastPopularCheese;                           sorted, so you can
    }                                                        take first food
}
```

Build a bundle containing the blueprint.xml and the `DesperateCheeseOffer` class (and a manifest). When you drop this bundle into the load directory, you should find that the front page of the Fancy Foods shop has gotten a lot more exciting (figure 3.10).

If you get the persistence wrong, you'll find that the cheese offer isn't listed. If the dependencies of the `DesperateCheeseOffer` aren't available, Blueprint won't instantiate the cheese offer and it won't publish a `SpecialOffer` service. Using the OSGi console's `ss` and `bundle` commands can usually help track down the weak link in the dependency chain.

After you've fixed and rebuilt the misconfigured bundle, you'll find that things kick into life without any restarts or manual interventions on your part. All that's required is a refresh of the web page for the cheese offer to appear. (And if you stop

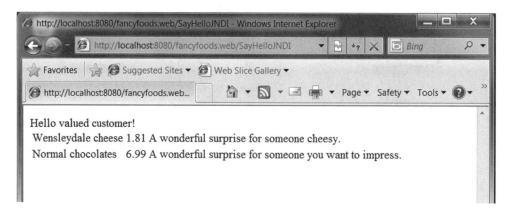

Figure 3.10   After the addition of the cheese department, datasource, and persistence bundles, the Fancy Foods shop has a new special offer, driven from the cheese stock levels in the database.

the cheese bundle or any of its dependencies in the OSGi console using the `stop` command, the cheese offer will vanish again. The authors can stop and start bundles and watch application behavior change a lot before they get bored of the trick.)

3.3 Transactions—the secret ingredient

Working through the inventory example, you'll have noticed a few references to transactions, XA, and JTA. You've written the `Inventory` class so it has full container-managed transaction support. Does it need this elaborate transaction infrastructure for its simple database reads and writes? Well, possibly not. But container-managed JPA (with or without OSGi) always requires a transaction to be present to update a database, so doing work without transactions means moving to unmanaged or application-managed JPA.

Even in the unmanaged case, it's difficult to do anything with databases *without* getting transactions involved. We don't recommend you try it, but rewriting the example so that it doesn't use XA and JTA requires *more* transaction-related metadata and an alarming quantity of transaction-related code. Getting it to work at all requires a pretty solid knowledge of transactions. Luckily, you can usually rely on container management of transactions and for the most part ignore them.

3.3.1 What is a transaction?

You may want to understand a bit more about what's going on with JTA transactions and enterprise OSGi. Particularly if you're writing an application where failures and data integrity matter, it's worth digging deeper into the world of enterprise transactions.

A transaction is a set of distinct operations that must behave like one atomic operation. If disaster strikes and one part of the group fails, the whole lot must be reversed.

LOCAL TRANSACTIONS

The simplest transactions are those that take place entirely on one resource. For example, a database may update several rows under a single transaction to ensure the state of the data remains consistent. In these cases there's no doubt about whether parts of the transaction have succeeded or failed. Local transactions are sufficiently straightforward that they don't really count as part of the enterprise programming model.

DISTRIBUTED TRANSACTIONS

In the distributed case, asynchronous and unreliable communication means that establishing whether any part of a transaction has been successful is rather more tricky. Has a remote database not reported success because it's crashed, or because of unusually heavy network traffic? When the transaction manager makes the decision to commit or roll back, it's also difficult to be sure all the participants in the transaction have followed along. Did that server fail before or after it applied the commit request?

Despite their difficulty, transactions are arguably even more essential in the distributed case. Transactions will almost certainly take longer, so the chances of multiple users trying to access the same data at the same time are higher. What happens if an online shopper buys a DVD and then cleans out their account by buying a car before the DVD payment has been processed?

These worries are addressed by using a transaction manager to coordinate the transaction across multiple resources using a robust transaction protocol known as a *two-phase commit*. Writing a transaction manager to coordinate a two-phase commit is complicated and error prone. Luckily, robust open source transaction manager implementations are available.

JTA

The *Java Transaction API (JTA)* is the Java EE implementation of the XA two-phase commit API. It defines an API for resources to communicate with the transaction manager, and also an API for applications to control transaction boundaries programmatically. JTA is the accepted standard for Java transaction managers.

DECLARATIVE TRANSACTIONS

Even with the support provided by the basic JTA, coordinating transactions can be time consuming and fragile. Rollbacks and commits need to be made in code, leaving the chance that some code paths, particularly unexpected exits, could fail to complete the transactions properly.

The process of handling transactions is made much simpler for container-managed declarative transactions. Transaction boundaries are declared simply in metadata and the container handles creating the transactions and managing failure cases. Container-managed transactions are so useful that they're arguably among the key attractions of application servers.

Updating an inventory with application-managed transactions

To see the difference, let's have a look at how the `InventoryImpl` implementation to persist a `Food` object would look if it were using application-managed persistence (and by extension application-managed transactions):

```
EntityManager em = entityManagerFactory.createEntityManager();
EntityTransaction tx = em.getTransaction();
em.getTransaction().begin();
try {
    em.persist(food);
    em.getTransaction().commit();
} catch (PersistenceException e) {
    if (em.getTransaction().isActive()) {
        em.getTransaction().rollback();
    }
} finally {
    em.close();
}
```

Not much fun, is it? Everything that's being done by hand here was automatically handled for you by the container (with much less hand-wringing and debugging) in section 3.2.4.

3.3.2 *Handling multipart transactions*

You may be feeling slightly suspicious about transactions you can't see and didn't do much work to create. Is the single line `<tx:transaction method="*" value=`

"Required" /> in your Blueprint enough to ensure complete transactional integrity? Aren't you better off keeping the transactions where you can see them?

The answers to these questions are, respectively, "not totally" and "almost never." There will be applications where you'll have to think a bit harder about what's going on with your transactions, but there will be few occasions indeed where this extends to having to code the transactions by hand.

Let's explore an example where the minimal transaction support isn't enough. So far, Fancy Foods has been a bit more like a printed flier than a modern shopping website. (And if it was a flier for your business, you'd probably fire the graphic designer responsible.) Users can see some of the available food, but they can't buy the food. Profits will be higher if people can buy things!

ENABLING FOOD SHOPPING

A `fancyfoods.foods.Customer` interface should be added to the API bundle, and a `fancyfoods.persistence.CustomerImpl` implementation class written. As with `Food-Impl`, the `@Entity` annotation should be added and a primary key declared:

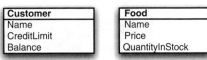

Figure 3.11 **The schema for the purchase-enabled Fancy Foods website. The schema is still simple, but there are now two entities, and two corresponding tables in the database.**

```
@Entity
public class CustomerImpl implements Customer {

    @Id
    private String name;
    private double creditLimit;
    private double balance;
[. . .]
```

If you're using a version of Aries persistence below 0.4, the new entity class needs to be listed in the persistence.xml so that it can be managed by JPA:

```
<class>fancyfoods.persistence.CustomerImpl</class>
```

We'll also add an `Accounting` interface and implementation to handle retrieving and updating customer details. Like the `InventoryImpl`, the `AccountingImpl` should be managed by Blueprint and exposed as a service:

```
<bean
    id="accounting"
    class="fancyfoods.persistence.AccountingImpl">
    <tx:transaction    method="*" value="Required" />
    <jpa:context property="entityManager" unitname="fancyfoods" />
</bean>

<service
    interface="fancyfoods.food.Accounting"
    ref="accounting" />
```

The `EntityManager` gets injected into the `AccountingImpl`, which makes handling the persistence easy. The `AccountingImpl` will do something we haven't done yet, which is to make changes to entity classes and persist them back.

Listing 3.9   The `chargeToAccount()` method of the `AccountingImpl` class

```
public void chargeToAccount(String name, double purchaseAmount) {
    CustomerImpl customer = getCustomer(name);
    if (customer == null)                               Make new customer
        customer = new CustomerImpl();                  if needed
        customer.setName(name);
        customer.setCreditLimit(20);
        em.persist(customer);                           Persist new
    }                                                   entity
    double currentLevel = customer.getBalance();
    double creditLimit = customer.getCreditLimit();
    double newBalance = currentLevel + purchaseAmount;
    if (newBalance <= creditLimit) {
        customer.setBalance(newBalance);                Update balance
        em.persist(customer);                           and persist
    } else {
        throw new IllegalArgumentException("'" +
                customer.getCreditLimit() +
                " is not enough credit for a '" + newBalance
            + " purchase.");
    }
}
```

If a request is made to charge a customer's account, the customer manager will first try to retrieve the customer record from the database. If the customer can't be found, the manager will—trustingly—set up a new credit account for that customer. The customer manager will then try to charge the customer's account. If the customer's credit limit is exceeded, no charge will be made and an exception will be thrown.

Not only will nothing be charged to the account, no changes at all will be made. In particular, no account will be created for the new customer. Although the new customer instance was created and persisted, the entire `chargeToAccount` method is wrapped in a single transaction. If any exception is thrown from the method, all changes made in the method will be rolled back.

You can update the food stock levels in a similar way in the inventory manager class:

```
public int removeStock(String name, int quantity) {
    FoodImpl food = getFood(name);
    int currentLevel = food.getQuantityInStock();
    int newLevel = currentLevel - quantity;
    if (newLevel >= 0) {
        food.setQuantityInStock(newLevel);
        em.persist(food);
        return newLevel;
    } else {
        throw new IllegalArgumentException(
            "Cannot have level below 0: " + newLevel);
    }
}
```

There should never be an attempt to purchase nonexistent food, so you don't add special code to handle that case. You automatically created customer accounts for new customers, but you definitely don't want to create entries for foods if they don't already exist in the database.

The final piece is a Shop service that coordinates purchases across the inventory and customer accounting classes. It can be created by Blueprint and automatically wired to the inventory and accounting beans:

```
<service
    interface="fancyfoods.food.Shop">
    <bean
        class="fancyfoods.persistence.ShopImpl">
        <tx:transaction
            method="*"
            value="Required" />
        <property
            name="inventory"
            ref="inventory" />
        <property
            name="accounting"
            ref="accounting" />
    </bean>
</service>
```

The shop implementation will have its inventory and account dependencies injected. To handle a purchase, it decrements the stock levels of the food, and debits the total cost to the customer's account:

```
public int removeStock(String name, int quantity) {
    FoodImpl food = getFood(name);
    int currentLevel = food.getQuantityInStock();
    int newLevel = currentLevel - quantity;
    if (newLevel >= 0) {
        food.setQuantityInStock(newLevel);
        em.persist(food);
        return newLevel;
    } else {
        throw new IllegalArgumentException(
            "Cannot have level below 0: " + newLevel);
    }
}
```

You don't want customers to be able to rack up credit indefinitely. If they've exceeded their credit limit, no changes are made to the database and an exception is thrown.

ADDING A WEB FRONTEND

All that remains now is to hook the Shop service up to the web frontend. Start by livening up the display of the special offers. Instead of a static list of special offers, users should be able to click on a food and bring up a purchase page (figure 3.12).

The link should lead to a new servlet that allows users to buy the food by filling in a customer name and a purchase quantity (figure 3.13).

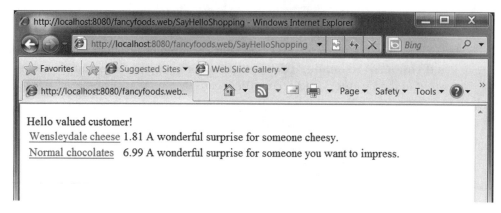

Figure 3.12   The SayHello servlet with links to allow users to purchase food

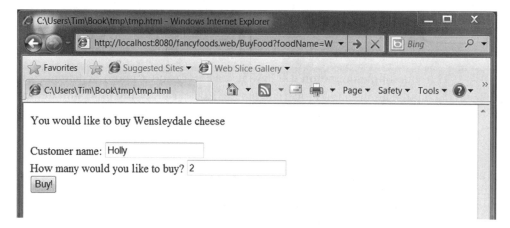

Figure 3.13   The BuyFood servlet prompts customers to fill in their name and how much food they'd like to buy.

The HTML for the GET method of the BuyFood servlet is a standard HTML form:

```
protected void doGet(HttpServletRequest request,
                     HttpServletResponse response)
                     throws ServletException, IOException {
    String foodName = request.getParameter("foodName");

    PrintWriter html = response.getWriter();
    html.append("<html>");
    html.append("<body>");

    html.append("You would like to buy " + foodName);
    html.append("<form method=post action="BuyFood">");
    html.append("Customer name:");
    html.append("<input type=text name=customerName> <br/>");
    html.append("How many would you like to buy?");
    html.append("<input type=text name=quantity><br/>");
    html.append("<input type=hidden name=foodName value=""
```

```
                        + foodName + "">");
    html.append("<input type=submit value=Buy!>");
    html.append("</form>");

    html.append("</body>");
    html.append("</html>");
}
```

The POST method takes the parameters passed across from the GET method, looks up a Shop service, and puts the purchase through.

```
protected void doPost(HttpServletRequest request,
                      HttpServletResponse response)
                      throws ServletException, IOException {
    PrintWriter html = response.getWriter();

    html.append("<html>");

    String customerName = request.getParameter("customerName");
    String foodName = request.getParameter("foodName");
    String quantity = request.getParameter("quantity");

    try {
        InitialContext ctx = new InitialContext();
        Shop shop = (Shop) ctx.lookup("osgi:service/"
                + Shop.class.getName());
        Inventory inventory = (Inventory) ctx.lookup(
            "osgi:service/" + Inventory.class.getName());
        Accounting accounting = (Accounting) ctx.lookup(
            "osgi:service/" + Accounting.class.getName());

        Customer customer = accounting.getCustomer(customerName);
        if (customer != null) {
            html.append(customer + "<br/>");
        } else {
            html.append(customerName + " is a new customer.<br/>");
        }

        Food food = inventory.getFood(foodName);
        html.append(food + "<br/>");

        html.append(customerName + " tried to buy " + quantity
                + " packs of " + foodName + "<br/>");

        try {
            shop.purchase(foodName, customerName,
                        Integer.valueOf(quantity));
            Customer refreshedCustomer = accounting
                    .getCustomer(customerName);
            html.append("Afterwards, " + refreshedCustomer +
                        "<br/>");
        } catch (Exception e) {
            html.append("A problem happened: " + e.getMessage() +
                        "<br/>");
        }
```

```
        Food refreshedFood = inventory.getFood(foodName);
        html.append("And after? " + refreshedFood);
    } catch (NamingException e) {
        html.append("We have no shop today. Try again tomorrow.");
    }

    html.append("</body>");
    html.append("</html>");
}
```

You may be dismayed by how long this method is. In fact, almost all of it's concerned with writing output to the page. The purchase itself could be managed in two or three lines of code. Part of the reason that writing out the object states is so verbose is that you have to retrieve the objects *twice*: once before the purchase and once after. If this wasn't a database application, you'd expect that each food or customer instance was unique. Changes to a food made in one part of the application (like the Shop) would automatically be reflected in food instances elsewhere.

Because this is a database, things aren't so easy. When they were passed to the Buy-Food servlet, the food and customer instances moved outside the boundaries of the persistence context and were *detached*. To see the latest state of the database after changes, it's necessary to request new instances of the entity classes.

Let's play with the shop. If a new user named Holly buys two packs of Wensleydale cheese, everything works exactly as you'd hope. The stock level of the cheese is decremented, and the purchase price is added to your account (figure 3.14). The only disappointing part is that you don't get the physical cheese to eat.

If Holly buys enough Wensleydale cheese, the stock levels will reduce to below the blue cheese levels, and the front page special offer will suggest that customers buy blue cheese instead.

What happens if Holly is more extravagant and buys three boxes of chocolates instead? See figure 3.15.

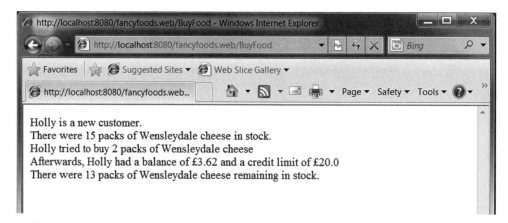

Figure 3.14 When a user purchases a small quantity of cheese, their account is created and then debited, and the cheese stock levels are reduced.

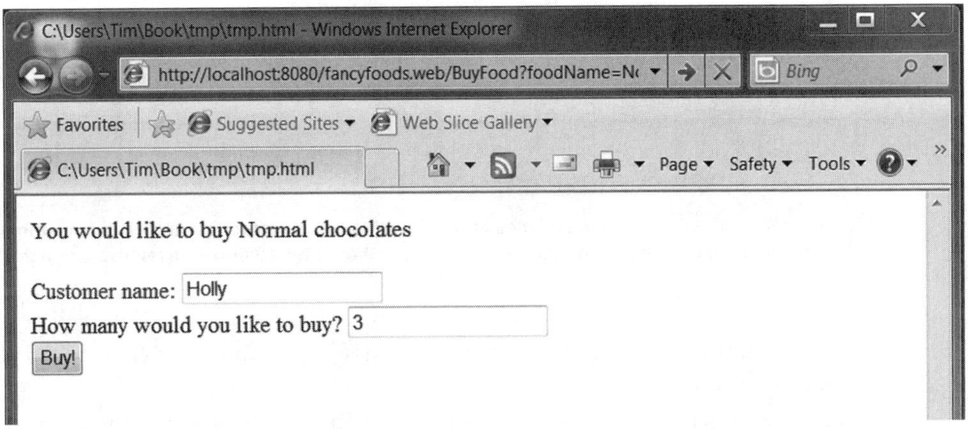

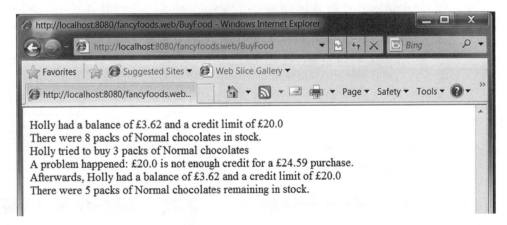

Figure 3.15 An attempt by Holly to buy three boxes of chocolates

This obviously shouldn't work, because there's not enough credit left in Holly's account. As expected, the web page reports that there was an issue and that the purchase wasn't successful (figure 3.16).

Looking at the web page more closely, though, it becomes clear that something is terribly wrong. The account wasn't debited, but the chocolates were still taken out of the stock. Holly is happy, but giving away chocolates to people with inadequate credit ratings isn't a sound way to run a business.

MAKING THE SHOP ROBUST

The core of the problem is the granularity of the transactions. The container-managed JTA is helpfully wrapping every method call to `InventoryImpl` or `AccountingImpl` in a transaction, and any failure in those methods will cause the transaction to be rolled back (figure 3.17). As you saw earlier, if a new customer doesn't have a

Figure 3.16 If a user tries to buy something that exceeds their credit limit, the purchase doesn't succeed and their account isn't debited. Unfortunately, the stock levels *are* reduced.

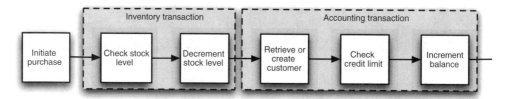

Figure 3.17   **The transaction boundaries in the default case. If a purchase exceeds a customer's credit limit, customer creation will be rolled back, but the purchased food will still be removed from the inventory.**

high enough credit limit for a purchase, the creation of their account will be reversed. (More accurately, the account creation is never committed, which looks the same from the outside.)

But the shop purchase uses methods from both `AccountingImpl` and `InventoryImpl`. Any failure in either method should cause the whole purchase to be rolled back and all database changes undone. You could do this by catching exceptions in the `purchase()` method and then writing new database operations to undo everything, but you risk getting into a world of trouble quickly. What if the attempt to reverse the problematic transaction fails? What if a `Throwable` is thrown and you don't remember to catch it?

By far the neater—and simpler—solution is to wrap the whole purchase in a single transaction (figure 3.18). That transaction is propagated to the `removeStock` and `chargeToAccount` methods. These methods need a transaction to be present when the method is entered, but there's nothing in their Blueprint metadata that says it has to be a *new* transaction. Any exception in either method causes everything to be rolled back.

How do you create this broad-scope transaction? Blueprint, again! All that's needed is to add the following line to the bean definition for `ShopImpl`:

```
<tx:transaction method="*" value="Required" />
```

This ensures that every method on the `ShopImpl` class gets a transaction. This transaction is propagated to other classes called by `ShopImpl` so that if one call within a method fails, the entire method is rolled back. What's so cool about this is how tiny the change is. It takes more characters to explain than it does to implement!

The coolness isn't over yet, though, because OSGi gives you something even cooler. The persistence bundle can be rebuilt and dropped into the load directory again without bouncing the OSGi framework. The runtime detects the new code in

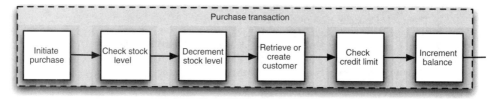

Figure 3.18   **Better transaction boundaries. If a purchase exceeds a customer's credit limit, no food will be removed from the inventory.**

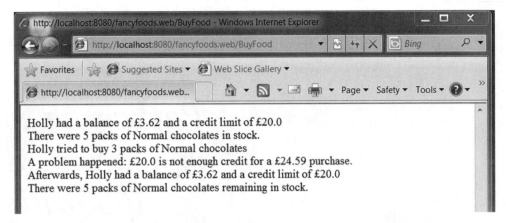

Figure 3.19 With appropriately scoped transactions, an attempt to buy chocolate that's beyond a customer's means won't result in a change to their balance or to the chocolate inventory levels.

the load directory and then uses the OSGi API to update the application with the new code without having to restart anything. If you try a second time to buy lots of chocolates, the result is much more reasonable (figure 3.19).

> **Is the shop enterprise-ready now?**
>
> We're cheerfully ignoring security here—as well as lots of other things. For example, it's still possible to remove stock or charge accounts without a surrounding transaction. This could easily be fixed by changing the transaction strategies for the remove-Stock and chargeToAccount methods from Required to Mandatory. Given these issues, we don't suggest you take this code literally as the basis of your high-turnover online shopping website. On the bright side, if you did, the transactional integrity would be pretty good and the modularity and dynamism would be *excellent*.

Although JTA is most closely associated with JPA and database access, it's not just for container-managed persistence classes. Any method, or set of methods, can be signed up for container-managed transactions.

3.4   Summary

A lot of code appeared in this chapter, so the Fancy Foods application is doing some powerful stuff now. It's not quite ready to make your fortune as an enterprise-grade cheese management system, but it's a lot closer than it was in chapter 2. You've got persistence fully integrated into your architecture without compromising modularity or dynamism. You know how to read from a database in a single line of code, and how to cocoon whole swathes of code in transactions with a single line of XML.

At this stage, the application has enough going on that it's no longer a few bundles. Let's move on to consider some of the patterns OSGi offers for packaging these more complex bundle groupings into self-contained applications.

Packaging your enterprise OSGi applications

Over the past couple of chapters you've put together an application consisting of a number of application bundles. As the number of bundles increased, it's quickly become unmanageable when you try to deploy it. Even with only a simple web front-end and the persisted backend that you added in the last chapter, the application has seven bundles to remember to install. It's time to look at how you can package your application in a more convenient form.

Packaging an application has changed over time, in much the same way as writing an application has. Originally programs were small, and could easily be packaged as a single binary file. As programs grew in complexity, they also grew in size and were split into a number of discrete units, usually based on function. As Java developers, you'll already be familiar with the concept of a JAR file and should also understand the structure of an OSGi bundle.

JARs and bundles are examples of coarse-grained packaging but, as you have already seen, they aren't coarse enough to describe an entire application. Most of this chapter is dedicated to describing application packaging concepts. With an understanding of the basic concepts behind enterprise OSGi application packaging, it becomes a straightforward exercise to package any application. To start with, let's try to understand the problem that application packaging is trying to solve. Why do you need something bigger than a bundle?

4.1 The need for more than modules

The OSGi specifications have described the interactions of bundles as a means for packaging code for many years, and before that the Java JAR specification defined a mechanism by which groups of classes could be delivered in a single unit. As a specialization of a JAR file, an OSGi bundle offers no greater structure than is present in Java SE. A single binary file may contain many classes or resources, logically arranged into packages, but it represents the largest packaging unit that can be deployed.

Because of their complex requirements and core business value, enterprise applications are usually quite large, and often are developed by distributed teams. Even if the entire development team works in the same location, in order for them to work effectively, it's typical to develop the application as a set of modules (JARs) rather than as a single monolithic unit.

It's almost certain that there will be classes that need to be shared between the individual modules of the application, but shouldn't be shared with other applications. If application internals are allowed onto the classpath of other applications, the encapsulation of the application as a whole will be poor, even if the individual bundles are nicely encapsulated. Multibundle applications can also behave unpredictably in multitenanted systems. Applications may also get inappropriate visibility of utility libraries from other applications. If the versions are incompatible, or if state is stored statically, this classpath contamination can have disastrous effects that surface only in production.

As you learned in chapter 1, modularity is good, and so it would be a shame to collapse that complex enterprise application back into a single JAR file to distribute it and ensure encapsulation. Java EE recognized this problem early in its development, and created the *Enterprise Archive (EAR)*.

4.1.1   Java EE applications

In the simplest sense, Java EE EARs can be thought of as bigger versions of Java SE JARs. EARs are in zip format, like JARs, but rather than containing Java classes, they contain enterprise modules such as WARs and EJB JARs. One other key difference between EARs and JARs is that an EAR contains an application descriptor called META-INF/application.xml rather than a standard manifest.

Listing 4.1   A simple application.xml

```xml
<?xml version="1.0" encoding="UTF-8"?>
<application xmlns="http://java.sun.com/xml/ns/javaee"
            xmlns:xsi="http://www.w3.org/2001/XMLSchema-instance"
            xsi:schemaLocation="http://java.sun.com/xml/ns/javaee
            http://java.sun.com/xml/ns/javaee/application_5.xsd"
            version="5">

    <display-name>My EAR Application</display-name>
    <description>An example EAR</description>

    <module>
        <ejb>ejb_module.jar</ejb>                          Included EJB
    </module>

    <module>                                               Included WAR
        <web>
            <web-uri>war_module.war</web-uri>
            <context-root>/migration</context-root>        Configuration for WAR
        </web>
    </module>

    <library-directory>shared</library-directory>          Folder for utility JARs
</application>
```

The application XML descriptor in listing 4.1 shows how a Java EE EAR provides a complete list of the content of the application (the WARs, EJBs, and library JARs that make up the application) and it can also contain security metadata. While it's possible for the application.xml to reference a module that isn't contained directly within the EAR, this is an extremely uncommon practice. Often the application.xml is used to do no more than restate the contents of the EAR and to provide context roots for any web modules.

> **Improvements to the EAR model**
>
> Starting with Java EE 5, the application.xml descriptor became optional, only being specified if you needed to override any defaults. This helps to reduce the duplication typically present in the EAR metadata as modules inside an EAR no longer need to be listed in application.xml as well.

THE PROBLEM WITH EARS

Although they add a different level of granularity to Java, EARs don't do much to help with Java modularity. EARs have no practical way to declare dependencies except to package all their required JARs inside themselves. This leads to big EARs! Carrying all your dependencies around with you is a blunt mechanism for dependency management, and it can cause considerable bloat at runtime. An application server can end up hosting many redundant copies of common libraries, one for each application.

A Java EE application server represents a large investment of money and computing resources, so they're typically used to run a number of applications. As you can see from figure 4.1, when two applications make use of the same library, which happens quite a lot, they end up running side by side. In the worst cases, the modules within an EAR will also package duplicate libraries, and without careful management when packaging this can lead to considerable bloat.

Some application servers have added extensions to allow libraries to be shared between Java EE applications, but these extensions are unique to each vendor. EARs with shared library dependencies are therefore necessarily less portable than their bulkier self-contained equivalents. Installing such an EAR involves an extra set of vendor-specific installation steps. ("Make sure there is a copy of something.jar in lib, unless you're on this other application server, in which case it's the ext folder it needs to be copied to.") Added to this complexity, there's no way of knowing what the shared dependencies of an EAR are except through documentation. If the documentation is incomplete or missing, the application will probably deploy without error only to fail with an unpleasant `ClassNotFoundException` at runtime. Some missing dependencies might not be discovered until well into production.

Even if all the shared dependencies of an EAR are identified and installed, success isn't guaranteed. What happens when different applications on the same server

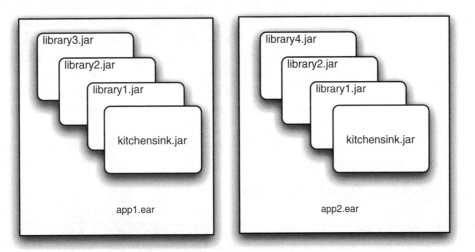

Figure 4.1 Duplication of common libraries between EARs

require different versions of the same common library? If the packages and class names are the same, one version will always come before the other one on the class-path. If the two versions have different sets of capabilities—or different sets of bugs—there may be runtime problems which are quite tricky to debug. The only solution for this problem is to repackage, redesign, or re-engineer the EARs and move the right version of each shared library back into an EAR. This can be particularly problematic for modules that you don't have the source for.

4.1.2 *Enterprise OSGi applications*

In Java EE, the application packaging role is fulfilled by the EAR. Until recently, in OSGi there was no similar concept; application packaging units began and ended with bundles. As we've already mentioned, bundles aren't a suitable packaging unit for large-scale applications. A typical application will be developed as several bundles, each with a well-defined API. In a standard OSGi framework, these bundles will need to be individually installed, which is far from ideal.

The lack of an aggregate deployment artifact in core OSGi is only one of its limitations. As we've previously discussed, OSGi provides an excellent platform for sharing code between different applications; however, because you never know what other bundles you might find in a framework, you often have no choice but to send all the bundles you might need to the application deployer, even though many of them may not be needed at runtime.

One final problem with enterprise OSGi application packaging is that it's possible to have too much sharing! While sharing common APIs and libraries is a good idea, there are some parts of an application that are distinctly private. This may seem counterintuitive at first, but an enterprise OSGi application is a bit like a larger version of an OSGi bundle where, instead of packages, you have modules. Some modules you're happy to have provided to you, like a bundle importing a package; some modules you're happy to provide to the outside world, like a bundle exporting a package. Most importantly, there are some modules (like your internal payment processing implementation) that you don't want other applications to be able to use! Application multitenancy is awkward in core OSGi frameworks, because there's only one level of granularity.

Don't let the previous paragraphs put you off. It's true that enterprise OSGi has some hurdles to overcome when it comes to application packaging, but as with many other problems in software engineering, there are some interesting solutions in open source, and useful new specifications. Let's start with a new standard for application packaging: *subsystems*.

4.2   *Enterprise OSGi subsystems*

OSGi subsystems are a new concept in release 5 of the OSGi Enterprise Specification. Subsystems are a more general concept than OSGi applications, which is why they're called subsystems, and not applications! Although they solve many of the same problems, subsystems are also definitely more than an OSGi equivalent to EARs. Subsystems are nestable collections of bundles with a shared lifecycle. The subsystem contents can be packaged into an archive with a .esa extension, and so we'll refer to them as *Enterprise Subsystem Archives (ESAs)*.

Like an EAR, an ESA contains metadata describing the contents of an application and how it should be deployed; however, unlike an EAR, the metadata for an ESA uses a configuration by exception model, and so is entirely optional. Even the metadata file may be omitted if no defaults need to be changed.

There are three distinct kinds of subsystems: applications, features, and composites. All represent collections of bundles, but how permeable the boundaries are varies.

4.2.1 *ESA structure*

One of the most important details about an application packaging model is the structure it places on the application. If the structure is too loose or complex, then the applications are usually hard to generate, requiring special tools, or they become impossible to understand for anything but simple examples. On the other hand, if an application's structure is too rigid, then it can end up being rather cumbersome and inflexible. The latter has plagued the EAR file format, requiring large monolithic files with redundant metadata.

In many senses, an ESA file is a lot like an EAR file. An ESA is a zip format archive that contains metadata in the form of an application manifest, and it also contains OSGi bundles in the root of the zip archive. An ESA file does differ from an EAR in structure in two key ways:

- Unlike an EAR file, the metadata for an ESA doesn't need to be complete. Every piece of ESA metadata has a default value that'll be used unless it's overridden. This defaulting is so extensive that the metadata for an ESA may be omitted entirely if the defaults are acceptable.
- As we mentioned in section 4.1.1, an EAR almost always contains the entire content of the application, including shared libraries. An ESA can contain all the bundles needed to run the application but, commonly, only a small subset of the bundles that make up the application are included in the ESA. The remaining bundles are then provisioned from a bundle repository when the application is installed. We'll talk about this more in section 4.2.5.

As you can see from figure 4.2, the structure of an ESA is similar to an EAR, but because the ESA doesn't need to package all of its dependencies, the file is much smaller. In addition, the reduced number of modules in the ESA makes it simpler to understand—there are fewer unimportant dependencies to wade through.

Although the metadata is optional in general, it's important to support applications that don't contain all their modules.

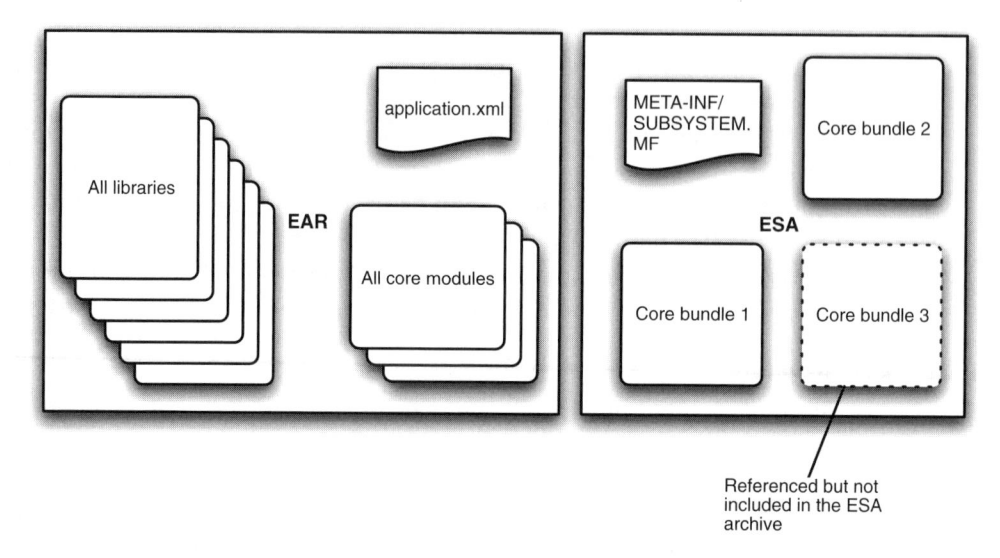

Figure 4.2 An EAR and an ESA representing the same application. The EAR must include all its component JARs and all the libraries it depends on. The ESA, on the other hand, need only include its component bundles, and even those may be loaded by reference from a bundle repository.

4.2.2 Subsystem metadata

The metadata in an ESA is similar to that of an EAR, but specified differently. The first key difference is that ESA metadata isn't stored as XML, as in an EAR, but using the Java manifest syntax in a file called META-INF/SUBSYSTEM.MF. This file defines the name and version of the application, which default to the name of the archive file and 0.0.0, and a human-readable description. Importantly, the subsystem manifest also defines the bundles that make up the *core content* of the subsystem, and any services that should be exposed or consumed by the application. For example:

```
Subsystem-ManifestVersion: 1
Subsystem-Name: The Fancy Foods online superstore
Subsystem-SymbolicName: fancyfoods.application
Subsystem-Version: 1.0
Subsystem-Content:
    fancyfoods.api; version="[1.0.0,2.0.0)",
    fancyfoods.business; version="[1.0.0,2.0.0)",
    fancyfoods.web; version="[1.0.0,2.0.0)",
    fancyfoods.department.chocolate; version="[1.0.0,2.0.0)",
    fancyfoods.department.cheese; version="[1.0.0,2.0.0)",
    fancyfoods.persistence; version="[1.0.0,2.0.0)",
```

SUBSYSTEM CONTENT

The core content of an application isn't an idea that exists in Java EE or standard OSGi, and so it's something many people find slightly unnerving. The concept is simple: the core content represents the bundles that provide the application's function, rather than common libraries, logging utilities, and so on. For most people, the core content of the application is exactly what they'd describe if asked what was inside their

EAR; however, the EAR also has to include libraries and other dependencies and describe them in the application.xml descriptor. Unlike an EAR, the core content of an ESA need not (and usually doesn't) represent the complete set of bundles that should be installed to run the application.

The core content of an ESA is selected using the `Subsystem-Content:` header in the application manifest:

```
Subsystem-Content: fancyfoods.web;version="[1.1.0,2.0.0)",
          fancyfoods.department.chocolate;version="[1.0.0,2.0.0)
```

Core content may be declared optional.

Aside from not specifying the complete set of modules, there's one other big difference between ESA metadata and EAR metadata. The content of an ESA subsystem selects bundles using their symbolic name and an OSGi-style version range. This means that the same OSGi subsystem may run different bundles over the course of its life! Because the metadata has a degree of flexibility built in, it allows the application to be updated with service fixes without being repackaged. This is a significant advantage over the static model used by EARs, which require a whole new application to be generated for even a minor update. When selecting by version range, the bundle used may be contained within the root of the ESA, like a module in an EAR file, or refer to a bundle within a bundle repository. In fact, unlike a typical EAR file, it's likely that an ESA file won't contain most of the modules that it needs. We'll discuss more about bundle repositories, version ranges, and dependencies when we look at provisioning and resolution, but first we should take a brief look at scoping and subsystem types.

SUBSYSTEM TYPES AND SCOPING

We mentioned earlier that there are three distinct types of subsystems: applications, features, and composites. Application is the default, but other types may be selected using a `Subsystem-Type:` header. For example, to declare a feature, the header would be this:

```
Subsystem-Type: osgi.subsystem.feature
```

An application doesn't export anything to the outside framework, but its contents have free access to the outside. A feature is designed for sharing, so it's totally unscoped. Not only can its bundles see everything in the outside framework, the outside world can see all the bundles in the feature. A composite is a group of bundles that behaves like a single bundle; everything is private to the composite unless explicitly exported, and external dependencies must be explicitly imported.

The type of a subsystem also affects how its content is handled. A feature has complete visibility of the outside framework, so there's no need to add content *inside* the feature beyond what's already included. Composites and applications are less porous, and so it's meaningful to ask what's inside the subsystem and what's in the outside framework. A `provision-policy:=acceptDependencies` directive may be added to the `Subsystem-Type` declaration. This tells the system that explicit content and indirect dependencies should be treated as *part* of the subsystem.

Stepping back, if content and dependencies aren't packaged up in the ESA archive, where do they come from? So far you haven't seen anything in the application manifest that shows how you cope when an ESA doesn't contain all the bundles it needs. There's a good reason for this, which is that none of this information is stored in the application metadata at all! To be run in an enterprise OSGi runtime, an ESA needs to undergo a process called *deployment*, where two important things happen: provisioning and resolution.

4.2.3   *Provisioning and resolution*

Provisioning and resolution are two different, but related, steps that are taken when deploying an enterprise OSGi application. Though both steps can occur independently, they're often performed simultaneously. Unfortunately, this often leads to some confusion about the difference between provisioning and resolution, with many people thinking the terms are interchangeable names for the same thing. For simplicity's sake, we'll attempt to separate the two operations from one another as much as possible; however, it will be pretty clear that the most useful applications will rely upon the interplay between the provisioner and resolver. We'll also come back to provisioning and resolution in chapter 7.

PROVISIONING

Fundamentally, provisioning is a relatively simple operation, but because it isn't part of the Java EE application model it's not immediately comfortable for many developers. Provisioning is a little more common in standard OSGi, but it's still not a process that many OSGi developers would think about in detail. At its most basic, provisioning is the operation by which modules are located and deployed into the correct location.

Because Java EE EARs package all their modules inside themselves, provisioning isn't necessary. The code needed to run the application is either available as a module within the EAR or from the application server itself. Nothing needs to be fetched from anywhere. As we've already discussed, ESAs are a bit different. Although an ESA may contain all the modules it needs, it will more commonly refer to bundles that aren't contained inside it. It won't be possible to run an OSGi application without having all of the bundles that it needs, so as part of the ESA deployment process it's necessary to locate and obtain any bundles that aren't already inside the ESA. This process typically makes use of one or more bundle repositories to locate and download the bundles that are needed (see figure 4.3).

For a typical enterprise OSGi application, one or more bundles will need to be downloaded as part of the deployment operation. This means that there needs to be some way of uniquely identifying the bundle and finding out where it can be downloaded from. Fortunately, OSGi provides a symbolic name for each bundle that, in conjunction with a version, uniquely identifies a particular bundle. A simple bundle repository can therefore be thought of as being a bit like an organized music store; you can search for music by a particular artist, and then pick a particular song. The store will then present you with a URL from which you can start downloading the song.

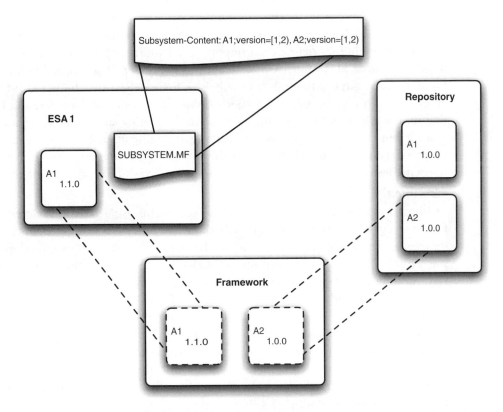

Figure 4.3 This subsystem refers to two bundles, both of which are available in the repository, but one of which is present in the ESA at a higher version. The higher-version bundle from the ESA is used at runtime, but the other bundle is provisioned from a remote location found in the repository.

VERSION RANGES, UNDECLARED DEPENDENCIES, AND PROVISIONING

We're sure you'll agree that provisioning is, at its heart, a fairly simple process. Why do so many people find it confusing? To start with, the example above is rather simplified! Provisioning an ESA that exactly specifies the symbolic names and versions of all the bundles it needs is indeed easy. In the real world, ESAs don't express themselves like this.

The most common reason that bundles can't be provisioned is because the bundles in an ESA aren't normally specified with an exact version. In fact, the ability to specify bundles with a version range is a key advantage of ESA metadata. If a range of versions is acceptable, it isn't possible to look for a single bundle in a repository. In this case, you could make the simplifying assumption that you want the highest available version of the bundle that fits within the version range, but what do you do about the dependencies of an ESA that aren't directly declared? For example, what happens when packages are imported by bundles inside the ESA? Even the symbolic name of the providing bundle won't be known!

One of the key drivers for the adoption of OSGi is classpath hell; it's difficult in Java SE and Java EE to know what classes you need and which JAR provides them. OSGi bundles are different: they define their imports and exports, making it clear whether the bundle will work at runtime. Unfortunately, the number of packages imported by a bundle can be large (although it usually isn't for a well-written bundle) and it isn't always easy to find a bundle that exports them. Even when you have found a bundle that supplies the required package, you also have to satisfy any packages requirements that the bundle has! This process can be long and difficult, and it would be annoying to have to do it manually for anything other than a trivial example. This problem illustrates the need for the resolution stage of an enterprise OSGi application deployment.

RESOLUTION

As with a provisioner, the fundamental job of a resolver isn't difficult to describe, but it's a concept that doesn't exist in Java EE or Java SE and so can be quite confusing for developers with those backgrounds when they first encounter it. OSGi developers, on the other hand, are familiar with the resolution process, even if they've never used a resolver to help them with it. This is because all OSGi bundles must be resolved within a runtime framework before they can be used. If you're still a little rusty about the OSGi classloading model and the bundle resolution process, it would be a good idea to get comfortable with section A.4.3 of appendix A before continuing here.

At the core of the resolution phase of ESA deployment is a single goal: to identify the set of bundles that need to be installed to satisfy the dependencies of this application. Without running through a resolution phase first, one of two things will happen to an ESA when it's started:

- If the ESA has no *missing* dependencies in its metadata, then it will already successfully resolve within the runtime. In this case, you're lucky and the application will work correctly when it's started.

- In the more common case where an ESA has external dependencies that aren't specified in the application manifest, for example, on a common utility library, the application won't be deployed properly. At the point the application is started, one or more of the application bundles won't be able to be resolved by the OSGi framework. These unresolved bundles won't be able to start, and the application won't work correctly.

In Java EE it would be almost impossible to identify missing dependencies in advance of a runtime failure; however, all OSGi bundles provide a detailed description of not only their dependencies, but also the capabilities they provide. Using this metadata, a resolver can identify all of the dependencies of the bundles within an ESA, find which dependencies are satisfied internally within the ESA, and then locate other bundles that satisfy any remaining dependencies.

Interacting with the provisioner

When the resolver is processing the application content of an ESA, it needs to know which bundles to look at, and what their bundle metadata is, to find out their dependencies.

What is a *missing* dependency?

The notion of a missing dependency is a little subjective. It boils down to your interpretation of what makes up the application and what makes up your server runtime. At its heart, a missing dependency is a package import, or for servers that offer OSGi service–based provisioning, a service dependency, made by a `Subsystem-Content` bundle that isn't satisfied by another bundle within the subsystem content. Some people argue that if this dependency is supplied by the server runtime rather than a shared library bundle, then the dependency isn't missing; however, as server runtimes differ, a dependency may be missing on one server but not on another. This scenario is the main reason that even though ESAs are portable artifacts, they still have to be redeployed if moved to a different server environment.

This is the point at which resolution and provisioning can become quite intertwined, and is the reason why many people struggle to understand the difference. If an ESA specifies a version range for its application content, then how are you ever going to find its dependencies—you don't even know which bundles to start with!

In essence, the resolver and the provisioner have to work together to provide a deployment for an ESA. The resolver typically only needs access to the metadata for a bundle, not the entire archive, so a typical resolver will generate a model from the metadata of the bundles available in a repository. This is a comparatively small amount of information, but provides the resolver with a complete description of all the bundle dependencies. The resolver can then use this information to calculate a *resolved* set of bundles for the ESA. This will include all of the application content bundles and any other bundles obtained via a repository to match missing dependencies (see figure 4.4).

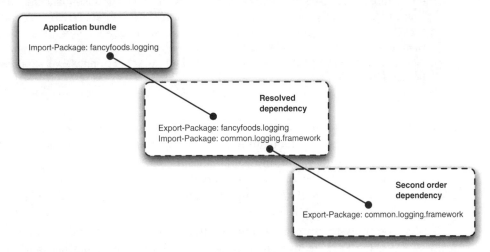

Figure 4.4   If you want to install this application bundle into a framework, then you need to ensure that the `fancyfoods.logging` package is available. This is provided by a bundle that has a dependency on the `common.logging.framework` package, which must also be satisfied by the resolution process. In this case, you pull in a third bundle that can supply the package and has no further missing dependencies.

It's possible that the resolver won't be able to find a set of bundles that has no missing dependencies, or even that it won't be able to locate one of the application content bundles. This is known as a *resolution failure*, and indicates that the ESA can't be deployed successfully. Resolution failures can typically be fixed either by adding missing bundles to the ESA archive, or preferably for shared bundles, by adding them to a bundle repository against which the ESA is being resolved.

When an ESA can be successfully resolved, you find that there's another constraint on the versions of bundles that make up the application content—it makes sense to take a version of a bundle that can resolve. Rather than selecting the highest version of a bundle that fits into the required range, deployments will select the highest version of the bundle that can be resolved given the other bundles known to the resolver. Having selected the bundles that are to be deployed, the result of the resolution is then passed to the provisioner. At this point, the provisioner can download *all* the bundles needed to run the ESA and the flexibility of the application manifest is collapsed into a single, repeatable deployment. (To ensure the deployment is repeatable, it's stored as a DEPLOYMENT.MF file.) This means that there's no risk of the application installing different bundles into the framework each time it's started, which would make problems hard to debug!

> ## ESA version ranges
> The version ranges used in ESAs are important, and as with any version range we strongly advise the use of semantic versioning to limit the range of acceptable bundles. For example, you may require a particular bug fix, establishing a micro version minimum, and wish to avoid function creep, with `version="[1.0.3,1.1.0)"`. Other applications may be a little looser and choose to allow functional enhancements. Critically, regardless of the version range you provide, after the application is deployed, a single version has been selected in the resolution phase. This is the bundle that will be used when running the application. Some runtimes will let you reresolve a deployed application to pick up updates, selecting a new fixed bundle version that will be used from then on.

As you've now seen, the interplay between provisioning and resolution can be quite involved, which is one of the main reasons that so many people struggle to differentiate the two processes. If you find yourself a little confused, remember the following: Provisioning is about locating and downloading bundles that aren't contained in the ESA. Resolution is about determining what additional bundles are needed to make the application content work at runtime.

Because subsystems were introduced after a number of alternate solutions such as EBAs, PARs, and Karaf features had already been developed, it may take a while for the fragmentation in this area to be eliminated. The OSGi subsystems specification standardizes many of the best bits of the earlier OSGi application models. We'll consider these alternatives in sections 4.3 and 4.4. (In case you're wondering, subsystems were also introduced after the first draft of this book was complete. This is the challenge of writing about exciting emerging technologies!) Subsystems implementations are being developed as we write, but it will take time for them to be finished. We expect support for plans, PARs, Karaf features, and EBAs will continue for some time, even after portable subsystems implementations have been released.

4.3 *The Enterprise Bundle Archive (EBA)*

Apache Aries defines a concept similar to the ESA called the *Enterprise Bundle Archive (EBA)*. The design of the EBA was one of the principal inspirations for the subsystems specification. If you understand subsystems, you'll understand a lot about EBAs by swapping the word *subsystem* for the word *application*. EBAs are packaged in .eba files, and the metadata is defined in an optional APPLICATION.MF file.

The headers are similar as well. For example, the core content of an EBA is selected using the `Application-Content:` header in the application manifest:

```
Application-Content: fancyfoods.web;version="[1.1.0,2.0.0)",
            fancyfoods.department.chocolate;version="[1.0.0,2.0.0)"
```

Like ESAs, EBAs may use a version range for the content bundles. Although ESAs can nest other ESAs, EBA content is restricted to bundles. The implications of being listed in the `Application-Content:` header are also different for EBAs.

4.3.1 *Sharing and isolation*

Although in general EBAs are similar to ESAs, one area where they differ significantly is scoping and isolation. Whereas ESAs offered lots of flexibility in terms of how content was scoped—with applications, features, and composites as precanned variants—options for EBAs are more limited.

As well as minimizing the amount of extra information that you need to supply when writing the metadata, the `Application-Content:` header has an important role to play in the structure of an enterprise OSGi application. The application content represents the core of an application, and will include APIs and services that the modules use to communicate with each another, but that aren't intended for public use. In Java EE this is accomplished by completely separating all parts of the applications. Enterprise OSGi could do the same thing by creating a separate OSGi framework for each application, but this would prevent any level of sharing or reuse within the runtime, essentially eliminating many of the advantages you switched to OSGi for in the first place!

Laying out the guts of your application for all the world to see isn't a good idea, but you don't want to hide everything else that could be shared, either. Fortunately, in enterprise OSGi you don't have to do either. The `Application-Content:` header of an EBA also defines the *isolated* content of the application. Isolated content is about as simple as it sounds; the isolated bundles can see each other, but can't be seen by shared bundles or by other applications. The clever part is that, because of the loose coupling that OSGi provides, the isolated bundles can still import packages from the shared bundles. This

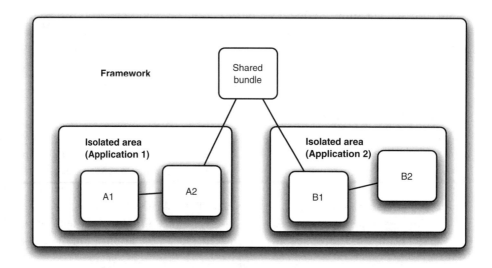

Figure 4.5   Isolation allows both Application 1 and Application 2 to share code with a single instance of a shared bundle without exposing their internal bundles.

means that shared code can contribute packages to multiple applications, but your payment processing system can only be seen by your online store web application (see figure 4.5). This is identical to the application semantics for subsystems.

But Aries EBAs don't have the notion of features or composites. They also don't have any option to accept dependencies; all dependencies listed in the Application-Content: header are included in the application, whether they were packaged in the application archive or not. All dependencies not included in the core content are considered to be *shared* and scoped *outside* the application, in the shared outer framework.

Bundles can be isolated from one another in several ways, with various advantages and drawbacks. From an application perspective, the mechanism by which isolation is achieved is relatively unimportant; the key detail is that services and packages exposed by isolated bundles can only be used by other isolated bundles in the same application.

You'll see an example of using an Aries application in section 4.5, but first we'll consider some of the other technologies that were also developed before OSGi subsystems.

4.4   Alternative approaches

The main focus of this chapter is the use of the EBA as a packaging model for enterprise OSGi, and the EBA will remain the application artifact for the rest of this book. Clearly you're keen to start packaging up your example application as soon as possible, but it wouldn't be fair to continue without at least briefly discussing some of the alternative application packaging approaches that have been offered for OSGi.

4.4.1 *Spring plan and PAR files*

The SpringSource dm Server runtime, which has now become the Eclipse Virgo project, was one of the first server runtimes that could host OSGi applications, and so it also encountered the limitations of the OSGi bundle as an artifact for application packaging. The first versions of dm Server allowed applications to be deployed as a PAR file.

THE PAR

In many senses a PAR file is like an EBA: it's a JAR file archive that contains a collection of OSGi bundles. In a way similar to an EBA, the PAR file defines an application scope. When the bundles in a PAR are deployed into an OSGi framework, they're isolated from other bundles in the runtime. Where the PAR file differs from the EBA is as follows:

- A PAR file doesn't provide metadata to allow bundles to be provisioned from elsewhere; they must be contained within the PAR file, increasing its size.
- When a PAR file is deployed into an OSGi framework, it doesn't allow for shared content to be deployed around it.
- Missing dependencies within a PAR aren't guaranteed to be satisfied when it's installed; this means that the only safe way to write a PAR that's portable across runtimes would be to contain all of your dependencies.

In an effort to improve upon the PAR file, later versions of dm Server added support for a new application descriptor known as a *plan file*.

THE PLAN FILE

To maintain a level of backward compatibility with PAR files, and to reduce cognitive load on developers, a plan file is similar in concept to a PAR file, and also to an EBA. Compared to a PAR file, though, a plan file goes to the opposite extreme, so where a PAR file must contain all its bundles, a plan file contains none!

A plan file is an XML descriptor for an OSGi application that has a .plan extension. Like a PAR file, it describes a collection of bundles; however, a plan file may also refer to other plan files or PAR files as sources of content. Plan files also loosen the scoping restriction of PAR files, in that a plan file need not isolate its bundles within the OSGi framework.

Interestingly, a plan file shares many characteristics with an EBA, but different ones than a PAR file shares with an EBA. Several key differences are these:

- A plan file doesn't provide any mechanism to allow bundles to be provided within the archive. All bundles, no matter how private, esoteric, or customized, must be made available in a centralized repository, either as the bundle itself, or within a PAR. There's also no way to easily provide a single artifact to machines with limited network connectivity.
- When a plan file is deployed into an OSGi framework, it may define shared content and use PAR files to provide isolated sections of the application, but this does require the generation of multiple deployment artifacts.

- Like a PAR file, a plan file provides no guarantees that missing dependencies
  will be satisfied when it's installed. Any dependencies must be listed at some
  scope within the application. This approach is brittle because you must encode
  the name of the bundle that provides your dependency, rather than the packages that need to be provided.

PAR files and plan files are, in many ways, similar to the EBA model, and in combination can be used to achieve almost identical results to EBA deployment. There are a
few ways to look at this. One mean-hearted way to look at it is to say that the EBA was a
case of *not invented here* syndrome; another, slightly kinder, viewpoint would be that an
EBA is a restatement of PAR and plan files to provide all the benefits within a single
packaging. In our (not completely unbiased) perspective, we suggest that there's one
other EBA idiom that's completely absent from the PAR/plan model, which is the concept of inclusion by version range. Both PAR and plan files require you to specify specific versions at development time. There's no flexibility for future bug fixes or feature
enhancements. New code can't be delivered as a new bundle, only as a completely
new application.

SpringSource dm Server/Eclipse Virgo isn't the only OSGi application platform
available that doesn't make use of EBA packaging. Another popular platform is
Apache Karaf, with its feature model.

4.4.2   Apache Karaf features

Karaf features are another way of describing an OSGi application, and are rather similar
to a plan file from Spring dm Server. Like plan files, Karaf features use XML to describe
the set of modules that are to be deployed. One key difference between Karaf features
and the other application packaging artifacts we've been looking at is that a single XML
file may define multiple features (applications). Even more flexibly, features can
depend on other features. These things are definitely not possible in Java EE EARs.

Because of their ability to define multiple features, Karaf features are sometimes
referred to as repositories. Each feature in the repository defines the bundles that
should be installed to activate the feature, because with plan files, the bundles are
referred to directly with no version range. One advantage of features over plan files is
that the bundles are defined as references within a Maven repository. The modules
referred to don't even have to be bundles; native JAR files can be automagically
wrapped into OSGi bundles.

Although wrapping a JAR might seem like the best feature in the world, allowing
the benefits of OSGi without any effort from the developer, it should be noted that
there are some big drawbacks. Automatic wrapping of bundles means there's no way
to distinguish an API from internals, so it typically exposes everything from the JAR.
It's also difficult to determine the dependencies of an arbitrary JAR file, so the imports
for a wrapped bundle aren't always correct. Automatic wrapping also has no context
for determining the versions at which packages should be exported, nor the version
ranges that should be used for imports. Finally, wrapping a JAR at runtime leaves no

way to determine dependencies ahead of time; there's no possibility of a resolution phase, so whether your application can run is a crapshoot.

In summary:

- Karaf features are simple XML files and so don't provide any mechanism to allow bundles to be provided within the archive. Bundles are expected to be retrieved from a Maven repository, or a repository available to the rest of the server runtime.
- Karaf features offer no real concept of scoping; applications share the same OSGi framework for all their bundles, allowing for unforeseen interactions when new applications are deployed.
- Like a plan file, a Karaf feature provides no guarantees that missing dependencies will be satisfied when it's installed and you must encode the name of the bundle that provides your dependency. Adding wrapped JAR files provides yet further uncertainty because it isn't clear what packages are needed or exported.

We believe that as implementations of the subsystems specification become available, the amount of fragmentation in the area of OSGi application packaging will reduce. But it may take a while because technologies are a bit like genies—it's hard to make them go away once they've been released! Although we think subsystems are the future of OSGi applications, we expect you want to try something out now. At the time of writing, Apache Aries is working on a subsystems implementation, but none have been released. But EBAs provide a good alternative. We hope it's clear to you what the advantages of an EBA are over the other models we've discussed, primarily around flexibility of management. Although the names have changed round, EBAs are also the starting point for subsystems, so time spent understanding EBA concepts won't be wasted. For now, we've spent enough time discussing what an EBA is, and we're ready to package our superstore application as an EBA.

4.5   *Developing an enterprise OSGi application*

Having learned about application packaging, and particularly about the EBA packaging model for enterprise OSGi applications, it's time to build an application from the bundles that you've been playing with so far. By the end of this section, you should have an EBA that can be deployed on your development stack or on top of an application server that supports EBA-packaged OSGi applications. The EBA you produce will, broadly speaking, follow the best practices for application packaging; however, at one or two points you'll have to make allowances for the limitations of the development platform.

The limitations of the development stack

The main limitation you face is that the development platform doesn't offer any way to configure bundle repositories to use for remote provisioning. As a result, although you could add an OSGi Bundle Repository (OBR) –based resolver to your platform, there wouldn't be much point!

(continued)

You'll therefore have to include all the bundles needed by the application (including shared code) inside the EBA, which acts as a local repository. On a beefier server this could be done more elegantly. One other limitation of this development platform is that it can't define datasources, so you have to build your own datasource bundles. To avoid complexity in this application, we'll ignore the datasource bundle, but to run the application it would need to be added. In the real world this wouldn't be necessary.

One more thing to note is that the development stack you're using doesn't enforce any of the application isolation boundaries. You could add a few more Aries bundles to enable this, but it isn't necessary for any of the examples covered here. The EBAs described in the enterprise OSGi 5 specification will include isolation.

4.5.1   Building your metadata

The most important part of the application, from a structural perspective, is the application manifest, but if you were happy to have no sharing between your application and others, then it could be entirely omitted. This sort of application isn't particularly interesting, but it does give you an excellent way to build up the application, filling in metadata as you go. Let's start with the most basic metadata—none!

THE ZERO METADATA APPLICATION

If you include no metadata in your application, then you must include the bundles that make it up inside the EBA. This tells the server that the bundles inside the EBA are the application content. The current application would look like figure 4.6.

This figure shows how simple an EBA can be; the zip archive `fancyfoods.eba` contains the six application bundles from chapter 3. No other metadata is required for this application, which is called *fancyfoods*, versioned at `0.0.0`, and it runs all six bundles as

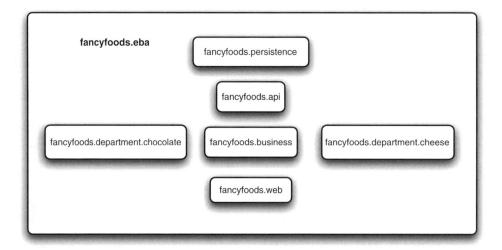

Figure 4.6   The minimum-effort EBA contains no metadata, only bundles.

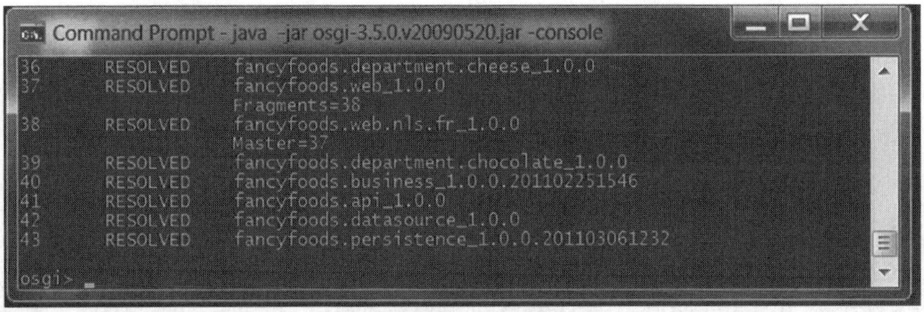

Figure 4.7 The installed EBA. Because the development stack doesn't support isolation, all of the application bundles are visible using the ss command. These bundles have been installed, but not started, by the application runtime.

isolated content. To run the EBA application, start the development stack with a clean load directory, and then drop the EBA into it. The runtime will detect the EBA, resolve it, and install it. With a little extra configuration you could get your development stack to automatically start the EBA as well. For the time being, if you want to check that the application still works, then you can start the bundles yourself from the Equinox console. You should be able to use the application as before (as long as you remembered to add the datasource bundle into the EBA!). See figure 4.7.

Although this EBA was easy to create, it doesn't offer much control. What if you want to change the name and version of your EBA?

TAKING CONTROL OF THE METADATA

When an application is under active development, it's convenient to avoid specifying any metadata, but this quickly becomes problematic as the application becomes more mature and needs to be passed to others for testing. At this point, it's much better to give the application a sensible name and, as with any OSGi artifact, a version. This information can be supplied as shown in the following listing.

Listing 4.2 The manifest for the Fancy Foods EBA

```
Manifest-Version: 1.0
Application-ManifestVersion: 1.0
Application-Name: The Fancy Foods online superstore
Application-SymbolicName: fancyfoods.application
Application-Version: 1.0
```

The example manifest in listing 4.2 contains two pieces of metadata describing the format of the application manifest itself and three pieces about the application. You'll start by describing the two pieces of formatting information that are required for any application manifest (if it's present):

- The Manifest-Version: 1.0 header and value is required by the Java manifest specification to indicate that this metadata file uses standard Java manifest syntax.

- The `Application-ManifestVersion: 1.0` header and value is required by the enterprise OSGi runtime to recognize this file as an application manifest. Don't worry that it might be out of date; at the time of writing only version 1.0 exists, and there are no plans to add a new version.

> **Building EBAs**
>
> If the idea of writing EBA manifests by hand doesn't appeal, don't worry—the Apache Aries project has developed a Maven plug-in, called the eba-maven-plugin, that generates EBA archives. We'll show it in detail in section 8.2.5, along with the other build tools. The Aries project is also working on an esa-maven-plugin for generating subsystem archives.

The other important information in listing 4.2 has to do with the application:

- Applications are easier to recognize if they have a human-readable name. This is added using the `Application-Name:` header. In this case, the name of your application is *The Fancy Foods online superstore.*
- It's also important to provide a unique name for your application that won't clash with others. This is like a bundle's symbolic name, so unsurprisingly it uses the `Application-SymbolicName:` header to call your application *fancy-foods.application.*
- Finally, it's vital to version your application. This, in conjunction with the application's symbolic name, provides a unique identifier just like a bundle. You'll use the `Application-Version:` header to version your application `1.0.0`.

> **Application symbolic names**
>
> Application symbolic names are exactly like bundle symbolic names. In fact, they are so similar that applications and bundles share the same namespace and can be confused in the OSGi framework. Because these names can clash, you should be careful when naming your application. It's easy to give the application the same name as one of your bundles, at which point you often have a painful debugging job before a rather embarrassing aha! moment...

If you add this manifest to the EBA from section zero metadata EBA at the location META-INF/APPLICATION.MF you end up with another deployable EBA. Feel free to try the new application; there should no difference at runtime, but more advanced stacks will display a sensible name for your application.

You're starting to get somewhere now, but you're still relying on defaulting to determine the structure of your application. It's time to take a deeper look at how your application fits together.

STRUCTURING YOUR APPLICATION

So far, your application bundles have been entirely isolated within the runtime. Clearly this works, but it isn't the best way to share code or reduce your runtime footprint. What you want to do is isolate the core content while sharing the API and library code. To do this, the first thing you need to do is look at the application to identify the bundles that can be safely removed.

As you can see from figure 4.8, the bundles in your application are interconnected.

At first glance it may seem as though all the bundles represent core content; however, looking deeper, this isn't quite correct. Core content bundles typically expose an endpoint (like a WAB) or provide an implementation of a service used within the application. In this case, the Fancy Foods API bundle does neither; it exposes packages to the implementation bundles, making it an excellent candidate for sharing.

Now that you've identified that the API bundle doesn't need to be isolated, but that the rest of the bundles do, you have two options. One option would be to add the API bundle to a repository and remove it from the EBA. This would mean it was no longer

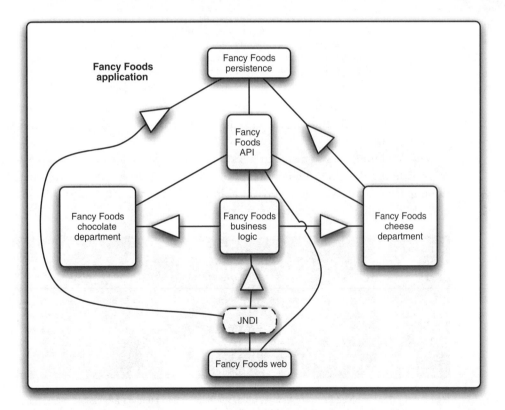

Figure 4.8   The relationships between bundles in your EBA. All of the bundles have a package dependency on the API bundle. The two department bundles expose services that are consumed by the business bundle. The web bundle consumes services from the business and persistence bundles indirectly, by JNDI.

> ### When to share and not to share
> In this example, the bundle you're sharing represents the core API of your application. We've chosen this bundle because it's a good example of the type of bundle that can be safely shared. In the general case, it's unlikely that you'd want to share the internal API of your application, so it isn't particularly valuable to do so. The best things to share are common libraries that are used, or are likely to be used, in multiple applications.

defaulted as core content and could be provisioned as a resolved dependency. Unfortunately, this isn't possible with the development stack you have. Your other option is to leave the API bundle in the EBA, which is what you'll do here.

This information is easily added to your application manifest. Note that the datasource bundle isn't part of your application content, but it's required for the EBA to run on your development stack:

```
Application-Content: fancyfoods.web;version="[1.0.0,2.0.0)",
            fancyfoods.web.nls.fr;version="[1.0.0,2.0.0)",
            fancyfoods.persistence;version="[1.0.0,2.0.0)",
            fancyfoods.business;version="[1.0.0,2.0.0)",
            fancyfoods.department.chocolate;version="[1.0.0,2.0.0)",
            fancyfoods.department.cheese;version="[1.0.0,2.0.0)"
```

Adding this line to your existing application manifest changes it significantly, but if you deploy the application again you can see the framework still contains the API bundle (see figure 4.9).

The API bundle is still installed because the resolver determined that it was needed to provide the dangling dependencies of your EBA. If your runtime supported provisioning from a repository, you'd be able to remove the API bundle from the EBA entirely, reducing the size and complexity of your EBA.

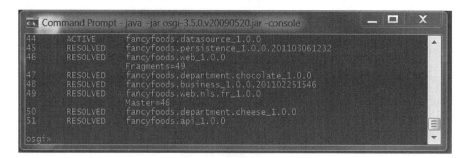

Figure 4.9 **The resolved EBA. As before, all of the application bundles are visible using the** `ss` **command. This also shows that the API bundle has been installed, even though it wasn't part of the application content, because it was needed as a dependency.**

4.6 *Summary*

In this chapter we've discussed the need for a packaging model beyond the OSGi bundle and we've also looked at what's provided by Java EE EARs, both the good and bad points. EBAs provide a familiar, powerful packaging model that leverages the modularity of OSGi bundles to provide great flexibility at runtime.

Most importantly, having packaged up the Fancy Foods application, you should now know enough about the structure of an EBA to be able to build your own. With a little experience, you'll quickly see how bundles can be packaged together to take advantage of resolution and provisioning, reducing the size and complexity of your applications. Having added to your knowledge of WABs, persistence bundles, and Blueprint, you can now begin to think of yourself as a real enterprise OSGi developer.

For those of you who are interested in more than a basic understanding of enterprise OSGi, our journey is far from over. In the next part of this book, we'll take a look at some of the more advanced features of enterprise OSGi.

Part 2

Building better enterprise OSGi applications

Now that you've written a complete enterprise OSGi application, what are the things you need to know to be a really effective enterprise OSGi developer? In this part, we'll explore best practices and the tools you should be bringing into your work flow.

Chapter 5 explains how to structure your applications and introduces a number of OSGi patterns and best practices. Of particular importance is the whiteboard pattern, a valuable pattern available in OSGi.

Chapter 6 considers dynamism and Blueprint in more depth. One of the reasons we really like Blueprint is how well it handles OSGi's dynamism.

Chapter 7 introduces OBR, a provisioning technology that allows you to dynamically install application dependencies.

Chapter 8 provides a guide to a number of useful build tools and test frameworks. These can considerably simplify the process of developing with OSGi.

Chapter 9 carries on the discussion of useful tools by exploring the OSGi support in a range of well-known IDEs.

Best practices for
enterprise applications

In the first part of this book, we took a focused look at the Apache Aries project and how it can be used to write useful enterprise OSGi applications that leverage a combination of base OSGi modularity, enterprise services, and a lightweight programming model. Although this was an incredibly fast way to get to grips with enterprise OSGi, we feel it's time now to take a step back and look at some of the principles underlying what we've been doing. Why did we structure the Fancy Foods application the way we did? What patterns should you be applying to your own applications?

5.1   *The benefits of sharing—and how to achieve them in your bundles*

You're probably wondering why we make such a big deal about sharing code; sure it sounds great in theory, but is it ever practical? Even if it's practical, is it worth the extra effort and loss of control?

Interestingly, both of these questions were initially raised about object-oriented programming (OOP), which was also introduced in an effort to increase reuse. Like OOP, the benefits of the new model in OSGi seem too good to be true, offering a theoretical reward that's almost impossible to achieve in practice. Thankfully, OOP has proved to be a much better model for writing code that needed to work in a large system, but only if you made use of the tools available. The same is true of OSGi, and there are some simple rules you can use to determine whether what you're writing will be a nice, reusable bundle, or if it will be a slightly mangled JAR.

Clearly there's a significant cost associated with writing a piece of code. Even volunteered development time isn't free; by spending time writing one piece of code, you're always taking time away from other pieces of code that need to be written. What isn't typically factored in is the cost of using code that has already been written. Sure, you don't have to pay to write it again, but repackaging code when you need to update a dependency for a bug fix is time consuming, uses computing resource, and may in the long term lead to the sort of JAR hell we saw in chapter 1. More problems arrive if you have to switch to a different implementation of a library that's ostensibly doing the same thing. It usually takes a lot of time and testing to find and fix all the places that were hooked into the old implementation.

The cost of using and maintaining code depends to a great extent on how well modularized the code is. It sometimes helps if you think of a bundle as a puzzle piece. If your bundle has a lumpy, bumpy shape, then it's almost certainly coupled to its dependencies (the other puzzle pieces around it) in a complex and brittle way. Although this shape may help in identifying the pieces of a puzzle, it doesn't help when reusing bundles. The chances are that if the bundle or its dependencies change in any way, the result will change the shape of the pieces so that they don't fit together anymore, causing a failure. If your bundle is well modularized, it will have a simple shape, meaning that it's much easier to find pieces that fit with it (see figure 5.1). Clearly this doesn't help you finish a puzzle, but it does make it much easier to reuse code!

Another cost that's almost always overlooked by developers, but significantly affects infrastructure, is how things are shared at runtime. Although you may have saved lots of money at development time by using a library in the twenty applications running on your system, if that library is loaded twenty times you still need to pay the footprint cost at runtime. In many systems this is a real problem, running to hundreds of megabytes, that adds a significant cost over the lifetime of the application. The problem is particularly obvious in cloud environments, where there's a direct price tag attached to application memory usage.

If you get your sharing right, then you can bypass both the cost of rewriting and the cost of repackaging your code. If you get your sharing *really* right, then you can reduce or even eliminate the cost of switching implementations, and the cost of loading the

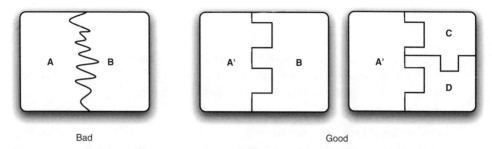

Bad   Good

Figure 5.1 Bundles that have complex dependencies (like A) can typically only be used in one way, relying on the dependencies they were compiled with. Bundles with a well-managed dependency graph can (like the refactored A') be reused in a variety of ways, because it's simple to satisfy their dependency requirements.

same library multiple times. One of the first, and most helpful, things you can do to start getting your sharing right is to get the basics of your bundles right. Unless you do this, everything else becomes difficult.

5.1.1 *Versioning bundles and packages*

As we discussed in section 1.2.1, versioning is a fundamental part of OSGi. Bundles and packages have versions, and getting them wrong can cause a lot of trouble. You can spend a lot of effort producing nice, well-proportioned bundles, but then waste it all by failing to version your imports and exports properly. A good explanation of the OSGi-recommended semantic versioning scheme is in section 12.1.2.

When we say versioning is vital, we mean it. In fact, a badly sized bundle with good versioning is better than any other bundle without versioning. If you don't provide version ranges for the packages you import and versions for your exports, it's *impossible* for anyone to reuse your bundle without having to find and install all the dependencies you originally compiled against. Even worse, if any of your bundle's package dependencies are the same as any of those from any other bundle, and the two bundles need different versions of that package—but don't express that in their package imports—then the application can't be made to work!

BUNDLE VERSIONS

Versioning bundles is probably the least well-defined versioning practice, and it's correspondingly less important than versioning package imports and exports. You mustn't let this mislead you into thinking that the bundle version isn't at all important. The version of your bundle should indicate to the world how the bundle's features and packages have changed over time. This will allow people to easily locate a bundle version that fits their needs.

How should you decide on a version for your bundle? Some people use the same semantic versioning principles for bundles as they do for packages, so that a bundle with backward-compatible changes might change from 2.1 to 2.2, for example, whereas a breaking change would be indicated by changing 2.1 to 3.0. Others align bundle versions with marketing versions, so that major functional improvements might warrant a change from 2.1 to 3.0, even if those changes are backward compatible. Whichever you choose, we feel that your bundle version should never change by a smaller increment than any of the packages it exports. If you've made a breaking change in a package that you provide, then this should be reflected in the bundle's version, as well as the version of the exported package.

VERSIONS FOR EXPORTED PACKAGES

Versioning API packages is extremely important; the version of an exported package is what allows providers and consumers of that API to determine if they're compatible with it. Semantic versioning is important because it provides detailed information about the types of changes that have occurred within the API. Versioning API packages is also crucial because if two packages have the same name and version, then they need to be identical. If you don't change your API version when the API changes, you'll hit the kinds of problems that feature in the section, "The problem with split packages."

IMPORT VERSION RANGES

Export versions are usually easy to define. Even if you don't follow the semantic versioning scheme (although you definitely should), it isn't too hard to decide on a version number. Things are less easy when it comes to package imports. This is because package imports use version ranges to define their future compatibility. In the absence of semantic versioning this is painfully difficult, but you should still try to pick a range of versions. What you absolutely *must not do* is add a single version matching the export you intend to use. For example, the following innocent-looking import is dangerous:

```
Import-Package: fancyfoods.offers;version="1.0.0"
```

Doing this says that your application is compatible with *all* future versions of this package (to infinity). This is extremely unlikely to be true, and causes major problems when an API does eventually make a breaking change.

5.1.2 *Scoping your bundles*

How many bundles is the right number of bundles? How big should bundles be? The answer to both questions, unfortunately, is "it depends." A bundle with one class in it is probably too small. A bundle with a hundred packages in it is almost certainly too big. In between those two extremes, however, it's up to you.

The aim of modularization is the same for bundles as it is for objects, high cohesion, and loose coupling. A good bundle is highly cohesive and loosely coupled. Bundles should be tightly focused in what they do, and they should be flexible in how their dependencies are satisfied. If a single bundle seems to be doing lots of different things, it's probably too big (incohesive). If it's tightly coupled to another bundle, then perhaps the two of them should be merged into one bigger bundle, or have some of their classes redistributed to reduce the coupling.

A bundle's package imports and exports can give a pretty good indication of both how cohesive it is and how coupled it is to its neighbors. If a bundle has a lot of package imports, perhaps it's trying to do too much in too many different areas (incohesive). For example, does the code for generating servlets and the code for sending JMS messages need to live in the same bundle? The number of imports doesn't show anything about coupling, but the nature of what's imported does. If a bundle imports low-level APIs or, worse yet, implementation packages, perhaps it's too closely coupled to its dependencies. Similarly, if a bundle has too many exports, it might be a bloated module trying to do too much in too many areas. If it's exporting lots of packages, it may be exposing too many of its innards to the outside world and encouraging an unhealthy level of coupling; if it's exposing packages containing implementation classes, the coupling is almost certainly too high. Keeping a handle on your imports and exports is a nicely complementary goal to achieving a well-structured modularization.

The `Require-Bundle` header is also a big clue that two bundles are tightly coupled. Ask yourself if you need those classes to come from that particular bundle rather than somewhere else. If you do need your dependencies to come from a fixed place, then the chances are that your classes should be packaged there too!

HOW TO MINIMIZE PACKAGE IMPORTS AND EXPORTS

The dependency graph of a well-architected application should look less like spaghetti and more like a fork. Try to keep both the package exports and package imports as small as possible. This can be a useful guide to sizing your bundles correctly. If the bundles are too small, function will be split between bundles and dependencies that should be internal are forced to be external (see figure 5.2).

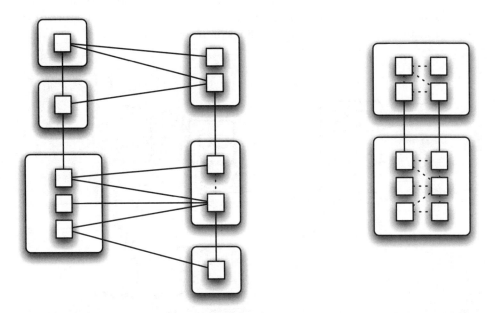

Figure 5.2   Bundles that are too granular will be forced to import and export lots of packages from other parts of the application (solid lines). If the bundles are made slightly larger, many of those dependencies become internal-only (dotted lines).

On the other hand, if bundles are too big, they may have sprawling external dependencies. For example, if the code for talking to both Oracle and DB2 databases is in the same bundle, that bundle will have dependencies on both the Oracle and DB2 database packages when both are unlikely to be present at the same time. In a less extreme case, a bundle that provides both a web frontend and a JMS backend will find itself depending on many unrelated bundles. Bundles that are too big are difficult to reuse in different contexts because they pull in piles of irrelevant dependencies, all of which have to be provided before you can call even a single method (see figure 5.3).

In the sweet spot, a bundle will—hopefully—have few dependencies on other bundles in the application, and few external dependencies. In day-to-day software development, bundles with tiny dependency sets and few exported packages are much easier to aspire to than to achieve! Both your authors have sometimes found themselves writing bundles with enormously long `Import-Package` statements, despite their best intentions.

If you end up in a similar situation, you shouldn't beat yourself up over it—we've all been there, and a lot of us are still there! But, it might be a good opportunity to look at how your code is divided between your bundles, and see if rearranging your bundle boundaries, or moving to a more service-oriented approach (see the section, "Expose services, not implementations"), could neaten things up a bit. It may be that after looking at your bundles, you decide they're highly cohesive and loosely coupled. In these cases you've done well, and no restructuring is required. Minimizing imports and exports is only a rough heuristic, and some highly cohesive and loosely coupled bundles do naturally have large dependency sets. What's most important is the cohesion and coupling, not how many lines there are in the manifest!

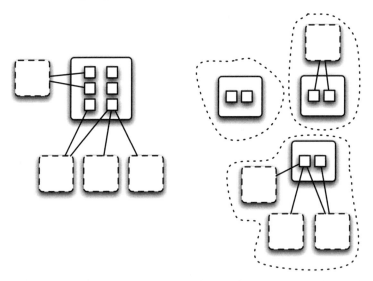

Figure 5.3 Bundles that are too big can have far too many unrelated dependencies. Splitting these bundles up doesn't reduce the number of dependencies, but it can make the dependencies easier to manage, and the bundles easier to reuse, by not requiring all the dependencies to be present all the time!

Having read the information in this section, you'll likely agree that structuring a bundle isn't too difficult. The skills you've developed writing Java objects are completely transferable, and once you get a feel for it you'll recognize a bad bundle in seconds. One important gotcha, which might seem perfectly innocuous and could easily be missed, is the cause of some of the most awkward headaches in OSGi development. This problem is called the *split package*.

THE PROBLEM WITH SPLIT PACKAGES

A split package is what you have when two bundles contain *and export* different bits of the same package at the same version. Although OSGi is well equipped to handle cases where the same package is exported by several bundles, the assumption is that the package implementations are interchangeable. Particularly, if two bundles export the same package at the same version, the OSGi framework could wire you to either. Importantly, the framework will only ever wire an importing bundle to one of the exported packages.

> ### When a split package isn't a split package
>
> If a bundle imports a package and contains extra bits of that package without exporting it, it isn't a split package. This is known as *shadowing*. Shadowing can cause as much of a mess as split packages, if you're not careful. We'll discuss shadowing more in a moment.

This works well when the packages are indeed interchangeable, but it can produce unexpected effects when different bundles claim to export the same package but contain different classes. Only the classes from the bundle you wire to will be visible at runtime! See figure 5.4.

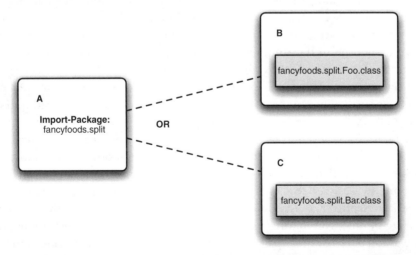

Figure 5.4   An importing bundle can only wire to a single instance of an exported package. If this client needs `fancyfoods.split.Foo`**, then you have a 50:50 chance of success. If it needs both** `fancyfoods.split.Foo` **and** `fancyfoods.split.Bar`**, then it can never work.**

It's possible to use attributes on your package exports to differentiate them, but this requires a corresponding attribute on the import. In the example manifests shown next, the importing bundle A will wire to the package from B and get fancy-foods.split.Foo every time:

```
Bundle-SymbolicName: A
Import-Package: fancyfoods.split;type="top"

Bundle-SymbolicName: B
Export-Package: fancyfoods.split;type="top"

Bundle-SymbolicName: C
Export-Package: fancyfoods.split;type="bottom"
```

Another way of differentiating the two packages is to explicitly select a providing bundle, either with the bundle-symbolicname or bundle-version attributes. These are the only way to choose a particular provider that doesn't specify any attributes:

```
Bundle-SymbolicName: A
Import-Package: fancyfoods.split;bundle-symbolicname="B"

Bundle-SymbolicName: B
Export-Package: fancyfoods.split

Bundle-SymbolicName: C
Export-Package: fancyfoods.split
```

Although using attributes does allow you to pick one export or the other, it's far from elegant. Using the bundle-symbolicname attribute introduces tight coupling between the importer and the exporter, as you force the framework to wire you to a particular bundle. This may indicate the two bundles should be merged. The type attribute you made up is a little more flexible, but still adds a degree of coupling. If you imagine a grand scale of coupling, this is much closer to an import without attributes than it is to the import with the bundle-symbolicname import. In either case, you're constraining the framework resolver, which can introduce other problems. Depending on how the rest of the bundles in the runtime are wired together, it may not be possible for the importer to resolve, even if the right version of the fancyfoods.split package is present in the runtime. This can happen when the bundle importing the split package needs to import a different package from another bundle that has wired to the *wrong* version of the fancyfoods.split package.

Attributes have another critical limitation when it comes to split packages: they allow you to choose one export or the other, but never both. If the importer needs classes from more than one part of the split package (packages can be split across as many bundles as there are classes in the package), then they're out of luck.

OSGi does offer a workaround for the split package problem that prevents the importing bundle from having to do anything messy, and that allows the importer to see the union of two or more parts of the split package. This requires one of the exporting bundles to use the Require-Bundle header to require the bundle that exports the other part of the split package. Require-Bundle is a bit like Import-Package:, except that you supply a bundle name and version, and it wires you to *every* exported package from that bundle. Unlike `Import-Package:`, `Require-Bundle` doesn't cause any code inside your bundle to be shadowed. This means that your bundle can see its original content and the required bundle's content for the split package, effectively combining them into one.

What do we mean by shadowing?

If a bundle contains a package without exporting it, and also imports it, the contained code will never be loaded. The semantics of OSGi classloading state that the load of any resource from an imported package is delegated to the exporting bundle to which you were wired. The content from the exporter *shadows* the entire content of the package inside the importing bundle, meaning that the contained content can't be loaded even if there's no corresponding resource in the exporting bundle. If you ever see a `ClassNotFoundException` for a class you know is in your bundle, then this is probably what has happened.

`Require-Bundle` doesn't cause shadowing of entire packages, but it can cause shadowing of individual resources. As with imported packages, required bundles are searched before the classpath of the bundle. This means that if a resource is present in a required bundle, then it overrides that resource inside the bundle that requires it. This can cause major problems if the resources in the two bundles aren't the same, or even if they are. When classes are loaded, their identity is defined by the `java.lang.ClassLoader` that loads them; this means that classes from required bundles are in a different package! This can cause havoc with default or protected visibility methods.

Using `Require-Bundle`, you can make one of the bundles export the entirety of the package. By adding an attribute with a mandatory constraint to the required bundle's export of the split package, importers of that package no longer need to worry about accidentally getting wired to the wrong export (see figure 5.5). (We'll look at the mandatory directive in more detail in section 7.1.3.)

```
Bundle-SymbolicName: A
Import-Package: fancyfoods.split

Bundle-SymbolicName: B
Require-Bundle: C
Export-Package: fancyfoods.split

Bundle-SymbolicName: C
Export-Package: fancyfoods.split; partial="true"; mandatory:="partial"
```

The use of `Require-Bundle` and mandatory attributes can eliminate the ambiguity created by the split packages, but it significantly reduces the modularity and flexibility of your application. The two halves of your split package are forever tightly tied together, and the whole thing is rather unpleasant. We hope that you agree with us that split packages are better off avoided!

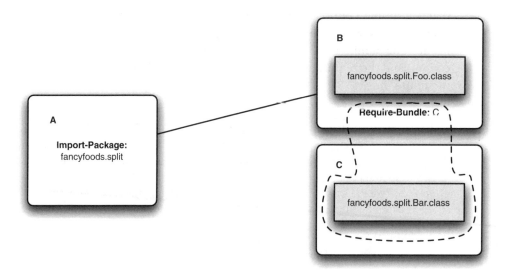

Figure 5.5   **In this case, the importing bundle, A, must wire to bundle B's package because the mandatory directive on bundle C's package requires that the importer specify** `partial="true"` **to wire to it. B uses** `Require-Bundle: C` **to unify the package, meaning that both** `fancyfoods.split.Foo` **and** `fancyfoods.split.Bar` **are visible to bundle A.**

> **WARNING:** `Require-Bundle` **AND ECLIPSE PLUG-IN DEVELOPMENT** If you're using Eclipse's Plugin Development Environment (PDE) to write your bundles, you may find you're using `Require-Bundle` instead of `Import-Packages` even if you don't have split packages. Historically, Eclipse used `Require-Bundle` internally, and its manifest editor occasionally defaults to requiring bundles rather than importing packages.

For those of you who develop in the Eclipse foundation, you're likely to see split packages. The reason for the split packages in Eclipse is architectural. The core Eclipse runtime is packaged as an OSGi bundle and is extended by other bundles that add extra classes to core packages. Clearly, if the core runtime is going to be extensible, it can't be tied to all the possible extensions by `Require-Bundle`. This left Eclipse with a solution similar to the one that we outlined earlier. Extensions to the Eclipse runtime bundle use `Require-Bundle` to unify the split package, and also export the package with an attribute that marks the *extended* view of the package. Clients that need a particular extension then supply a matching attribute on their import and find all the classes they need. Although this may sound elegant, it does mean that no client can make use of two extensions at once in a reliable way, and that clients need to be extra careful about what they import. As before, we strongly discourage you from splitting packages across bundles that you write.

So far we've been focusing on package imports and exports, but equally important is what you don't share with the outside world.

5.1.3   Why isolation is important to sharing

An old adage in computing says "All you need to solve any problem is another layer of abstraction." The grain of truth behind this saying is that problems often become much more tractable if the gory details are hidden away so that you can deal with a set of simple base cases instead. This fact applies generally across software, and most applications make use of frameworks or other services that deal in these abstractions.

INVASION OF PRIVACY

One of the most important things about levels of abstraction is that the underlying details don't bleed through, breaking the abstraction. In Java code this is typically accomplished through interfaces, factories, and changeable implementations. Unfortunately for Java, there's little to prevent someone bypassing your API and starting to work directly with the underlying implementation classes. Clearly this is a gross violation of the abstraction, but what if there's a method on the implementation object, but not on the interface, that does exactly what you want, what you *need*? Aren't you tempted? Most people are; after all, expediency is what gets projects delivered on time, right?

The previous paragraph is clearly a bad idea, and yet so many of us are guilty of doing it. When people start casting objects to specific implementation types, the API becomes brittle. Any change to *private* content risks breaking clients, even though it's not supposed to. Even without change, casting to implementation types is a risky business. What if the internal documentation says you're supposed to `synchronize` on a particular object in a lock hierarchy before calling it to avoid a potential deadlock?

KEEPING YOUR BUNDLES MODEST

Given that we'll never stop being tempted to make use of implementation specifics for expediency, sacrificing long-term benefit for a quick win despite the cost, developers won't stop doing it. The only way to stop this sort of hack from happening is to make the hack less convenient than doing things properly. Fortunately, this is easy to accomplish in OSGi; if an implementation isn't part of your API, then don't export it. There's no reason to expose the implementation type to other bundles. If other bundles can't see your implementation type, it's impossible for them to cast to it, and it takes a dirty hack for reflection to look like a good idea! When in doubt, cover up.

If your bundles do meet Victorian standards of decency, then how do they communicate? Bundle A may contain an implementation of an interface, but it's not much use unless you can get it in to Bundle B somehow, and if you can't cast to a type you certainly can't instantiate it...

The answer is to use the OSGi Service Registry.

EXPOSE SERVICES, NOT IMPLEMENTATIONS

As we've already mentioned, a great way of ensuring that bundles neither import nor export too many packages is to never export implementation classes. This also prevents people from violating any abstractions you've made, or doing things that are plain wrong. Using services isn't just good for keeping manifest sizes down. It entirely avoids compile-time dependencies on implementation bundles and keeps the coupling between bundles much looser than it would be otherwise.

If you catch yourself exporting an implementation package from a bundle, stop and think carefully. Why are you doing this, and is it the best way? Is your bundle granularity too fine? Could a service be used instead?

5.2 *Structuring for flexibility*

You already know that how you structure and scope your bundles has a big impact on the modularity of your application. It's also important to realize that the structure of your bundles affects how dynamic they can be as well. There are a few important things to remember.

5.2.1 *Separate interfaces from implementation*

Not exporting implementation packages is important for modularity, but for dynamism it's best if they aren't even in the same bundle as the interfaces. This is in fact one of the most important things you can do to allow dynamism. But why?

HOT SWAPPABILITY

Keeping APIs separate from implementation matters more in an OSGi application because OSGi makes it possible to add and remove things from a bundle's class space. If your implementation is packaged in the same bundle as its API, then their lifecycles are permanently tied together. If you had done this with your buggy persistence layer, then, to replace the implementation, you'd also have to replace the API. After the old API bundle has been replaced, any consumers of the API would need to be restarted and refreshed to wire to the new copy of the API classes. Keeping APIs separate gives you much more flexibility to swap implementations in and out without affecting other bundles in the runtime (see figure 5.6).

5.2.2 *If you can't separate out your API*

Sometimes, for perfectly good reasons, it's not possible to keep your API and implementation in separate bundles. Perhaps your architecture, or corporate policy, forces your API to be colocated with your implementation classes. The best solution is to come up with a more OSGi-friendly API, but often you have to play the cards you're dealt.

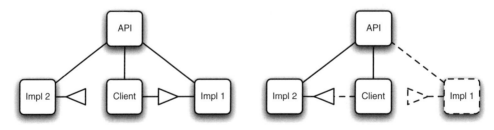

Figure 5.6   When the API for a service is separated from the client and implementations, then implementations can easily be switched. On the left you see the client using implementation 1. If you remove implementation 1 from the system, then the client can switch to implementation 2 with no loss in function or availability.

In cases like this it's important to ensure that you keep your class space as wide as possible. If three implementations of this API were present in the runtime, then clients would only be able to use one implementation at a time, determined by the API package they're wired to, making the other two implementations redundant. Clearly this isn't ideal.

SUBSTITUTABILITY

Do you remember learning about shadowing (section 5.1.2)? In your current predicament, shadowing becomes useful. If your bundles both import *and* export the API packages, then the runtime will play a clever trick. If the API packages *aren't* already available when your bundle is resolved, then the *import* statement is ignored and the API packages are *exported* from your bundle. If the API packages *are* available, then the *export* statement is ignored and the API packages are *imported* into your bundle. This arrangement means that there will only be one instance of the API package available in the framework, shared between all of the implementations. This means that clients can use any of the implementations.

If dependencies are only on interfaces, to the point where implementations can be swapped in and out at will, how does anything get hold of concrete instances of these interfaces? If you're thinking in terms of conventional Java, you probably already have an answer ready—the factory pattern.

5.2.3 *Avoid static factory classes*

The factory pattern is extremely prevalent in Java; static factories are used to provide indirection between interfaces and implementations. Although this pattern is technically possible in OSGi, it's unable to cope with OSGi's dynamism. If you do create an object using a static factory, then you won't get any notification when the bundle that provided it is stopped or even uninstalled. What's worse is that because the static factory is unlikely to be OSGi aware, it won't be tracking its dependencies either. This means that watching the lifecycle of the bundle that hosts the static factory isn't always good enough to tell you that your object has become invalid.

The ability to register for Service Registry event notifications as well as the Service Registry's get/release semantics provide exactly the lifecycle structure that's missing from the static factory model. If you had used static factories to build your superstore, then you wouldn't be able to dynamically add and remove special offers. What's worse, you wouldn't have been able to prevent people from seeing the special offer even if you removed the department, causing failures elsewhere. And you could never have separated out your interface and implementation bundles if you had to provide a static factory that was closely coupled to implementation internals.

As you try to break the static factory habit and replace it with services, you may find you have to change how you're thinking in other areas. For example, the apparently inoffensive listener pattern often relies heavily on the factory pattern. Just as they allow you to avoid static factories, OSGi services also allow you to get more from your listener while writing less code.

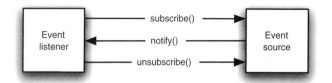

Figure 5.7 The listener pattern. A listener registers with an event source.

5.2.4 *Building a better listener with the whiteboard pattern*

A common pattern in many applications is the *listener pattern.* An event source maintains a list of event listeners; when events happen, it notifies each listener in turn. Interested listeners register and unregister with the event source (see figure 5.7).

What happens when the listener's useful life comes to an end? Depressingly little, in some cases. Unless the listener is careful, the event source still holds a reference to the listener. You risk ending up with unused objects hanging around, leaking memory, and being notified of events that they don't care about and probably can't handle without throwing an exception. The only way to avoid the issue is to be scrupulously careful about manually unregistering listeners when they no longer require events.

If you think about it a bit more, you can see that the event source is in fact maintaining a registry of listeners. It's a pretty simple registry—often nothing more than a Set or List managed by register() and unregister() methods. Even though the registries aren't particularly complex, they still need writing. It seems kind of crazy to re-implement a private registry for every class that could produce events. It seems extra crazy when even the best-written registries are still prone to memory leaks and runtime errors from obsolete entries. Less well-written registries can also be crippled by threading issues.

OUTSOURCING THE REGISTRY

Wouldn't things be better if there were already a registry you could use? One that supported dependency injection? In OSGi, there is, and it does. Using the Service Registry as a convenient way of implementing a listener registry is known as the *whiteboard pattern* (see figure 5.8).

The big advantage of the whiteboard pattern is that it avoids the explicit dependency between the event source and the listener. The listener merely needs to advertise that it's interested in events, instead of tracking down a reference to a named event source. If needed, service properties and filters can be used to ensure listeners are registered only for events from the right sources; we'll cover more about those in section 6.4.2.

Figure 5.8 The whiteboard pattern. A listener registers with the Service Registry. When an event occurs, the event source obtains an up-to-date list of listeners to notify from the Service Registry.

> **Why whiteboards?**
>
> If you struggle to get the whiteboard pattern first time 'round, you're not alone. One of the most puzzling things about the whiteboard pattern is its name! The idea behind the name, apparently, is that the Service Registry acts a bit like a whiteboard in an office. People can subscribe to an event—a picnic, say—by adding their name to the shared whiteboard. They don't need to contact the picnic organizer directly, or even know who's organizing the picnic.

At first, the whiteboard pattern can seem backward. After all, surely it's the event source that's providing the useful service, and the listeners that benefit from the service, right? The event source doesn't need any of its listeners, but the listeners need the event source a great deal!

The thing to do is think less about the *service* part of the Service Registry and more about the *registry* part. The Service Registry, in combination with Blueprint, is a handy general-purpose registry. By using the Service Registry to collect your listeners you dramatically reduce the complexity of your event source. You also don't have to worry about what happens when listeners are stopped; the Service Registry elegantly ensures that you only ever see services from running bundles. When you get used to the whiteboard pattern, you'll find that it can be used to simplify many different situations. It even crops up when writing remote services, as you'll see in chapter 10.

The whiteboard pattern is most effective when you want the same event, or the same processing, to occur multiple times. This could involve calling a number of listeners, counting up a number of objects, or even reacting to the presence and absence of particular services. You've been using the whiteboard pattern in the Fancy Foods online superstore since chapter 3; rather than registering each of the departments in your superstore with the business beans, you expose them as services, and let the business beans look them up as necessary. This is part of what makes the superstore so simple to extend.

Taking full advantage of OSGi doesn't just means changing how you think about low-level patterns like factories and listeners. You may also need to have a bit of a rethink about some of your habits for structuring enterprise applications.

5.3   *A better enterprise application architecture*

If you're used to writing Java EE applications, you probably have a toolkit of application architectures and development patterns you're in the habit of using. Many of the patterns that work well for Java EE applications work equally well for enterprise OSGi ones.

How do these Java EE patterns translate in the dynamic world of OSGi? Some work pretty much unchanged. For example, you'll probably want a business tier, a presentation tier, and a data access tier. But some of the familiar Java EE patterns need a bit of rework to make the most of OSGi's modularity and dynamism, and there are some new patterns in enterprise OSGi.

A complete lesson on designing Java EE applications is well beyond the scope of this book, but we'll walk you through some of the variations and exciting new possibilities that come with enterprise OSGi.

5.3.1   *Use small WABs*

Many Java EE WARs are pretty big beasts. Not only does the WAR include its own code and image resources, it often packages all of its dependencies in the WEB-INF/lib folder. The WAR is acting almost like a mini-EAR, only with less explicit metadata.

Nobody likes massive WARs, but sometimes keeping all your JARs inside the lib directory is such an ingrained habit that you do it automatically. Remember—unlike WARs, WABs can be small, compact, and modular—and they're better that way (see figure 5.9).

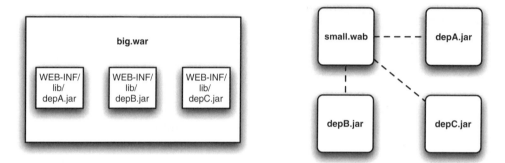

Figure 5.9   Whereas a WAR often needs to package all its code and dependencies inside the WAR itself, WABs can be much more modular.

5.3.2   *Make a persistence bundle*

If your application is using persistence, it's a good idea to use a purpose-built persistence bundle for the persistence.xml and the entity classes. This may be a bit different from how you structured your persistence code for Java EE, but there's a good reason for grouping everything together (see figure 5.10).

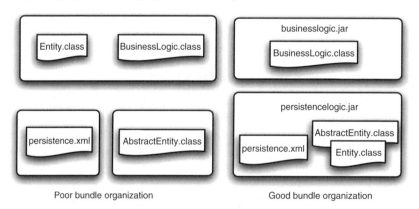

Figure 5.10   In an enterprise OSGi environment, it's important to package persistence classes in the same bundle in which the persistence units are defined.

Why should the persistence unit and the entities be kept together? A persistence unit and its entities are intimately related; one without the other doesn't give a complete picture. In combination, the persistence unit defines not only the database backing the entity classes, but also the way in which the entity classes are mapped into tables within the database. This is a tight coupling, and so the artifacts should live in the same bundle; making a change to an entity without reference to the persistence unit is usually disastrous, which is why storing them independently is a bad idea. Not only is keeping the persistence unit and its entity classes together wise, it's required by the JPA Service Specification. If the entities are separated from the persistence unit, features like runtime entity enhancement will stop working.

Having a discrete persistence bundle has a second advantage. If the persistence code and domain model aren't tangled in with application business logic, the same persistence services may be reused by several different applications. Having multiple persistence units talking to the same database is far less efficient in terms of implementation and maintenance effort. If either the implementation or the maintenance goes wrong, there's the possibility of inaccurate entity mappings causing data corruption.

Packaging all of an application's entities together may not feel like the most natural pattern to you. If your database is complex, your persistence bundle might be quite large, or even—say it isn't so—monolithic. Ultimately, your persistence bundle will have the same modularity characteristics as your backing database. If the tables in your database split nicely into separate groups with the entities representing them having no mapped relationship (that is, they can be put into separate persistence units), then those persistence units can be happily packaged in different persistence bundles. On the other hand, if your entities are all interconnected, then they need to be in a single persistence unit, and therefore a single persistence bundle. When you think about it, this is exactly what you should be doing with classes in a bundle anyway.

Luckily, just because all of your entity classes are in a single bundle doesn't mean they all have to be exposed to the rest of your application. Large domain models should at least be divided across multiple packages. Consuming bundles should only import the packages they need for their part of the business logic.

You may remember that in the section, "Expose services, not implementations," we explained that hiding your implementation classes is a good idea. Sadly, JPA entity classes

Inheritance, object-orientation, and entities

In more complex applications with multiple persistence units, it's sometimes nice to pull out elements common to several JPA entities (such as numeric primary keys or creation dates) into a superclass or embedded class. This is enabled by JPA's `@MappedSuperclass` and `@Embedded` annotations. Unfortunately, this pattern doesn't always translate into an OSGi environment. The specification requires the persistence.xml to be in the same bundle as the entity implementations. This restriction applies to mapped superclasses, as well as the named entities. (Any interfaces are exempt!) This means mapped superclasses must be packaged in the same bundles as their subclasses, which can limit their reuse.

don't fit particularly well with this model. By definition, entity classes aren't interfaces, and they do contain a reasonable level of mapping metadata. When working out how best to deal with your JPA entities, you have two main options, which we'll discuss next.

EXPOSING ENTITY CLASSES

The simplest option is to bite the bullet and export the JPA entity classes. This has the important, and sometimes unwanted, effect of making your entity classes part of your API. Exposing the entity classes directly makes it quick and easy for clients to use them, and also allows other bundles to make use of your persistence units by directly using your `EntityManagerFactory` services. This works well if the entity classes are simple, JavaBeans-style objects with getters and setters. It's also important that the entity classes offer a reasonably stable API, and particularly one that isn't specific to the underlying database implementation.

The main problems with exposing entity classes stem from the fact that the entities have become part of your API. First, you can no longer replace your persistence bundle without having to refresh all your persistence clients. Second, and probably more awkward, you can no longer make structural database changes, or add new features to your entity classes without potentially breaking the rest of your application. The more complex the logic in your entity classes is, the more likely this is to happen. Finally, if you do expose your entity classes, then you're implicitly accepting the fact that other bundles can directly use your persistence units without going through a data access layer. If your database model is complex, or you wish to enforce some rules about valid data values, this is often a deal breaker.

HIDING ENTITY CLASSES WITH INTERFACES

Normally, there's no reason for any code to have a direct dependency on the persistence bundle, a fact that helps makes the persistence bundle easy to upgrade. If you add a data access service to your persistence bundle, you can use this to load and store objects but only refer to them by interface. This is exactly what you do in the Fancy Foods application, where `Inventory` and `Accounting` from section 3.2.4 take interfaces instead of implementations. Not only does this keep your business layer loosely coupled to your persistence bundle, but this has the big advantage that you can force *every* bundle to use your data access methods. This means that you can enforce rules about minimum stock and credit levels much more easily.

There are clear advantages to using interfaces to hide your entity classes; however, it isn't a perfect solution. It's easy for the data access service to return data objects that have been looked up—either the entity types will implement the interface directly, or there can be a wrapper class. Storing or updating the entity instances in JPA requires instances of the entity class. This means that the data access service must be able to create new instances of the entity classes from raw data (or other implementations of the interface) that get passed in. Sometimes you might get lucky, and find that you can cast the instance you were passed to an entity implementation (if, say, it came from a previous lookup), but other cases can involve significant amounts of copying.

5.3.3 *The rewards of well-written bundles*

Given the level of effort you spent making your bundles, you would hope for some sort of pay-off, and unsurprisingly there's a big one. If you've written your bundles well, it becomes extremely easy to reuse them. Because you have a small list of imports, it's trivial to supply your dependencies, and because the imports are versioned, you also know what version of the dependencies to supply. Furthermore, if you want to make use of a third-party bundle, then later change version or implementation, you know exactly which bundles are affected; there's no need to scour the entire codebase of your application. Finally, because all of your exports and imports are versioned, it doesn't matter if the dependency of a dependency clashes with another; if the versions are semantically compatible, you can provide one implementation that both can use, or if not, you can provide two implementations knowing that there's no risk of failure at runtime!

For those who embrace OSGi, hiding implementation classes adds yet more benefits. Bug fixing and refactoring become trivial because there are no compile-time dependencies between implementation bundles, only between an implementation and its API. This significantly reduces the time it takes to debug, fix, build, and deploy.

Although the benefits mentioned are all incredibly worthwhile achievements, OSGi wouldn't have achieved the popularity it has if that were all it had to offer. For many people who know OSGi, they're fringe benefits—services are OSGi's killer feature. We've seen one of the ways OSGi services can be put to use in our discussion of the whiteboard pattern. We'll discuss OSGi services more in the next chapter.

5.4 *Summary*

Although this chapter hasn't extended your superstore, it has taught you a lot more about what was already there. The main reason that you haven't had to make changes to your application is that it was already following the guidelines for ensuring good modularity and dynamism. We hope that you have a new-found appreciation for your little superstore, and that by better understanding the principles that underpin it, you'll find it easier to recreate its modularity in your own applications.

Building dynamic
applications with
OSGi services

6

This chapter covers

- What OSGi dynamism means for your application
- Your dependency injection options
- How to become a Blueprint power user
- How Blueprint interacts with OSGi dynamism
- Detecting system changes

Dynamism is probably the most powerful, and often the most underrated, feature of the OSGi framework. A lot of people think that their applications are already dynamic because they have plug points that can be easily extended, or that dynamism isn't that useful. It's true that dynamism isn't important to everyone, but it can do a lot more than most people think!

What does dynamism mean for you? Is it your friend or your foe? If you decide it's all too hard, can you ignore it entirely? How does it affect how you write your enterprise application?

One of the key enablers of OSGi dynamism is OSGi services. Services form the basis of an extremely powerful programming model, and OSGi's dependency injection frameworks extend that programming model to make it simple to use, too.

In this chapter, we'll discuss how OSGi dynamism works and how to get the most out of it. We'll also cover in detail how dependency injection and services can be used to handle dynamism with as little work as possible.

We'll start by looking more closely at what dynamism means for OSGi applications.

6.1 OSGi dynamism

One of the defining characteristics of OSGi is its dynamism. This dynamism was critically important in the environment for which OSGi was originally conceived: embedded devices. How does it play out in the enterprise space? Many of the concerns of enterprise applications are surprisingly similar to those of embedded ones; modules may be deployed to a variety of different environments, and those environments might change over the lifetime of the module, as other devices (in the embedded case) and components (in the enterprise case) come and go.

We first introduced the concept of dynamism way back in chapter 1, so far back that you might not remember it now. Since then we've covered a lot of ground, some of it making use of OSGi's dynamism without calling it out. Going back to chapter 1, we discussed how in OSGi bundles can be started and stopped and even uninstalled from a running OSGi framework. This is the core of OSGi's lifecycle model, and ties in closely with dynamism.

In OSGi, *ACTIVE* (that is, started) bundles are roughly equivalent to what Java EE developers would think of as *running* modules. In Java EE, running modules can load classes and have managed objects such as servlets or EJBs available for use by clients. In OSGi, things are similar: ACTIVE and STARTING bundles can load classes and expose services in the Service Registry. (A bundle may be in the STARTING state either because its bundle activator is still being run, or because the bundle has chosen lazy activation and none of its classes have been loaded.) Importantly, OSGi bundles have other states; you may remember that RESOLVED bundles can still load classes, but are not able to register services. If a bundle is stopped, then all of its services are unregistered. This has an important consequence for other bundles; because services can come and go, it's possible that a service you're using may cease to exist. Clearly your code might still have an object reference to call, but it's important to stop using it because its behavior is no longer guaranteed. The stopped bundle will have lost access to any services it was using, and will probably also have done some tidy-up to free up resources.

The most surprising difference between Java EE and OSGi is that, in OSGi, modules can be completely removed from a running system or added to it. Can you imagine removing an EJB JAR from a running EAR without stopping the other EJB JARs and WARs? Doing this in OSGi is surprisingly easy; if you've been following our examples, then you've already done it! Do you remember fixing a bug in the superstore's persistence layer? You had an in-memory database that continued running throughout. You didn't even lose your HTTP session because the WAB was running throughout.

> **WARNING: DISMANTLE WITH CARE** Just because you *can* remove parts of a running OSGi application, doesn't mean it always ends well! Your application must be written to cope safely with things appearing and disappearing. How to do that is the subject of this chapter.

Fixing the superstore was a powerful example of how OSGi's dynamism can be used. You were able to apply a critical fix to your running application without stopping it. This is one of OSGi's lesser-known features, but it's the sort of thing that makes administrators squeak with joy. Your dynamic fix was only possible because you followed the good modularity practices described in section 5.1, keeping your bundles small and focused. If your persistence logic had been mixed in with your web layer, or implementation details had bled through, it wouldn't have been possible. Good modularity on its own isn't enough—you also had to follow good patterns for dynamism in the superstore's design, handling the dynamic nature of the OSGi services you used to communicate between bundles.

6.2 *Using OSGi services*

Although services are an excellent way to decouple bundles from one another, they're *essential* in a dynamic system. As you saw in the persistence layer of the superstore, service implementations can be replaced at runtime without even restarting the application. If implementation classes had been hardcoded, on the other hand, replacing one implementation with another would have required a complete recompile, as well as a restart.

> **The value of the Service Registry**
>
> One school of thought says that OSGi services are the most useful features of the entire OSGi specification, more valuable even than modularized classloading and versioning. In our opinion, it's rather difficult to separate the two, although there have been a number of recent attempts to bring the OSGi Service Registry to Java SE, such as the pojosr project (http://code.google.com/p/pojosr/). This dynamic Service Registry has value, but without the underlying module lifecycle and classloading we can't help but feel that there's something missing. Equally, if you were to take the Service Registry out of OSGi, then you'd take many of the valuable usage patterns with it. Projects like pojosr are an excellent way to shrink the gap between Java SE and OSGi. We just hope that people don't end up missing out on the real value of OSGi, thinking that OSGi is Java SE with a Service Registry.

6.2.1 *Registering and looking up services the old-fashioned way*

You've already been using OSGi services extensively in chapters 2 and 3. If you don't recall a discussion of OSGi services, you're probably not alone—you've always used Blueprint to manage your services. As you'll see, there was a good reason for this!

REGISTERING OSGI SERVICES

Let's see what OSGi services look like without a helper framework. Registering OSGi services is easy; it's a single API call. The following listing shows how to register a service of class `DesperateCheeseOffer` that exposes the interface `SpecialOffer`.

> **Listing 6.1 Registering an OSGi service using the OSGi API**

```
public void registerService(BundleContext ctx) {

    String iface = SpecialOffer.class.getName();          ◁── Interface name

    Dictionary<String, Object> props =
            new Hashtable<String, Object>();
    props.put("myStringProperty", "foo");                 ◁── Optional properties
    props.put("myBooleanProperty", Boolean.TRUE);

    SpecialOffer impl = new DesperateCheeseOffer();        ◁── Service object

    ServiceRegistration reg =
    ctx.registerService(iface, impl, props);               ◁── Register the service

}
```

The service is registered under a string representing an interface name, and to prevent an error at runtime, the service object has to implement that interface. Optional properties describing the service can also be added. An object representing the service is instantiated, and then the name, properties, and instance are passed to the bundle context for registration with the OSGi framework. The returned `Service-Registration` can be used to unregister or update the service if you need to at some point in the future.

LOOKING UP OSGI SERVICES

Consuming OSGi services appears to be equally easy, requiring only two API calls. But this isn't the whole story. You may have guessed that we're keen to impress upon you that an OSGi framework is a dynamic place. Services can come and go at any moment, including the instant that you have looked them up! If you want to use services properly, it takes more code than the bare minimum two calls. You have to be particularly careful to always unget a service when you're done with it. Listings 6.2 and 6.3 show code calling out to services in the Service Registry.

> **Ungetting services**
>
> The get/release pattern can be the source of a lot of problems in computing, and many people are confused by why it's needed in the OSGi Service Registry. Typically, in Java the only things that you release after use are I/O streams.

(continued)

These need to be closed to free up resources, and that's exactly the same reasoning used in OSGi. As we mentioned in section 1.2.3, OSGi began life in constrained systems. Every byte of memory was precious, so reducing the footprint was important. You'll see in more detail in section 6.3.4 how services can be lazily created, but for now it's enough to know that you can create a service object dynamically when it's requested. The framework caches this result, speeding up future lookups and reducing memory usage. If the service is no longer being used, then this caching is a waste of memory. By ungetting the service you're letting the framework know that it can invalidate its cache (assuming nobody else needs the service), and that any resources associated with the service can be cleaned up.

Listing 6.2   Consuming a single OSGi service using the OSGi API

```
public void callService(BundleContext ctx) {                    Find service that
    String name = SpecialOffer.class.getName();                 advertises right interface
    ServiceReference ref = ctx.getServiceReference(name);

    if (ref != null) {                               Check that service exists
        SpecialOffer s = (SpecialOffer) ctx.getService(ref);            Get
                                                                        instance
        if (s != null) {              Service instance could
            try {                     have been unregistered!
                Food f = s.getOfferFood();                     You can finally
            } finally {                                        call service
                ctx.ungetService(ref);              You must
            }                                        unget service
        }
    }
}
```

You first use the bundle context to find services that are registered under an interface name you supply. A null return indicates that you couldn't find any services with the right interface name. Then you can use the bundle context to get the service instance for the service you looked up. But between doing the initial lookup and getting the instance, the service might have been unregistered, in which case it's no longer available. (Have we mentioned OSGi is dynamic?) After you have a service instance, you're safe to use it. But you need to remember to unget the service when you're done with it.

The best way to get services?

Even though listings 6.2 and 6.3 aren't short, they don't show all the possible complexity of getting services using the low-level OSGi APIs in a real application. If you showed this code to an OSGi expert, you'd get a lot of furrowed brows and concerned noises. This sample may not perform well, because it doesn't keep hold of the service for long.

(continued)

It also risks losing state if `unget()` is called with a stateful service. Even worse, nothing is done to handle the case when the service is dynamically unregistered. For more correct behavior, you'd need to introduce service listeners or service trackers. If your head is spinning at this point with all the APIs and complications, don't worry—treat listings 6.2 and 6.3 as examples of what you won't be doing, because you'll be using dependency injection for your services instead!

Even if multiple services which implement the `SpecialOffer` interface are available, the code in listing 6.2 will only return the top-ranked service. To get all the available services, use the `getServiceReferences` method instead. You'll also need to use `getServiceReferences` if you want to filter the returned services based on their service properties.

Listing 6.3   Consuming multiple OSGi services using the OSGi API

```
public void callServices(BundleContext ctx)                          Filter services
                    throws InvalidSyntaxException {                   based on
    ServiceReference[] refs = ctx.getServiceReferences(    ◁──────    properties.
            "fancyfoods.food.SpecialOffer",
            "(myStringProperty=foo)");

    if (refs != null) {                          ◁──── Check for null ...
        for (ServiceReference ref : refs) {
            SpecialOffer s = (SpecialOffer) ctx.getService(ref);
            if (s != null) {                                         ◁──    ... and check
                try {                                                        again.
                    Food f = s.getOfferFood();
                } finally {
                    ctx.ungetService(ref);                   ◁──    You must unget every
                }                                                   service found.
            }
        }
    }
}
```

As before, you need to be diligent about checking for null service references and null service instances, and also in ungetting any services you get.

Type safety and the Service Registry

You may have noticed that listings 6.2 and 6.3 have to cast the service object to its interface type. Newer versions of the OSGi framework offer methods that take `Class` objects rather than `String` class names. These methods use Java generics to ensure type safety and remove the need to cast your service objects.

You could have used these methods to get slightly neater code in your examples, but existing code you see in the real world will almost certainly have been written using the older `String` versions of these methods.

The problem with consuming OSGi services is greatly magnified when a bundle relies on more than one; in fact this code is sufficiently complex that most people get it wrong. You can use a simpler OSGi API, called the `ServiceTracker`, to consume services (see appendix A for more detail). The `ServiceTracker` makes consuming a service easier, but things quickly become unmanageable if you need to consume more than one in a thread-safe way. It's for this reason that we always recommend using a dependency injection framework to consume OSGi services. It's not that you can't do it yourself, but we don't recommend it. (We suspect the complexity of the OSGi services API may be one of the reasons OSGi services haven't yet taken the software world by storm, despite their usefulness.) Dependency injection frameworks eliminate almost all of the hassle of using OSGi services. But avoiding complexity isn't the only reason to use dependency injection—there are lots of other advantages to using a dependency injection framework in OSGi.

Not only is it tricky to get right, consuming services programmatically isn't terribly efficient unless you're super-careful to optimize. Service instances (or service factories) need to be instantiated, even if nothing ever ends up looking up those services. If `unget()` isn't called on looked-up services, classloaders may be held in memory unnecessarily. And OSGi dynamics mean that using services can be like walking through quicksand. At its best, dependency injection offers identical performance to using the programmatic service API and protects developers from the sometimes hairy dynamics of OSGi services without sacrificing anything in terms of dynamism or even the ability to respond to system changes. As you'll see, there's no shortage of dependency injection frameworks to choose from, either. We'll discuss four of the more popular OSGi-enabled frameworks: Blueprint, Declarative Services, iPojo, and Peaberry.

6.2.2 *Blueprint*

In general, we believe the most suitable dependency injection framework for enterprise OSGi programming is Blueprint. Not only is it well integrated with other enterprise OSGi technologies, it acts as an integration point for many of them. For example, container-managed persistence and container-managed transactions use Blueprint for their metadata.

Because Blueprint is an open standard based on the Spring Framework, the XML syntax will be familiar to most Java EE developers. Blueprint also offers the best support of all the dependency injection frameworks for combining service injection with normal Java constructs like static factory methods and constructed objects. Finally, by using proxies, Blueprint insulates you and your application most effectively from some of the less welcome parts of OSGi dynamism.

6.2.3 *Declarative Services*

But Blueprint isn't the only technology in town for managing OSGi services declaratively. An earlier specification, Declarative Services (DS), is also popular. In broad terms, Declarative Services is lighter-weight but less feature-rich than Blueprint-managed services. You may therefore find that Declarative Services offers slightly better performance than Blueprint, although well-optimized implementations are likely to show little measurable difference from one another. Like Blueprint, Declarative Services uses XML to expose a managed object as an OSGi service, inject dependencies, and chain services together. Also like Blueprint, managed objects are only exposed as services if all of the services that they're injected with are also available or have been marked as optional. Declarative Services also helps manage OSGi dynamism, but unlike Blueprint it exposes you to more of the details.

Declarative Services doesn't have the same level of support as Blueprint for building and describing networks of managed bean instances within a bundle. In Declarative Services, a managed component can easily be injected with a reference to a service and exposed as another service (see figure 6.1), but, for example, it isn't possible to inject a component with another managed component that was created using an arbitrary static factory method.

What's in a name?

Instead of Blueprint beans, Declarative Services describes managed classes in terms of components and service components. For this reason, the Declarative Services technology is often referred to as Service Component Runtime (SCR). When we use the term *SCR*, we're referring to one implementation of Declarative Services, the Apache Felix Service Component Runtime.

Like beans, service components may be wired to one another and optionally exposed as services. Listing 6.4 shows the Declarative Services equivalent of listing 3.7. The XML file should be referenced from the bundle manifest using the `Service-Component` header. Wildcards can be used to pick up several XML files.

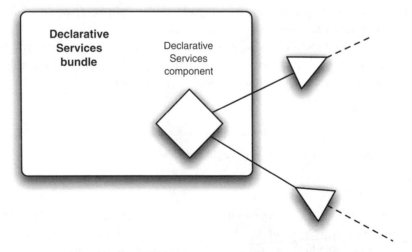

Figure 6.1   A bundle using Declarative Services to consume a service into a managed component, which is then exported as a service itself

Listing 6.4   Declaring special offer service that has an `Inventory` dependency

```xml
<?xml version='1.0' encoding='utf-8'?>
<component name='fancyfoods.cheese.offer' enabled='true'>
  <implementation
    class='fancyfoods.department.cheese.offers.DesperateCheeseOffer'/>
  <service>
    <provide interface='fancyfoods.offers.SpecialOffer'/>
  </service>

  <reference name='inventory' interface='fancyfoods.food.Inventory'
             bind='setInventory' unbind='unsetInventory' />
</component>
```

Expose this
component
as service

Inject Inventory instance using
named set and unset methods

Because it's an older technology than Blueprint, Declarative Services has a wider
range of tooling support. Some of the more popular tools, such as bnd and bndtools,
support both of them, which makes it convenient to use whichever dependency injection technology you prefer. (More on bnd can be found in chapter 8.)

ANNOTATIONS

One limitation of both Declarative Services and Blueprint is that, in their original,
strictly specified forms, neither supported annotations. Annotations are a frequent
feature request for both Declarative Services and Blueprint, and unofficial support
has been developed for both platforms. Annotation support for Blueprint has been
prototyped in Apache Aries, but not developed further at the time of writing. Annotation support for Declarative Services is available in Apache Felix's SCR subproject.
The SCR support has now been standardized. As well as being more concise than
XML metadata (which isn't hard!), annotations are less brittle if you refactor your
code frequently.

Felix's annotation support works by using a Maven plug-in to convert the annotations
to normal Declarative Services XML at compile time. To use the support, you'll first need
to add a Maven dependency on the `maven-scr-plugin`. The annotation syntax is rich,
supporting almost everything that can be specified in DS XML, but in its simplest form,
to identify a class as a component and expose it as a service, you'd write this:

```
@Component
@Service
public class DesperateCheeseOffer implements SpecialOffer {
```

To inject a reference to another service, it's even simpler:

```
@Reference
Inventory inventory;
```

Handy as it is, the Felix SCR annotation support does feel slightly tacked-on. Although
Declarative Services is part of the existing OSGi specifications, annotations aren't
(although there are plans to add them soon). Other dependency injection frameworks support both XML and annotations as first-class programming models.

6.2.4 *iPojo*

We mentioned earlier that you'd be spoiled for choice in terms of dependency injection frameworks—or perhaps confused! Not only does the OSGi alliance specify two different dependency injection frameworks, Blueprint and Declarative Services, the Apache Felix project itself includes several subprojects for dependency injection: Service Component Runtime (a Declarative Services implementation), Dependency Manager, and iPojo. iPojo isn't a standard, so you're restricted to the one iPojo implementation. But it supports configuration by XML, annotations, and even API. It uses bytecode instrumentation internally, which makes it more invasive than Declarative Services, but also more powerful.

iPojo is extremely sophisticated, and we'll only scratch the surface of it here. In its simplest form, iPojo looks a lot like SCR annotations, except that it uses a `@Provides` annotation instead of an `@Service` annotation to indicate that a component should be exposed as a service:

```
@Component
@Provides
public class DesperateCheeseOffer implements SpecialOffer {
```

Similarly, injected services are marked with a `@Requires` annotation:

```
@Requires
Inventory inventory;
```

More fundamental differences become apparent when you try to do more involved things; iPojo has more support for lifecycle callbacks and complex dependency relationships than Declarative Services. It also supports stateful services by providing guarantees that a thread in a given context will always see the same service instance.

Because it uses bytecode instrumentation, in general iPojo requires an extra build step to insert the required bytecode. Build tasks and plug-ins are available for Ant, Maven, and Eclipse. iPojo does also provide a runtime enhancement feature, although this adds an unpleasant ordering dependency between iPojo and the bundles it extends.

6.2.5 *Google Guice and Peaberry*

Blueprint, Declarative Services, and iPojo were all designed with OSGi in mind, but dependency injection isn't restricted to the OSGi world. Some of the non-OSGi dependency injection frameworks can also be adapted to work in an OSGi environment. In particular, a framework called *Peaberry* has been added to Google Guice that allows OSGi services to be exposed and consumed.

One feature of Peaberry that makes it different from the other frameworks here is that there's nothing OSGi-specific about it. It can be extended to use any service registry (for example, integrations with the Eclipse extension registry are available). It can also use ordinary Guice injection. This means it's easy to use the same client code in a variety of different contexts. The big problem with Peaberry comes from the fact that it isn't specifically designed for OSGi, and there isn't a specification describing it. Some of the more advanced features that are present in other OSGi dependency injection models are missing, or are more difficult to use than if they'd been designed in at the start.

A mix-and-match principle applies to any of the OSGi service-based injection frameworks we've described. If you want one of your modules to run outside of OSGi, but want to take advantage of Blueprint's tight integration with the rest of the Apache Aries runtime, you can use Blueprint for most of your bundles and Peaberry in the module that needs to run elsewhere. Regardless of which implementation you choose to use, underneath they are all using normal OSGi services, so compatibility is guaranteed. Alternatively, if you like Blueprint's tidy handling of OSGi dynamics, you could consume services using Blueprint but publish them using iPojo, or any other framework, or even register them programmatically.

Covering Declarative Services, iPojo, and Peaberry in detail is beyond the scope of this book; although these frameworks have many nice aspects and distinct advantages over Blueprint in some contexts, we think that Blueprint is the framework most suited to enterprise programming. Even though you've seen quite a bit of Blueprint already, it has lots of sophisticated features that we haven't had a chance to explore yet. Let's have a look at some of this extra power in more detail.

6.3 *Getting the most out of Blueprint*

As you've been writing the Fancy Foods application, we've been demonstrating the most important bits of the Blueprint syntax. But Blueprint is a rich specification language, and there's lots more to it than what you've seen so far. We won't cover all the dark corners of the Blueprint syntax in this chapter, but we'll show you a few more capabilities.

6.3.1 *Using Blueprint for things other than services*

Although we've been talking about Blueprint as a tool for managing OSGi services, it can do a lot more than register and inject services. If you're used to programming in *core* OSGi, you may have some jobs that you automatically do with a `BundleActivator`. (If you're used to Java EE programming, you might be using static factories to do the same sorts of jobs.) All of this is still possible in enterprise OSGi, but we're firmly convinced that it's easier, cleaner, and better using Blueprint.

For example, an eager singleton bean can play the role of a bundle activator. The main difference is that a bean has much more flexibility in terms of its interface because a bundle activator has to implement `BundleActivator`, whereas a Blueprint bean can implement whatever it likes (or nothing at all).

> **WARNING: WIRING WITHIN A BUNDLE** One area where Blueprint is useful but OSGi services *shouldn't* be used is for wiring within a bundle.
>
> One good reason for this is that services are public; unless you want the entire framework to see your internal wiring, you should keep it out of the Service Registry.

Another good reason comes from Blueprint. Wiring beans from the same bundle together needs to be done using bean references instead of services. Otherwise, a circular dependency is created, where the Blueprint container for the bundle won't initialize until it's found all the unsatisfied service references. Because the unsatisfied service references are supposed to get registered by the waiting Blueprint container, this doesn't usually end well.

6.3.2 *Values*

Blueprint allows you to declare a wide variety of Java objects using relatively simple XML. These values can be passed to beans using `<property>` and `<argument>` elements.

SPECIAL TYPES

Lists, sets, arrays, maps, and properties objects can also be specified in XML. To define a map of foods and prices, you could use the following XML:

```
<map>
    <entry key="Bananas"
           value="1.39" />
    <entry key="Chocolate ice cream">3.99</entry>
</map>
```

The two forms of the `<entry>` element are equivalent. To define the same relationship as a `Properties` object, the XML would be

```
<props>
    <prop key="Bananas"
          value="1.39" />
    <prop key="Chocolate ice cream">3.99</prop>
</props>
```

Null can be specified using `<null>`.

TYPE CONVERSION

Beans can be instantiated with simple Java types or references to more complex Blueprint-managed classes. The container will try to construct an appropriate object to pass to the class's setter object from the XML parameters. It will automatically convert XML strings into Java primitives, and it can initialize arbitrary Java classes if they have a constructor that takes a simple `String`. Most impressively, Blueprint can use generic type information to perform implicit type conversion for collection types. For example, the following snippet calls a `setShopClosedDates(List<Date> dates)` method that expects a `List` of `Date` objects:

```
<property
    name="shopClosedDates">
    <list>
        <value>November 6, 1980</value>
        <value>February 14, 1973</value>
    </list>
</property>
```

When implicit conversion isn't good enough (or if you have nongeneric code), you can explicitly specify types:

```
<entry>
    <key type="java.lang.String">Bananas</key>
    <value type="java.lang.Double">1.39</value>
</entry>
```

Blueprint also allows you to define your own type converters, turning `String` values from the XML into arbitrary `Objects`, but because the default Blueprint type converter works in so many situations, it's unlikely you'll ever need to write your own.

SPECIAL PROPERTIES

In chapter 3, you saw how special `<jpa:context>` elements could be used to inject JPA persistence contexts. Blueprint also has a number of other predefined properties that can be used to get hold of special objects. For example, in the following example, the `blueprintBundleContext` reference is a precanned reference to the bundle's `BundleContext`:

```
<bean class="SomeClass">
    <property name="context" ref="blueprintBundleContext"/>
</bean>
```

(If you followed our advice about always using Blueprint instead of old-style OSGi, you shouldn't ever need to get hold of a bundle context. But there are exceptions to every rule!)

6.3.3 *Understanding bean scopes*

Blueprint beans may have one of two scopes: *singleton* or *prototype*. If you're keen, you can also write your own custom scopes. The scope determines the lifespan and visibility of the beans.

THE SINGLETON SCOPE

When the singleton scope is used, a single instance of the bean is created. As figure 6.2 shows, the exact same instance is used every time the bean is required, even if it's already in use. The singleton scope requires—but doesn't enforce—that beans are stateless and thread safe. There's only one instance created, regardless of the number of requests, so it's an extremely scalable model.

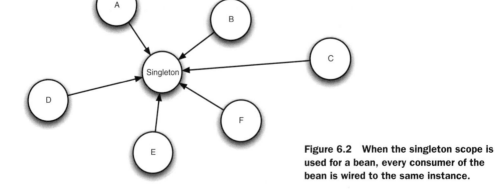

Figure 6.2 When the singleton scope is used for a bean, every consumer of the bean is wired to the same instance.

THE PROTOTYPE SCOPE

The prototype scope is the exact opposite of the singleton scope. Every time the bean is wired to a consuming bean, a new instance is created. This means beans can safely hold internal state, although they still need to be careful about thread safety. Although holding state can be a convenient programming model, its scalability is more limited. Figure 6.3 shows how the number of bean instances can rapidly multiply with the prototype scope.

The singleton scope is the default Blueprint scope for top-level beans (beans that are immediate children of the <blueprint> element). Inlined beans (bean declarations that are nested within other elements), on the other hand, have a default scope of prototype. Not only is the scope prototype by default, the scope is always prototype for beans declared inline. Because Blueprint is designed to be extensible, the schema does allow you to specify a scope for inlined beans; however, unless you're using a custom namespace for your particular Blueprint implementation, any value other than prototype will be ignored, or cause an error creating the Blueprint container.

For example, the following Blueprint snippet declares a top-level bean with a prototype scope:

```
<bean
    class="fancyfoods.department.cheese.offers.DesperateCheeseOffer"
    scope="prototype"
    id="cheeseOffer" />
<service
    interface="fancyfoods.offers.SpecialOffer"
    ref="cheeseOffer">
</service>
```

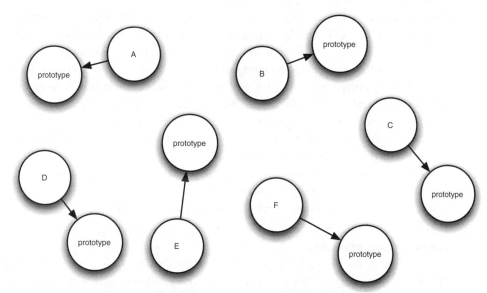

Figure 6.3 When the prototype scope is used for a bean, every user of the bean is wired to a new instance. This allows beans to maintain internal state, but it's less scalable.

The previous example demonstrates a pattern that's occasionally useful. Because the bean exposed as a service is prototype scoped, a new one will be created for each bundle that requests the service (though successive requests return the same object; see `ServiceFactory` in appendix A for details).

The following Blueprint snippet declares the same bean inline, which therefore has an implicit prototype scope. The runtime behavior is identical to the previous example:

```
<service interface="fancyfoods.offers.SpecialOffer">
  <bean
    class="fancyfoods.department.cheese.offers.DesperateCheeseOffer"/>
</service>
```

The scope of a bean affects more than how many `Object` instances you end up with. It also has implications for how the bean is constructed and how its lifecycle is managed.

6.3.4   Constructing beans

Beans can be instantiated lazily or eagerly. Eager instantiation is the default for singleton beans; however, this default can be changed for all the singleton beans in a Blueprint XML file. Beans with prototype scope are always constructed lazily because that's the only way that makes sense. You may find for some singletons lazy activation is more efficient:

```
<bean
      id="microwaveMeal"
      class="fancyfoods.food.MicrowaveMeal"
      activation="lazy"/>
```

Lazy activation is often a good thing in enterprise applications, because otherwise they can take rather a long time to start. As a result, the Blueprint container offers much more laziness than bean instantiation. For reasons we'll discuss further in the section on damping, Blueprint `<reference>` objects are proxies to the real service. This means that the Blueprint container doesn't have to look up the service until it's first used. Another place in which Blueprint is particularly lazy is when it comes to registering services on your behalf. Rather than eagerly creating the service object, the Blueprint container registers a `ServiceFactory` object. A `ServiceFactory` allows you to create your service object when it's first looked up, rather than when it's first registered. If you want more control, then you can write your own `ServiceFactory` and then treat it like a normal Blueprint service. The Blueprint container is smart enough to delegate to your `ServiceFactory` when a service is needed. If you're interested in writing a `ServiceFactory`, we suggest having a look at *OSGi in Action* (Hall et al., Manning Publications, 2011).

CONSTRUCTOR ARGUMENTS

So far, you've always used Blueprint beans with a no-argument constructor. But this is by no means required. Any number of `<argument>` elements may be used to pass arguments to a constructor. The order in the Blueprint file determines their order in the constructor. Arguments may even refer to other beans or services:

```
<bean
        id="offer"
        class="fancyfoods.fruit.BananaOffer">
        <argument value="Bananas" />
        <argument ref="anotherOffer" />
        <argument value="5.42" />
        <argument ref="time" />
    </bean>
```

FACTORIES

Although the easiest way of instantiating a Blueprint bean is by direct construction, this doesn't always line up well with how the bean class works. In that case, factories can be defined instead. Factories can be used to drive any static method, even on code you don't control.

The following snippet cunningly uses a bean factory to generate a timestamp. Notice the use of the prototype scope to ensure that the timestamp is regenerated each time, rather than once at application initialization:

```
<bean
        id="time"
        class="java.lang.System"
        factory-method="currentTimeMillis"
        scope="prototype"/>
```

Is construction all the initialization a bean will ever need? Sometimes yes, but sometimes beans need initialization in multiple phases.

6.3.5 *Lifecycle callbacks*

You've already seen in section 3.2.2 that it can sometimes be handy to do some bean initialization after all the properties have been set by specifying an `init-method`. (Constructors are also good at initializing objects. In some cases, `init-methods` can be avoided by passing everything to a constructor using `<argument>`s instead of relying on injected `<property>` elements.)

Blueprint also offers a `destroy-method` callback. The `destroy-method` is only supported for beans with singleton scope; beans with prototype scope must be destroyed by the application.

The `destroy-method` can be used to clean up resources used by the bean. Because singleton beans are only destroyed when a bundle is stopped, `destroy-methods` can also be used more generally for bundle-level cleanup (see figure 6.4).

IS CLEANING UP IN DESTROY METHODS WISE?

How much can you rely on destroy methods for resource cleanup? Some Java programmers have an instinctive twitchiness whenever the subject of callbacks for resource cleanup is mentioned. They remember the excitement they felt when they first learned about Java finalizers, and the creeping disillusionment that followed when they learned that JVMs don't guarantee calling finalizers, because they don't guarantee garbage collecting unused objects. Many JVMs optimize garbage collection

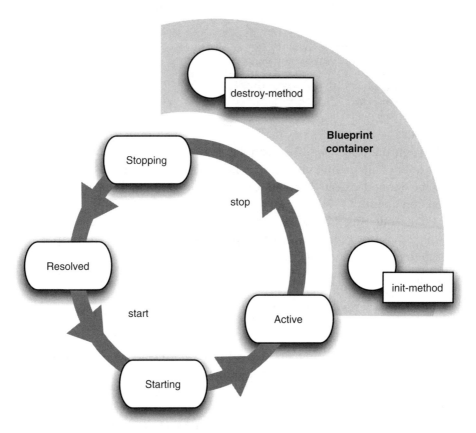

Figure 6.4   The lifecycle of a bundle's Blueprint container and Blueprint beans is closely tied to the bundle's lifecycle. The `init-method` is called on eager singleton beans after the container is started; the `destroy-method` is called when the bundle is stopped.

times by doing everything they can to avoid collecting objects with potentially expensive `finalize()` methods.

Will you fall into the same trap if you rely on destroy methods? Yes and no. Your destroy methods will certainly be called by the Blueprint container, unlike a finalizer, but you should still exercise some caution in using them.

In particular, you should try to avoid calling other services (including injected services) in destroy methods. If your Blueprint bean is in the process of going away, there's a chance that the system is shutting down or in some unstable state, and other services have already disappeared. If you try to use those services, you risk a long Blueprint timeout, and a `ServiceUnavailableException` at the end. In principle this should never happen, because the Blueprint specification requires that beans be destroyed in reverse dependency order. But this doesn't help you when using services that aren't managed by Blueprint. A bug in versions of Aries Blueprint below 0.4 also meant that calls to Blueprint-injected services in destroy methods were unreliable.

More fundamentally, a destroy method may not be the best place to do your cleanup. A destroy method will be called when a bundle is stopped, but after it's been called you're only guaranteed that your bean won't be used by the Blueprint container, not by poorly written clients. Even ignoring this, if a resource is only used by a bean for a short period of time, a destroy method probably isn't the best way of cleaning it up. For example, holding a file handle open for the whole life of a bean may not be ideal. On the other hand, if a resource is genuinely required for the lifespan of the bean (that is, until the bundle is stopped), a destroy method is an appropriate and safe way of cleaning up. However you tidy up, make sure that you correctly handle calls when tidy-up is complete, even if that's by throwing an `IllegalStateException`.

There's a further catch—destroy methods can only be declared for singleton scope beans. Even though destroy methods are a safe way of cleaning up resources, their utility is limited. If you were busily plotting to use destroy methods for all of your object cleanup, we're afraid you'll have to go back to the drawing board!

6.3.6 Service ranking

What happens when multiple services are registered, but a client requires only one? Services may have a service ranking specified when they're registered:

```
<service
    ref="specialOffer"
    interface="fancyfoods.offers.SpecialOffer"
    ranking="100"/>
```

When more than one service is available, the container will choose the highest-numbered service available.

6.3.7 Registering services under multiple interfaces

In the examples so far, you've always used only one interface for each service you've registered. But beans can be registered under multiple interfaces at the same time (as long as they implement those interfaces):

```
<service
    ref="specialOffer">
    <interfaces>
        <value>fancyfoods.offers.SpecialOffer</value>
        <value>fancyfoods.some.other.UsefulInterface</value>
    </interfaces>
    </service>
```

Blueprint can also reflectively determine the interfaces under which a service should be made available. In this case, it will be all the interfaces implemented by the bean:

```
<service
    ref="specialOffer"
    auto-export="interfaces"/>
```

6.4   *Blueprint and service dynamism*

As we've been working through enterprise OSGi programming, we've said several times that OSGi is a dynamic environment. You've even seen OSGi dynamism in action in chapters 2 and 3. Uninstalling a bundle fragment removed translations, and stopping and starting bundles made special offers appear and disappear. This dynamism is amazingly powerful and allows OSGi applications to do things that aren't possible for conventional applications.

6.4.1   *The remarkable appearing and disappearing services*

What this dynamism means is that *services can come and go at any time.* It's possible that a required service isn't available when you need it. It's possible that there's more than one potential match for the service you need. It's possible that a new service becomes available at runtime, or that a service you're currently using goes away while you're using it! Put like that, OSGi dynamism sounds scary. How can you write a solid program on quicksand?

Luckily, your application is only as dynamic as you want it to be. If you have good control over your application environment and have no need to add or remove services on the fly and no desire to upgrade your application without restarting everything, you can probably assume that a lot of the scenarios in figure 6.5 won't apply to you.

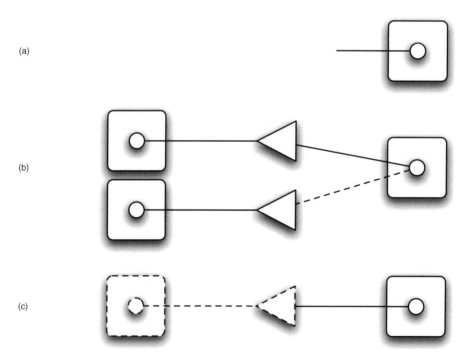

Figure 6.5   It's possible that (a) a required service isn't available, (b) there's more than one match for a required service or that a new service becomes available at runtime, or (c) a service that's in use goes away.

Be careful, though—even relatively static applications aren't completely free from OSGi dynamics. Even if your application never changes after it's installed, there will be a period during server startup and shutdown when not every service is available to everyone who might want it. In general, the OSGi bundle start order is undefined, so your services may not appear in the order you expect.

The good news is that Blueprint insulates you from almost all of this uncertainty, both during bundle startup and later, during runtime.

STARTUP AND GRACE PERIOD

When a bundle starts, there's no guarantee that other bundles within the application that it requires have already been started. (The start order on your test system may end up being quite different from the start order on the customer's production box.)

What happens when a bundle declares Blueprint beans that depend on services from other bundles, but those services aren't there? Starting the bean anyway and hoping the services appear before the bean tries to use them would be rash. In this position, Blueprint allows a *grace period* for the required services to appear.

Each bundle that defines Blueprint components has its own Blueprint container. (This is probably at odds with your mental model, which may have a single Blueprint container for the whole system.) The Blueprint container for a bundle won't start unless all the mandatory dependencies are available.

By default the Blueprint container will wait five minutes for all required services to appear. You may see messages relating to GRACE_PERIOD in the log during this time (see figure 6.6). If all the required services don't appear, the container won't start for the dependent bundle. You can change the duration of the grace period if you want things to fail more quickly, or even eliminate it entirely, but we can't think of any good reasons why you'd want to do that!

Figure 6.6   The Blueprint container reporting that it's waiting for a Blueprint dependency to become available

WARNING: THE IMPACT OF ONE MISSING SERVICE   If any service dependency of a bundle can't be satisfied, the Blueprint container won't start. This can be hard to spot, because the bundle itself will reach the started state. No Blueprint container means no Blueprint services at all will be registered by that bundle, and there will be no managed Blueprint beans for the bundle. You may not have expected that a missing service dependency for one bean would prevent all your other beans from running. If you're hitting problems in this area, consider declaring some of your service dependencies optional (see section 6.4.2) or dividing your bundle into smaller independent bundles. If you have several independent dependency networks in the same bundle, it may be a sign that you haven't got the modularity right.

Blueprint also has an elegant way of handling services that appear, disappear, or change at runtime. Like the grace period, it's a sophisticated variant of *container-managed wait and hope*. It's a lot more robust than this description makes it sound, and it's also more granular than the startup case. This is known as *damping*.

DAMPING

OSGi Blueprint aims to reduce the complexity of consuming OSGi services by performing *service damping*—rather than injecting a managed bean with a service, the Blueprint container injects a proxy. This means that if the service implementation needs to be replaced, then this can be performed transparently, without interrupting the normal operation of the bean. Figure 6.7 shows how a proxy allows the provider to be transparently swapped.

   If no other implementation is available, any services registered by the consuming bean will automatically be unregistered. This management of dependency chains is one of the benefits of using Blueprint. You can see this behavior in action in the Fancy Foods application by stopping the persistence bundle. The Blueprint container will automatically unregister the desperate cheese special offer, because that special offer required the persistence service (see figure 6.8).

   The offer aggregator uses a reference list rather than a single reference. The cheese service is transparently removed from the aggregator list when it's unregistered, and the aggregator service itself isn't affected.

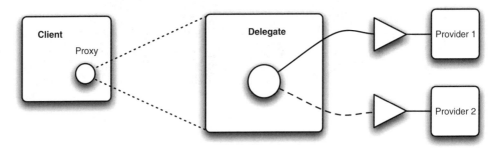

Figure 6.7   If the proxied implementation of a Blueprint-provided service becomes unavailable, the proxy will be transparently wired to another implementation.

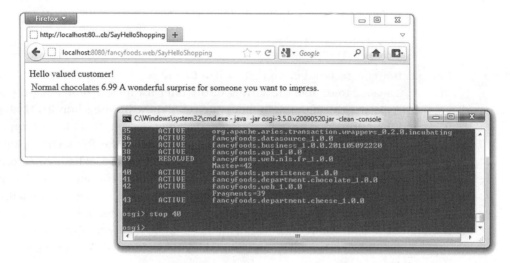

Figure 6.8　If the persistence bundle is stopped, the Blueprint container automatically makes the cheese special offer unavailable and removes it from the reference list in the offer aggregator. Subsequent requests won't see the cheese offer.

Timeouts

What happens if an attempt is made to use an injected service after it goes away? Nothing—literally! If a method is invoked on the service proxy, the proxy will block until a suitable service becomes available or until a timeout occurs. On timeout, a `Service-UnavailableException` will be thrown.

In practice, timeouts don't occur often, because the automatic unregistration of chained dependencies eliminates most opportunities to use nonexistent services. You can see this behavior in the Fancy Foods application if you try hard, but with a little tweaking you can make it happen much more often. What's required is a bit of surgery so that you can stop a service before it's been used, but after any services that depend on it have been invoked. What you're trying to simulate here is a minor concurrency disaster, rather than normal operation.

The code you need to modify is in the cheese department of your application. You'll modify the `getOfferFood()` method on the `DesperateCheeseOffer` to insert a pause so that you can reliably stop the persistence bundle in the middle of the method execution:

```
public Food getOfferFood() {
    long start = System.currentTimeMillis();
    System.out.println("INVOKED, PAUSING, STOP THAT BUNDLE!");
    try {
        Thread.sleep(5000);
    } catch (InterruptedException e) {
    }
    System.out.println("RESUMING after "
            + (System.currentTimeMillis() - start) + " ms");
    List<Food> cheeses =
        inventory.getFoodsWhoseNameContains("cheese", 1);
```

```
System.out.println("Cheese returned after "
        + (System.currentTimeMillis() - start) + " ms.");
Food leastPopularCheese = cheeses.get(0);//
return leastPopularCheese;
```

Rebuild the cheese bundle, and drop it into the load directory. Also update the
OfferAggregator to disable the sorting of the offer list for the moment (so that you
get the persistence call at the right time) and rebuild the business bundle. Hit the web
page, and then stop the persistence bundle when you see your first message appearing
in the console. You'll see that instead of returning after the five-second pause you
introduced, the load request on the web page hasn't returned. What's going on? The
call on the inventory object will block until a persistence provider becomes available
again, or until the Blueprint timeout happens after five minutes (see figure 6.9).

The nice thing about the Blueprint damping is that the disappearance of a service
need not be fatal. If you restart the persistence bundle before the five-minute timeout
expires, the cheese offer will miraculously kick back into life. But you may get more
than you bargained for, as figure 6.10 shows.

What's going on? You certainly didn't expect that the removal of the cheese offer
service would give you *two* cheese offers.

The list of offers is injected into the OfferAggregator, which passes a reference to
the same list to the servlet. When the servlet starts iterating over the list, there are two
elements in the list. It requests the details for the chocolate offer, and then it requests
the details for the cheese offer, which is where you disable the persistence bundle,
causing the cheese offer to block when asked for its details. Re-enabling the persistence bundle unblocks the call and allows the servlet to see the details of the cheese
offer. Meanwhile, however, the cheese offer has been removed from the aggregator's
reference list and then added back to it. When the iterator finishes printing out the

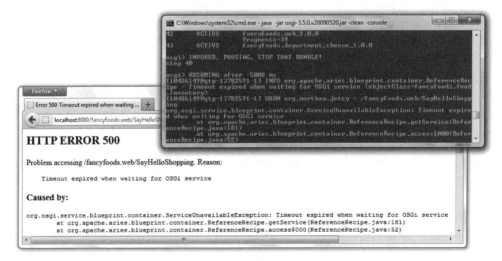

**Figure 6.9   If a Blueprint service is unregistered after services that depend on it have been invoked, the
proxy to the service will block for five minutes before throwing a `ServiceUnavailableException`.**

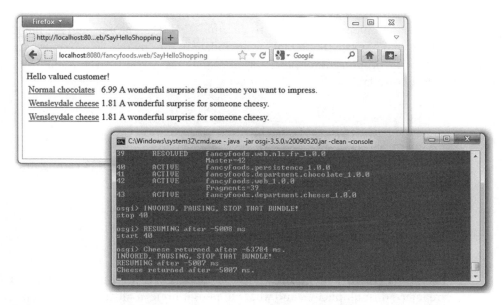

Figure 6.10   If a proxied service reappears after disappearing, blocked service calls will resume and complete almost normally. But dependent services will be removed and reregistered, which could allow iterators to traverse them twice.

details of the cheese offer, it checks to see if there are any more offers, and discovers that a new offer has been added to the list—a cheese offer, apparently. At the end of the procedure, the reference list still only has two offers, cheese and chocolate, but if the timing is right (or you insert lots of pauses, as we did!), an unlucky iterator could see both the old and new occurrences of the cheese offer.

In this case, the only consequence of a potentially disastrous outage of the persistence bundle is that the cheese offer is included twice in the printed list of offers. It looks a bit stupid, but there's no harm done. If iterating over the same service twice is more serious, you may want to consider making unmodifiable copies of reference lists before passing them around or iterating over them.

Test, test, test, and test again

In our opinion, this is incredibly cool. We must be honest, though, and disclose that it took a few tries to get the right pictures! If you expect to support these extreme dynamics in your application, it's important that you test properly. As you've seen, hanging on to references to services that might have been compromised can cause problems (an offer appearing twice). In this case, you might see problems if there were multiple calls to `getOfferFood()` from the web frontend that returned different answers. If you make sure to synchronize access to your sorted list (and return a copy to the web layer), you should avoid any concurrent modification problems. One more issue is that if the web frontend holds on to the returned instance from `getOffer-Food()`, then it could end up using a stale service.

Setting timeouts

The default Blueprint timeout is five minutes, but it can be adjusted per bundle or per reference. For example, the following update to the Inventory reference ensures that method invocations never block for more than two seconds, even when no Inventory service is available:

```
<reference
    id="inventory"
    interface="fancyfoods.food.Inventory"
    timeout="2000" />
```

Timeouts can also be set for an entire bundle in the manifest by setting directives on the symbolic name:

```
Bundle-SymbolicName: fancyfoods.persistence; blueprint.timeout:=2000
```

If the timeout is set to 0, a service invocation will block indefinitely.

6.4.2   *Multiplicity and optionality*

Part of the power of Blueprint services is that you can easily tune how many instances are injected (multiplicity), and what happens if none at all are available (optionality).

OPTIONAL SERVICE REFERENCES

When declaring a Blueprint service reference, one of the things you can do is declare that it's optional:

```
<reference
    id="specialOffer"
    interface="fancyfoods.offers.SpecialOffer"
    availability="optional"/>
```

This means that if no satisfactory service can be found, the Blueprint container will still start up and initialize the rest of your beans. This is useful; you often don't want a single missing service to be fatal. But what happens if you try to use an unsatisfied optional service?

SERVICE DAMPING AND OPTIONAL REFERENCES

As it happens, after the Blueprint container has been initialized for a bundle, optional services are indistinguishable from mandatory services. Even if the backing service goes away—or was never there—any method invocation on the injected service (which is a proxy, remember) will block until the service reappears or until a timeout happens. Whether your service is optional or mandatory, you'll need to remember that a timeout could occur and a ServiceUnavailableException could be thrown.

A service being unavailable is arguably much more likely if the service was optional in the first place, and so using your optional services as if they were mandatory services may lead to some long delays. How can you handle missing services gracefully? One option is to set a short timeout and catch the ServiceUnavailableException. A cleaner option is to use a reference listener to monitor the lifecycle of the service (more on those in a moment). Alternatively, the sneakily lazy option is to use a reference list instead of a reference for your service.

So far we've been talking about how damping works for service references. Reference lists are subtly different from references in how they handle dynamism, and sometimes this difference comes in handy.

REFERENCES AND REFERENCE LISTS

A reference refers to one, and only one, instance of a service. Reference lists, on the other hand, refer to several instances of a service. Although reference lists still use proxies, they make it much more apparent when services come and go. As services appear and disappear from the system, they'll pop in and out of a reference list (see figure 6.11). A reference list will never contain entries for services that are unavailable. So dynamic is the reference list, services can even appear in an existing iterator. (No ConcurrentModificationExceptions here!)

How does this help with optional services? If you use an optional reference list rather than an optional reference to inject a service, then the service's absence still won't prevent the bundle's Blueprint container from starting. The key difference is that if a service arrives and then goes away again, you'll find a zero-length list rather than a long wait and a ServiceUnavailableException.

Coping with multiplicity

On the other hand, if you use a reference list, you may get more than you bargained for. What will you do if multiple instances of a service are present? You could decide you want to call all the services in the list, but on the other hand you may never want more than one service. If you do only want to call one service, then which service do you call? Will the first service be the most appropriate one?

It turns out that this is an issue that affects you even if you're using references instead of reference lists. With references, the container will choose the service for you, but how does it decide which service to pick?

One strategy for ensuring you get supplied with the most suitable service is to specify a ranking for each service. (We showed you how to do this in section 6.3.6.) The downside here is that the ranking must be specified at the time the service is registered by the service provider. If that's not you, you'll have some work to do persuading

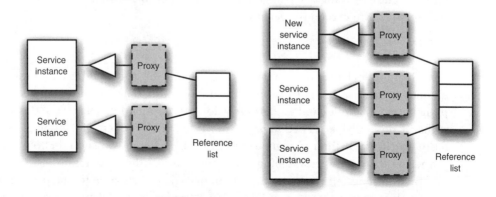

Figure 6.11   As services appear and disappear in a system, they're automatically added to or removed from reference lists.

all your dependencies to rank themselves. More seriously, what should the ranking even be? Can you be sure that every consumer of the services will agree on the same relative ranking? Should a faster service implementation be ranked highest, or a more reliable one? Sometimes a clear ranking of services is possible—for example if one service wraps another one and is intended to supersede it—but more often, different services are...different.

> **Being choosy about services**
>
> Although it's usually easy to distinguish services, it's also worth remembering that a well-designed application shouldn't normally need to. If you've done things right, then any service in the list should be up to the job.

Sometimes the differences between services can be an issue; happily, these differences can be expressed using service properties. You can identify your service precisely by adding specific service properties to it. As it does for other parts of the service API, Blueprint offers some handy XML for adding properties to a service:

```
<service ref="specialOffer"
    interface="fancyfoods.offers.SpecialOffer">
  <service-properties>
      <entry key="magic.word"
            value="Abracadabra"/>            String service property

      <entry key="magic.number">
          <value type="java.lang.Integer">
            42
          </value>                            Typed service property
      </entry>
  </service-properties>
</service>
```

When you have some service properties to pick from, you can tie down your choice of service tightly by using a service filter in your Blueprint XML. Filters can be used to pick services with certain properties:

```
<reference interface="fancyfoods.offers.SpecialOffer"
      filter="(magic.number=42)"/>
```

If you want to lock down your service usage completely you could even set the implementation name as a service property and filter on it. This drastically increases coupling between bundles and we definitely don't recommend it! The risk of this strategy is that if no available service satisfies your filter, you'll be left with none at all. The more specific your filter, the greater the risk. In general, you should choose service properties that express something about the contract the service satisfies (for example, is.transactional=true), rather than ones that are unique to one particular service (such as vendor=SomeCorp). Filters are extremely powerful and use the full range of syntax allowed by the LDAP filter specification. If you're keen to use filters in your application, then there's more information about them in appendix A, but we find that we don't usually need them in our applications.

Being flexible about what service gets used can feel uncomfortable at first. How can you possibly test your code (it's possible—wait until chapter 8)? What happens if the provided service turns out to be terrible? What if it doesn't do what you need? Nonetheless, it's best to trust the application deployer and leave the decision about what service gets used to deploy time, rather than trying to specify everything at development time. It can be hard to give up control, but being service-oriented and loosely coupled means—well, just that!

SERVICES AND STATE

Holding much state in services presents some problems. An injected service may be transparently swapped for another implementation if the original service goes away, or if a higher-ranked service comes along. More fundamentally, a bundle can be restarted or upgraded at any time, which destroys state. Persisting data is so easy that you should consider using a persistence bundle or data grid to ensure that information survives.

If it's absolutely essential that your services store state, all isn't lost. After all, in many realistic application environments the system is, by design, stable—services *won't* be dynamically swapped out or bundles arbitrarily bounced, even though such things are possible in principle.

As a starting point, you'll almost certainly want to use the prototype scope for beans that represent stateful services, rather than the singleton scope. The prototype scope ensures each bundle that uses the service gets its own instance (though a bundle will get the same instance if it does more than one lookup). Don't forget that using prototype scope can have scalability implications.

The prototype scope ensures no service instance is being used by more than one bundle, but it doesn't solve the problem of more than one service instance being used by the *same* bundle. Ultimately, even in a relatively stable system, nothing can stop a service instance from going away if an unexpected catastrophe occurs. (We've been imagining a mischievous cat sneaking into the ops center and walking all over the keyboard, disabling parts of the system, but feel free to invent your own entertaining mental pictures!)

If you're programming defensively, you'll protect yourself against the disappearance of stateful services, even if such things are extremely unlikely. (The system is stable, maintenance is done in scheduled downtime windows, and you keep a dog in the ops center.) Nothing can get the stateful service back after it's gone, but as long as you can detect the disappearance, you can initiate data recovery procedures or throw an exception to indicate a catastrophic event.

Both the core OSGi programming model and Blueprint allow you to closely monitor the lifecycle of services. Not only does this allow you to be confident that your stateful services aren't disappearing, it has a variety of other uses, particularly for services that are optional.

> **Stateful services**
>
> OSGi services don't fit well with the stateful model. The default usage pattern has only a single service instance for the whole framework, and even if you use a `ServiceFactory`, you still only get one instance per client bundle. Added to this, services have to be thread safe, which becomes much more difficult if they have state. All in all, we recommend steering clear of stateful services if you can, but it's perfectly possible to use them if you're careful.

6.4.3 *Monitoring the lifecycle*

Closely monitoring what's going on with the services you care about is a convenient way of handling optional services and service multiplicity.

If a service has been declared optional, how do you know if it's there and safe to use or not? If you have a reference list, how can you know when things magically get added or removed? If you're interested, you can register service listeners that are notified when services are registered or unregistered. (If you're not using Blueprint, you *have* to care when these things happen. With Blueprint, caring is optional!)

REFERENCE LISTENERS

Reference listeners have a number of potential uses, but you'll start with a straightforward case—caching. For example, in the Fancy Foods application, the current implementation of the offer aggregator re-sorts the offer list every time a request is made (listing 2.11). Users are likely to hit the offer page far more often than the Fancy Foods business updates its special offers, so caching the sorted list is a performance optimization.

The code changes to use a cache instead of recalculating the sorted list are straightforward:

```
private synchronized void sortOfferList() {
    if (offers != null) {
        sortedOffers = new ArrayList<SpecialOffer>(offers);
        Collections.sort(sortedOffers, new OfferComparator());
        int offerCount = Math.min(MAX_OFFERS, sortedOffers.size());
        sortedOffers = sortedOffers.subList(0, offerCount);
    }
}

@Override
public synchronized List<SpecialOffer> getCurrentOffers() {
    return new ArrayList(sortedOffers);
}
```

The challenge is to know when the cache should be updated, and this is where the reference listeners come in. Registering a reference listener ensures the `OfferAggregator` bean is notified every time an offer is added to or removed from the list. To register the reference listener, a `<reference-listener>` declaration is added as a child of the `<reference>` or `<reference-list>` element from listing 2.10:

```
<reference-list
    id="specialOffers"
    interface="fancyfoods.offers.SpecialOffer">
    <reference-listener
        ref="offerAggregator"
        bind-method="bind"
        unbind-method="unbind" />
</reference-list>
```

The reference listener need not be the same as the bean that uses the services. It can even be a completely new bean declared with an inlined <bean> element, although in that case the bean will always have a singleton scope.

The bind method is only called if the new service is consumed by the bean. In the case of a reference list, this is every time a matching service is added to the Service Registry. When a reference is used, on the other hand, the consumed service will only be changed (and the bind method called) if the new service has a higher service ranking than the existing one.

The bind method for the offer aggregator is simple; when something gets added to the list, the cache should be updated. If you're interested in the service properties, your bind and unbind methods can also be written to take an optional `Map` that lists all of the service properties:

```
public void bind(SpecialOffer offer) {
    sortOfferList();
}
```

The bind method is called after the new service has been added to the list, so the sorted list will be accurate. The unbind method, on the other hand, is called *before* the reference is removed. Calling the method to re-sort the offer list and update the cache in the unbind method isn't much use, because it's the old list that will be sorted. Instead, you'll need to get your hands dirty and remove the obsolete offer from the cache manually:

```
public synchronized void unbind(SpecialOffer offer) {
    if (sortedOffers != null) {
        sortedOffers.remove(offer);
    }
}
```

> **WARNING: PROXYING OBJECTS** One side effect of the proxying of services is that you'll find that the service you get injected with isn't == to the service in the Service Registry, even though you might expect it to be. The proxied object may not even be of the same type as the real service object! Rest assured, if you've implemented equals() and hashCode() on your service, then the proxy code does the correct unwrapping to make sure that they work properly.
>
> Somewhat unfortunately, a bug in the early releases of the Aries proxy code (prior to 0.4) sometimes fails to do this unwrapping if your service uses the default version of equals().

If you're using version 0.4 or higher, then there's nothing that you need to do. If, on the other hand, you're using, or might need to use, an older version of the proxy bundle and are relying on default equality, you'll need to provide your own implementation of `equals()` and `hashCode()`—adding these also documents the fact that you rely on the default behavior for anyone else maintaining your code, which is a good thing too.

You've got one little change to make for your cache to work. Remember that OSGi is dynamic (we might have mentioned that once or twice already!). Bundle startup order isn't deterministic, and so the collection of references may be populated before it's injected into the `OfferAggregator`, or after. If the list is populated first, then the `bind()` method will be called when the `offers` field is still null. You've guarded against this in the `sortOffersList()` method, so there's no risk of a `NullPointerException` from the `bind()` method. But there's a risk the `sortedOffers` field will never be initialized at all, if all the `bind()` calls happen before the injection. Luckily, there's an easy solution, which is to ensure you also sort when the offers are injected:

```
public void setOffers(List<SpecialOffer> offers) {
    this.offers = offers;
    sortOfferList();
}
```

If you build the updated bundle and drop it into your load directory, you should find that everything works as it did before. You can test your caching by using the OSGi console to stop and start the chocolate and cheese bundles. If you've got things right, your stopped services will continue to appear and disappear appropriately from your web page when you refresh it.

Other uses for monitoring

Caching is a nice use for reference listeners, but it's not the only one. In the case of our example, when new special offers appear, they could be highlighted or bumped to the top of an otherwise sorted list. Reference listeners can also act as a fail-safe when using stateful services, as we discussed earlier. Finally, reference listeners allow you to avoid calling a service that has gone away and blocking in the proxy, or to disable parts of your application if a service goes away.

> **WARNING: DETECTING SERVICE SWAPS**   If you're planning to use reference listeners to detect when an injected service has been swapped out (for example, to reconstitute a stateful service), be careful. If you're using a reference, the bind-method and the unbind-method aren't symmetric. The bind-method will be called every time a new service is bound—every time the service changes. But the unbind-method will only be called if a service goes away and can't immediately be replaced—if your bean is left without a service. Only the bind-method, therefore, can be reliably used to detect when the service has changed, whereas the unbind-method is most useful to detect periods of service unavailability.

REGISTRATION LISTENERS

Usually, when services appear and disappear, it's the users of the service that need to be notified. But the services themselves can be notified of their registration and unregistration using a *registration listener.* Remember that a service being registered is a necessary prerequisite for anyone to be able to consume it, but it's not the same thing as it being consumed. Just because a service is registered doesn't mean it's used by someone, or ever will be.

Why would you want to know if a service has been registered and unregistered? Notification of unregistration has a clear use case for teardown and tidy-up. An unregistration listener can serve the same function as a Java finalizer, but without the issues of finalizers.

There are fewer uses for service registration listeners, but they can sometimes be useful for initialization. If nothing else, they're handy for tracing the dynamics of your system!

6.5 *Summary*

OSGi services are sometimes described as a replacement for conventional Java factories. You've seen in this chapter that services can do an awful lot of things that factories can't—they can come and go, they can be managed at runtime, they can be filtered using properties, and they form the basis of a handy pattern for handling event notifications.

The dynamism of OSGi services isn't without its downside; in their raw form, registering them is a little verbose, and accessing them, if done in a safe way, is extremely verbose. Blueprint and other dependency injection frameworks neatly eliminate these issues. They make providing services easy and insulate applications from the dynamism of services. Perhaps most conveniently, Blueprint manages dependency chains so that services (and ordinary Blueprint beans) only become available when all their dependencies are present; if services go away, the services that depend on them are automatically unregistered.

7
Provisioning and resolution

This chapter covers

- How to find the dependencies your bundles need to work properly
- Using additional constraints to avoid resolution problems
- How repositories and resolvers model bundles and other resources
- How to take advantage of provisioning when writing applications

You may remember that, back in chapter 4, we discussed the concepts of provisioning and resolution. These are two fundamental parts of enterprise OSGi deployment and, as such, are worth a second, deeper look. Although we stand by the statement that "provisioning is a relatively simple operation," and the fact that many OSGi developers will succeed by treating provisioning as a black box, there are a few subtleties that you can use to your advantage. Understanding subtleties like these marks the difference between a competent enterprise OSGi developer and an expert. Now, adding in the more detailed understanding of OSGi packaging you learned in chapter 5 and armed with your Service Registry experience from chapter 6 we're ready to discuss provisioning and resolution in more detail.

OSGi provisioning and resolution is covered by the OSGi Resource API Specification, the Resolver Service Specification, and the Repository Service Specification. Historically, these specifications were part of a single OSGi Bundle Repository Specification (often known as OBR). These specifications explain how bundles should be described, how dependencies between bundles are resolved, and how resolvers interact with bundle repositories, and describe a text format for representing bundle repository metadata. Although they define the standards for provisioning and resolution in OSGi, there are several other popular systems that also allow bundles to be automatically downloaded and installed based on analysis of their dependencies.

Let's return to the world of provisioning and resolution by considering *what* gets provisioned and resolved—how do you tell the provisioner about your bundles?

7.1 Describing OSGi bundles

You already know that OSGi bundles contain a lot of metadata describing themselves. Metadata describes a bundle's dependencies, the packages it exposes to the outside world, the bundle's name and version, and more. As you've seen in section 5.1.2, some of a bundle's metadata has metadata of its own; Import-Package and Export-Package allow packages to be decorated with attributes and either version ranges or versions, respectively. This metadata is rich with information, most of which is used by the OSGi framework resolver to determine whether a bundle is able to load classes.

As you learned in chapter 4, provisioning and resolution are closely related. That this processed information is necessary in the resolution process means that it's also critical for provisioning. When attempting to resolve a partially complete dependency graph, a resolver may need to query a bundle repository to fill in the missing dependencies. To answer these questions from the resolver, a bundle repository must be able to describe the bundles it has to offer by modeling them, including all the information needed by the resolver.

If the resolver and the repository are to agree in their descriptions of bundles, then they need a common definition for describing OSGi bundles and their interactions with the outside world. This common description is provided in OSGi by the Resource API Specification through the use of generic Resource, Capability, and Requirement objects. Together these form a model for bundles—and lots of other things!

7.1.1 Describing bundles as resources

In the generic sense, a Resource is a vague object. A Resource can represent anything, from a binary or text file to a web service, an OSGi bundle, or something more bizarre like a treacle sponge pudding! The key details about a Resource object are as follows:

- All resources define a capability named `osgi.identity` that determines their type.
- Resources provide a set of `Capability` objects describing the features they provide.
- Resources provide a set of `Requirement` objects describing the features they need to run.
- Resources use the `osgi.identity` and the optional `osgi.content` capabilities to provide a set of named attributes describing the resource.

Despite the vague nature of `Resource` objects, these rules mean that they aren't as complicated as you might think. In figure 7.1, you can see that a `Resource` is not much more than a holder for `Requirement` and `Capability` descriptions.

Figure 7.1   Resources may have requirements and capabilities.

Every resource exposes three mandatory attributes through the `osgi.identity` capability:

- `type`—The type of the resource
- `osgi.identity`—The symbolic name or identity of the resource
- `version`—The version of the resource

Other attributes, such as the license, description, and links to documentation, may also be included. Further predefined attributes that broadly correspond to other informational headers in the bundle manifest file are defined by the `osgi.wiring.bundle`, `osgi.wiring.package`, and `osgi.wiring.host` capabilities. Any of a resource's capabilities may also contain arbitrary keys and values that are used in a resource type-specific way.

IDENTITY OF RESOURCES

The identity of a resource is, unsurprisingly, defined by the attributes of the `osgi.identity` capability. For a particular `type` of resource, the combination of `osgi.identity` and `version` attributes provides a unique identifier, but it's important to remember that, when comparing resources, they may not be of the same type. This is why it's always important to refer to the whole `osgi.identity` capability. With the cornucopia of potential resource types, OSGi defines a standard type for OSGi bundles (`osgi.bundle`) and fragments (`osgi.fragment`). Any OSGi bundle modeled as a resource will have an identity type of `osgi.bundle` and an `osgi.identity` corresponding to its symbolic name, instantly separating it from the crowd of configuration property and steamed pudding resources in the repository, even if one of those puddings has exactly the same name and version as your bundle (see figure 7.2).

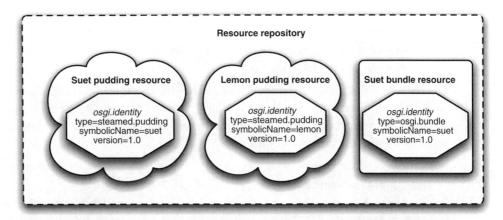

Figure 7.2 **Resource repositories may contain resources of any type including, but not restricted to, bundles. Two resources may share a symbolic name and version as long as they're different types.**

7.1.2 *Requirements and capabilities*

As with a `Resource`, both a `Requirement` and a `Capability` are generic objects that can be used to express *any* dependency or exposed feature. As such, they're more than capable of expressing the potential range of bundle dependencies and features. Requirements and capabilities define a namespace, which is like the `type` of the `osgi.identity` capability, indicating what sorts of things they require and provide. Requirements and capabilities are related in that a capability can *satisfy* a requirement if it meets three rules (see figure 7.3):

1 The requirement and capability share a namespace.
2 The requirement's filter matches the attributes of the capability.
3 Any relevant *directives* are satisfied. We'll cover these in more detail in section 7.1.3.

Requirements and capabilities share a similar structure. They both expose the following:

- A link back to the resource that *owns* this requirement or capability.
- A namespace. A particular resource may define requirements and capabilities from many namespaces. Critically, a capability and requirement can only match if they're in the same namespace.
- A set of attributes that describe the required or provided feature. The attributes for a requirement are used to

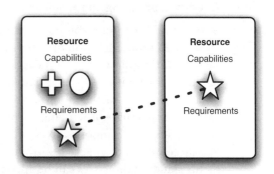

Figure 7.3 **A requirement is satisfied by a capability if that capability is of a matching namespace, provides the attributes needed by the requirement, and has no conflicting constraints.**

define the filter used for matching capabilities. The attributes for a capability *must* contain an entry whose key matches the capability's namespace.

- A set of directives that are used to provide instructions to the matching algorithm, or to the OSGi runtime.

For OSGi bundles, there are standard mappings for the specification-defined capabilities and requirements. Headers such as `Import-Package`, `Require-Bundle`, and `Fragment-Host` correspond to requirements, whereas `Export-Package` and the existence of the bundle are capabilities.

The bundle capabilities

Aside from the packages it exposes, a bundle still has other capabilities, though you probably wouldn't think of them that way normally. These are the capability to be *required* by another bundle using `Require-Bundle`, and the capability to host a fragment when specified by `Fragment-Host`. These capabilities both loosely correspond to the `Bundle-SymbolicName` and `Bundle-Version` headers, and are therefore similar to the `osgi.identity` capability!

It may seem odd to model the bundle like this, but it makes a lot of sense. `Require-Bundle` and `Fragment-Host` are clearly dependencies that need to be mapped as requirements—therefore, there must be matching capabilities to satisfy them! The two capabilities are in the `osgi.wiring.bundle` and `osgi.wiring.host` namespaces for `Require-Bundle` and `Fragment-Host`, respectively.

We've discussed how requirements and capabilities are structured, and that a capability must provide the right attributes to *satisfy* a requirement. Although this model has an elegant simplicity, it isn't, unfortunately, the full story. In addition to attributes and their namespaces, both requirements and capabilities can express directives that affect the way they resolve.

7.1.3 *Directives affecting the resolver*

As we've said before, resolution is closely tied to provisioning. Nowhere is this more clear than in the resolution directives that can be passed to the resolver through capabilities and requirements. Directives aren't usually used directly to match requirements to capabilities (the mandatory directive is a notable exception), but instead offer instructions to the resolver saying how they should be processed. If you find yourself scratching—or banging!—your head about why a bundle won't resolve when all the packages it imports are clearly available, check to see if there are any unsatisfied directives on the packages—there almost certainly will be!

Six standard directives can be applied to any namespace, which makes them particularly important to understand. These are the `resolution` directive, the `mandatory` directive, the `cardinality` directive, the uses directive, the `effective` directive, and the `filter` directive.

THE RESOLUTION DIRECTIVE

The resolution directive serves a fairly simple purpose; it determines whether a requirement is optional or not. The resolution directive has two allowed values, optional and mandatory. The default value of this directive is mandatory.

The resolution directive can be applied to any requirement, and it's also possible to specify it on requirement-like manifest headers:

```
Import-Package: fancyfoods.optional; resolution:=optional
Require-Bundle: fancyfoods.needed.bundle; resolution:=mandatory
```

> **WARNING: DIRECTIVES IN THE BUNDLE MANIFEST** At first glance, there doesn't seem to be any difference between the resolution directive and any other attribute on an Import-Package; however, if you look closely you'll see that it's specified using :=, not =. This is the key difference in syntax between an attribute and a directive. If you were to write resolution=optional, then your package import would still be mandatory and the resolver would try to find an exported package that defined an attribute called *resolution* with a value of *optional.*

THE MANDATORY DIRECTIVE

The mandatory directive is somewhat more complicated than the other directives, primarily because it doesn't apply to a requirement, but instead to a capability. Many people get confused by what the mandatory directive does, but there's a reasonably simple way to think about it. When you specify attributes on a requirement, it means that the requirement can only be satisfied by a capability that provides *all* of those attributes; however, *any* capability that provides those attributes will do, even if it specifies a hundred extra attributes. The mandatory directive effectively provides the reverse mapping of this behavior. By using the mandatory directive, a capability can specify a set of attributes that a requirement *must* specify to be matched. Even if the capability supplies all of the attributes needed by the requirement, it won't match unless the requirement supplies all of the mandatory attributes:

```
Bundle-SymbolicName: A                                        Importing
Import-Package: fancyfoods.mandatory; chocolate=nice          bundle manifest

Bundle-SymbolicName: B
Export-Package: fancyfoods.mandatory; chocolate=nice;         Exporting bundle
 cheese=yummy; mandatory:="chocolate,cheese"                  manifest
```

In this code snippet, you can see that the package import from bundle A looks as though it should match the export from bundle B. Bundle B, however, only allows importers that specify both that chocolate is nice *and* that cheese is yummy. As a result, poor bundle A must look elsewhere for its package (see figure 7.4).

The mandatory directive is a specialized tool, and we recommend avoiding it unless you really need it. One example of why you might want to use the mandatory directive is if you have a private SPI package that needs to be shared between two bundles (yuck!). In this case, you can add a mandatory attribute to the exported package so that you can't wire to it accidentally, only if you supply the necessary attribute. Even

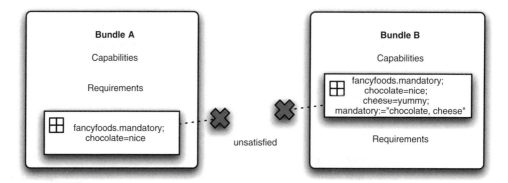

Figure 7.4   If a capability includes the `mandatory` **directive, requirements must specify the mandatory attributes to be satisfied. In this case, a bundle with a requirement for the** `fancyfoods.mandatory` **package must also specify that chocolate is nice and cheese is yummy for bundle B to satisfy the requirement.**

though it's unlikely that you'll need to use it, we think it's important that you know what it looks like and what it does, in case you see it in a bundle manifest somewhere.

The remaining directives are different from the `resolution` and `mandatory` directives in that they don't have a corresponding entry in a bundle manifest. On the other hand, they're extremely useful!

THE CARDINALITY DIRECTIVE

The `cardinality` directive is simple to understand; it's applied to a requirement and determines the number of capabilities that can be wired to that requirement by the resolver. It has two values: `single` and `multiple`. The default value is `single`; however, the cardinality is determined by the interaction between the `resolution` directive and the `cardinality` directive (see figure 7.5 and table 7.1).

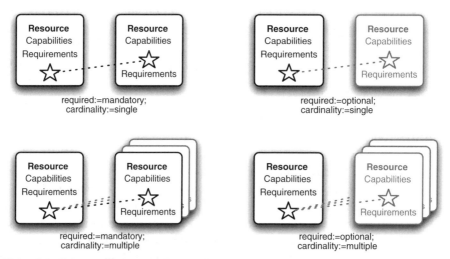

Figure 7.5   How many instances of a capability are resolved is determined by the combination of the `cardinality` **directive and the** `resolution` **directive.**

Table 7.1 Interaction between the `resolution` and `cardinality` directives

`resolution` directive	`cardinality` directive	Number of wired capabilities
mandatory	single	Exactly one
mandatory	multiple	One or more
optional	single	Zero or one
optional	multiple	Zero or more

THE USES DIRECTIVE

The uses directive is a comma-separated list of packages used by a capability. The reason this information is interesting is because it helps the resolver ensure that the class space is consistent. Although you could generate uses directives by hand, it's better to have a tool do it. We'll come back to uses constraints in section 7.2.1.

THE EFFECTIVE DIRECTIVE

The effective directive is almost certainly the one that you'll have the least contact with. The effective directive applies to both requirements and capabilities, and is used to determine at what time that requirement is needed, or when the capability becomes available. There's only one defined value, which is the default. This value is resolve. If a requirement is effective at *resolve* time, it must be taken into account during the resolution process. If a requirement is effective at any other time, it isn't processed by the resolver because it has no resolution impact. Similarly, a resolve-time capability can be used by the resolver to satisfy requirements, but a capability with any other effective time can't, and is ignored.

Given that an effective directive of anything other than resolve is more or less ignored by the OSGi resolver, you might think that it isn't useful. This isn't true, although its use is fairly specific. A good example of a nonresolve time requirement is configuration. The OSGi Compendium Specification defines the Configuration Admin service, which can inject configuration into managed services. To be injected with configuration, your managed service must specify a persistent identifier (PID), which identifies the configuration dictionary to be injected. This clearly has no impact on the resolution of your bundle; however, without the configuration dictionary your service will be relatively useless. Some proposed provisioning systems allow you to express an active time requirement on a configuration dictionary with a particular PID. This requirement allows the provisioning system to identify a configuration resource (with the right PID) and make the configuration available for you at runtime. The OSGi Resolver Service Specification suggests using a value of active for this case, but implementations are free to choose a value that makes sense within their requirement's namespace.

THE FILTER DIRECTIVE

As far as the resolution process is concerned, the filter directive is probably the most important of all the directives. The filter directive exists on a requirement and contains an LDAP filter that's used to determine whether a particular capability satisfies this requirement. Despite being so important, the `filter` directive is almost always generated programmatically (the framework generates them for bundles), so it's unlikely that a user would ever have to write one.

We've spent a reasonable amount of time looking at how bundles can be modeled programmatically using the OSGi Resource Specification, and how this fits into the OSGi resolver service, but we haven't explained how these fit together with provisioning. We're now ready, however, to look at provisioning using the OSGi Repository Service. One of the key aspects of the OSGi Repository Service is hinted at in its name, the *repository*. Repositories are a vital part of provisioning; without a repository it's not possible to provision anything in a meaningful sense.

7.1.4 *Repositories*

Modeling bundles is an important job for an OSGi resolver, and it's critical that the framework understand the relationships between OSGi bundles so that they can be resolved. This information isn't just important to a framework resolver, but is also necessary in provisioning. A repository is a standard place in which bundles can be located and, if necessary, downloaded and installed. As the collection of OSGi bundles within your enterprise grows, you'll almost certainly need a repository to store your bundles and allow applications to be provisioned against them. You may also want to make use of a number of publicly available repositories (more on public repositories in section 7.4.1).

Repositories make use of exactly the same `Capability` and `Requirement` interfaces as the resolver, which makes it easy for them to interoperate. Although a resolver is capable of large-scale complex dependency analysis, a repository can only provide responses to simple queries, listing the capabilities that match a supplied requirement. On the other hand, although a typical repository can contain a large variety of resource types, a resolver can typically only understand a limited number of resource types. For example, a framework resolver is only required to understand OSGi bundles.

REPOSITORY SERVICES AT RUNTIME

Repositories serve an important function at runtime. When the resolver is asked to determine whether a set of bundles can resolve or not, it makes use of an `Environment`. You can compare the `Environment` or a `Repository` to a helpful waiter in a restaurant that's run out of menus. You might want to eat steak, or to order something served with asparagus. To find out what was available, you'd ask the waiter if they had any steak or asparagus on the menu. When the resolver comes across a dependency, it does more or less the same thing; it queries the environment for resources that expose particular capabilities. The resolver then attempts to determine the *correct* resolution for the bundles. Depending on how deep the dependency graph is (whether you want side dishes), this may involve further queries to the environment. The link between the environment and repositories is that the environment can be used to join the current state of the framework (the bundles that are already installed) with one or more repositories. This allows additional bundles to be dynamically provisioned into a system as necessary (see figure 7.6).

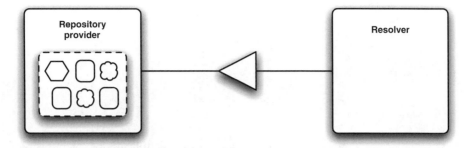

Figure 7.6 A resolver can make use of one or more repository services via the `Environment` to find out what capabilities are available.

When the resolver has finished determining a resolvable set of resources, the repository services are no longer needed; however, it would be wasteful to get rid of them. If you needed the repositories for another resolution, you'd have to rebuild them by modeling all of the bundles, all over again. Even if you keep the repository services around for the entire lifetime of the framework, but they only exist in memory, they'll still have to be rebuilt after every restart.

XML REPOSITORIES

A rather large amount of computational effort is required to generate the model for a bundle, so after it's been done once, it's preferable to save the information away. It's clearly even better if this data is saved in a format that's human-readable and freely interchangeable. This is why the Repositories Specification includes a standard XML form for a repository. The following listing shows a small snippet of a serialized repository.

Listing 7.1 An excerpt of a repository XML serialization

```
<repository
    xmlns='http://www.osgi.org/xmlns/repository/v1.0.0'
    name='Fancy Foods repository'>

    <capability namespace='osgi.identity'>
        <attribute name='osgi.identity' value='fancyfoods.api' />
        <attribute name='version' type='Version' value='1.0.0'/>
        <attribute name='type' value='osgi.bundle' />
    </capability>

    <capability namespace='osgi.wiring.bundle'>
        <attribute name='osgi.wiring.bundle'
                    value='fancyfoods.api' />
        <attribute name='bundle-version' type='Version' value='1.0.0' />
    </capability>
    <capability namespace='osgi.wiring.package'>
        <attribute
            name='osgi.wiring.package'
            value='fancyfoods.food' />
        <attribute
            name='version'
            type='Version'
```

```
            value='1.0.0' />
        <attribute
            name='bundle-version'
            type='Version'
            value='1.0.0' />
        <attribute
            name='bundle-symbolic-name'
            value='fancyfoods.food' />
    </capability>
...
```

As you can see, one consequence of the repository allowing generic resources is that the XML form is verbose!

Repositories are important, and we'll talk about them again later in this chapter. First, now that you have a better understanding of how bundles are modeled, we should take a deeper look at dependency provisioning, particularly how packages and services can be located within a repository.

7.2   *Provisioning bundles*

Now that you understand the generic descriptions of resources used by OSGi resolvers and repositories, it's time to look back at how to provision bundles, and how you can achieve finer control with your applications if you need to.

> **WARNING: BEST PRACTICES**   One or two of the examples in this section may seem to deviate from the best practices outlined in chapter 5. As in all things, context is king. The examples we provide aim to demonstrate best practices; however, sometimes this doesn't offer the most elucidating examples. The best practices from chapter 5 are good rules to follow, and we encourage you to do so, but sometimes they aren't 100% appropriate. Perhaps in the future you too will find that the right thing to do in your project is to ignore one or more of the best practices. If it is, we wish you luck!

7.2.1   *Package-based provisioning*

When we looked at provisioning applications, we primarily focused on how an application manifest can require bundles within a range of versions. We also discussed the concept of a *missing dependency*. You may have noticed, at the time, that we never dug into how these missing dependencies were identified; more probably, you took for granted that it would work.

Now that you know how bundles can be modeled and made available through repositories, hopefully you can see how it might be possible to provision based on package dependencies. What you can do is provide an example of a real-world resolution involving a repository. Your repository will contain three bundles (listing 7.2 and figure 7.7).

Listing 7.2   The bundles in your repository

```
Bundle-SymbolicName: A
Bundle-Version: 1.0.0
Import-Package: fancyfoods.pkg; version="[1,2)"; foo=bar
```

```
Export-Package: fancyfoods.a; version=1.2.0

Bundle-SymbolicName: B
Bundle-Version: 1.0.0
Export-Package: fancyfoods.pkg; version=1.1; foo=bar; type=old

Bundle-SymbolicName: B
Bundle-Version: 1.1.0
Export-Package: fancyfoods.pkg; version=1.2; foo=bar; type=new;
 mandatory:="foo,type"
```

Example repository

Bundle A
Bundle-SymbolicName: A
Bundle-Version: 1.0.0
Import-Package: fancyfoods.pkg; version="[1,2)"; foo=bar
Export-Package: fancyfoods.a; version=1.2.0

Bundle B
Bundle-SymbolicName: B
Bundle-Version: 1.0.0
Export-Package: fancyfoods.pkg; version=1.1; foo=bar; type=old

Bundle B
Bundle-SymbolicName: B
Bundle-Version: 1.1.0
Export-Package: fancyfoods.pkg; version=1.2; foo=bar; type=new; mandatory:="foo,type"

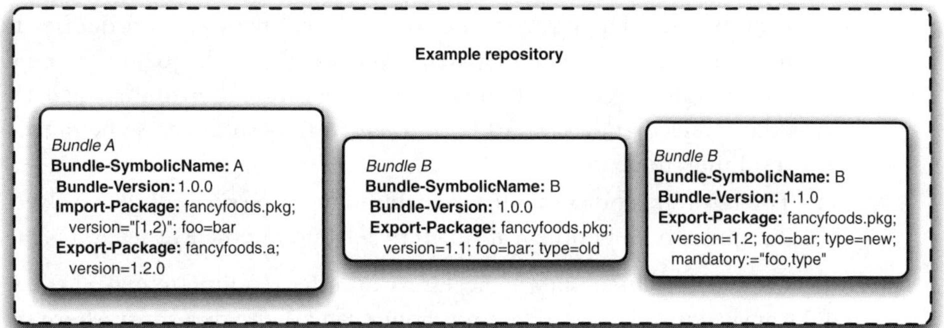

Figure 7.7   Your example repository contains three bundles with a variety of package exports, versions, attributes, and directives.

Given the content of your repository, you'll try to resolve the following bundle:

```
Bundle-SymbolicName: Test
Bundle-Version: 1.0.0
Import-Package: fancyfoods.a; version="[1.1,2)",
 fancyfoods.z; version="[1,2)"; resolution:=optional
```

If you ask the resolver whether your test bundle can resolve, the following things will happen under the hood (we've represented the resolution logic as a flowchart in figure 7.8):

1 The resolver will model the Test bundle, determining that it has two dependencies: one for the fancyfoods.a package, and one for the fancyfoods.z package.

2 Having determined that the requirements can't be satisfied by any other bundles known to the resolver (because there aren't any!), the resolver asks the environment if there are any resources that can supply a package capability for fancyfoods.a between versions 1.1 and 2. The environment has no matches locally (because there are no other bundles) and so delegates to the repository.

3 The repository returns the resource A as a possibility, which the resolver determines to be a valid match, but requiring further dependencies. To determine whether these dependencies can be satisfied, the resolver asks the environment if there are any resources that can supply a package capability for fancyfoods.pkg between versions 1 and 2 that also specify the attribute foo with a value of bar.

4   The environment queries the repository and finds one match. Even though bundle B at version 1.0.0 and at version 1.1.0 both look like possible matches, the mandatory directive on version 1.1.0 of B means that the requirement doesn't match (because it doesn't specify type=old). Because of this, the repository returns fancyfoods.pkg exported at version 1.1 from B at version 1.0.0.

5   Neither A nor B has any further requirements. The resolver continues to process the Test bundle.

6   The resolver queries the environment for the second package import from the Test bundle. The environment has no local matches and queries the repository, which also returns no matches because there are no bundles exporting the fancyfoods.z package. Rather than fail the resolution at this stage, the resolver determines that the import is optional and doesn't need to be satisfied for this resolution to be valid.

7   The resolver reports that the Test bundle can be successfully resolved, and that it requires both bundle A at version 1.0.0 and bundle B at version 1.0.0 to do so.

After you've determined that the necessary bundles required to make Test resolve are A and B at version 1.0.0, then the provisioner can ask the repository where the bundles are located and download them. If Test were the *core content* of an application, then you'd now have successfully determined the shared content you need to deploy it!

EXPORT-PACKAGE AND THE USES CLAUSE

Packages have a rather special place in OSGi because they represent the unit of modularity. The problem with Java packages, however, is that they aren't particularly well-defined units. On one level, a package is easy to define: every class declares which package it's in. But overlaps between packages exist. Methods on an interface in one package can accept parameters, or return things, that are declared in another package. This causes a problem for you in OSGi.

The identity of a class is determined by two things: its fully qualified name and the ClassLoader that loaded it. Because each bundle has its own classloader, but also imports classes from other bundles, it's possible that a class will exist more than once in a framework, but none of them will be the same class! Normally this isn't a problem, because the resolver ensures that you're only wired to a consistent set of bundles, but what if one of the packages you imported returned you an object from a different package? You would need to be certain that your view of that object was the same as the one from the imported package. If it wasn't, you would get a ClassCastException!

This is where the uses clause comes in. The uses directive can be applied to almost any header, but it's most often applied to Export-Package entries. It tells the framework about the other packages that are *used* by the exported package. This may mean that the exported package has method parameters or return values from those packages, or that they're used internally by classes in the package in a way that might cause problems. The directive instructs the resolver that when someone imports this package, the user *must* share the same class space for *all* of the packages in the uses directive, as shown in listing 7.3.

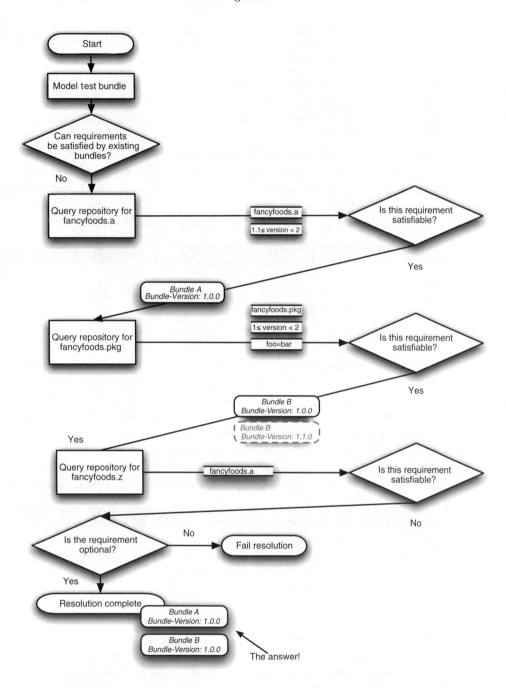

Figure 7.8 To resolve a bundle, a resolver will first model its requirements, and then query an environment for matching capabilities and any transitive requirements of the matching resources. It will then further refine possible matches based on the resource's attributes and directives.

Listing 7.3   Successfully resolving with a uses clause

```
Bundle-SymbolicName: Exporter
Export-Package: fancyfoods.special; uses:="fancyfoods.used"
Import-Package: fancyfoods.used; version="[1,2)"

Bundle-SymbolicName: Importer
Import-Package: fancyfoods.special,
 fancyfoods.used; version="[1,2)"
```

In listing 7.3, you can see two bundles. One bundle exports a package, fancy-foods.special, with a uses constraint of fancyfoods.used. The other bundle imports the fancyfoods.special and fancyfoods.used packages. The resolver knows that the importing bundle *must* be wired to the same instance of fancy-foods.used that the exporting bundle is, as shown here.

Listing 7.4   Successfully resolving with a uses clause

```
Bundle-SymbolicName: Exporter
Export-Package: fancyfoods.special; uses:="fancyfoods.used"
Import-Package: fancyfoods.used; version="[1,2)"

Bundle SymbolicName: Importer
Import-Package: fancyfoods.special
```

In listing 7.4, you can see two bundles similar to those in listing 7.3—one that exports package fancyfoods.special with a uses constraint of fancyfoods.used, and another that imports fancyfoods.special but not fancyfoods.used. In this case, the importing bundle can't see the fancyfoods.used package at all. Because of this, the importing bundle is class-space compatible with *any* view of that package. This might sound odd, but think of it this way: the importing bundle has no way to get the fancy-foods.used package; therefore it can't have an incompatible view! The end result of this is that, as in the following listing, we can successfully wire these bundles together.

Listing 7.5   Failure to resolve with a uses clause

```
Bundle-SymbolicName: Exporter
Export-Package: fancyfoods.special; uses:="fancyfoods.used"
Import-Package: fancyfoods.used; version="[1,2)"

Bundle SymbolicName: Importer
Import-Package: fancyfoods.special,
 fancyfoods.used; version="[2,3)"
```

Listing 7.5 is another variation on listing 7.3. Again, the Exporter hasn't changed, but the Importer has a different import version range for fancyfoods.used. In this case, the importing bundle can see the fancyfoods.used package, but can never wire to the same package that the Exporter bundle does. Because of this, you can guarantee that the uses constraint on the fancyfoods.special package will *never* be satisfied. This means that the resolver can't wire the import and export together, even though they look like they should match.

WARNING: COMPLEX USES CONSTRAINTS The examples in this section show reasonably simple situations involving the uses directive, ones that are easy to understand. You should, however, be aware that resolution problems involving uses constraints can be nasty to debug. This is because the class space of a bundle includes not only the packages it imports, but any packages that are used by those packages. In a complex case, you may find that the uses constraint violation occurs because of a third bundle, one that isn't even supplying the package you're trying to import!

To minimize the risk of unpleasant uses problems, you should try to avoid making use of too many API packages from other bundles when defining your API. In general, this isn't a huge problem; good API design tends to minimize the dependencies on other packages, and even in cases with large uses clauses, problems are comparatively rare.

WRITING USES CLAUSES

You may have noticed that you haven't been adding uses clauses to your example bundles. There are three main reasons for this. The first is that you don't want to overload your samples with new concepts. The second is that because all your API comes from a single, separate bundle, it must all be class-space consistent with itself, making you unlikely to suffer from uses problems (another good reason for doing what we suggest in section 5.2.1). The third reason is that writing accurate uses clauses is hard to do and hard to keep up to date. In the real world, almost all uses clauses are generated by tooling, which you'll hear more about in chapter 8.

Package-based provisioning is extremely handy and is probably the most commonly used feature of an OSGi bundle repository. A well-structured repository, however, can offer more than packages for provisioning.

7.2.2 *Service-based provisioning*

Service-based provisioning works in exactly the same way as package-based provisioning, and it's easy to see why. If you look back at the resolution process, you can see that despite the specific example, there was no reason that the requirements and capabilities had to be packages at all. In terms of your restaurant example, if your Test bundle had a requirement for toffee sauce (a requirement we can all get on board with!), then it could have been satisfied by a sticky toffee pudding in your repository. Fundamentally, there's no difference between the two scenarios.

Having identified that service-based provisioning is a trivial extension of the package-based provisioning model, why does it warrant all of section 7.2? To answer that question, you need to look back at the most critical part of the resolution and provisioning process, the generation of the capabilities and requirements. For packages, all the information you need is handily expressed in the bundle manifest, making package dependencies easy to model. Unfortunately, for services the problem isn't so simple, providing a key difference between services and packages.

MODELING OSGI SERVICES

If an OSGi bundle uses the OSGi API to register and consume services, then there's no metadata that describes the dependencies or capabilities offered. This causes a significant problem for modeling. How do you model things that are only expressed in the bytecode of a class file?

Bytecode analysis is a possibility for determining service registrations and lookups; however, it's an extremely expensive operation. To model the bundle, you would need to perform an in-depth analysis of *every* class contained within it. If computational complexity were the only issue, then it probably wouldn't be a problem; however, it isn't. Analyzing the bytecode can't always give you all the information you require.

It may seem odd that scanning the bytecode isn't able to supply all the information you need, but in bytecode you can't always tell what the value of variables are going to be at runtime. This means that if the interface name, the service properties, or the filter expression used when interacting with the Service Registry are able to vary at runtime, then it can be impossible to know what they'll be. This isn't the end of your problems, either. What if the registration of the service occurs in some other bundle that you import a package from? Also, how can you ever know if a service is optional or not?

Clearly, bytecode analysis is only feasible if you've found a way to solve the halting problem, which seems rather unlikely. What would be useful would be manifest headers like `Import-Package` and `Export-Package`. These would allow you to process the services in the same way you process packages.

IMPORT-SERVICE AND EXPORT-SERVICE

Earlier versions of the OSGi core specification described two headers, `Import-Service` and `Export-Service`. These headers are fairly self-explanatory, and seem like the perfect solution to your problems. Unfortunately, there were several problems with these headers, which means that they were deprecated and withdrawn from the core specification. In case you're worried that this means the OSGi alliance makes breaking changes to your bundles, be assured that this doesn't constitute a breaking change. The fact that this wasn't a breaking change even provides a good example of why the header wasn't that useful in the first place.

The problems with `Import-Service` and `Export-Service` are rather wide ranging. First, the headers are purely informational—they have absolutely no effect on the resolver at all. This is why it wasn't a problem for the OSGi alliance to remove them from the core specification. The informational nature of these headers, and the fact that they don't affect resolution, was a big reason for removing them. Because they look so similar to `Import-Package` and `Export-Package`, most people mistakenly believed that the resolver would ensure that the necessary services were available for their bundle. Another problem with the headers was that, because they were informational, they were also optional. This made them impossible to rely upon, and therefore rather useless.

Furthering their confusing nature, `Import-Service` and `Export-Service` weren't expressive enough to describe the myriad of services that can be exposed in the Service Registry. The big problem with these headers is that they have no way to type their attributes (the service properties), and no way to specify multiple values for the same property, either as an array or as a collection. Finally, the headers offered no way to identify the optionality or cardinality of required services. All in all, the headers were something of a disaster, which explains why they were removed from the specification.

Some people argue that, despite their shortcomings, `Import-Service` and `Export-Service` are the only sensible way to model dependencies and should be used to build `Requirement` and `Capability` descriptions. Others argue that co-opting headers that were (and still are) reserved by the OSGi alliance for something other than their original purpose is a bad idea. For what it's worth, we don't think that using `Import-Service` and `Export-Service` is a particularly good idea. They're hard to keep in sync with your code, they can't express more complex services and requirements, and it's not a good idea when there's a better alternative. If there's an alternative, what is it?

MODELING BLUEPRINT SERVICES

The reason that you can't easily provision against OSGi services is because you don't have anywhere to find reliable descriptions of them. Luckily, this isn't true for all OSGi services. Services that are exposed using the OSGi Blueprint container have an easily available, easily readable, and complete expression of all their properties—the Blueprint itself! By parsing the Blueprint definitions in a bundle repository, generators can quickly locate the services exported. As you saw in section 6.4.3, the service properties for a Blueprint exposed service are also easily accessible, as illustrated here.

Listing 7.6 A Blueprint service definition

```
<service ref="specialOffer"
    interface="fancyfoods.offers.SpecialOffer">
  <service-properties>
    <entry key="shop" value="chocolate"/>
    <entry key="open">
      <value type="java.lang.Boolean">true</value>
    </entry>
  </service-properties>
</service>
```

Looking again at the Blueprint, you can see that all the relevant information describing your service is available to the modeler. You can see the advertised interface and all of the service properties. From this XML snippet, it's a trivial exercise to build a `Capability` describing the service.

From this example, it's clear that Blueprint offers a mechanism through which you can model exposed services, and fortunately service requirements are as easy.

MODELING BLUEPRINT REFERENCES

In Blueprint the logical partner of the `service` element is the `reference` element. Where `service` exposes a Blueprint bean in the Service Registry, `reference` defines a

Blueprint bean representing a service from the Service Registry. Just as Blueprint services make good capabilities, Blueprint references can be turned into requirements, as shown in the following listing.

Listing 7.7   A Blueprint reference definition

```
<reference id="reference"
    interface="fancyfoods.offers.SpecialOffer"
    availability="optional"
    filter="(open=true)">
</reference>
```

Once again, the Blueprint XML snippet provides you with all the information you need to build a requirement, in this case the required service interface, and an LDAP filter expression that can easily be turned into the requirement's filter. Importantly, there are a few other pieces of information contained within this XML snippet that allow you to determine the directives, as well as the attributes, that you should add to this requirement.

The easiest directive to spot from listing 7.7 is the availability directive. In this case, your Blueprint reference is optional, which can be communicated to the resolver easily. The second directive is somewhat more difficult to spot because there's no attribute that corresponds to it. It's the element itself that defines it. Because you're using a reference element, you're looking for a single service instance. This means that your `Requirement` object should have a `cardinality` of `single`.

REQUIRING MULTIPLE SERVICES

As you may remember, in Blueprint it's possible to require multiple services with the same service interface. This is done using the `reference-list` element. The `reference-list` element is similar to the `reference` element, and again provides an excellent way to model service dependencies, as can be seen in this listing.

Listing 7.8   A Blueprint `reference-list` definition

```
<reference-list id="ref-list"
    interface="fancyfoods.offers.SpecialOffer"
    availability="mandatory"
    filter="(open=true)">
</reference-list>
```

In listing 7.8, you can see that the attributes for your `Requirement` will be exactly the same as the attributes for listing 7.7. The directives, however, will be different. In listing 7.8, your `Requirement` is now mandatory not optional, and because this is a `reference-list` element, the `Requirement` must have `multiple` cardinality.

Now that you've seen how bundles can be modeled to support provisioning by package and by service, it's time to take a look at some of the technologies that can be used to provision bundles at runtime.

7.3 *Provisioning technologies*

We've taken a good look at how provisioning works, and the things you can do to describe your bundles. Now that you're armed with all this knowledge, we can take a look at the implementations available to you for provisioning your bundles. Provisioning technologies are responsible for integrating one or more repositories, such that you can identify, locate, and obtain your dependencies from them. Because the final version of the OSGi repositories standard is new, implementations are still emerging. But the precursor to the OSGi Repository Specification (Felix OBR) is an excellent provisioner, and there are other provisioners not related to the OSGi specification that are still more than up to the job. We'll focus on a selection of open source provisioners.

7.3.1 *Apache Felix OBR*

The OBR subproject in Apache Felix was originally known as the Oscar Bundle Repository, and was introduced as a way of easily provisioning dependencies to get bundles up and running. OBR offers the following useful features:

- Support for exposing XML-based repositories in the runtime
- A mechanism for federating multiple repositories into a single repository view
- The ability to automatically install identified dependencies into the framework

Is it Felix OBR, or OSGi OBR, or OSGi Bundle Repository?

Felix OBR has been around for a long time, and predates both the OSGi Repository Service and the OSGi Resource API. In fact, the work done in Felix OBR was used to create both of these specifications! Although both the name and concepts are similar, the OSGi Repository Service and historical releases of Felix OBR aren't the same thing. To further muddy the waters, the OSGi Repository Service Specification was known as OBR during its—long—gestation. Because OBR predates the standardized OSGi Repository Specification, it's currently more widely used. You'll have to work out for yourself whether products with OBR support mean Felix OBR, a draft version of the OSGi repositories specification (also known as OBR or RFC-112), or the final version of the specification. Critical differences exist between the technologies that may make compatibility difficult. For example, in their XML serializations, the draft specification uses `<require>` elements and attributes, whereas the final version uses `<requirement>` elements and namespace elements.

Felix OBR is widely used because of its simple API and long history, but there are other popular OSGi provisioners.

7.3.2 *Equinox p2*

The Eclipse Equinox project provides the reference implementation for the core OSGi framework, but it also provides a number of other projects. Equinox p2 is a provisioning system, but not just for OSGi. The p2 system is a generic constraints resolver, and has been applied to a wide variety of problems. Importantly, p2 is the provisioning system used by the Eclipse project where it manages updates that can be applied to Eclipse applications.

One of the key criticisms leveled at p2 is that it's perceived as being difficult to use. This is probably because p2 is a more general provisioning solution, and so it's typically more effort to achieve specific use cases. Despite this drawback, p2 offers two particularly useful features that other provisioners don't.

TRANSACTIONAL INSTALLATION

If you have multiple dependencies that need to be provisioned, which you almost certainly do, then p2 can install them as a single logical unit within a transaction. If any failures occur, then *all* the bundles will be uninstalled. This is different from other provisioners, where a provisioning failure can leave you in an inconsistent state.

GARBAGE COLLECTION

Over multiple provisioning operations, you may find that the same dependency is needed by multiple bundles. In OSGi this is a good thing, because you gain the benefits of runtime, as well as development time, reuse. Unfortunately, this can cause problems when you want to uninstall a particular bundle; you may know that no other bundle is relying upon the bundle you want to remove, but what about the rest of its dependency graph? After you remove one bundle, you may find that there are other bundles that are no longer needed. This can be a long and difficult process, and may remind you of Java's garbage collection model. With p2, these bundles can be garbage collected automatically, saving effort for the runtime.

7.3.3   *Apache ACE*

Apache ACE is a fundamentally different kind of provisioner than either Felix OBR or p2. OBR and p2 operate on a *pull* model, where the client tries to find out what additional bundles it needs to get a particular bundle running. ACE, on the other hand, operates with a *push* model. With ACE, you pick a set of bundles to install on remote targets and then, as new remote targets become available, the ACE runtime will push these resources out to the target. It should be noted that neither of these models is truly *pull* or *push*, but it's a useful analogy.

Apache ACE doesn't provide the same resolution capabilities that you get with OBR or p2, meaning that it doesn't fill many of the use cases we've discussed in this chapter. ACE is, however, able to do something neither of the other provisioners we've discussed can: ACE can manage multiple OSGi application environments at once. This facility is useful for enterprise OSGi where, as your scaling requirements grow, you'll need to maintain more and more servers. Ideally, you would combine ACE with another provisioning technology to get the best of both worlds.

7.3.4   *Standard OSGi repositories*

Several implementations of the OSGi Repository Specification are being developed at the time of writing. JBoss is working on a well-supported implementation of the specification. Karaf Cave is a promising implementation, with support for both OSGi bundles and Karaf features. Karaf can also proxy other repositories and generate metadata on the fly. It will be interesting to see how these projects mature. The Apache Felix Sigil project provides another implementation, as well as a set of UI tools and build plug-ins. We also expect that the Felix OBR project will update its implementation to comply with the standard.

No matter which technology you choose, to get the most from a provisioner you need access to a repository of bundles to provision from. Fortunately, there are a number of public repositories and repository generation tools available for you to use.

7.4 Bundle repositories

Much like the word *database*, the phrase *bundle repository* is overloaded. *Database* can refer to a technology system that manages data, or to a collection of data. Similarly, *repository* can refer to the technology for describing a collection of bundles, or to the collection of bundles itself. Earlier, thinking of repository technology, we compared a repository to a waiter in a restaurant with no menus. In its other meaning, a repository is also like the food the restaurant has available. If he has bills to pay, the same waiter might work in multiple restaurants, serving different menus. A single restaurant might also employ multiple waiters, so that customers can inquire about asparagus, *asperges*, or *Spargel*.

So far we've been talking about repository technologies such as the standardized OSGi repositories, OBR, and p2. But you're going to need food as well as waiters! A number of public repositories make open source bundles available for provisioning against, and you can also generate your own repositories for internal hosting. You'll most likely want to take advantage of both options and use a mix of public bundle repositories and ones specific to your project.

7.4.1 Public bundle repositories

Several open source projects host bundle repositories that support one or more of the repository technologies we've discussed. If you don't need OSGi-specific metadata for provisioning, there are also a number of public repositories and projects that expose OSGi bundles as Maven artifacts. We'll cover these simpler repositories later in section 12.1.1.

XML repository formats

At the time of writing, none of the repositories we'll discuss support the new standard OSGi XML repository format. The repository specification has been under active development for a *long* time, and most OBR repositories are based on a relatively old public draft of the specification, when the specification was still called OBR! This XML is supported by current releases of Felix OBR and other tools in Apache Aries, but isn't up to date with the final specification.

THE FELIX OBR REPOSITORY

As well as providing a repository implementation, the Felix OBR project hosts a repository of around three hundred Felix bundles. Unlike most other public repositories, the Felix repository includes information about service requirements and capabilities. It can be accessed at http://felix.apache.org/obr/releases.xml.

THE APACHE SIGIL REPOSITORY

The Apache Felix Sigil project offers enriched OBR metadata for bundles hosted by SpringSource in the SpringSource Enterprise Bundle Repository (EBR).

THE KNOPFLERFISH BUNDLE REPOSITORY

Knopflerfish is another open source implementation of the OSGi core specification, but it also offers a number of other OSGi services through its bundle repository. It supports both the old-school Oscar Bundle Repository format, at http://www.knopflerfish.org/repo/repository.xml, and the draft OSGi specification, at http://www.knopflerfish.org/repo/bindex.xml. The Knopflerfish repository is considerably smaller than the SpringSource EBR, but it still contains a number of useful dependencies.

THE SONATYPE OSS REPOSITORY

Although Sonatype Nexus is best known for hosting Maven repositories, it can also generate and host OBR data for its Maven repositories. The Nexus public repositories therefore can be used for OSGi provisioning.

THE ECLIPSE MARKETPLACE

If you're using p2 instead of OBR, a number of repositories, also known as *update sites*, are available. An Eclipse update site uses XML metadata to describe one or more OSGi bundles, typically deployed as a set that make up an Eclipse plug-in. Eclipse update sites don't model the bundles they describe in the same way that we've described in this chapter, but are commonly used, particularly in conjunction with the p2 provisioner. The Eclipse Marketplace is an example of one of the many available Eclipse update sites.

What happens if the bundle you need isn't available in one of the public repositories? If you want to provision against bundles you've written yourself, this is almost certainly the case. Even widely distributed bundles may not be available in a public OBR repository. The good news is that generating repositories is so easy, you may already be doing it.

7.4.2 *Building your own repository*

A number of tools are available that can generate repositories from Maven repositories or the filesystem. They can even be integrated into your build process.

BINDEX

The most popular tool for generating OBR XML repositories is called *Bindex*. Bindex models the dependencies that are declared in the bundle manifest, and recent versions are able to use Blueprint and Declarative Services metadata to create requirements and capabilities for services.

THE MAVEN BUNDLE PLUG-IN

Although Bindex has excellent function, it does need to be downloaded and explicitly run. A more convenient alternative is the `maven-bundle-plugin`, which embeds Bindex. The `maven-bundle-plugin` will automatically generate OBR metadata in a repository.xml file in the local Maven repository, so you may already be creating OBR repositories without even knowing it! The bundle plug-in has extra goals to deploy bundles to remote OBR repositories and generate an OBR repository from all the files in an existing Maven repository:

```
mvn org.apache.felix:maven-bundle-plugin:index
```

Listing 7.9 shows part of an OBR repository automatically generated by building the Fancy Foods application with Maven. If you compare it to the OSGi standard repository from listing 7.1, you'll see it's less generic but also more human-readable. We anticipate later versions of the Maven bundle will be able to produce both OBR and standard repository serializations.

Listing 7.9 An OBR repository.xml generated by the Maven bundle plug-in

```
<repository lastmodified='17874783'>
    <resource
        id='fancyfoods.department.chocolate/1.0.0'
        symbolicname='fancyfoods.department.chocolate'
        presentationname='Fancy Foods Chocolate Department'
        uri='fancyfoods/fancyfoods.department.chocolate/1.0.0/
            fancyfoods.department.chocolate-1.0.0.jar'
        version='1.0.0'>
    <size>5151</size>
    <capability name='bundle'>
      <p n='symbolicname' v='fancyfoods.department.chocolate'/>
      <p n='presentationname' v='Fancy Foods Chocolate Department'/>
      <p n='version' t='version' v='1.0.0'/>
      <p n='manifestversion' v='2'/>
    </capability>
    <capability name='service'>
      <p n='service' v='fancyfoods.offers.SpecialOffer'/>
    </capability>
    <capability name='package'>
      <p n='package' v='fancyfoods.chocolate'/>
      <p n='version' t='version' v='0.0.0'/>
      <p n='uses:' v='fancyfoods.food,fancyfoods.offers'/>
    </capability>
    <require
        name='package'
        filter='(&amp;(package=fancyfoods.food)(version&gt;=1.0.0)
                  (!(version&gt;=2.0.0)))'
        extend='false'
        multiple='false'
        optional='false'>
    </require>
```

The bundle plug-in can read an obr.xml file for supplemental information about requirements and capabilities. For example, if you need to document toffee sauce requirements, you can handle them with an obr.xml fragment.

APACHE ARIES REPOSITORY BUILDER

Apache Aries also provides a command-line repository building tool that models package dependencies, but also makes use of the Aries Blueprint implementation to model Blueprint services and references. The command syntax is as follows:

```
java -jar
    org.apache.aries.application.tooling.repository.generator-1.0.0.jar
    [repository xml location] url1 [url2...]
```

NEXUS REPOSITORIES

If you're using Nexus for Maven hosting, Nexus's ability to expose an OBR-compatible view of the repository can be convenient. This provides an excellent way to share existing artifacts without impacting existing infrastructure.

MODELING BY HAND

As we discussed in section 7.2.2, the ability of these tools to generate repositories that allow service-based provisioning depends on service metadata being available. For those of you that don't want to use an injection container, or if you want to describe nonstandard requirements, all isn't lost! Because there's a standard XML serialization for OSGi repositories, it's entirely possible to author your own resource descriptions. You need to be careful to keep the description of your resource up to date if your bundle ever changes, but it does give you all the flexibility you could ever need. You can also hand decorate the repository descriptions generated by a tool with additional service capabilities and requirements as necessary. The schema for the bundle repository format is available at http://www.osgi.org/xmlns/repository/v1.0.0/repository.xsd. Services should use the osgi.service namespace and objectClass attribute.

You can provision directly against repositories generated using one of these tools, or you can use one of the repository implementations we discussed in section 7.3 to create a federated view of your local repository and one or more of the public repositories.

7.4.3   *Generating your repository*

The Apache Aries repository generation tool processes a set of bundles in a directory, turning them into an XML repository. To start with, let's put your application bundles in a directory on disk.

Now that you have a location on disk to scan, you need to get hold of the repository generator. The repository generator uses a live OSGi framework to model the bundles, which ensures that it can validate any extra namespaces used in your Blueprint bundles. To validate these namespaces, the repository generator also needs the bundles that provide these extra namespaces.

The Apache Aries modeler is new, and so isn't available as a set of released modules. To get hold of the application modeler, you can either get one from a nightly snapshot of the Aries build, or by building Aries yourself. The bundles you need exist in the target directory of the application/application-tooling-repository-generator. If you copy the contents of this directory to somewhere a little more accessible, then you can use them to build your repository.xml using a single, simple command. Before you can launch the generator, you must remember to add the bundles that supply the namespace extensions that you used in your application. In this case, you need the transactions and JPA namespace handlers.

The transactions namespace handler is available as a released bundle called transaction.blueprint, or from a build in the transaction/transaction-blueprint/target directory. It also depends on the JTA API; this bundle can easily be retrieved from the test stack you used in chapter 3:

```
java -jar
   org.apache.aries.application.tooling.repository.generator-<version
   id>.jar [repository xml location] url1 [url2...]
```

In the command to launch the repository generator, you need to replace the `<version id>` with the build ID of your repository generator JAR. The `repository xml location` parameter is optional, and defaults to ./repository.xml. The URL that you supply points to a directory of bundles that you wish to build a repository from, and you may optionally supply further URLs to scan and aggregate into a single repository.

7.5 *Summary*

This chapter has covered the provisioning process in a lot of depth. We hope that by now you have a good understanding of how resolvers can solve the constraint problems offered by bundle dependency graphs. You've also learned how bundle repositories work and, if you wanted to, you could probably write your own tool for generating a repository, both at runtime and in XML.

You may have come to the end of this chapter thinking that there isn't much reason for you to know about repositories and modeling to this level of detail. We, on the other hand, would disagree. The most common problem we come across when people are building enterprise OSGi applications is that their application doesn't resolve. The next-most-common problem is that the application *does* resolve, but not in the way the developer was expecting. For many people, the errors output by the resolution process are completely opaque, as is the underlying process itself. Armed with the information in this chapter, you should have no difficulty in diagnosing any resolution problems you see; other developers will probably seek you out to help them as well!

Now that you've seen how repositories can be a useful tool for locating dependencies, it's time for us to look at other tools that can speed and ease the enterprise OSGi development cycle.

8

Tools for
building and testing

This chapter covers

- Strategies for building OSGi bundles
- How to choose a set of tools that works for you
- Useful command-line OSGi tools
- Using Maven and Ant to build OSGi bundles and EBA applications
- How to unit test OSGi bundles
- How to run tests on bundles inside an OSGi framework

As you've been working through the OSGi examples in this book, we've cheerfully assumed that you didn't need much help building your example bundles. After all, an OSGi bundle is a JAR with some extra metadata, and even an enterprise OSGi bundle is only an OSGi bundle with even more extra metadata. But just because you *can* build OSGi bundles the same way that you build ordinary JARs doesn't mean you *should*. A lot of specialist tools are out there that can make the process of building your OSGi application easier and more robust.

With a few notable exceptions, most of the tools we'll discuss aren't specific to enterprise OSGi. This is partly because you don't necessarily need *enterprise* tools—the most important thing is support for core OSGi concepts like compile classpath and launching an OSGi framework. A second reason we don't cover many enterprise OSGi tools is that enterprise OSGi itself is new, and the tools are still catching up!

We won't specifically discuss IDEs—we'll get to them in chapter 9. But we can't ignore IDEs, because for building OSGi bundles your choice of command-line tooling and your choice of IDE are interconnected. Which command-line tooling you use will influence which IDE works best for you, and the opposite is true as well; you may find your choice of IDE makes the decision about your command-line build for you. In particular, you'll need to decide early on whether you want to use *manifest-first* tools or *code-first* tools.

8.1   *Manifest-first or code-first?*

One of the great debates in the OSGi world is whether it's better to write manifests or generate them automatically. Unlike a conventional JAR manifest, which is pretty boring, an OSGi manifest is absolutely critical to how an OSGi bundle works. Because manifests are so pivotal, some people think they're much too important to be left to a computer to write. Others argue that they're too important to be left in the hands of software developers!

Writing the manifest for a complex bundle can be *hard*, and getting it right can be even harder. For this reason, many developers prefer to write and compile their Java code as though it were going to run in a normal Java environment. Tools can then use this code to generate a manifest that's guaranteed to accurately reflect the code's dependencies. This style of development is known as code-first. Some developers, on the other hand, prefer to be more involved with the OSGi side of things. In particular, they want to see and control what's going into their manifests.

Opponents of code-first development argue that although it's easy to automatically produce an accurate list of packages a bundle should import, it's much harder to produce a list of packages the bundle should export. Generated manifests often export more packages than you might have intended, particularly if you're using a service-oriented style of OSGi. To keep your bundles as private as they should be, you may find yourself having to pay as much attention to package exports as you would if you were writing the manifest yourself.

Even the bundle imports might not turn out how you want them. Because the packages you use are hidden with code-first development, you may end up using packages you would have avoided if you'd had to introduce an explicit dependency on them. This can create bundles that fail to resolve at deploy time because of code dependencies you don't even want or need. Manual tweaking is also required to ensure that optional dependencies are flagged appropriately.

Manifest-first development, on the other hand, has its own difficulties. Development can be slower because you may find yourself constantly interrupting coding to go add required imports to your manifest. Although the tools should automatically tell you if you're missing required imports, they won't, in general, flag unused imports. This means you can end up with bundles with dangerously bloated package imports, unless you make a point of cleaning up regularly. Maintaining accurate versions on your exported packages is also almost impossible without some level of byte-code analysis and partial manifest generation.

Whether you prefer manifest-first or code-first development, one thing is certain: for projects of any size, you'll need *some* sort of OSGi-aware tooling. Managing small manifests by hand is reasonable, but it rapidly becomes impossible without a compiler to either tell you that you got it wrong or generate the manifest for you.

> **OSGi and the dreaded `ClassNotFoundException`**
> It's often said that OSGi eliminates class-not-found exceptions. This statement needs to be qualified—OSGi can only eliminate class-not-found exceptions *if all the bundle manifests are correct*. A bundle that forgets to import packages is guaranteed to fail if it tries to use classes from those packages. Both styles of OSGi development try to guarantee accurate manifests, but a determined developer can introduce manifest errors with either process!

The flagship tool for code-first OSGi development is a command-line tool, bnd. Bnd is also well integrated into a higher-level stack of more general build tools like Ant and Maven, and IDE tools. The star tool for manifest-first development, on the other hand, is Eclipse's built-in OSGi tooling, Eclipse PDE (we'll discuss PDE much more in chapter 9). Eclipse PDE itself has only limited support for command-line builds, but several tools integrate with PDE to support command-line building. We'll begin with a survey of the command-line tools available, starting with bnd.

8.2   *Building OSGi applications*

Although setting up a command-line build may not be the first thing you do when you start developing a new project, you'll almost certainly need an automated build sooner or later. Even if you're not wading into build scripts as your first development step, thinking in advance about what kind of build you want can help you make the right choices about what kind of IDE tools are best suited for your project.

Your choice of which command-line tools to use will usually be guided by whether you prefer a manifest-first or code-first style of development. (Alternatively, if you already know which build tools you want to use, that may make the decision about manifest-first or code-first for you!) Figure 8.1 shows how the various styles of development and tools we'll discuss in this chapter connect to one another.

8.2.1   *Bnd*

We'll start our discussion with the bnd tool. If you're sharp-eyed, you'll notice that bnd only appears in one path in figure 8.1. Nonetheless, if you opt for a code-first style of OSGi development, you'll almost certainly use either bnd directly or—more likely—

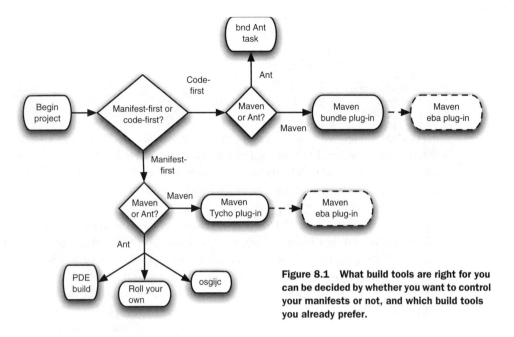

Figure 8.1 What build tools are right for you can be decided by whether you want to control your manifests or not, and which build tools you already prefer.

one of the many tools that incorporate bnd under the covers. For this reason, it's important to understand what bnd is and what it can do for you. Bnd analyzes a bundle's bytecode to work out what packages it would *need* to import to work properly, and then it uses that information to generate a manifest. Bnd is extremely powerful and could easily fill a chapter of its own. In this chapter, we'll cover the bits of bnd you're most likely to use at build time, but we'll come back to some of bnd's other features again in section 12.1.3.

Why are we only getting to bnd at this late stage?

The bnd tool is widely used for OSGi development; some people argue that OSGi development on any kind of serious scale is impossible without bnd, and will be wondering why we've waited so long to introduce bnd. In our view, using bnd is like using a calculator. When you learn addition and multiplication in school, you don't use a calculator, because it's important to properly understand the basic principles; after you've got the basics mastered and move on to more advanced math, you use a calculator to handle the basics for you. In our opinion, even if you opt for a code-first style of development, you must understand OSGi manifests so that you can understand what the tools have generated for you.

BUILDING WITH BND

Bnd works from a configuration file that it uses to guide the generation of your manifest. Simple .bnd files are almost indistinguishable from MANIFEST.MF files. Let's have a look at the bnd file for the fancyfoods.persistence bundle in the next listing.

```
Bundle-Name: Fancy Foods Persistence Bundle
Bundle-SymbolicName: fancyfoods.persistence
Bundle-Version: 1.0.0
Meta-Persistence:
Private-Package: fancyfoods.persistence
Import-Package: *
```

This is almost exactly the same as the manifest you wrote in chapter 3. One little difference is that the bnd file is parsed as a properties file, so line breaks must be escaped with a backslash, rather than indenting the following line with a space. But the two most important differences are the extra header, `Private-Package:`, and that you're allowed to use the value * for pattern matching.

`Private-Package:` is used to indicate that a package should be considered private to the bundle, and that it should not be exported. Bnd will assume that any code not mentioned in a standard `Export-Package:` or bnd-specific `Private-Package:` header should be ignored; bnd won't put code into the bundle it builds unless you explicitly tell it to do so. This may surprise you the first time you do a bnd-based build.

Even though there are three of them, getting all the package declarations right isn't as time consuming as you might initially guess, because of the second difference between the bnd file and a manifest—*patterns*. Notice how listing 8.1 uses a wildcard for the package imports. You can also use wildcards and other regular expression constructs such as !, when setting your private and exported packages.

CREATING A BUNDLE

To see how the bnd file works, let's get bnd to produce the `fancyfoods.persistence` bundle. Navigate to the folder that contains the compiled `fancyfoods.persistence` classes and create the `bnd.bnd` file (or the folder with your Eclipse .classpath folder if you imported `fancyfoods.persistence` into Eclipse). (If you name the file `fancyfoods.persistence.bnd`, bnd will automatically work out the bundle symbolic name and JAR name.) Then type the following

```
java -jar ${bnd.path}/biz.aQute.bnd.jar buildx -classpath
 ${bin.dir} bnd.bnd
```

where ${bin.dir} is the location of the compiled `fancyfoods.persistence` classes. If you have the `fancyfoods.persistence` bundle set up as an Eclipse project, you can use the following command from the root of the Eclipse project:

```
java -jar ${bnd.path}/biz.aQute.bnd.jar bnd.bnd
```

Bnd will create a `fancyfoods.persistence.jar` file in the current directory. Open it up and have a look at what classes were included and the manifest. You'll see that bnd has helpfully included what the `Private-Package:` header looked like after wildcard expansion. It's also added in required manifest headers like the `Bundle-ManifestVersion`.

WARNING: WHEN BND GOES BAD When using bnd, it's essential to inspect both your bundle contents and your manifest after building, at least while you're getting started. Small misunderstandings between you and bnd can result in

- Every package in your bundle being exported
- *All* of your dependencies being included in your bundle
- None of your classes being repackaged in your bundle

The authors are aware of these possibilities because we've made all of these mistakes ourselves! You'll quickly discover if your classes haven't been included in your bundle, but the other two issues may take much longer to notice; your built bundle will be perfectly valid, but it won't be at all encapsulated, or at all modular, so it's not in the *spirit* of OSGi.

We've been talking about building using bnd, but what you're doing here is somewhere halfway between building and packaging. The way you're using it, the bnd tool isn't compiling anything; all it's doing is using the precompiled code to generate a manifest, and then packaging everything up into a JAR.

PACKAGE VERSIONS

When you used bnd to build the `fancyfoods.persistence` bundle, it added in package imports, but no versions. Because specifying versions is an OSGi best practice, it would be annoying if bnd always ignored them. Luckily, bnd will take good care of your versions if provided with the right information.

Bnd can't guess the version of exported packages from their bytecode, so the version must be specified somewhere. One option is to explicitly list the packages in the `Export-Package` and provide a version for each one, but this is manual, and undoes some of the benefits of bnd wildcards. A nicer solution is to make use of bnd's support for Java `package-info.java` files. A `package-info` file is a special class whose only content is an annotation specifying the version. Because the `package-info` files are right next to the source, it's easier to remember to update them when making code changes.

> ### An alternative to `package-info.java`
> Some people dislike the extra overhead of maintaining a class to represent information about their Java packages. As an alternative option, bnd also looks for text files called `packageinfo` in each package. These `packageinfo` files use the properties format, but otherwise can contain exactly the same information as `package-info.java`.
>
> Any of the tricks we show you for managing `package-info.java` will work equally well in a `packageinfo` file.

Bnd will automatically detect `package-info` files and use them to determine the version of exported packages. For example, to set the version of the `fancyfoods.food` package to 1.0.0 (as we did in chapter 2), it's sufficient to create the following `package-info.java` file in that package:

```
@Version("1.0.0")
package fancyfoods.food;

import aQute.bnd.annotation.Version;
```

But you can do even better than that. The semantic versioning scheme suggests adding a fourth qualifier part to the version string to identify the individual build. While generating the manifest, bnd will automatically expand variables in the `package-info.java` files:

```
@Version("1.0.0.${buildLabel}")
package fancyfoods.food;

import aQute.bnd.annotation.Version;
```

To set the build label, add the following to the `bnd.bnd` file:

```
buildLabel = build-${tstamp}
```

Even more usefully, bnd will automatically add version ranges to its package imports. It does this based, not on information you provide, but rather on what's in the manifest of the bundles on the build path. Bnd will work out an appropriate version range based on the semantic versioning policy. API implementation providers will be less tolerant to changes in the API than consumers of the API, so you'll need to give bnd a hint to choose the right range for API providers. Explicitly including the API package in the `Import-Package` list and adding the `provide:=true` directive will do the trick. API providers will import packages between versions on the classpath up to, but not including, the next minor increment. Other consumers of an API can handle versions up to, but not including, the next major version. If you're at all confused about the difference between consumers and providers, or why they need different version ranges, then we suggest taking a look at appendix A (A.2.5), as well as looking back at section 1.2.1.

SETTING THE CLASSPATH FOR BND

How does bnd work out what version you're importing? When you repackaged the `fancyfoods.persistence` bundle, no versions were specified for the imported packages, because bnd didn't have access to them (or rather, to their exporting bundles). To allow bnd to work out package versions, bnd needs to see both the compiled classes and the compile-time classpath. These two groups of classes are collapsed into a single bnd classpath. Bnd will read Eclipse .classpath files to work out a default classpath, but it won't unpack Eclipse classpath containers (like those used by Eclipse PDE). If you're not using Eclipse, or if bnd is struggling to interpret the Eclipse classpath files, classpaths can be specified using the `-classpath` option.

The lack of a distinction between the compiled classes for the target bundle and the classpath used to compile those classes is why it's necessary to specify the `Private-Package` header. Otherwise, bnd won't have any way of knowing which classes belong to the bundle it's building. It also means caution must be exercised when using wildcards in the `Private-Package` header—make the regular expression too general, and bnd will package up the *entire* classpath into a single bundle. (This brings us neatly back to the importance of double-checking the bundles produced by bnd in case of disaster!)

> **WARNING: WRONG VERSION? WRONG CLASSPATH** Bnd's automatic versioning of package imports is incredibly useful, but if you get things wrong it can leave you with bundles that won't start when you deploy them in production. If you compile against a package with version 1.1.0, bnd will (correctly) set the minimum version for that package import as version 1.1.0. What happens if you then deploy into an environment where that package is only available at version 1.0.0? The OSGi framework will refuse to start your bundle because its minimum requirements aren't met, even if all your code *really* needed was version 1.0.0. You *can* fix this problem by manually specifying the version range for the import in your bnd.bnd file, but a cleaner solution is to make sure that what you're compiling against lines up with what you're deploying against. You'll want to compile against the *lowest* compatible version of a bundle.

Let's look in more depth at what can go into a bnd configuration file.

MAKING THE MOST OF THE BND FILE

The bnd file is an extremely flexible and powerful configuration tool. As well as the wildcards we've already seen, it supports variable substitution, macros, inheritance, and even Declarative Services.

The `Import-Package`, `Export-Package`, and `Private-Package` headers all allow wildcards. This means bundle exports can be specified concisely. For example, if you adopt a naming convention that assumes packages ending with `.impl` are private, the following `.bnd` snippet will automatically export only what it should:

```
Export-Package: !*.impl, *
Private-Package: *
```

If the same package is included in both `Export-Package` and `Private-Package`, the export takes precedence.

One nice thing about the variable substitution is you can include as much or as little detail as you like. You can specify nothing but `*`, or copy and paste whole import declarations from existing manifests, or add in package versions or other package directives where needed. Even if you do explicitly list out a bundle's package imports, it's a good idea to add a catch-all `*` at the end of the list to import anything you've forgotten—or didn't even know you needed. If you don't import everything you need, then bnd will issue warnings to tell you so. If you choose to continue from there, then you expose yourself again to the dreaded `NoClassDefFoundError`.

So far all the bnd functionality we've seen has been about generating manifests—better, smarter, cleaner manifests, but still manifests. Bnd can also use the information in the bnd.bnd file to generate other types of resources. In particular, it can be used for Declarative Services.

DECLARATIVE SERVICES

If you're planning to use both bnd and Declarative Services, you may find the bnd support for Declarative Services handy. Service components can be declared within bnd files; bnd will generate the component XML files. The bnd format for service components is another syntax to learn, but it's more concise than the XML.

For example, the cheese bundle can be packaged so that it uses bnd Declarative Services instead of Blueprint, with the following bnd file. (We've switched from the persistence bundle to the cheese department bundle, both for variety, and because you can't do the sort of container-managed JPA Blueprint made possible with Declarative Services.)

```
-include= ~../common.props

Bundle-SymbolicName: fancyfoods.department.cheese
Export-Package:
Private-Package: fancyfoods.dept.cheese*

Service-Component=fancyfoods.cheese.offer; \
 implementation:=fancyfoods.dept.cheese.offers.DesperateCheeseOffer;\
 provide:=fancyfoods.offers.SpecialOffer;\
 enabled:=true; \
 inventory=fancyfoods.food.Inventory
```

If you drop the rebuilt cheese bundle into your Aries assembly's load directory in place of the original cheese bundle, you should find everything works exactly as before. The cheese offer gets to the Service Registry by a different mechanism, but the service is the same. (Don't forget, you'll need to add a Declarative Services implementation to your Aries assembly.)

Just as there's more to bnd files than generating better manifests, there's more to bnd than building. Bnd is also useful for working with existing conventional JARs and bundles. You'll see more about these parts of bnd in section 12.1.3.

Although bnd on its own is useful, its mechanisms for specifying classpaths and build paths are fairly limited. Some large projects build with bnd alone, but most opt to use one of the bnd integrations with more general build tools. The bnd project provides Ant tasks, and it's also extremely well integrated with Maven through the bundle plug-in.

8.2.2 *The Maven bundle plug-in*

Maven considerably simplifies the dependency management required when building with Ant. If Maven is your build tool of choice, you'll find that the decision about whether to control your manifests directly or generate manifests automatically has been mostly made for you. Although it's technically possible to use Maven to build bundles while using existing manifests—and the sample code for the earlier chapters of this book did that—it's not a natural way of using Maven. (If you need convincing, you need only to look at the build scripts packaged with the sample code!)

In many ways, Maven is a natural fit with OSGi, because Maven's modules and dependencies map relatively neatly to OSGi bundles. Both modules and bundles are uniquely identified by their symbolic names and versions. Maven's bundle plug-in combines *module-level* (or bundle-level) dependencies declared in the pom.xml with bnd bytecode analysis to produce OSGi manifests that declare package-level dependencies. The convenient thing about this process is that it involves almost no extra work compared to normal Maven JAR packaging.

Let's see what the pom.xml file looks like for a simple bundle with no external dependencies, `fancyfoods.api`, in this listing.

Listing 8.2 The pom.xml build file for the `fancyfoods.api` bundle

```
<project xmlns="http://maven.apache.org/POM/4.0.0"
        xmlns:xsi="http://www.w3.org/2001/XMLSchema-instance"
        xsi:schemaLocation="http://maven.apache.org/POM/4.0.0
        http://maven.apache.org/xsd/maven-4.0.0.xsd">

    <modelVersion>4.0.0</modelVersion>
    <groupId>fancyfoods</groupId>
    <artifactId>fancyfoods.api</artifactId>          The critical bit that
    <packaging>bundle</packaging>                    enables bundle plug-in
    <version>1.0.0</version>
    <name>Fancy Foods API</name>

    <build>
        <plugins>
            <plugin>
                <groupId>org.apache.felix</groupId>
                <artifactId>maven-bundle-plugin</artifactId>
                <version>2.2.0</version>              ❶ Configure what
                <extensions>true</extensions>            goes in generated
                <configuration>                          manifest
                    <instructions>
                        <Bundle-SymbolicName>
                          ${pom.artifactId}
                        </Bundle-SymbolicName>
                        <Bundle-Name>
                          ${pom.name}
                        </Bundle-Name>
                        <Bundle-Version>
                          ${pom.version}
                        </Bundle-Version>
                        <Export-Package>
                            fancyfoods.food,          Versions from
                            fancyfoods.offers         package-info files
                        </Export-Package>
                    </instructions>
                </configuration>
            </plugin>                                 API bundle has no
        </plugins>                                    dependencies

    </build>
</project>
```

The manifest generation is controlled by the plug-in configuration for the bundle plug-in ❶. We've kept all the plug-in configuration in the same file for clarity, but it's more likely you'd want to move the generic parts of it up to a parent pom. Almost anything that can go into a bnd file can be added—in XML form—to the bundle plug-in configuration, and the cautions that apply to writing bnd files also apply to configuring the bundle plug-in.

TAKING ADVANTAGE OF DEFAULTS
The Maven bundle plug-in uses the information available elsewhere in the pom file to provide some nice defaults. If you don't specify the bundle symbolic name, the plug-in will construct it from the group ID and default ID. In general, it will be `${pom.groupId}.${pom.artifactId}`, but overlaps between the group ID and artifact ID will be stripped out. Maven will automatically use the artifact ID and version for the JAR name, but it's good OSGi practice to use the symbolic name (and version) for the JAR names. Therefore, we suggest ensuring that your artifact ID matches your intended bundle symbolic name. For example, to get a bundle symbolic name of `fancyfoods.api` and a JAR name of fancyfoods.api-1.0.0.jar, choose an artifact ID of `fancyfoods.api` and a group ID of `fancyfoods`.

The bundle version will be set to the module version. Similarly, the bundle name, description, and license will all be taken from ones specified elsewhere in the pom.

The bundle plug-in also overrides some of the more counterintuitive bnd defaults for what's included in and exported by the bundle, because it's able to distinguish between your local Java source and the binaries on your classpath. It assumes that you do want to export packages you provided the source code for, but don't want to export all the other packages on your classpath. Packages containing `impl` or `internal` in the name won't be exported. Recent versions of the bundle plug-in default `<Private-Package>` to include classes in the module, rather than the empty default you get with raw bnd.

> **WARNING: THE IMPORTANCE OF DOUBLE-CHECKING** As with plain bnd, it's a good idea to validate your configuration of the bundle plug-in by having a look in the bundle that comes out and making sure the manifest is what you hoped for, and there aren't too many or too few classes packaged into the JAR.

You may find that, with bundles that are using service dependencies instead of package dependencies, even the bundle plug-in's defaults are too generous and you'll need to restrict the exports further. In listing 8.2, they're listed explicitly. Versions will be inferred from package-info files, as we discussed in section 8.2.1.

ENTERPRISE OSGI AND THE BUNDLE PLUG-IN
You can also add any other custom headers you need as XML elements. This enables enterprise OSGi headers like `Meta-Persistence:` to enable container-managed JPA, or `Bundle-Blueprint:` file to point to a Blueprint file.

To see how the nondefault headers work in a pom, let's have a look at the pom file for the persistence bundle. This is a more complex pom than the API pom, because the persistence bundle has a Blueprint configuration and dependencies on other bundles. But using the bundle plug-in's defaults can reduce the amount of configuration it needs, as shown next.

Listing 8.3 A sample pom.xml for the `fancyfoods.department.cheese` bundle

```xml
<project xmlns="http://maven.apache.org/POM/4.0.0"
    xmlns:xsi="http://www.w3.org/2001/XMLSchema-instance"
    xsi:schemaLocation="http://maven.apache.org/POM/4.0.0
    http://maven.apache.org/xsd/maven-4.0.0.xsd">
    <modelVersion>4.0.0</modelVersion>
    <groupId>fancyfoods</groupId>
    <artifactId>fancyfoods.persistence</artifactId>
    <packaging>bundle</packaging>
    <version>1.0.0</version>
    <name>Fancy Foods Persistence Bundle</name>
    <build>
        <plugins>
            <plugin>
                <groupId>org.apache.felix</groupId>
                <artifactId>maven-bundle-plugin</artifactId>
                <version>2.2.0</version>
                <extensions>true</extensions>              ◁──┐ Accept defaults for bundle
                <configuration>                               ┘ name and version
                    <instructions>

                        <Export-Package />      ◁── No package exports

                        <Meta-Persistence>
                            META-INF/persistence.xml    ◁── Add header and value
                        </Meta-Persistence>
                    </instructions>
                </configuration>
            </plugin>
        </plugins>
    </build>

    <dependencies>                                  ┌ Standard Maven
        <dependency>                              ◁─┤ dependencies on
            <groupId>fancyfoods</groupId>           └ other bundles
            <artifactId>fancyfoods.api</artifactId>
            <version>1.0.0</version>
            <scope>provided</scope>
        </dependency>
        <dependency>
            <groupId>org.apache.geronimo.specs</groupId>
            <artifactId>geronimo-jpa_2.0_spec</artifactId>
            <version>1.1</version>
        </dependency>
        <dependency>
            <groupId>org.apache.geronimo.specs</groupId>
            <artifactId>geronimo-jta_1.1_spec</artifactId>
            <version>1.1.1</version>
        </dependency>
    </dependencies>
</project>
```

You'll notice we didn't add a `<Bundle-Blueprint>` element. Although there's nothing stopping you adding this header, the bundle plug-in is smart enough to hunt out Blueprint files and automatically add the `Bundle-Blueprint:` headers for you.

The `org.osgi.service.blueprint` dependency

If you look at the manifest generated for you by the bundle plug-in, you'll see an extra imported package, `org.osgi.service.blueprint`. Where did this import come from? When the Maven bundle plug-in detects that your bundle uses Blueprint, it will automatically add that package dependency. Although this package doesn't include any code, the Blueprint specification encourages Blueprint bundles to import it to ensure that Blueprint is available in their runtime environment. (The specification also insists that Blueprint implementations must export this package.) If you need your bundle to run in non-Blueprint environments too, you can make the package optional by specifying it explicitly in your pom:

```
<Import-Package>
  org.osgi.service.blueprint;resolution:=optional
</Import-Package>
```

If you're using code-first development, you've got a lot of build tools open to you. You can use bnd on its own, you can use it in combination with Ant, or you can use the powerful Maven build plug-in. If you're doing manifest-first development, you have a similar choice between Ant and Maven. Several tools allow manifest-first building using Ant, although most involve some degree of duplication of information with the IDE. There's also a nice set of Maven plug-ins that neatly share information with the Eclipse PDE IDE.

8.2.3   *Ant and Eclipse PDE*

With manifest-first development, one of the main challenges of building an OSGi bundle vanishes; there's no need for the tools to work out a manifest, because you've already written one. But it's still necessary to work out a classpath for compiling. Ideally, this classpath should be the same as the one used by the Eclipse IDE, without having to duplicate it between IDE and command-line environments. For bonus points, the compile stage should pay attention to the manifest and only allow imported packages onto the compile-time classpath.

THE ECLIPSE HEADLESS BUILD

It turns out that this is a challenging set of requirements. The only Ant tool that fully satisfies them is a miniaturized headless version of the IDE.

Despite running without a GUI, the Eclipse headless build is fairly heavyweight. Even projects that want to take advantage of Eclipse's metadata often try to build without the direct dependency on the Eclipse runtime. The Eclipse headless build is also fairly inflexible, so integrating extra build steps like coverage instrumentation or custom packaging can be painful.

OSGIJC

An alternative to the Eclipse headless build is a third-party tool called osgijc. Osgijc is a replacement for the Ant `<javac>` task that reads the contents of an Eclipse .classpath file and adds it to the compile classpath. Users will need to manually add in their own classpath entries for bundles that haven't been explicitly included in the .classpath file. The most convenient way of doing this is to add the directory containing the target runtime to the Ant classpath.

Unlike the Eclipse headless build, osgijc doesn't validate that a bundle imports all the packages it needs to compile, or that those packages have been exported by some other bundle. Despite the name, osgijc does a conventional Java compile in a flat and open class space.

The osgijc tool, therefore, relies on manifest validation having been done earlier, in the IDE environment. If team members inadvertently deliver code that couldn't compile in Eclipse because of missing manifest imports or exports, osgijc will build the broken bundle without complaint. Problems will only be discovered during the test phase when classes can't be loaded.

ROLLING YOUR OWN, CHEATING, AND OTHER OPTIONS

The osgijc tool isn't complex, and many teams opt to roll their own Ant tasks to consume Eclipse metadata instead. Parsing the Eclipse .classpath file allows you to identify what other projects need to be on an individual project's classpath, and then you can bulk-add the bundles from the target OSGi environment. If you're feeling enthusiastic, you can even read in all the .classpath files to work out the right order to build the projects, so that all the dependencies get built in the right order. But unless you parse the MANIFEST.MF files themselves (at which point you're venturing dangerously close to writing your own OSGi framework), you'll still be dependent on the Eclipse IDE to validate that the manifests are as they should be.

A more basic approach, which can be effective for many smaller projects, is to manually maintain both the IDE .classpath and Ant or Maven build files in parallel. Although this violates the software engineering practice of not writing anything down more than once, you may find it's a simple and pragmatic solution to getting things building. (This is how the Fancy Foods sample code is built, for example.)

8.2.4 *Maven Tycho*

Although most attempts to build OSGi bundles from Eclipse projects have focused on Ant, a promising new project called Eclipse Tycho brings together Eclipse and Maven. Tycho reuses Eclipse metadata to keep pom files small and ensure that automated builds behave the same way as builds within the IDE. Tycho appears to be providing a *true* manifest-first OSGi build, rather than building in a flat classpath and relying on the IDE to catch manifest problems.

Because it's so tightly integrated with Eclipse PDE, Tycho is a peculiar hybrid of Maven and Eclipse. Many familiar Maven idioms have disappeared. The default disk layout for source and resources is an Eclipse layout, rather than a Maven one. You no longer need to use <dependency> sections to declare your dependencies—Tycho ignores them. Although Maven repositories still have their place, how they're used and what gets put into them are different. If you're a long-time Maven user, you may find the Tycho experience unsettling; but if your heart lies with Eclipse, Tycho will feel warm and comforting, like an old pair of slippers.

Because it's so different from conventional Maven, Tycho works best if you've already got your projects set up in Eclipse, but haven't yet written an automated build for them. If you already have everything laid out on disk in the standard Maven way, you can make Tycho work with Maven's build layouts, but it will require extra plug-in configuration.

Tycho is a Maven plug-in, so getting started with Tycho is easy. All you'll need is Maven 3 and a pom file. One of the nice things about Tycho is that Tycho poms are small, especially if you put the plug-in configuration in a parent pom (which we haven't done here!). Almost all of the information needed to build the plug-in is shared between the IDE and the build tooling.

Listing 8.4 The pom.xml file for a Tycho build of the `fancyfoods.business` bundle

```
<project xmlns="http://maven.apache.org/POM/4.0.0"
    xmlns:xsi="http://www.w3.org/2001/XMLSchema-instance"
    xsi:schemaLocation="http://maven.apache.org/POM/4.0.0
    http://maven.apache.org/xsd/maven-4.0.0.xsd">
    <modelVersion>4.0.0</modelVersion>
    <groupId>fancyfoods</groupId>
    <artifactId>fancyfoods.department.cheese</artifactId>      To generate bundle,
    <packaging>eclipse-plugin</packaging>                      use eclipse-plugin
    <version>1.0.0</version>                                   packaging
    <name>Fancy Foods Cheese Department Bundle</name>

    <build>                                                    Tycho plug-in
        <plugins>                                             must be explicitly
            <plugin>                                          referenced
                <groupId>org.eclipse.tycho</groupId>
                <artifactId>tycho-maven-plugin</artifactId>
                <version>0.12.0</version>
                <extensions>true</extensions>
            </plugin>
        </plugins>
    </build>
</project>
```

Like Eclipse PDE, Tycho uses the terms *plug-in* and *bundle* somewhat interchangeably, so to build a normal bundle, you'll have to use Tycho's eclipse-plugin packaging type. Don't worry, Tycho will build you a standard OSGi bundle, despite the name!

Almost all of the information about how your bundle should be built is drawn from the bundle manifest and the eclipse metadata, rather than the pom. This avoids duplication, and it has the added bonus that you can use Eclipse's nice tools (which we'll come to in section 9.1.1) to control things. The symbolic name and version strings should exactly match the ones in your manifest, but that's the only information you'll need to duplicate.

You may need to adjust your Eclipse build.properties file (using the Eclipse GUI or a text editor) to ensure nonstandard resources like the OSGI-INF folder are included in the built JAR.

Unlike many OSGi-aware build solutions, Tycho fully honors your bundle manifest at compile time. It doesn't take the common shortcut of working out what bundles should be on the classpath, and then treating that classpath as a flat classpath after that. Tycho uses the rules of OSGi to work out what's visible to your plug-in.

But how does Tycho work out what should be on the classpath in the first place? You'll notice that there's no <dependency> section in the pom.xml—any <dependency> elements are ignored. The answer is that Tycho *provisions* as it builds your plug-ins.

PROVISIONING

Provisioning is nothing new for Maven users—every time Maven downloads a JAR from the Maven repository, it's provisioning—but the way Tycho provisions is both sophisticated and convenient. Dependencies are implicitly declared by Import-Package: statements, rather than explicitly declared with <dependency> elements. Tycho will look for bundles with matching package exports in its repository.

Where do the repositories come from? Tycho can't provision against a normal Maven repository, because it doesn't know which bundles export which packages. Clearly, downloading *everything* in the Maven repository to read all the bundle manifests isn't practical. (You may suspect your normal Maven builds already download *everything*, but trust us, there's more in there!)

When Tycho runs the *install* goal, it adds extra metadata to the local Maven repository along with the built bundles. This metadata allows it to quickly identify and download bundles with appropriate package exports when building. For example, this allows it to work out that it should add the fancyfoods.api bundle to the classpath when building the fancyfoods.cheese.department bundle (assuming you built the api bundle first, using Tycho!).

But you're not going to build all your external dependencies using Tycho before trying to build your product. Tycho can be configured to provision against external repositories. Unfortunately, these repositories must be in the p2 format. (For a refresher on p2, see section 7.3.2). Although p2 repositories are widely available for Eclipse-based projects, the format isn't common outside the Eclipse ecosystem. This limits the utility of Tycho for non-Eclipse-based OSGi development. But with elbow grease you can make Tycho provisioning work for enterprise OSGi, and you may find the benefits of Tycho outweigh the clunkiness of getting the provisioning going.

You have two options for making your external dependencies visible to Tycho's provisioner. The first is to step back to a slightly modified version of Maven's normal dependency declarations. The other is to generate your own p2 repository.

USING MAVEN DEPENDENCIES

Although Tycho normally ignores Maven's <dependency> elements, it can be configured to consider them in its provisioning by adding the following plug-in configuration:

```
<plugin>
    <groupId>org.eclipse.tycho</groupId>
    <artifactId>target-platform-configuration</artifactId>
    <version>${tycho-version}</version>
    <configuration>
        <resolver>p2</resolver>
        <pomDependencies>consider</pomDependencies>
    </configuration>
</plugin>
```

Sadly, at the time of writing, Tycho would not resolve transitive dependencies (the dependencies of your dependencies). This means you'll have to list more dependencies in your pom files than you would if you weren't using Tycho! But you may find that listing the dependencies isn't too onerous if you list all the external dependencies for your project in a single parent pom file. Internal dependencies will still be handled automatically by Tycho.

You may find that managing your dependency list quickly becomes tedious. One way of managing it is to write scripts that autogenerate it from your runtime environment. Files in the JAR's META-INF/maven folder can be used to work out every JAR's group and artifact ID, and so you can work out a complete <dependencies> element by scanning every JAR in the deploy directory.

Generating your own p2 repository

Another option is to bypass the <considerDependencies> route entirely and generate your own p2 repository. Eclipse provides command-line tools for doing this. Generating your repository directly from your runtime environment has some advantages over normal Maven dependency management; because you know the compile-time environment is identical to the runtime environment, you don't risk building bundles that compile against the latest and greatest available from a Maven repository, but then fail miserably at runtime when required bundles are either back-level or missing entirely.

To generate the p2 repository, you'll first need to copy all your runtime bundles into a folder called plugins, inside a holding folder, ${bundles.dir}. Then run the following command

```
${eclipse.home}/eclipse -nosplash -application
  org.eclipse.equinox.p2.publisher.FeaturesAndBundlesPublisher
  -metadataRepository file:${repository.dir}
  -artifactRepository file:${repository.dir}
  -source ${bundles.dir} -compress -publishArtifacts
```

where ${eclipse.home} is an Eclipse installation and ${repository.dir} is the output directory for your repository.

You now have a p2 repository that exactly represents the bundles available in your runtime environment. To configure Tycho to use it, add the following to your pom.xml (or to a parent pom.xml):

```
<repositories>
    <repository>
        <id>runtime-environment</id>
```

```
            <layout>p2</layout>
            <url>file://${repository.dir}</url>
        </repository>
</repositories>
```

In section 8.2.2, we described how the Maven bundle plug-in could automatically find Blueprint files. As far as we know, the Tycho plug-in hasn't achieved this level of support for enterprise OSGi. But whether you're using Tycho or the bundle plug-in, Maven does have some more enterprise OSGi tricks up its sleeve.

8.2.5 *The Maven EBA plug-in*

Apache Aries provides a useful Maven plug-in for building EBA archives. All dependencies listed in the EBA pom are zipped up into a generated .eba file.

Listing 8.5   The pom.xml file to build the Fancy Foods EBA

```
<project
    xmlns="http://maven.apache.org/POM/4.0.0"
    xmlns:xsi="http://www.w3.org/2001/XMLSchema-instance"
    xsi:schemaLocation="http://maven.apache.org/POM/4.0.0
    http://maven.apache.org/xsd/maven-4.0.0.xsd">
    <modelVersion>4.0.0</modelVersion>
    <groupId>fancyfoods</groupId>
    <artifactId>fancyfoods.application</artifactId>      ← Packaging is EBA
    <packaging>eba</packaging>
    <version>1.0.0</version>
    <name>Fancy Foods Application</name>

    <dependencies>
        <dependency>
            <groupId>fancyfoods</groupId>
            <artifactId>fancyfoods.api</artifactId>
            <version>1.0.0</version>                     ← More EBA contents
        </dependency>
    </dependencies>

    ...

    <build>
        <plugins>
            <plugin>                                     ← EBA plug-in must be referenced
                <groupId>org.apache.aries</groupId>
                <artifactId>eba-maven-plugin</artifactId>
                <extensions>true</extensions>            ← By default, no manifest is generated
                <configuration>
                    <generateManifest>true</generateManifest>
                </configuration>
            </plugin>
        </plugins>
    </build>
</project>
```

By default, the EBA plug-in will look for an APPLICATION.MF file in src/main/resources/META-INF. If none is found, it won't include an application manifest (don't worry, the manifest is optional, so your application will still work). To have the EBA plug-in automatically generate a manifest based on the .eba contents and the pom symbolic name, set `generateManifest` to true.

Whichever style of OSGi build you go for—manifest-first or bundle-first, Maven or Ant, tightly integrated to your IDE or relatively standalone—compiling and packaging up your OSGi bundles and applications should only be the first half of your build automation. The second, equally important, half is automated testing. As with compiling, testing OSGi bundles presents some unique challenges, and a range of tools have sprung up to help.

8.3   *Testing OSGi applications*

If you're like a lot of developers, you'll probably divide your testing into a few phases. The lowest-level tests you'll run are simple unit tests that exercise individual classes, but not their interactions with one another. The next group of tests in your test hierarchy are the integration tests, which test the operation of your application. Finally, at the highest level, you may have system tests, which test the complete system, preferably in an environment that's close to your production one.

When you're testing OSGi bundles, each of these types of testing requires a different approach—different from the other phases, and also different from how you'd do similar testing for an application intended to run on a Java EE server or standalone. We'll start by discussing unit testing, because that's the simplest case in many ways. We'll then show you some tools and strategies that we hope you'll find useful for integration and system testing.

Unit testing OSGi bundles is straightforward, but you'll find you've got choices to make, and a bewildering array of tool options when you start looking at integration testing. The good news is that if you've already decided how to build your bundles, some of the choices about how best to test them will have been made for you. The bad news is that you've still got a few choices! Figure 8.2 shows some of these choices.

8.3.1   *Unit testing OSGi*

By definition, unit tests are designed to run in the simplest possible environment. The purest unit tests have only the class you're testing and any required interfaces on the classpath. In practice, you'll probably also include classes that are closely related to the class that's being tested, and possibly even some external implementation classes. But unit tests needn't—and shouldn't—require big external infrastructure like an OSGi framework.

How can code that's written to take advantage of the great things OSGi offers work without OSGi? How can such code be tested? Luckily, the answer is *easily*.

MOCKING OUT
If you followed our advice in chapter 5, you probably don't have many explicit dependencies on OSGi classes in your code. The enterprise OSGi features of your runtime environment will ideally be handling most of the direct contact with the OSGi libraries for you.

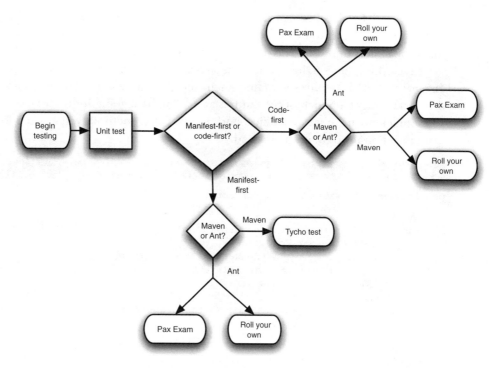

Figure 8.2 Testing OSGi applications can be done in many ways. Any test process should include a simple unit test phase, but the best way to do integration testing depends on a number of factors, including which build tools are already being used.

Even if you need to reference OSGi classes directly, you may feel more comfortable writing your application so that it doesn't have too many explicit OSGi dependencies. After all, loose coupling is good, even when the coupling is to a framework as fabulous as OSGi.

If you do have direct OSGi dependencies, using mocking frameworks to mock out OSGi classes like BundleContext can be helpful. You can even mock up service lookups, although if you're using Blueprint or Declarative Services you'll probably rarely have cause to use the OSGi services API directly. Using Blueprint has a lot of testability advantages beyond eliminating direct OSGi dependencies.

BLUEPRINT-DRIVEN TESTING

One of the nice side effects of dependency injection frameworks like Blueprint is that unit testing becomes much easier. Although Blueprint won't do your testing for you, testing code that was written with Blueprint in mind is an awful lot easier than otherwise.

Separating out the logic to look up or construct dependencies from the work of doing *things* with those dependencies allows dependencies to be stubbed out without affecting the main control flow you're trying to test. The key is to realize that although you certainly need a Blueprint framework to be present to run your application end to end, you don't need it at all to test components of the application in isolation.

Instead, your test harness can inject carefully managed dependencies into the code you're trying to test. You can even inject mock objects instead of real objects, which would be almost impossible if your intercomponent links were all hard-wired.

To see this in action, look at the `DesperateCheeseOffer` again. It depends on the `Inventory`, which requires container-managed JPA and a functioning database. You don't want to get a bunch of JPA entities and a database going for a unit test. Instead, you'll mock up an `Inventory` object and use the setter methods you created for Blueprint injection for unit testing instead.

Listing 8.6   Using mocked injection to unit test the desperate cheese offer

```
public class DesperateCheeseOfferTest {

    @Test
    public void testOfferReturnsCorrectFood() {            Use Mockito to
        Food food = mock(Food.class);                      mock out classes
        when(food.getName()).thenReturn("Green cheese");
        Inventory inventory = mock(Inventory.class);
        List<Food> foods = new ArrayList<Food>();
        foods.add(food);
        when(inventory.getFoodsWhoseNameContains("cheese", 1))
                .thenReturn(foods);                        Initialize
                                                           cheese
        DesperateCheeseOffer offer = new DesperateCheeseOffer();    offer
        offer.setInventory(inventory);

        assertNotNull(offer.getOfferFood());
        assertEquals("Green cheese", offer.getOfferFood().getName());
    }
}                                                      Test that cheese offer
                                                       behaves as expected
```

This sort of testing allows you to verify that if the injected `Inventory` object behaves as expected, the `DesperateCheeseOffer` does the right thing. You could also add more complex tests that confirmed that the cheese offer tolerated the case when `Inventory` had no cheeses in it at all, or the case when there was more than one cheese present in the inventory.

Although tests running outside an OSGi framework are straightforward and can spot a range of problems, there are several classes of problems they can't detect. In particular, unit tests will still continue to run cleanly, even if bundles fail to start or Blueprint services never get injected. To catch these issues, you'll also want to test the end-to-end behavior of your application, inside an OSGi framework.

How closely this OSGi framework matches your production environment is a matter of taste. You may choose to do automated integration testing in a minimal environment, and follow it up with a final system test in a mirror of your production system. Alternatively, you may find you flush more problems out more quickly if you test in a more fully featured environment. The tools and techniques we'll describe for testing inside an OSGi environment are broadly suitable for both integration and system testing.

8.3.2 *Pax Exam*

The gold standard for OSGi testing tools is a tool called Pax Exam. Pax Exam is part of a suite of OSGi-related tools developed by the OPS4J open source community. In contrast to other open source communities like the Apache and Eclipse Foundations, OPS4J has an interestingly flat structure that emphasizes open participation as well as open consumption. There's no notion of a *committer*, no barrier to committing source changes, and little internal hierarchy.

Pax Exam builds on other tools developed by OPS4J, such as Pax Runner, to provide a sophisticated framework for launching JUnit—or TestNG—tests inside an OSGi framework and collecting the results. Under the covers, the Pax Exam framework wraps test classes into a bundle (using bnd to generate the manifest), and then automatically exposes the tests as OSGi services. Pax Exam then invokes each test in turn and records the results.

HOW CLEAN IS YOUR FRAMEWORK?

By default, Pax Exam will start a fresh framework for each test method, which means Pax Exam tests may run slowly if you've got a lot of them. In recent versions, you can speed things up—at the risk of interesting side effects—by specifying an `@ExamReactor-Strategy` annotation. You can also choose whether Pax Exam launches the OSGi frameworks inside the main JVM or forks a new JVM for each framework, and runs tests by RMI (Remote Method Invocation). Not spawning a new JVM makes things far faster, and it also means you can debug your tests without having to attach remote debuggers. But many of the more useful options for configuring frameworks are only supported for the remote framework case.

Which container to use is determined by which container you list in your Maven dependency. To use the quicker nonforking container, add the following dependency:

```
<dependency>
    <groupId>org.ops4j.pax.exam</groupId>
    <artifactId>pax-exam-container-native</artifactId>
    <version>${paxexamversion}</version>
    <scope>test</scope>
</dependency>
```

To use the more powerful, but slower, Pax Runner–based container, specify the following:

```
<dependency>
    <groupId>org.ops4j.pax.exam</groupId>
    <artifactId>pax-exam-container-paxrunner</artifactId>
    <version>${paxexamversion}</version>
    <scope>test</scope>
</dependency>
```

ENABLING TESTS FOR PAX EXAM

A JUnit test intended for Pax Exam has a few key differences from one that runs standalone. Running your test code in an entirely different JVM from the one used to launch the test, with RMI and all sorts of network communication going on in the middle, isn't something the normal JUnit test runner is designed to handle. You'll need to run with a special Pax Exam runner instead by adding a class-level annotation:

```
@RunWith(org.ops4j.pax.exam.junit.JUnit4TestRunner.class)
```

Pax Exam can also inject a bundle context into your test class:

```
import javax.inject.Inject;
    @Inject
    protected BundleContext ctx;
```

> **WARNING: WHY IS NOTHING BEING INJECTED?** If you're using Pax Exam injection, make sure to use the `javax.inject.Inject` annotation and not `org.ops4j.pax.exam.Inject`. The Pax Exam annotation is nonfunctional in Pax Exam 2.0 and up.

It's a good pattern to use the bundle context for querying the state of the framework, but to use Pax Exam's API to configure the framework and install bundles.

CONFIGURING A FRAMEWORK

Pax Exam configuration of the framework is done in a method annotated `@Configuration`. Pax Exam provides a fluent API for building up configuration options and gives you detailed control over the contents and configuration of your OSGi framework. You can specify the OSGi framework implementation (Equinox, Felix, Knopflerfish) and version, or any combination of implementations and versions, system properties, and installed bundles. You can specify a list of bundles to install, as well as JVM options, and OSGi frameworks. All of these can be controlled using methods statically imported from `org.ops4j.pax.exam.CoreOptions` and combined into an array using the `CoreOptions.options()` method:

```
@Configuration
public static Option[] configuration() {
    MavenArtifactProvisionOption foodGroup = mavenBundle().groupId(
            "fancyfoods");
    Option[] fancyFoodsBundles = options(
            foodGroup.artifactId("fancyfoods.department.cheese").
                version("1.0.0"),
            foodGroup.artifactId("fancyfoods.api").
                version("1.0.0"),
            foodGroup.artifactId("fancyfoods.persistence").
                version("1.0.0"),
            foodGroup.artifactId("fancyfoods.datasource").
                version("1.0.0"));
    Option[] server = PaxConfigurer.getServerPlatform();
    Option[] options = OptionUtils.combine(fancyFoodsBundles,
                                    server);

    return options;
}
```

Here you're installing the `fancyfoods.department.cheese` bundle, along with its dependencies and the bundles that make up the hosting server. Most of your tests will probably run on the same base platform (or platforms), so it's worth pulling out common configuration code into a configuration utility, `PaxConfigurer` in this case. If you do this, you can use `OptionUtils.combine()` to merge the core option array and `Option` varargs parameter into one big array.

Using Maven

Pax Exam is well integrated with Maven, so one of the most convenient ways of specifying bundles to install is using their Maven coordinates and the `CoreOptions.maven-Bundle()` method. Versions can be explicitly specified, pulled from a pom.xml using `versionAsInProject()`, or left implicit to default to the latest version.

Using an existing server install

As well as your application bundles themselves, you'll need to list all the other bundles in your target runtime environment. If you think about using `mavenBundle()` calls to specify every bundle in your server runtime, you may start to feel uneasy. Do you *really* need to list out the Maven coordinates of every bundle in your Aries assembly—or worse yet, every bundle in your full-fledged application server?

Luckily, the answer is *no*—Pax Exam does provide alternate ways of specifying what should get installed into your runtime. You can install Pax Runner or Karaf features if any exist for your server, or point Pax Exam at a directory that contains your server. For testing applications intended to run on a server, this is the most convenient option— you probably don't need to test your application with several different OSGi frameworks or see what happens with different Blueprint implementations, because your application server environment will be well defined. Listing 8.7 shows how to configure a Pax Exam environment based on the Aries assembly you've been using for testing.

Using profiles

Pax Exam also provides some methods to reference convenient sets of bundles, such as a `webProfile()` and a set of `junitBundles()`. Remember that Pax Exam installs only the bundles you tell it to install—your server probably doesn't ship JUnit, so if you point Pax Exam at your server directory, you'll need to add in your test class's JUnit dependencies separately. Because it can be complex, even with profiles, we find it can be convenient to share the code for setting up the test environment. The following listing shows a utility class for setting up a test environment that reproduces the Aries assembly we've been using throughout.

Listing 8.7 A class that provides options that can be shared between tests

```
package fancyfoods.department.cheese.test;

import org.ops4j.pax.exam.Option;
import org.ops4j.pax.exam.options.extra.DirScannerProvisionOption;

import static org.ops4j.pax.exam.CoreOptions.*;

public class PaxConfigurer {

    public static Option[] getServerPlatform() {            Path to Aries
        String ariesAssemblyDir = "$[aries.assembly]/target";  assembly
```

```
        Option bootPackages = bootDelegationPackages(
            "javax.transaction", "javax.transaction.*");
        String f = "*-*.jar";
        DirScannerProvisionOption unfiltered =                      Only include JARs
            scanDir(ariesAssemblyDir);                          ◁─┘ with "-" in name
        Option ariesAsembly = unfiltered.filter(f);
        Option osgiFramework = equinox().version("3.5.0");
        return options(bootPackages, ariesAsembly, junitBundles(),
            osgiFramework);
    }
}
```

Here $[aries.assembly] should be replaced with a path—there's no clever variable substitution going on!

> **WARNING: ONE OSGI FRAMEWORK GOOD, TWO OSGI FRAMEWORKS BAD**   Pax Exam will install all the bundles in the scanned directory into an OSGi framework. Because the scanned directory contains its own OSGi framework bundle, this means you may getting slightly more than you bargained for. Installing one OSGi framework into another is possible, but the classloading gets complicated! To avoid installing multiple frameworks, you can either copy all your server bundles except for the OSGi framework itself to another directory, or rename the OSGi bundle so that it's not captured by your filter. For example, if you rename the bundle to osgi.jar (no dash) and then specify the filter `"*-*.jar"`), Pax Exam will install every JAR except for your framework JAR (assuming all the other JARs have dashes before the version number).

All this setup might seem like a lot of work, and it is. Luckily, once you've done it for one test, writing all your other tests will be much easier.

THE PAX EXAM TEST

What kind of things should you be doing in your tests? The first thing to establish is that your bundles are present, and that they're started. (And if not, why not!) Bundles that haven't started are a common cause of problems in OSGi applications, and if anything, these problems are even more common with Pax Exam because of the complexity of setting up the environment. Despite this, checking bundle states isn't a first-class Pax Exam diagnostic feature. It's worth adding some utility methods in your tests that try to start the bundles in your framework to make sure everything is started, and fail the test if any bundles can't start.

   After this setup verification, what you test will depend on the exact design of your application. Verifying that all your services, including Blueprint ones, are present in the Service Registry is a good next step—and the final step is to make sure your services all behave as expected, for a variety of inputs. The following listing shows a test for the cheese bundle.

Listing 8.8   A Pax Exam integration test

```
@Test
public void testOfferReturnsCorrectFood(BundleContext ctx) {
```

```
        Bundle bundle = getInstalledBundle(ctx,
                      "fancyfoods.department.cheese");
        try {
            bundle.start();
        } catch (BundleException e) {                    If bundle can't start,
            fail(e.toString());                          find out why
        }
        SpecialOffer offer = waitForService(bundle,      Get offer
                          SpecialOffer.class);           service
        assertNotNull("The special offer gave a null food.",
              offer.getOfferFood());
        assertEquals("Wrong food.", "Wensleydale cheese",
            offer.getOfferFood().getName());
    }

    protected Bundle getInstalledBundle(BundleContext ctx, String name) {
        assertNotNull("No bundle context was injected.", ctx);
        for (Bundle b : ctx.getBundles()) {
                System.out.println("Checking bundle " + b);
            if (b.getSymbolicName().equals(name)) {
                return b;
            }
        }
        return null;
    }

    protected <T> T waitForService(Bundle b, Class<T> clazz) {
        try {
            BundleContext bc = b.getBundleContext();
            ServiceTracker st =
                new ServiceTracker(bc, clazz.getName(), null);
            st.open();                                         Give service
            Object service = st.waitForService(30 * 1000);     30 seconds
            assertNotNull("No service of the type " + clazz.getName()  to appear
                    + " was registered.", service);
            st.close();
            return (T) service;
        } catch (Exception e) {
            fail("Failed to register services for " +
                b.getSymbolicName() + e.getMessage());
            return null;
        }
    }
}
```

> **The `ServiceTracker`**
>
> The eagle-eyed among you will have noticed that the test in listing 8.8 uses a `ServiceTracker` to locate the service. We did mention this briefly in section 6.2.1, but for a more detailed explanation we suggest that you look at appendix A.

Unlike normal JUnit test methods, Pax Exam test methods can take an optional `BundleContext` parameter. You can use it to locate the bundles and services you're trying to test.

WARNING: BLUEPRINT AND FAST TESTS   An automated test framework will generally start running tests as soon as the OSGi framework is initialized. This can cause fatal problems when testing Blueprint bundles, because Blueprint initializes asynchronously. At the time you run your first test, half your services may not have been registered! You may find you suffer from perplexing failures, reproducible or intermittent, unless you slow Pax Exam down. Waiting for a Blueprint-driven service is one way of ensuring things are mostly ready, but unfortunately just because one service is enabled doesn't mean they all will be. In the case of the cheese test, waiting for the `SpecialOffer` service will do the trick, because that's the service you're testing.

RUNNING THE TESTS

If you're using Maven, and you keep your test code in Maven's src/test/java folder, your tests will automatically be run when you invoke the `integration-test` or `install` goals. You'll need one of the Pax Exam containers declared as a Maven dependency. If you're using Ant instead, don't worry—Pax Exam also supports Ant.

8.3.3   *Tycho test*

Although Pax Exam is a popular testing framework, it's not the only one. In particular, if you're using Tycho to build your bundles, you're better off using Tycho to test them as well. Tycho offers a nice test framework that in many ways is less complex than Pax Exam.

Tycho is a Maven-based tool, but like Tycho build, Tycho test uses an Eclipse PDE directory layout. Instead of putting your tests in a test folder inside your main bundle, Tycho expects a separate bundle. It relies on naming conventions to find your tests, so you'll need to name your test bundle with a `.tests` suffix.

> **Fragments and OSGi unit testing**
>
> Tools like Pax Exam will generate a bundle for your tests, but with Tycho you've got control of your test bundle. To allow full white-box unit testing of your bundle, you may find it helpful to make the test bundle a fragment of the application bundle. This will allow it to share a classloader with the application bundle and drive all classes, even those that aren't exported.

CONFIGURING A TEST FRAMEWORK

Tycho will use your bundle's package imports to provision required bundles into the test platform. Like any provisioning that relies solely on package dependencies, it's unlikely that all the bundles your application needs to function properly will be provisioned. API bundles will be provisioned, but service providers probably won't be. It's certain that the runtime environment for your bundle won't be exactly the same as the server you eventually intend to deploy on.

To ensure Tycho provisions all your required bundles, you can add them to your test bundle's manifest using `Require-Bundle`. (At this point, you may be remembering that in chapter 5 we strongly discouraged using `Require-Bundle`. We're making an exception here because it's such a handy provisioning shortcut, and it's only test code. We won't tell, if you don't!)

Tycho will automatically provision any dependencies of your required bundles, so you won't need to include your entire runtime platform. But you may find the list is long enough that it's a good idea to make one shared `test.dependencies` bundle whose only function is to require your test platform. All your other test bundles can require the `test.dependencies` bundle.

Your test bundles will almost certainly have a dependency on JUnit, so you'll need to add in one of the main Eclipse p2 repositories to your pom so that Tycho can provision the JUnit bundle:

```
<repository>
    <id>eclipse-helios</id>
    <layout>p2</layout>
    <url>http://download.eclipse.org/releases/helios</url>
</repository>
```

As with Pax Exam, you may find it takes you a few tries to get the Tycho runtime platform right. Until you've got a reliable platform definition, you may spend more time debugging platform issues than legitimate failures. Don't be deterred—having a set of solid tests will pay back the effort many times over, we promise!

8.3.4 Rolling your own test framework

So far, the OSGi testing tools we've discussed have all provided some way of integrating a unit test framework, like JUnit, into an OSGi runtime. To do this they've required you to do some fairly elaborate definition and configuration of this runtime, either in test code (Pax Exam) or in Maven scripts and manifest files (Tycho). Sometimes the benefits of running JUnit inside an OSGi framework don't justify the complexity of getting everything set up to achieve this.

Instead of using a specialized OSGi testing framework, some developers rely on much more low-tech or hand-rolled solutions. A bundle running inside an OSGi framework can't interact with a JUnit runner without help, but this doesn't mean it can't interact with the outside world. It can provide a bundle activator or eager Blueprint bean to write out files, or it can expose a servlet and write status to a web page. Your test code can find the file or hit the servlet and parse the output to work out if everything is behaving as expected. It can even use a series of JUnit tests that hit different servlets or read different log files, so that you can take advantage of all your existing JUnit reporting infrastructure.

This method of testing OSGi applications always feels a little inelegant to us, but it can work well as a pragmatic test solution. Separating out the launching of the framework from the test code makes it much easier to align the framework with your production system. You can use your production system as is, to host the test bundles. It's also much easier to debug configuration problems if the framework doesn't start as expected. Both authors have witnessed the sorry spectacle of confused Pax Exam users shouting at an innocent laptop, "Where's my bundle? And why won't you tell me that six bundles in my framework failed to start?" at the end of a long day's testing.

If you're planning to deploy your enterprise OSGi application on one of the bigger and more muscular application servers, you may find that it's more application server than you need for your integration testing. In this case, you may be better off preparing a sandbox environment for testing, either by physically assembling one, or by working out the right minimum set of dependencies.

The Aries assembly you've been using to run the examples through the course of the book is a good example of a hand-assembled OSGi runtime. You've started with a simple Equinox OSGi framework and added in the bundles needed to support the enterprise OSGi programming model. Alternatively, there are several open source projects that aim to provide lightweight and flexible OSGi runtimes.

PAX RUNNER

Pax Runner is a slim container for launching OSGi frameworks and provisioning bundles. We've already met Pax Runner in section 8.3.2 because Pax Exam relies heavily on Pax Runner to configure and launch its OSGi framework. You may find it easier to bypass Pax Exam and use Pax Runner directly as a test environment. Pax Runner comes with a number of predefined profiles, which can be preloaded into the framework. For example, to launch an OSGi framework that's capable of running simple web applications, it's sufficient to use this command:

```
pax-run.sh --profiles=web
```

At the time of writing, there isn't a Pax Runner profile that fully supports the enterprise OSGi programming model. But profiles are text files that list bundle locations, so it's simple to write your own profiles. These profiles can be shared between members of your development team, which is nice, and fed to Pax Exam for automated testing, which is even nicer. Pax Runner also integrates with Eclipse PDE, so you can use the same framework in your automated testing and your development-time testing:

```
pax-run.sh --file:///yourprofile.txt
```

Although Pax Runner is described as a provisioning tool, it can't provision bundles like the provisioners we discussed in chapter 7. You'll need to list every bundle you want to include in your profile file.

KARAF

An alternative to Pax Runner, with slightly more dynamic provisioning behavior, is Apache Karaf. Like the name implies, Karaf is a little OSGi container. Karaf has some handy features that are missing in Pax Runner, like hot deployment and runtime provisioning. This functionality makes Karaf suitable for use as a production runtime, rather than as a test container. Karaf is so suitable for production, it underpins the Apache Geronimo server. But Karaf isn't as well integrated into existing unit test frameworks as Pax Runner, so if you use Karaf for your testing you'll mostly be limited to the "use JUnit to scrape test result logs" approach we described above.

Karaf has a lot of support for Apache Aries, which makes it a convenient environment for developing and testing enterprise OSGi applications. So well integrated is Karaf with Aries, Karaf comes with Blueprint support by default. Even better, if you list the OSGi bundles using the `osgi:list`, there's a special column that shows each bundle's Blueprint status.

Hot deployment

Like the little Aries assembly we've been using, Karaf can install bundles from the file-system dynamically. Karaf monitors the ${karaf.home}/deploy directory, and will silently install any bundles (or feature definitions) dropped into it. To confirm which bundles are installed and see their status, you can use the `list` command.

Karaf features

Karaf features, like Pax Runner profiles, are precanned groups of bundles that can easily be installed. As an added bonus, Karaf features have been written for many of the Apache Aries components. To see all the available features, type `features:list`. To install new features, type `features:install -v` (the `-v` option does a verbose install). To get a working Apache Aries runtime with Karaf features, it's sufficient to execute the following commands:

```
features:install -v war
  features:install -v jpa
  features:install -v transaction
  features:install -v jndi
```

You'll also need to enable the HTTP server by creating a file called ${karaf.home}/etc/org.ops4j.pax.web.cfg and specifying an HTTP port:

```
org.osgi.service.http.port=8080
```

To get the Fancy Foods application going, the final step is to install a database by copying one into the deploy directory, and then copy your Fancy Foods JARs into the deploy directory. You can also install the bundles from the console using Maven coordinates.

The Karaf console is nice, but it doesn't lend itself so well to automation. Luckily, repositories can be defined, features installed, and bundles started, by changing files in ${karaf.home}. If you're keen to automate, the Karaf console can even be driven programmatically.

8.4   Collecting coverage data

When you're running tests against your application, how do you measure the effectiveness of your tests? How do you make sure you haven't forgotten anything? Code coverage tools instrument your application classes to produce reports on which code was exercised. We feel collecting coverage data should be an integral part of your development and testing process.

The good news is that a range of coverage tools are available. Most either make Ant tasks available or integrate neatly into Maven. The bad news is that instrumenting classes is different in an OSGi environment, so most coverage tools will spectacularly fail to work out of the box.

Why doesn't bytecode modification work with OSGi? The problem is that code that's instrumented to collect coverage data will have extra dependencies. In a non-OSGi environment, the classpath is flat, so it's sufficient to have the coverage library on the classpath. In an OSGi environment, with its structured classpath and limited class visibility, a bundle must explicitly import any new dependencies added at runtime.

> **OSGi support for load-time weaving**
>
> Version 4.3 of the OSGi specification includes new support for load-time bytecode weaving of classes. Although at the time of writing no coverage tools exploit this capability, expect future tools to take advantage of this extremely useful facility.

If you want to collect coverage data for your enterprise OSGi application (you do), there are two options. A few tools have been specifically designed to support OSGi coverage collection. Alternatively, you can carry on using your favorite tools by doing creative classpath manipulation.

The most well-known coverage tool with built-in OSGi support is EclEmma. But as the name suggests, EclEmma only supports Eclipse Equinox.

8.4.1   Getting coverage tools onto the classpath

If you're fond of another tool, like Cobertura, or using Felix as your OSGi framework, there are ways to make non-OSGi-aware tools work. One option is to explicitly import the coverage library packages in the manifests of your instrumented bundles. You'll either need to produce two versions of the bundle, one for testing and one for production, or make the coverage imports optional. Another option, which is less disruptive to your manifests, is to add the coverage classes to your boot classpath and use boot delegation to ensure all bundles can see them.

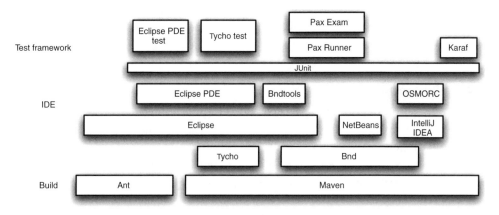

Figure 8.3   A range of tools for building, developing, and testing OSGi applications is available. Many of the tools build on or integrate with other tools, or even several other tools.

8.5 Summary

The OSGi tools ecosystem is big, and many of the tools are powerful (or complicated!). We could probably write a whole book on OSGi tools. Hopefully this chapter has given you an overview of what kind of tool options are out there, and some starting points to find more information on individual tools.

The key differentiators between many of the tool stacks is whether your OSGi development starts with an OSGi manifest or starts with plain code. After you've made this decision, you'll find the choice between tools like bnd and Tycho starts to get made for you. As you move on to test your bundles, you'll find that many of your build-time tools have natural testing extensions. In particular, almost all testing tools offer some level of Maven integration. How do all these tools fit together?

Figure 8.3 shows how the tools we've been discussing relate to one another and the broader tooling ecosystem. We'll cover the middle section of figure 8.3, IDE tools, in the next chapter.

IDE development tools

This chapter covers

- OSGi development with Eclipse PDE
- The bndtools Eclipse plug-in
- Eclipse Libra
- Other Eclipse plug-ins for enterprise OSGi
- OSGi support in NetBeans and IntelliJ IDEA

At the beginning of chapter 8, we mentioned that whichever build tool you choose, you'll probably want to use it in concert with a complementary IDE. What choices do you have for IDEs? Do any of them offer special support for enterprise OSGi? The good news is that there's rich support for OSGi in development tools, and support for enterprise OSGi is growing.

Your decision about which set of IDE tools to use will partly be determined by whether you prefer a code-first or manifest-first development style, and which build tools you're using. On the other hand, you may already have an IDE in mind, and that might determine your choice of build tools! Figure 9.1 shows one possible route to making a decision about which IDE to use—but feel free to work from right to left instead if you already know which IDE you want to use.

Although the range of IDEs that support OSGi is growing, Eclipse is the most popular and mature platform for OSGi development, so we'll start our discussion there.

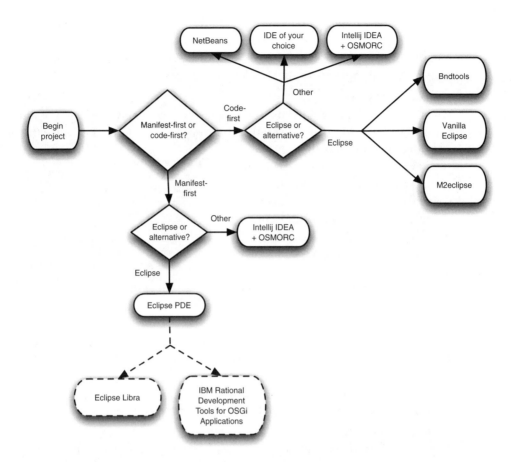

Figure 9.1 When choosing an IDE, the most important factor to consider is whether you're developing code-first or manifest-first. Good tools based on the Eclipse platform are available in both cases, but other options are also available, particularly in the code-first case. No matter which development style you're using, if you're using Eclipse as your IDE you may also want to use one of the development tools specifically designed to support the enterprise OSGi programming model.

9.1 *Eclipse-based OSGi development*

Why is the Eclipse IDE so popular for OSGi development? One reason is that Eclipse is generally popular, and this dominance has naturally extended into the OSGi space. More fundamentally, though, Eclipse itself is an OSGi application and supports OSGi natively.

9.1.1 *Eclipse Plug-in Development Environment*

Eclipse's built-in OSGi development environment is known as the Plug-in Development Environment (PDE). It's one of the quickest ways to get started developing bundles in Eclipse, although its manifest-first style isn't to everyone's taste. PDE comes integrated with many Eclipse distributions. You'll need the Classic distribution, also known as the SDK distribution, rather than the default Java-development version.

As the name implies, PDE was originally designed to support development of plug-ins to Eclipse itself. In a sense, OSGi development is a side effect, and this shows in the naming of many of the perspectives and views. If you mentally substitute *bundle* for *plug-in*, the purpose of various GUI elements may become clearer!

SETTING A CLASSPATH

If you've done normal Eclipse development, you've probably spent a lot of time editing the project classpaths to add in all the libraries you need. One of the nice things about

OSGi development in Eclipse PDE is that you never need to touch the .classpath file (or the classpath GUI) again. If you find yourself editing it, you've most likely done something wrong. Adjusting the classpath directly bypasses PDE's manifest valida-tion mechanism, so it's both unnecessary and risky.

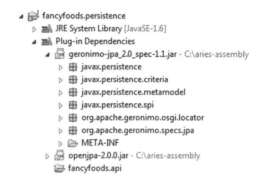

Instead of using a user-defined class-path, PDE creates a plug-in dependencies *bucket* and adds that to the project class-path. When you import a package from a bundle, PDE adds that bundle to the plug-in dependencies bucket. You can explore the contents of the imported bundles in the package explorer, as shown in figure 9.2.

Figure 9.2   Eclipse adds a plug-in dependencies container to each project's classpath. Required projects and JARs from the target platform are added. If you're curious about what's on the classpath, you can look inside each bundle by expanding it.

DEFINING A TARGET PLATFORM

The contents of the plug-in dependencies container are drawn from other projects in the workspace and the bundles in the *target platform*. By default, Eclipse uses itself as the target platform, but it's easy to change it to point to a different runtime, folder, or remote site (or any combination of the above!).

To define a new target platform, bring up the Eclipse preferences and navigate to Plug-in Development > Target Platform. Choose Add and accept the default on the next panel to start with nothing. You're developing for the Apache Aries sample assembly, so point your target platform to your Aries install by clicking Add, and then Directory, and then navigating to the directory where you've built the Aries assembly. After clicking OK and selecting the Show Location Content check box, you can see that Eclipse has added all the bundles in the Aries runtime to its target platform (figure 9.3).

SHARING A TARGET PLATFORM

The target platform definition can be saved as a .target file and checked into source control, which makes it easy to ensure all members of a team are developing against the same set of libraries.

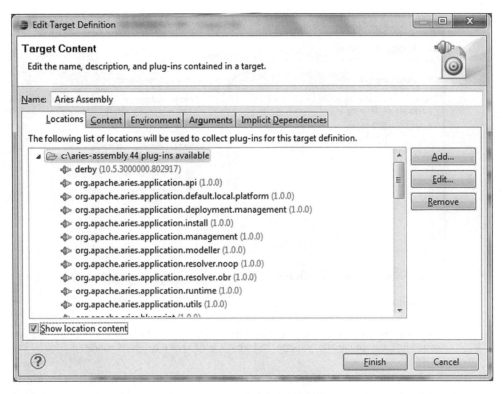

Figure 9.3 Eclipse PDE makes it easy to define a target platform from the Aries assembly. This platform is used for both compiling and running.

Tycho and target platforms

If you're using Tycho to build and generate your own p2 repository, you can—and probably should—use that repository as your target platform instead, by adding it as a repository of type `Software site`. Before the IDE will recognize your p2 repository, you'll also need to follow some extra repository generation steps, creating at least one category for the repository, and then adding the repository contents to it.

EDITING MANIFESTS

Eclipse PDE is a manifest-first IDE, and as you'd expect it provides a sophisticated tabbed editor for bundle manifests (see figure 9.4).

WARNING: `Require-Bundle` AND ECLIPSE If you're using Eclipse's PDE to write your bundles, it's easy to inadvertently use `Require-Bundle` instead of `Import-Package`. `Require-Bundle` should only be used in the case of split packages, and even then other alternatives should be sought! Historically, Eclipse used `Require-Bundle` internally, and the manifest editor still makes it slightly easier to require bundles than to import packages by positioning it more prominently on the dependencies panel.

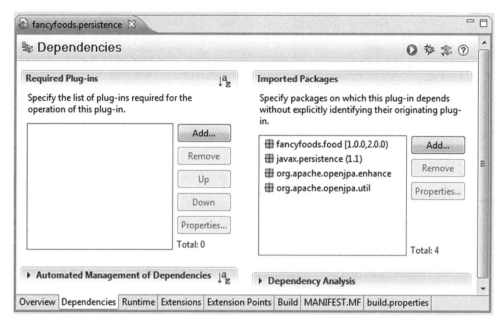

Figure 9.4   Eclipse PDE offers a nice manifest editor. As well as a source view, there are tabs for controlling package imports, exports, and what's packaged into a built bundle.

PDE uses the target platform to automatically validate package imports, and it can also do more advanced validation and visualization of a bundle's dependencies. We mentioned earlier that accumulating dead layers of unused dependencies in your manifests is one of the hazards of manifest-first development. Eclipse PDE addresses this problem by providing an option to search for unused dependencies; sadly the detection isn't always entirely reliable! See figure 9.5.

Eclipse also provides some tooling for visualizing and generating manifests. For example, clicking on the Dependency Analysis link in the Dependencies tab of the

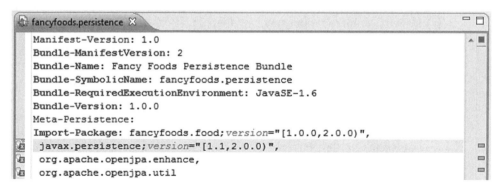

Figure 9.5   If imported packages aren't available in the target platform, Eclipse will highlight them in the manifest. In this case, `fancyfoods.food` is available, because it's another Eclipse project, but the `javax.persistence` and `openjpa` APIs can't resolve.

manifest editor (see figure 9.6) brings up a tree view of bundles that depend on the current bundle (see figure 9.7).

For example, the dependency hierarchy of the Fancy Foods application is shown in figure 9.7.

Finally, Eclipse PDE includes support for declarative services components, although it's well hidden! Choose New > Plug-in Development > Component Def-

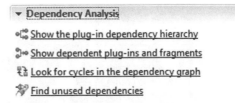

Figure 9.6   The manifest editor's dependency analysis view shows which bundles depend on the current bundle, and also which bundles the current bundle depends on.

inition. Eclipse will bring up an editor with both GUI and source views. It will also update the project's manifest to reference the SCR XML.

Although Eclipse PDE has a number of good features, none of them are much use to you if you don't want to write your own manifests. But if you're using bnd directly (or embedded into Ant) to generate your manifests, good Eclipse-based OSGi tools are still available to you.

9.1.2   *Extending bnd into the GUI world with bndtools*

The bndtools plug-in extends bnd's code-first command-line support into the Eclipse environment. As well as providing syntax highlighting and a forms-based editor for .bnd files, it integrates into the Eclipse compiler so that Eclipse automatically produces OSGi bundles on compile.

SETTING UP THE BND REPOSITORY

Bndtools maintains a local bundle repository, which serves the same function as a Maven repository or an Eclipse PDE target platform. When developing your classes, there's no need to explicitly add imports or project dependencies; bndtools will find your dependencies in its internal repository. Before this works, you'll need to set up the repository.

When you create a new OSGi bundle project, bndtools will automatically set up a configuration project. This project includes useful Ant boilerplate, but its most important

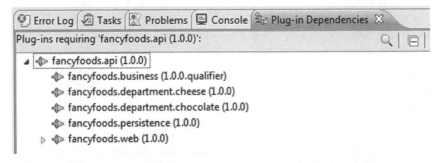

Figure 9.7   Eclipse PDE's visualization of the dependency hierarchy of the Fancy Foods application.

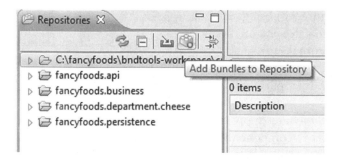

Figure 9.8   Bnd maintains a list of bundle repositories that are used for compiling and running bundles. To ensure your compile-time dependencies are available, you can add them to the internal bndtools repository.

role is to define the bnd repository. Bndtools prepopulates the repository with various useful bundles, like JUnit and the Felix Declarative Services implementation, but you'll need to add bundles for your enterprise OSGi runtime environment, like a Blueprint implementation, and perhaps a database.

You can populate the repository using the bnd file, but the simplest way is to use the bndtools' Repository View, in the bottom left corner of the OSGi perspective, which has an Add Bundles to Repository icon. You'll need to add your bundles to a specific repository, so the icon isn't active unless an existing repository is highlighted (see figure 9.8).

SETTING THE BUNDLE BUILD PATH

Although the bnd repository is similar in several ways to the PDE target platform, the two aren't the same. One important difference is that it's not sufficient to add a bundle to the bnd repository for it to be part of a bundle's compile path; the bundle must also be added to the bndtools build path. This makes getting everything compiling in bnd harder than it could be, but it does ensure no unwanted dependencies creep into a bundle's package imports. In a way, setting the bnd build path is like adding package imports in PDE, although you'll probably have to add fewer bundles to the build path than imported packages (see figure 9.9).

Figure 9.9   You'll need to add the bundles your project depends on in the Build tab in the bndtools bnd file editor.

EDITING BND FILES

The bndtools include a nice .bnd file editor. As well as editing the .bnd source directly, you can use a GUI to specify your private and exported packages, and see bnd's calculated imports (see figure 9.10).

Figure 9.10   Bndtools will show you the calculated imports for each bundle, which can help avoid runtime surprises. You can even see which classes are using the imported packages.

Like PDE, the bndtools bnd file editor also includes a nice GUI interface for defining Declarative Services. More accurately, bndtools provides a GUI to generate a bnd file, and the bnd file is then used to generate XML files that define the Declarative Services!

9.2 OSGi support in other IDEs

Although we've talked about a range of development tools, they've all been based on the Eclipse IDE. What if you prefer a different IDE? Well, you do have some options. Because of its early internal adoption of OSGi, Eclipse is dominant in the field of OSGi development, but other IDEs are catching up.

9.2.1 NetBeans

NetBeans is a free IDE that integrates closely with the GlassFish server. In recent years, both NetBeans and GlassFish have greatly increased their OSGi support. NetBeans has a concept of *modules*, and these modules map reasonably well to OSGi bundles; Net-Beans modules encode module information in a module's MANIFEST.MF, and these headers map nicely to OSGi headers. NetBeans modules have the notion of names, versions, public packages, and required module dependencies (but not package-level dependencies). When creating a NetBeans module, you can mark it as an OSGi bundle by ticking Generate OSGi Bundle (see figure 9.11).

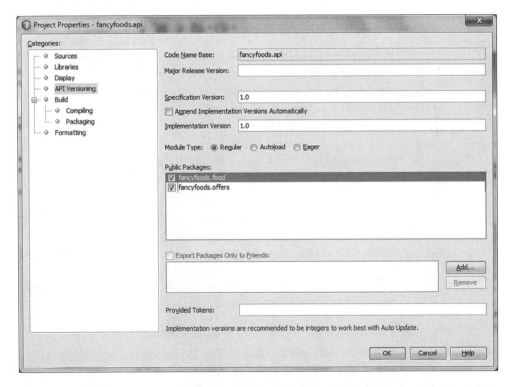

Figure 9.11   NetBeans provides a GUI editor to choose which packages you want to export from a module.

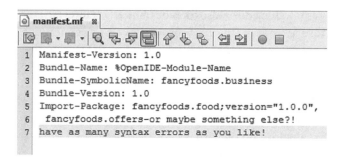

Figure 9.12   **The manifests for NetBeans OSGi bundles allow variable substitution. The editor doesn't have autocompletion or error detection.**

Despite the similarities between OSGi bundles and NetBeans modules, NetBeans' OSGi support is limited. Developing OSGi bundles in NetBeans is like doing code-first development, except instead of the code, NetBeans is guided by its project.xml file. For example, private packages are shown with a cute little padlock decorator, but this information is stored in the project file. Dependencies are also always per-module (or, equivalently, per-bundle) rather than OSGi's preferred package-level dependencies (see figures 9.12 and 9.13).

Figure 9.13   **When you add a module explicitly to one of your NetBeans modules, it shows in the Libraries twisty of the module. This is similar to the plug-in dependencies twisty in Eclipse, and Eclipse's referenced libraries twisty.**

9.2.2   *Osmorc and IntelliJ IDEA*

Recent premium versions of the IntelliJ IDEA IDE bundle a set of OSGi tools called Osmorc. Osmorc is also available independently as a plug-in to IntelliJ's Community Edition. One nice feature of Osmorc is that it supports both a manifest-first and a code-first approach to OSGi development. Existing manifests can be used to generate module dependencies, and manifests can also be generated from project bytecode. Like many OSGi tools, Osmorc embeds bnd for the manifest generation support.

> **What's an Osmorc?**
>
> If you're curious what *Osmorc* stands for, it's *OSGi Module Layer and Eclipse RCP Support*. The second part of the name has to do with another of Osmorc's features, the ability to run applications based on the Eclipse Rich Client Platform GUI framework inside IDEA. It doesn't have anything to do with the Eclipse IDE (confusingly!).

Figure 9.14 shows what the fancyfoods application looks like when edited with IntelliJ IDEA.

Like Eclipse PDE and bndtools, Osmorc allows you to set up a compile-time and runtime environment, called a *framework instance*.

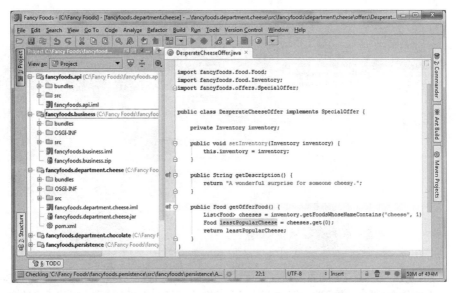

Figure 9.14   The Osmorc IDE being used to develop the `fancyfoods` application

WORKING WITH MANIFESTS

Osmorc provides syntax highlighting and autocompletion for manifest files, but no forms-based editor. In principle, it will automatically work out required bundles and add them to the dependencies of a project, although at the time of writing, it's not clear if this feature works properly. Figure 9.15 shows Osmorc's manifest editor in action.

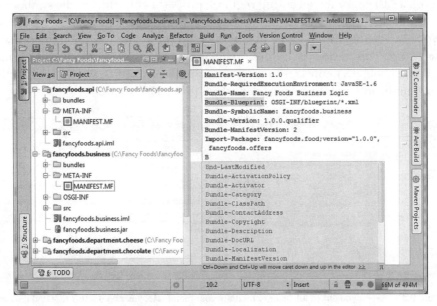

Figure 9.15   Osmorc's manifest editor has fewer features than Eclipse's, but it does provide syntax highlighting, error-detection, and autocompletion.

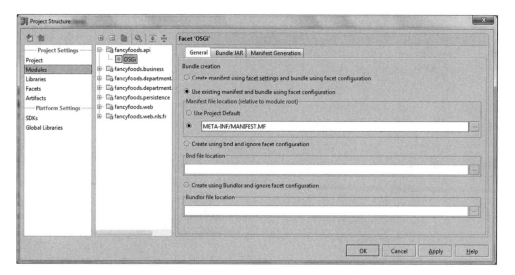

Figure 9.16   One nice feature of Osmorc is that it allows you to choose whether to manage your manifests yourself, or to have your manifests managed for you based on your module dependencies.

Unlike most of the tools we've discussed, Osmorc is designed to support both manifest-first and code-first styles of development (see figure 9.16).

If you opt to have Osmorc manage your manifests for you, you have a choice between using Osmorc's native support (which is based on bnd under the covers), providing .bnd files, or using SpringSource's Bundlor. If you use the Osmorc support, there's a GUI editor for specifying required properties like the bundle symbolic name. You can also specify extra required entries in a text box. These entries are passed to bnd before being written to the manifest file, so you're not restricted to normal manifest syntax. This means you can use regular expressions and variable substitution. As with plain bnd, it's important to specify your package exports, rather than allowing all your bundle internals to be exported (see figure 9.17).

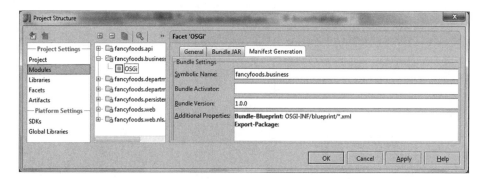

Figure 9.17   When you opt to let Osmorc manage your manifests, you can point it to a bnd file, or fill in a simple panel on the module settings page with bnd-style settings. Don't forget to narrow down the default package exports.

Neither Osmorc nor NetBeans provides OSGi support that's as rich as that of bndtools and Eclipse PDE. If you're using NetBeans as your development environment, you may have to make some compromises in terms of how you structure your OSGi bundles, or work against the IDE to some extent. Osmorc is more flexible and more closely aligned with OSGi best practices, but you may find that it's adding only limited value compared to using IntelliJ IDEA in its normal mode alongside a bnd-based Maven build.

9.2.3 Do you need OSGi support in your IDE?

If you're developing OSGi bundles using a code-first style, and you're not writing your own bnd files, how much OSGi support any IDE—even Eclipse—can give you is limited. Luckily, this isn't such disappointing news as you might initially think. One of the defining characteristics of the code-first style of OSGi development is that the code development itself doesn't necessarily involve much OSGi. It arguably doesn't involve *any* OSGi at all—the OSGi-ness gets added later, at build time. This means you can choose to develop with whatever development tools you're most comfortable with.

If you're using Maven and the bundle plug-in, a popular choice is to use the Maven Eclipse plug-in to align your IDE and your Maven build. The Eclipse plug-in creates Eclipse projects for each of your Maven modules and ensures Eclipse knows where to find all the source files and resources. If you'd like more complete integration, you can use Eclipse's m2eclipse (m2e). The m2eclipse plug-in hooks the Eclipse compile process into the Maven build process, so that Maven builds get used by Eclipse to compile your code. This is the approach taken by the Apache Aries project, for example. Maven also integrates nicely with other IDEs, including some we've discussed, like NetBeans and IntelliJ IDEA, and some we haven't, like Embarcadero's JBuilder.

9.3 Tools for the enterprise OSGi extensions

Although they offer varying levels of support for core OSGi, none of the development tools we've discussed so far offer much support for the enterprise OSGi programming model. Bndtools and PDE do have handy built-in support for Declarative Services, but that's about the extent of enterprise OSGi support in what we've seen so far. But there are several free tools built on top of Eclipse PDE that allow it to support development of enterprise OSGi applications. Although this support isn't essential to code enterprise OSGi applications, you may find it useful.

9.3.1 IBM Rational Development Tools for OSGi Applications

The more mature of these tools, IBM Rational Development Tools for OSGi Applications, is a set of free tools that support Apache Aries development. The Rational tools know about Blueprint, WABs, JPA persistence bundles, and also EBA applications. They also offer support for WebSphere Application Server concepts like composite bundles.

To install the tools, you'll need the Java EE version of Eclipse, version 3.6 or higher. Bring up the Eclipse Marketplace from the Help menu and search for OSGi. The Rational tools should be the first option.

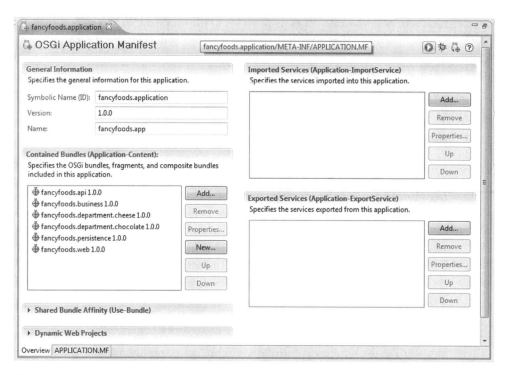

Figure 9.18   The Rational tools support Aries-style EBA applications. The APPLICATION.MF files may be edited as text files or in a GUI editor.

The Rational tools have special project types for OSGi bundles and applications, and nice editors for APPLICATION.MF files (see figure 9.18).

The Rational tools also allow you to take advantage of Eclipse's existing support for programming models like servlets and JPA (see figure 9.19).

The Rational tools do have a slightly different source layout, which you may find inconvenient if you've set your build up to use a normal PDE layout. On the other hand, if you're used to using Eclipse's WTP (Web Tools Platform) tools, you may find the code layout more natural. Certainly, its integration with both the enterprise and enterprise OSGi programming models may make it a handy addition to your toolkit.

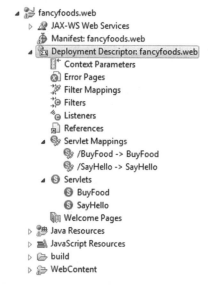

Figure 9.19   In the Java EE perspective, the web.xml files of OSGi bundles with the web facet can be easily visualized and manipulated.

9.3.2   Eclipse Libra

An alternative set of tools based on Eclipse PDE and the Eclipse Web Tools Platform is the Eclipse Libra project. Unlike the Rational tools, Libra's scope is strictly what's in the enterprise OSGi specification; extensions (like Aries applications or Virgo plans) won't be supported.

Instead of starting with OSGi bundle projects and adding web or JPA facets, Libra reuses the existing JPA and web projects and adds an OSGi bundle facet (see figure 9.20).

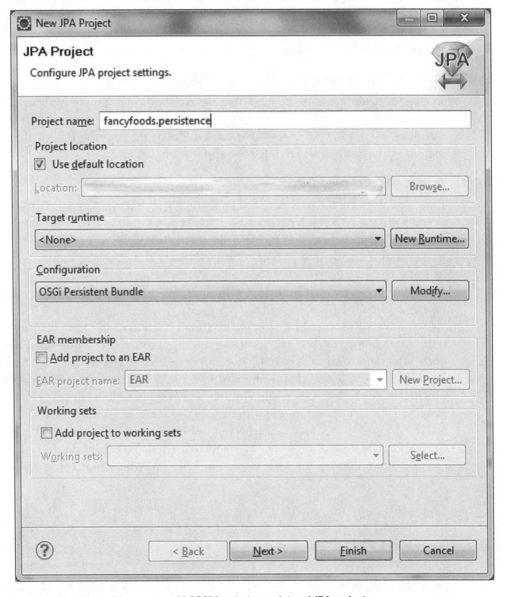

Figure 9.20   Libra allows you to add OSGi facets to servlet and JPA projects.

Like the Rational tools, Libra integrates with Eclipse's existing web, JPA, and OSGi tools rather than re-inventing wheels. This makes both tools attractive options if you're used to using Eclipse for your Java EE development. At the time of writing, Libra is still an incubator project in the early phases of development, but it has significant promise as a development tool.

A good IDE isn't a substitute for a good automated build system—instead, your IDE and your build system should work together. When chosen well, an IDE and an automated build complement each other, making code easier to write and debug. The same principles apply to testing code—for all but the smallest projects, you'll need some sort of automated testing. But you'll find your development process a lot slower if these tests can *only* be run from your automated framework.

9.4 Testing OSGi applications inside IDEs

In chapter 8, we mentioned that getting the runtime environment for your tests right can sometimes be as tricky as getting your tests functionally correct. A good IDE setup will allow you to run your tests so that you can debug the tests themselves, debug automation problems, and also debug your application.

9.4.1 Testing with Eclipse PDE

If you're using PDE for your development, you'll find it natural to run the tests in PDE as you write them. If you have the target platform set up to mirror your runtime environment, integration testing inside Eclipse PDE is simple. After you've written your unit tests, running them is a matter of right-clicking and choosing Run as > JUnit Plug-in Test (see figure 9.21).

Results are presented in the same form as any other JUnit tests run from Eclipse (see figure 9.22).

So far, so convenient. PDE's test environment will allow you to run your integration tests and debug problems with your tests and applications. The one thing missing is deep integration with a command-line build system. If you're using Tycho as your build system, you'll find that Tycho and PDE use a different system for working out which bundles to include in the runtime environment. This means that the automated tests may not be running with exactly the same set of bundles as you're using inside PDE, and in the worst case, this will cause behavior differences. PDE will launch your entire target platform when it runs tests, whereas Tycho will carefully provision a minimal runtime platform. Instead of launching every bundle it knows about, it will

Figure 9.21 Eclipse allows unit tests to be run in an OSGi framework from within the IDE using a simple menu option. The target platform is used to generate the list of bundles to install in the OSGi framework.

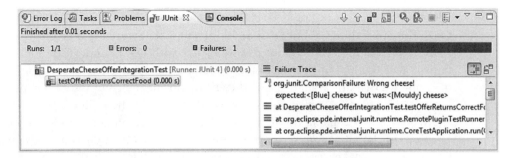

Figure 9.22 **Eclipse presents test results from JUnit tests that were run inside a framework in the same GUI format as normal JUnit results.**

launch only your test bundle and any required bundles. If you're not using Tycho, you can easily launch an OSGi framework that's identical to your Eclipse target platform, but you may not have much command-line support for running the tests.

9.4.2 Testing with bndtools

If you're using bndtools instead of Eclipse PDE, you still have options for running your unit tests inside Eclipse. To run a JUnit test from inside Eclipse, right-click on the test and choose Run As > OSGi JUnit Test (see figure 9.23).

Just as Eclipse can use the target platform to provision and launch an OSGi framework, bndtools can provision a framework from its repository.

By default, Eclipse launches with the whole target platform, although subsets of the target platform can be specified in the run configuration. Bndtools, on the other hand, requires you to explicitly list each bundle from the repository that should be included in the run configuration. Bundles that your project explicitly depends on will be automatically included. (This may sound a lot like Tycho right about now!)

9.4.3 Pax Exam

Even Pax Exam includes some Eclipse support for testing. The 2.2 release of Pax Exam includes an Eclipse plug-in that flags common configuration problems as compile errors. Pax Runner also provides an Eclipse plug-in that provides launch configurations for all the OSGi frameworks Pax Runner supports.

Figure 9.23 **Bndtools can run JUnit tests inside an OSGi framework from within Eclipse.**

9.5   *Summary*

One of the nice things about OSGi development is that you have a great deal of flexibility about whether you choose to use an IDE with OSGi support, or stick to your favorite IDE and add in your OSGi bits at build time. Some excellent IDE plug-ins for developing OSGi are available, but they're by no means compulsory. Eclipse is the most popular base for developing OSGi, both because of the built-in PDE tooling and alternative toolsets, like bndtools and the Maven Eclipse plug-ins. Both bndtools and Eclipse PDE also allow you to run your tests inside the IDE as well as on the command line, which can make writing and debugging tests much faster.

Tools are only a small part of the OSGi ecosystem. In part 3, we'll take a tour of the broader enterprise OSGi ecosystem—extra technologies, bigger and higher stacks, and the messy edges between the OSGi world and the non-OSGi world.

Part 3

Integrating enterprise OSGi with everything else

Now that we've reached part III of our book, it's time to start looking at how OSGi relates to the environment you already have. Our main focus so far has been developing new applications from scratch. Although we're sure you'd agree that this is a fun approach, it isn't realistic to assume that you'll always be starting with a clean slate. Java has a rich and successful history, and this means that there will be a lot of existing code that you want to use.

Despite our description of the enterprise as a large distributed system in section 1.1.2, your applications so far have been firmly tied to a single virtual machine. You'll remedy this in chapter 10, where we look at how to extend enterprise OSGi applications between frameworks.

In chapter 11, we consider how to connect OSGi frameworks to non-OSGi containers using SCA and ESBs. We also present suggestions for how to migrate applications running in these non-OSGi containers to OSGi.

In chapter 12, we'll look at how to use existing Java libraries. You may hit a number of pitfalls using libraries that weren't designed for OSGi in an OSGi environment, so we'll explain what to watch out for and how to make everything work.

Finally, we'll review the available enterprise OSGi servers in chapter 13. Many of the popular application servers support OSGi applications, and you can also assemble a good OSGi stack starting with a simple OSGi container.

By the time we finish this part, our work here will be done, and you should have a thorough mastery of enterprise OSGi. But first, let's have a look at distributed OSGi.

Hooking up remote systems with distributed OSGi

This chapter covers

- The Remote Services Specification
- How remote services differ from local services
- Exposing an OSGi service as an external endpoint
- Transparently calling a remote endpoint as an OSGi service
- SCA as an alternative distribution mechanism

In previous chapters, you've spent a great deal of effort building a scalable, extensible online superstore application. Although it's unlikely that this exact application will ever be used in a production system, it does demonstrate the sorts of patterns that real enterprise applications use, such as that the application can be added to over time.

Given the small loads and small amounts of data that you've been using in the Fancy Foods application, you aren't stretching the limits of a typical development laptop, let alone a production server, but it's easy to see that if you were to increase the number of departments, increase the user load, and increase the volume of data involved, then things might be a little more constrained. These sorts of scaling requirements mean that many enterprise applications can't run on a single server because the volume of data and users would overwhelm the system. At this point, you have no choice but to distribute the application over more than one machine. This distribution process can be extremely painful if the application hasn't been designed for it. Fortunately, well-written OSGi code lends itself well to distributed systems, and the OSGi Enterprise Specification offers us a standard mechanism for expanding OSGi beyond a single framework using remote services.

Before we dive straight into the details of authoring a remote service, let's first make sure you understand some of the reasons why you might want to access a remote service. It's also important that you know about the drawbacks of using remote calls instead of local ones, particularly that you understand the limitations that being remotely available places on the design of the service you wish to access. It would be embarrassing to author a remote service only to find that you can't use it remotely!

10.1   *The principles of remoting*

Enterprise applications have to cope with huge scales, both in terms of the application and the user base. As an application and the demands upon it get bigger, it becomes impractical, or even impossible, to host the whole application on a single machine. Accessing services hosted on another machine is therefore a vitally important part of enterprise programming.

10.1.1   *The benefits of remoting*

The primary benefit of remoting is obvious: by allowing applications to access services and/or resources on another machine, you can dramatically reduce the computational load on a single machine. Spreading computationally difficult and memory-intensive tasks out to remote machines ensures that the server hosting your frontend has ample resources to accept new HTTP connections from other clients.

Remoting isn't the only way to scale out applications. As you've seen from the example applications in this book, it's perfectly feasible to write an enterprise application that can live comfortably on a single machine. But if this application needs to support a large number of concurrent users, then that single machine may not be capable of servicing every request without overloading its CPU or network adapter. Often applications like these are scaled out *horizontally* by adding more machines running the same application. Using a simple router fronting, these machines' clients can be transparently redirected to an instance of the application. Most routers are even able to remember which machine a client has previously been redirected to and ensure subsequent requests are sent to the same machine (see figure 10.1). Given that this sort of design is possible, why would you bother physically separating parts of your application with remoting?

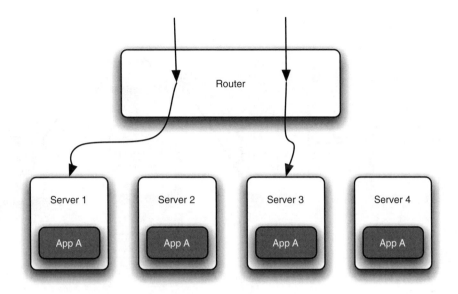

Figure 10.1 Horizontal scaling allows client requests to be transparently distributed across a number of servers to increase throughput.

ALLOWING SPECIALIZATION

As with many things, not all computers are created equal. Laptops are small, light, use comparatively little power, and, as a result, produce little heat. Laptops also have reduced processing speed, less memory, and slow disks. Mainframe computers are large, require specialized power supplies and cooling, and you certainly would struggle to lift one; on the other hand, they have vast quantities of memory, a number of fast processors, and usually fast disks.

Laptops and mainframes represent two ends of a large scale of computing equipment; one where processing power, reliability, size, and cost vary hugely. In terms of cost effectiveness, it's usually best to pick a system that suits the type of work that you're going to give it. Running your corporate directory database on a laptop is inadvisable (and probably impossible), but running a small internal web portal on a mainframe is also a waste (unless you also have that mainframe doing a number of other things at the same time). What remoting allows you to do is to put services on machines that fit the type of work that they perform.

If you look at the Fancy Foods superstore as an example, there's an obvious way in which it will fail to scale. A typical machine for hosting a web application like the superstore would be a rack-mounted blade server. These machines have reasonably fast processors and network adapters, but only moderate memory and disk performance. This makes blades excellently suited for handling web traffic and running servlets, but if your database runs on the same system, this is likely to have a significant negative impact on performance. As the number of clients increases, the amount of

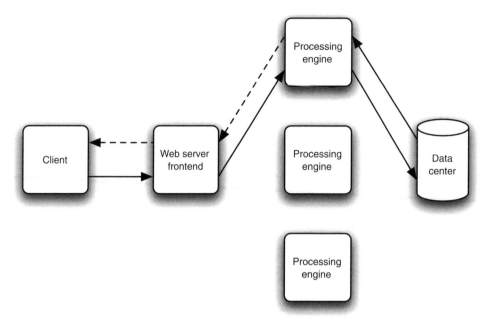

Figure 10.2 **A simple web server can forward complex processing tasks out to dedicated machines for execution, returning results when the task is complete.**

resource available to run the database drops significantly. By moving the database out to another machine, you can dramatically improve the performance of your application (see figure 10.2).

This is a common model, particularly for databases, but it also applies to other types of work. If, for example, you wanted to batch update 100,000,000 files, or run a vector-calculus-based fluid dynamics simulation, then it's unlikely that your local machine, or a central access point, are the best tools for the job.

Allowing for specialized workloads isn't the only reason that you might want to use remoting; probably the most common requirement has nothing to do with performance—it's all about reliability.

INCREASING AVAILABILITY

If you have a single system responsible for performing a large number of tasks, then in some senses you're doing well. The utilization of the system is likely to be high, and the management costs are lower because there's only one machine. On the other hand, the more services you cram onto a single machine, the bigger the risk you're taking. Even if the machine is able to cope with the work load, what happens when it needs to be maintained or restarted? What if one of the services needs to be updated? If all the services need to be accessed at once, this is less of a problem. If the services are used by different groups of users, then things are rather more difficult to manage. Can user X afford to take a total production outage, so that user Y can get a fix for the intermittent problem they're seeing?

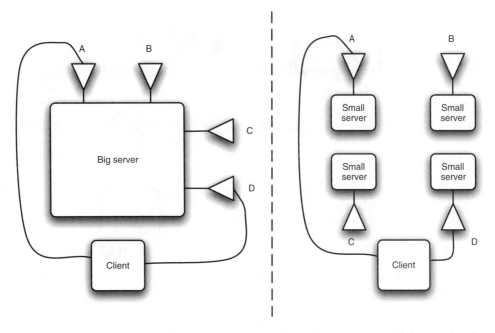

Figure 10.3 **If all your services exist on one big server, then maintenance to any of them can break a client. In this case, the client only needs to access services A and D, but suffers an unnecessary outage whenever B or C needs updating. If the services all exist on separate servers, then the client can continue to operate even if B and C are no longer available.**

Remoting allows you to separate services onto different machines so that they can be more independently maintainable; you can even think of this as being like modularity. If all of your services are tightly coupled (by being on the same machine), then you have problems making a change to any of them. Furthermore, having the services on different machines makes it easier to decouple them, meaning that horizontal scaling for performance or reliability in the future will be much easier (see figure 10.3).

Sometimes availability concerns cut both ways: not only is it necessary for a service to be accessible independently of another, but sometimes you may not want a service to be accessible from the outside world.

PROTECTING ACCESS AND ENCOURAGING CO-LOCATION

Computing systems are a large investment, and almost always contain sensitive data or provide a mission-critical function. As a result, they need to be protected from external influences, both malicious and poorly written ones. Firewalls are a vital piece of infrastructure in enterprise networks, preventing access from one area of a network to another, except for specific, configurable types of traffic. It's extremely rare for an enterprise system, such as a corporate database or server room, not to be protected by one or more firewalls.

Using firewalls is essential, but it does cause some problems. If the Fancy Foods superstore protects its database behind a firewall and users can't access it, then it won't be

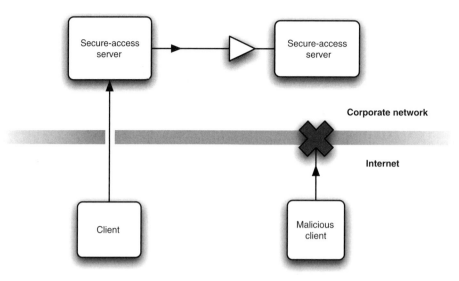

Figure 10.4   In combination with a firewall, an intermediate server can be used to provide safe access to a secure system without allowing direct access to it.

much use at all. On the other hand, you don't want users to have free access to the database machine, or probably even access to the network port exposing the database.

Remoting allows you to get around these sorts of problems by accessing a third party. If you have a reasonably secure intermediary system, then you can use that to access the backend service that you need. The intermediary is trusted to only access the database in a safe way, and so can be allowed through the firewall, whereas the client speaks to the intermediary and is shielded from the valuable content of the database (see figure 10.4).

This model isn't useful only for improving security; it also has a significant role to play in the performance of your system. It's best if services you access regularly can be accessed quickly. This is most likely if you're physically close (co-located) to the service you want to access. If performing a particular task requires you to access a service multiple times, then sending a single request to an intermediary, which then makes the rest of the calls and returns the result, can provide a significant performance boost.

Although remoting does have a number of advantages, it should be noted that there are some drawbacks when accessing remote systems.

10.1.2 *The drawbacks of remoting*

Although remoting is a critical part of enterprise programming, there are good reasons why it isn't used a lot of the time. Probably the single biggest reason that people avoid remoting is because of performance.

WHY REMOTING IS SO SLOW

One of the big lessons for most programmers is to avoid prematurely optimizing your code; still, it's worth thinking about trying to avoid things that have a negative impact on performance. Typically, people learn that data stored in a processor cache can be accessed so quickly that it's effectively free; that data in memory can be accessed fast; that large data structures can begin to cause problems; and that data stored on disk is extremely slow. This advice boils down to "avoid I/O operations where you can."

Remoting, by its nature, requires some level of network communication, which is the key reason for its comparatively abominable performance. Even if you're making a method call that passes no arguments and has no return value, the speed of the network is a critical factor. In a typical modern system, a processor will have to wait for less than a nanosecond to load the next operation instruction from an internal cache, or up to a few tens of nanoseconds to load instructions or data from main memory. On a typical, small-scale network, fetching even a few bytes of data would be measured in hundreds of microseconds or possibly milliseconds; on a large network, or perhaps over the Atlantic, this latency can easily reach more than 100 milliseconds. As you can see from figure 10.5, any method invocation that you need to make over the local network is likely to be *a thousand times slower* than performing it locally.

Invocations over the internet can be *a million times* slower than local ones. In this measurement, we're ignoring the length of time it takes for the method to run. If the method takes a second to complete, then the remoting overhead is comparatively small. We're also assuming that the method parameters and return value are sufficiently small that transferring them will take negligible time. If the data to be transferred is large, say, 50 kilobytes, then this can be a much larger factor than the network latency (about a millisecond on a fast local network, or 10 to 15 seconds over a slow mobile phone network). Any way you slice it, making remote calls isn't a cheap thing to do.

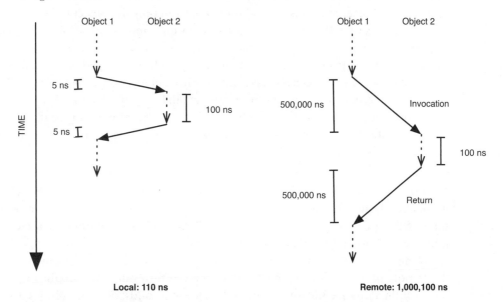

Figure 10.5   The execution times for remote methods are dramatically increased by the latency of the network, even on a local network with a 500 microsecond latency.

REMOTE CALL SEMANTICS

One of the things that often surprises people about calling remote objects in Java is a subtle change in the semantics of the language. Java inherits a lot of its syntax and behavior from C. This includes its behavior when calling methods that use a pass-by-value mechanism for method parameters. This means that when you pass a value to a method (say, an `int`) the method gets a *copy* of the `int`, not the original. Therefore, if you modify the `int` in your method, the `int` the caller had will remain unchanged. This initially surprises many people, because they're used to the fact that if you pass an object as a method parameter, then the method operates on the same object, not a copy. There isn't a difference between objects and primitives passed as parameters, but you do need to know that what you pass to a method isn't the object itself, it's a *reference* to the object, and that's passed as a copy. If object references weren't passed as copies, then you would be able to re-assign your caller's object reference to some other object. This would be confusing and open to abuse; what if someone were allowed to replace the unmodifiable collection you gave them with a modifiable `Hash-Set` without you knowing!

Even though it doesn't always feel like it, Java uses pass-by-value semantics for local calls. You can, however, modify objects that are passed to you and expect those modifications to be visible to the person who called you. This is why you can write methods like `public void fillMap(Map<String,String> map)` to add entries to a map passed to a method. Remote Java calls are different. The local call in your `Map` filling method relies on the fact that the method has access to the same `Map` in memory that the caller has. If the method were running on a remote machine, then this wouldn't be the case. In a remote call, all of the method parameters have to be serialized over the network to the remote machine. This forces Java to copy not only the object reference, but the whole object as well. If your `Map` filling method were running on a remote server, then it would be operating on a copy of the `Map`, not the original reference, and you'd find that any `Map` you tried to fill would remain completely unchanged on the client.

The fact that remote calls behave differently from local ones isn't necessarily a disadvantage, and in many cases doesn't matter at all; however, it's a significant change to the normal flow of Java code. As such, you should be careful to ensure that any interface you write that you might want to expose remotely doesn't rely on changing the state of objects passed in.

RELIABILITY AND REMOTING

Performance isn't the only thing that suffers when you make remote calls. When you make a local call, you can usually rely on an answer coming back. You can also rely on the fact that the data you need to execute will be available and not corrupted. Unfortunately, networks give you no such guarantee.

When you make a remote call, you usually need to wait for a reply indicating that the remote process has completed, often with a return value. You might receive your reply within a millisecond, or it might take several seconds, or even minutes. Crucially, you might *never* receive a reply from the remote server if, say, the server went down after receiving your request, or if a network problem has cut off the route between you and them.

It's impossible to know if a response is about to arrive, or if it will never arrive. As a result, you need to be careful when making remote invocations. Error conditions aren't uncommon, and you must be careful to avoid ending up in an inconsistent state. To ensure this is the case, almost all enterprise applications that make use of remoting use transactions to coordinate any resources they access. Advanced remoting models assist the user here by allowing the transaction context to be propagated across to the remote machine. At this point, you're running in a *distributed* transaction, namely, one that's spread across more than one machine. The transaction is coordinated such that both systems can recover from a failure on either side of the remote link.

10.1.3 *Good practices and the fallacies of remoting*

The problems with remoting are well known, and a particularly good description of them is encapsulated in "Fallacies of Distributed Computing Explained" (Arnon Rotem-Gal-Oz; see http://www.rgoarchitects.com/files/fallacies.pdf). People make assumptions about distributed systems that are rarely, and often never, true:

- The network is reliable
- Latency is zero
- Bandwidth is infinite
- The network is secure
- Topology doesn't change
- There's one administrator
- Transport cost is zero
- The network is homogeneous

You may notice that we used a number of these pieces of information to explain why remoting isn't used all the time. In general, they indicate a few good practices for remoting:

- Make as few invocations across the remote link as you can.
- Try to keep parameter data and returned data small.
- Avoid hardcoding any locations for remote services.
- Be prepared to handle timeouts, badly behaved clients, and erroneous data.

Now that you know a little more about the principles of remoting, it's time for us to look at the enterprise OSGi standard for remoting, the Remote Services Specification.

10.2 *The Remote Services Specification*

One of the primary aims of the Remote Services Specification is that it should be as natural as possible to make use of a remote service from within an OSGi framework. One of the big drawbacks in many remoting models is that there are a number of hoops you have to jump through to access a remote service. OSGi minimizes this problem by leveraging existing OSGi service mechanisms. In normal OSGi, bundles communicate via the OSGi Service Registry, which shields service clients from service providers. It turns out that not only is this a good thing for modularity within the local system, but that it provides excellent modularity for remote services as well!

The Remote Services Specification defines a mechanism by which a service can be exported from the Service Registry in one OSGi framework, making it appear in another OSGi framework. As far as the client is concerned, it can then consume both local and remote services in exactly the same way. From the provider's perspective, things are equally simple; they register a service into their local Service Registry, and then wait for incoming requests. These requests may be from local bundles, or from remote ones; the provider doesn't need to know or care.

To achieve this model, the Remote Services Specification defines two different roles for the remoting implementation, which is usually known as the *distribution provider.*

10.2.1 Exposing endpoints

When a local OSGi service is made available for remoting, it needs to be exposed as an endpoint. This endpoint could be anything from a web service to a proprietary bitstream format; the important thing is that the endpoint is accessible from outside the framework. This part of the process is relatively simple, and it's correspondingly easy to indicate to a distribution provider that a service should be made remotely accessible. To do this, you make use of the whiteboard pattern. Rather than looking up a remoting provider and providing it with a remotable object, you register that remotable object as a normal OSGi service. To indicate that your service should be made available remotely, you add the `service.exported.interfaces` property to your service. The value of this property defines the interface names that should be exposed remotely. This is a good example of section 5.2.4 in action (see figure 10.6).

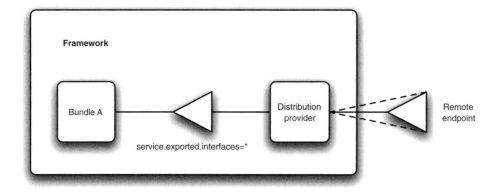

Figure 10.6   A distribution provider uses the whiteboard pattern to locate remotable services and expose them outside the OSGi framework.

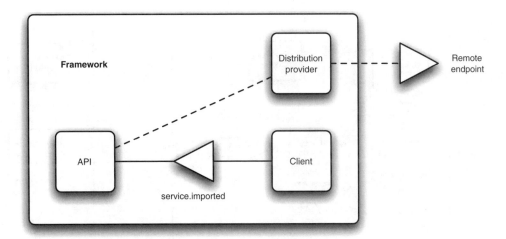

Figure 10.7 A distribution provider can also create OSGi services within an OSGi framework that delegate to remote endpoints.

10.2.2 *Discovering endpoints*

Both registering and consuming remotable services is easy, mostly because of the service discovery part of the distribution provider. This part of the distribution provider is responsible for detecting when new remote services are available, and they're for registering proxy services in the local framework. These proxy services mirror the backing services in the remote framework, including any changes in their service properties. The proxy services are also unregistered if the remote service becomes unavailable. Imported services (ones that proxy a service in a remote framework) also have a number of other properties registered by the distribution provider. Importantly, if the service.imported property is set to *any value*, then this service is a proxy to a remote service in another framework (see figure 10.7).

One further detail to note is that distribution providers are only required to support a limited set of parameter types when making remote invocations. These are primitive types, wrapper types for primitives, and Strings. Distribution providers must also cope with arrays or collections of these types.

Now that you understand the basics of the Remote Services Specification, let's try extending your superstore with a remote department.

10.3 *Writing a remotable service*

In chapter 3, you built an extensible facility for special offers. This is an excellent opportunity for you to add a remote special offer service. Writing a remote department for your superstore will be simple. It'll be the foreign foods department, and you'll base it heavily on the departments you've written before. Also, thanks to OSGi's modular, reusable bundles you can take the fancyfoods.api, fancyfoods.persistence, and fancyfoods.datasource bundles from chapter 3 without making any changes at all. Figure 10.8 shows the architecture of the distributed Fancy Foods system.

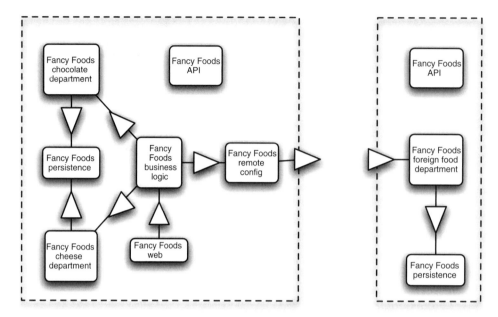

Figure 10.8   The distributed Fancy Foods system includes two frameworks. The original framework includes a new `fancyfoods.remote.config` **bundle; the remote framework reuses some Fancy Foods bundles and adds a new** `fancyfoods.department.foreign` **bundle.**

The first thing you need is an implementation for your remote service.

10.3.1 Coding a special offer service

To simplify things, your `SpecialOffer` implementation is effectively identical to the cheese department one, with a slightly different query, as shown in the following listing.

Listing 10.1   A foreign foods special offer service

```
public class ForeignFoodOffer implements SpecialOffer {

    private Inventory inventory;

    public void setInventory(Inventory inventory) {
        this.inventory = inventory;
    }

    @Override
    public String getDescription() {
        return "Something exotic to spice up your weekend.";
    }

    @Override
    public Food getOfferFood() {
        List<Food> foods =
            inventory.getFoodsWhoseNameContains("Foreign", 1);
        Food mostStocked = foods.get(0);
        return mostStocked;
    }
}
```

You'll also reuse the trick for populating the database, as follows.

Listing 10.2   Populating the foreign food database

```
public class InventoryPopulater {

    private Inventory inventory;

    public void setInventory(Inventory inventory) {
        this.inventory = inventory;
    }

    public void populate() {
        boolean isInventoryPopulated = (inventory.getFoodCount() > 0);

        if (!isInventoryPopulated) {
            inventory.createFood("Foreign Sushi", 3.45, 10);
            inventory.createFood("Foreign Borscht", 1.81, 15);
        }
    }
}
```

Once again, you can use Blueprint to glue everything together, as shown in the following listing.

Listing 10.3   Exposing your remote service

```
<?xml version="1.0" encoding="UTF-8"?>
<blueprint
    xmlns="http://www.osgi.org/xmlns/blueprint/v1.0.0">

    <service interface="fancyfoods.offers.SpecialOffer">          Mark your service
                                                                  remotable
        <service-properties>

            <entry key="service.exported.interfaces"
                   value="fancyfoods.offers.SpecialOffer"/>

        </service-properties>

        <bean class="fancyfoods.department.foreign.ForeignFoodOffer">

            <property name="inventory" ref="inventory"/>

        </bean>
    </service>

    <reference id="inventory" interface="fancyfoods.food.Inventory"/>

    <bean class="fancyfoods.department.foreign.InventoryPopulater"
          activation="eager" init-method="populate">             Eagerly populate
        <property name="inventory" ref="inventory"/>             database
    </bean>
</blueprint>
```

Having built your bundle, you can deploy it into your test environment along with the API, datasource, and persistence bundles. You can also see your remote service registered in the Service Registry (see figure 10.9).

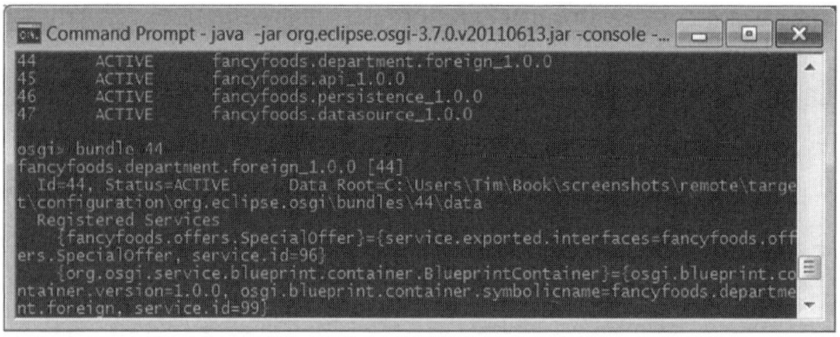

Figure 10.9 The local view of your remote service

Your foreign foods department can't do much at the moment; it's not even available remotely. For that you need a remote services implementation.

10.4 Adding in your remote service using Apache CXF

Apache CXF hosts the Distributed OSGi project, which is the reference implementation of the Remote Services Specification. (Other implementations, such as Eclipse ECF and Paremus Nimble, are also available.) Distributed OSGi makes use of CXF's web services runtime to expose OSGi services as web services. Distributed OSGi then uses CXF's web service client code to implement local OSGi service proxies to remote web services. By gluing these two pieces together, you get a complete remote services implementation.

Distributed OSGi is easy to use and will allow you to quickly and simply expose your foreign foods special offers to the outside world.

10.4.1 Making your service available

Distributed OSGi is available in two forms: as a set of OSGi bundles, or as a single bundle that packages its dependencies (sometimes known as an *uber bundle*). Both forms are reasonably common ways to release OSGi services; the former gives good modularity and fine control, whereas the latter is useful for getting up and running quickly. Because you want to start selling your foreign food as soon as possible, you'll be using the single bundle distribution of Distributed OSGi 1.2, which is available at http://cxf.apache.org/dosgi-releases.html.

You need to get the Distributed OSGi implementation into your framework, which can easily be achieved by dropping it into the load directory of your running framework. Adding this bundle will cause a huge flurry of activity, but importantly it will create a web service for any service that declares a `service.exported.interface`!

CONFIGURING YOUR DISTRIBUTION PROVIDER

It isn't immediately clear where Distributed OSGi has registered your web service, and it also isn't clear how you could get the service to be registered somewhere else. At this point, it's worth knowing that the Remote Services Specification defines a configuration property, `service.exported.configs`. This property can be used to define *alternatives* (different places where the same service should be registered) and *synonyms* (different configurations for the same service endpoint). If more than one configuration is required, then the service property can be an array of configurations.

In Distributed OSGi, `service.exported.configs` can be used to define the URL at which your web service is registered. To start, set the `service.exported.configs` property value to `org.apache.cxf.ws`. When Distributed OSGi sees this value for the `service.exported.configs` property, it begins looking for other, implementation-specific properties. The property for setting the web service URL is `org.apache.cxf.ws.address`. By default, Distributed OSGi URLs are of the form http://localhost:9000/fully/qualified/ClassName.

Distributed OSGi offers a number of other mechanisms for exposing your service, such as JAX-RS (all of this is implementation-specific). The Remote Services Specification requires implementations to support services that don't specify any implementation-specific configuration. As such, you'll keep your service clean and vendor-neutral by not specifying any configuration.

VIEWING YOUR REMOTE SERVICE

Although you haven't imported your service back into an OSGi framework, you shouldn't underestimate the power of what you've achieved. What you've got here is a remotely available OSGi-based web service. You can even get hold of the WSDL (Web Services Description Language) for your service by going to http://localhost:9000/fancyfoods/offers/SpecialOffer?wsdl. For those of you who know a little about web services, this is exciting stuff: you can see a complete description of your OSGi service (see figure 10.10).

Figure 10.10   The WSDL for your remote service

Figure 10.11 Invoking your remote service

> **WARNING: WHO'S THAT URL FOR?**   In some cases, Distributed OSGi tries to be
> too helpful in determining the default URL that it should use to register ser-
> vices. Rather than using localhost, the default becomes the current external
> IP address of your machine. If you find that your WSDL isn't visible on local-
> host then you should try using your current IP address instead. Unfortu-
> nately, you'll have to substitute this IP for localhost throughout the rest of
> this example.

We do understand that many of you won't get as excited by WSDL as we do, so as a treat
why don't you try visiting http://localhost:9000/fancyfoods/offers/SpecialOffer/
getDescription? We think you'll be rather pleased by what you find. See figure 10.11.

   You now have conclusive proof that CXF and Distributed OSGi have successfully
exposed your OSGi service as a publicly accessible web service. Now it's time to look at
how you can get that service into another running OSGi framework.

10.4.2 *Discovering remote services from your superstore*

We're sure you'll agree that exposing your OSGi service was extremely easy. Happily
for us, Distributed OSGi makes consuming the service back into another OSGi framework just as easy.

   To start with, you need to get your application from chapter 3 up and running in a
different OSGi framework. At this point, you can use the application happily, but you
won't see any offers for foreign foods (see figure 10.12).

Figure 10.12 Without your remote service

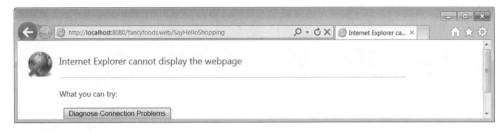

Figure 10.13   After adding Distributed OSGi

To get a remote service imported into your framework, you need to install the Distributed OSGi bundle, which again you can do by dropping it into the load directory of your framework. Sadly, this is enough to cause a problem. As you can see from figure 10.13, adding Distributed OSGi has caused something to go wrong with your application.

Although the problem may look severe, it's not as bad as it looks. Distributed OSGi makes use of the Jetty Web Container project to provide its HTTP web service hosting. This is exactly the same web container that your basic runtime uses, and when the Distributed OSGi bundle starts up, it ends up accidentally reconfiguring your runtime's Jetty instance as well as its own!

Unfortunately, the reconfiguration that happens moves Jetty onto a randomly assigned free port. Luckily, it's easy for you to find out what port Jetty was reassigned to. If you look at your runtime's `pax-web-jetty-bundle` in the OSGi console, you see something like figure 10.14.

If you look closely at figure 10.14, you can see that `pax` has registered an OSGi HTTP Service implementation in the Service Registry, and that one of the service properties for this service is called `org.osgi.service.http.port`, and it has a numeric value. This value is the port that you can access your application on. If you change your URL to use this port instead, then things look much rosier again (see figure 10.15).

Although your application is still working happily, notice that your foreign foods special offer is nowhere to be seen. This is because you haven't given Distributed OSGi any information about the remote endpoints you want it to connect to. If you want to go any further, you'll need to learn more configuration.

```
Command Prompt - java  -jar org.eclipse.osgi-3.7.0.v20110613.jar -console -...
osgi> bundle 7
org.ops4j.pax.web.pax-web-jetty-bundle_0.8.1 [7]
  Id=7, Status=ACTIVE      Data Root=C:\Users\Tim\Book\screenshots\local\target\
configuration\org.eclipse.osgi\bundles\7\data
  Registered Services
    {org.ops4j.pax.web.service.spi.ServerControllerFactory}={service.id=32}
    {org.osgi.service.cm.ManagedService}={service.pid=org.ops4j.pax.web, service
.id=33}
    {org.osgi.service.http.HttpService, org.ops4j.pax.web.service.WebContainer}=
{org.ops4j.pax.web.ssl.keystore=C:\Users\Tim\.keystore, org.osgi.service.http.po
rt.secure=8443, org.ops4j.pax.web.listening.addresses=, org.osgi.service.http.po
rt=54786, org.ops4j.pax.web.ssl.clientauthneeded=false, org.osgi.service.http.us
eNIO=true, org.osgi.service.http.enabled=true, org.osgi.service.http.secure.enab
led=true, org.ops4j.pax.web.ssl.clientauthwanted=false, javax.servlet.context.te
mpdir=C:\Users\Tim\AppData\Local\Temp\.paxweb4379256695361620314, service.id=43}
```

Figure 10.14   Your Jetty service properties

Figure 10.15   Using your new Jetty port

CONFIGURING ACCESS TO A REMOTE ENDPOINT

Before describing the details of configuring remote endpoints in Distributed OSGi, we feel that it's important to say that configuration isn't always required. A number of *discovery* services can be used to automatically locate endpoints, but these aren't part of the OSGi standards. What you'll do is use part of an OSGi standard called the Remote Service Admin Service Specification. This specification has an odd-looking name, but effectively it's a standard describing a common configuration and management model for different Remote Services Specification implementations.

You'll provide your configuration using the Endpoint Description Extender Format. This is a standard way of providing remote services endpoint configuration inside a bundle using the Remote Services Admin Service, and an alternative to dynamic discovery. To start with, you'll need a basic manifest, as shown in the following listing.

Listing 10.4   A remote services endpoint configuration bundle manifest

```
Manifest-Version: 1.0
Bundle-ManifestVersion: 2
Bundle-SymbolicName: fancyfoods.remote.config
Bundle-Version: 1.0.0
Remote-Service: OSGI-INF/remote-service/*.xml
```

The new and interesting entry in your manifest is the `Remote-Service` header. This header signals to the extender that this bundle should be processed for remote service endpoint descriptions. The value of the header is a comma-separated list of XML endpoint descriptions, potentially including wildcards.

Other than its manifest, your bundle will only contain one file, OSGI-INF/remote-service/remote-services.xml. This file matches the wildcard description described in the `Remote-Service` header of the bundle's manifest. This file uses a standard XML namespace to describe one or more endpoints that should be exposed by the remote services implementation. As a result, this file could be used with any remote services implementation, not just Distributed OSGi, as follows.

Listing 10.5   A remote services endpoint configuration file

```
<endpoint-descriptions xmlns="http://www.osgi.org/xmlns/rsa/v1.0.0">
  <endpoint-description>
```

```
    <property name="objectClass">
        <array>
<value>fancyfoods.offers.SpecialOffer</value>
        </array>
    </property>

<property name="endpoint.id"
        value="http://localhost:9000/fancyfoods/offers/SpecialOffer"/>

<property name="service.imported.configs"
        value="org.apache.cxf.ws"/>
    </endpoint-description>
</endpoint-descriptions>
```

Service interface(s) exposed

Your endpoint location

Type of endpoint to import

As you can see in listing 10.5, you provide the URL for your endpoint, as well as its interface type and some information about how the service was exported, in this case as a CXF-generated web service. This is rather brittle, unless you have a known proxy server that can get the routing right for you. For now a fixed URL is fine. If you build your manifest and XML configuration into a bundle and drop it into the load directory of your client system, then something rather magical happens when you refresh the front page of your superstore.

As you can see in figure 10.16, your special offers now include some foreign food from your remote system! Note that you didn't make any changes to your API or to the client application, and that you wrote a total of two manifests, two classes, and two XML files. This is how easy life can be when you have a modular OSGi application. We hope it's as exciting for you as it is for us!

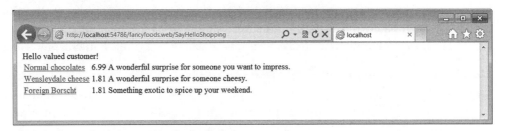

Figure 10.16   Your remote-enabled superstore

10.5   *Using your remote application*

You could stop adapting your application here, now that you know how to expose and consume a remote OSGi service in a transparent way using only standard configuration. On the other hand, there was more to your application than the special offers on the front page. What happens if you try to buy some of the foreign food that you've added? Clicking on the link to your special offer yields the page shown in figure 10.17.

The page in figure 10.17 is promising; everything looks about right, but what happens if you attempt to complete a purchase? See figure 10.18.

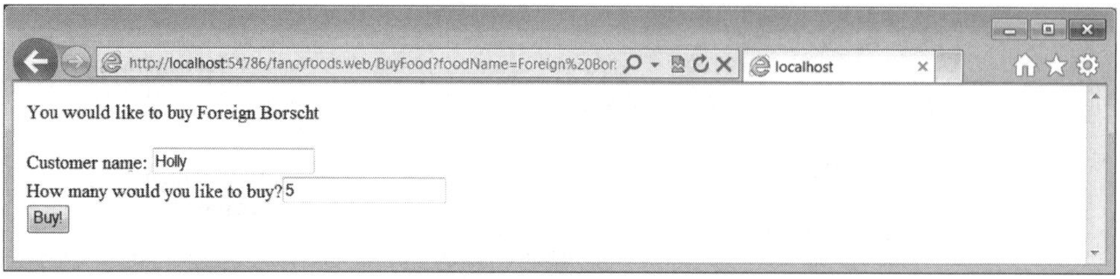

Figure 10.17   Trying to buy some foreign food—part 1

Figure 10.18   Trying to buy some foreign food—part 2

Oh dear. Clearly there's something wrong here; your purchase should be able to proceed, but it fails. The reason for this is simple, and it has to do with your database. You may remember that you've been using a local, in-memory database. Hopefully, you'll remember that you copied your datasource bundle into both the local and the remote framework. Doing this did let you get up and running more quickly, but it also created a second copy of your database, which definitely isn't good for your application!

Fortunately, the fix for this situation is simple. You need to build a new version of your datasource bundle that speaks to a remote database, rather than creating a local one.

10.5.1 *Setting up your remote database connections*

A huge number of powerful, scalable, network-enabled database implementations exist, any one of which would be more than capable of handling your new requirements. For simplicity you'll stick with the Apache Derby database, but you should feel free to use another if you fancy an extra challenge.

Setting up datasources for a remote Derby instance will require some changes to the Blueprint for your datasource bundle. Because there's no code in your datasource bundle, it's nontrivial to say what the new version of your datasource bundle should be. Our view is that moving the database to a remote machine, making it possible for a number of clients to concurrently share access, and making the database persistent is a major change, and therefore warrants an increment to the major version of the bundle.

The changes to your Blueprint are simple. You can leave the `service` elements untouched; what you need to do is to make some changes to the beans that they reference. In listing 10.6, you can see that all you need to do is to change the implementation class of your beans and supply some additional properties to indicate where your Derby server will be running. After you've made those changes, all you need to do is to increase the version of your bundle and package it up again.

Listing 10.6 Exposing your remote service

```
<bean id="derbyDataSource"
    class="org.apache.derby.jdbc.ClientDataSource">    ◁— Network Derby driver
    <property name="createDatabase" value="create"/>
    <property name="databaseName" value="fancyfoodsDB"/>      ◁—┐ No longer an in-
    <property name="portNumber" value="1527"/>                  │ memory database
    <property name="serverName" value="localhost"/>     ◁─┐
</bean>                                                     │ Remote Derby
                                                           │ location
<bean id="derbyXADataSource"
    class="org.apache.derby.jdbc.ClientXADataSource">
    <property name="databaseName" value="fancyfoodsDB" />
    <property name="createDatabase" value="create" />
    <property name="serverName" value="localhost"/>
    <property name="portNumber" value="1527"/>
</bean>
```

STARTING YOUR DERBY SERVER

It's easy to get your Derby server running. First you need to download a copy of Derby, because the one in your basic runtime doesn't have any network Derby support. Copies of Derby can be obtained from http://db.apache.org/derby/derby_downloads.html.

When you have a copy of Derby, you need to start the server running. This can be done by unzipping the Derby zip and issuing a single command from the Derby lib directory:

```
java -jar derbyrun.jar server start
```

Now that your Derby instance is running, you need to alter your basic runtime to support remote client connections to Derby. To do this, you need to replace the existing Derby JAR, which will be called something like `derby_10.5.3.0_1.jar`, with the `derbyclient.jar` from the Derby you downloaded. To get this bundle picked up in your basic runtime, you'll also have to edit the configuration for your framework. This configuration file is called configuration/config.ini.

> **WARNING: DERBY'S SPLIT PACKAGE** The version of Derby in your basic framework only provides support for embedded databases. As a result, it doesn't include the remote client drivers. Unfortunately, the remote client drivers and embedded drivers are in the same package. This means that you don't get a resolve-time error about the missing class. If you don't update your basic framework to replace the embedded Derby package, then you'll see a `ClassNotFound-Exception` from the Blueprint container trying to create your datasource.

After you replace the Derby bundle with the remote client, you may find that you start seeing a `ClassNotFoundException` from another datasource bundle. You aren't using this bundle, so it's nothing to worry about. You can remove the bundle from your basic runtime if the exception makes things difficult to follow.

When you open configuration/config.ini, you'll see a large number of framework properties used to determine the bundles that get started in your basic runtime. You're looking for the Derby entry that's something like the following:

```
derby-10.5.3.0_1.jar@start,\
```

You need to change the JAR name in this entry to `derbyclient.jar` so that the Derby network client code is available, as follows:

```
derbyclient.jar@start,\
```

After you've done this in both of your frameworks (the service provider and consumer frameworks), it's time to start up your application again. Initially there should be no difference at all; after all, your previous database had perfectly good read-only behavior (see figure 10.19).

Figure 10.19   Running with a remote database

If you attempt to buy some of your foreign food, then, as before, you're allowed to put some values into the form (see figure 10.20).

Figure 10.20   A second attempt to buy from your foreign foods department

This time, however, the result is a lot more pleasant! See figure 10.21.

Now that you have a single backing database, you're able to interact with the same data that your remote system is. As a result, your superstore can be distributed across

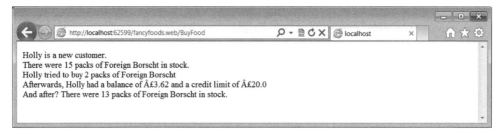

Figure 10.21   A successful purchase

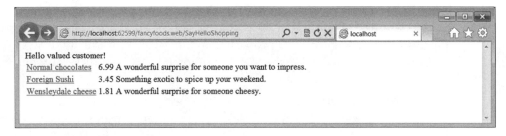

Figure 10.22   A new special offer!

as many machines as you want. As a final proof that the remote service is behaving properly, try making a bulk order for some more of your foreign food. This will cause your stock to drop, and if you buy enough, should cause your foreign foods department to select a new special offer (see figure 10.22).

We hope that you're now convinced that your remote service is not only live, but operating on the same data as the consuming framework. One thing you haven't done is propagate distributed transactions. This isn't always a problem—for example, your special offer service is read-only, and it isn't a disaster if you advertise an offer that's been changed by another user's large order. Sometimes, however, it's vitally important that both ends of the remote call run under the same logical transaction, and this isn't an area where CXF is strong. Although Apache CXF is probably the simplest way to take advantage of OSGi remote services, it's not the only one.

10.6   Using SCA for remoting

The Apache Tuscany project provides an alternative remote services implementation based on the Service Component Architecture (SCA). SCA is designed to enable component-oriented programming, in which discrete components are wired together through well-defined endpoints. These components may be co-located on the same system or—more usefully for remote services—distributed across a network.

10.6.1   Apache Tuscany

The Apache Tuscany project is an open source implementation of the SCA specification based on a Java-language runtime. As well as the core SCA runtime, Tuscany includes a number of SCA component implementation types. Importantly for OSGi, the Tuscany project hosts the reference implementation of the OSGi SCA component type, known as `<implementation.osgi/>`.

Because service component architecture is all about services, and OSGi services are one of the great features of the OSGi programming model, you may be guessing that these two technologies are a good fit. Unsurprisingly, SCA's OSGi component type makes use of the OSGi Service Registry to provide and consume SCA services. An OSGi SCA descriptor (following the typical SCA syntax) can be used to select particular OSGi services from the Service Registry using service properties to identify particular implementations. These services are then exposed as endpoints through the SCA runtime.

In addition to exposing existing OSGi services to SCA applications, the OSGi SCA component type also allows SCA endpoints to be advertised and consumed as services in the OSGi Service Registry. The properties and interface with which the SCA service is registered are also defined in the SCA descriptor, but OSGi bundles can then consume the SCA service as if it were any other OSGi service.

USING TUSCANY AND ARIES TOGETHER

Much like CXF, you can integrate Tuscany into your little Aries runtime by downloading a Tuscany distribution and copying all the bundles into the load directory. Alternatively, you can merge the config.ini configuration files for the Aries and Tuscany runtimes. Tuscany can be downloaded from http://tuscany.apache.org/sca-java-releases.html.

> **WARNING: GETTING TUSCANY WORKING WITH ARIES** You may find that combining Tuscany and Aries isn't as straightforward as it was for CXF and Aries. When we tried it, we hit several issues and we needed to do some tweaking to get everything working together. At a minimum, you'll need a Tuscany release more recent than 2.0-Beta3, because some OSGi bundles didn't resolve in that release. Some of Tuscany's dependencies required Declarative Services, but no implementation was included in the Tuscany distribution we tried. You'll need to make sure a Declarative Services implementation like Felix SCR is present in your runtime. Finally, Tuscany includes a bundle for the JPA API that's incorrectly labeled version 3.0, and this needs to be removed.

If getting a combined Tuscany-Aries runtime up and running is sounding like too much hard work, you might consider one of the prebuilt server stacks that have already done the integration for you. Remember that Apache Aries isn't intended to be an application server—it's a set of components that can be included in a server. IBM's WebSphere Application Server includes both an SCA runtime, based on Apache Tuscany, and an enterprise OSGi runtime, based on Apache Aries. We'll discuss other options for an enterprise OSGi stack more in chapter 13.

10.6.2 *Importing a remote service*

After you've got your Tuscany runtime up and running, you'll find that remote services with Tuscany looks a lot like remote services with CXF. Because you started off exporting a service with CXF, this time you'll go in the opposite order and start by importing a service using Tuscany. As with CXF, you'll need a remote services configuration file, as shown in the following listing.

Listing 10.7 The remote services endpoint configuration file for SCA

```
<?xml version="1.0" encoding="UTF-8"?>
<endpoint-descriptions
    xmlns="http://www.osgi.org/xmlns/rsa/v1.0.0"
    xmlns:sca="http://docs.oasis-open.org/ns/opencsa/sca/200912"
```

```
    xmlns:tuscany="http://tuscany.apache.org/xmlns/sca/1.1">
    <endpoint-description>
        <property
            name="objectClass"
            value="fancyfoods.offers.SpecialOffer" />
        <property
            name="remote.configs.supported"
            value="org.osgi.sca" />
        <property
            name="service.imported.configs"
            value="org.osgi.sca" />
        <property
            name="org.osgi.sca.bindings">
            <list>
                <value>{http://fancyfoods}ForeignFood</value>
            </list>
        </property>
    </endpoint-description>
</endpoint-descriptions>
```

Type of endpoint to import ⟵

Pointer to endpoint configuration ⟵

This is similar to the remote services configuration file you defined in listing 10.5. But the details of the configuration are different, because you're using a different remote services implementation. You set the `service.imported.configs` property to `org.osgi.sca`. Instead of providing lookup information for the service directly, as you did in listing 10.5, you provide a reference to an SCA *binding* by specifying a `org.osgi.sca.bindings` property.

The SCA bindings are set in a small SCA configuration file, as shown in the following listing.

Listing 10.8 The SCA configuration for a WSDL binding of a remote service

```
<scact:sca-config
    targetNamespace="http://fancyfoods"
    xmlns:scact="http://www.osgi.org/xmlns/scact/v1.0.0"
    xmlns:sca="http://docs.oasis-open.org/ns/opencsa/sca/200912">
    <sca:binding.ws
        name="ForeignFood"
        uri="http://localhost:8081/foreignfood" />
</scact:sca-config>
```

Finally, you'll need to add two extra headers to your manifest, so that SCA can find the remote services and SCA configuration files:

```
Manifest-Version: 1.0
Bundle-ManifestVersion: 2
Bundle-SymbolicName: fancyfoods.remote.config.sca
Bundle-Version: 1.0.0
Import-Package: fancyfoods.food;version="[1.0.0,2.0.0)",
 fancyfoods.offers;version="[1.0.0,2.0.0)"
Remote-Service: OSGI-INF/remote-service/*.xml
SCA-Configuration: OSGI-INF/sca-config/food-config.xml
```

TRYING OUT THE SCA IMPORTED SERVICE

Let's have a look at how the remote services behave in your SCA runtime. Build the
`fancyfoods.remote.config.sca` bundle and drop it into the load directory. You
should see the bundle appear, but more interestingly, you should also see some new
services appear. List the services that implement the `SpecialOffer` as follows:

```
osgi> services (objectClass=fancyfoods.offers.SpecialOffer)
```

As well as the familiar cheese and chocolate offers, there's a new offer, with lots of extra
SCA-specific service properties. You may expect the bundle that registers the service
would be the `fancyfoods.remote.config.sca` bundle. But it's the bundle that *consumes*
which registers its remote representation. If no bundles consume the remote service, it
won't even be registered. (And if you stop the `fancyfoods.remote.config.sca` bundle,
the `SpecialOffer` service will be unregistered.)

At this point, you may be slightly suspicious. You haven't written the SCA foreign
food service implementation, much less deployed and started it. How can a service be
available when there's no backend?

If you try to access the Fancy Foods front page, you'll discover that the backing
remote service is definitely missing, which makes a mess (see figure 10.23).

The SCA runtime registers services based on what's in the bundle metadata, but it
doesn't require the backing services to be available until they're used. This may seem
error prone, and in a sense it is—but it's merely reflecting the fact that remote invocations are naturally subject to service interruptions. Networks are inherently unreliable,
and remote services may come and go, so even if the remote service is available at the
time of registration, it might have vanished by the time it's used. This volatility is something to be aware of when using services that could be remote; more error handling

**Figure 10.23 If the remote implementation of a remote service is missing, the service will still be
available, but using it will cause errors.**

may be required than you're used to. Remember that local proxies of remote services will have the `service.imported` property set.

10.6.3 *Exporting remote services*

We're sure you know how to write code for handling errors, so rather than demonstrating that, we'll skip straight on to ensuring the remote service is available, which is much more fun.

You'll use a bundle similar to the foreign food department bundle from section 10.3. The Blueprint for the foreign food service is nearly identical to listing 10.3, but you'll need to add some extra service properties to tie together the exported service and some extra SCA configuration:

```
<service interface="fancyfoods.offers.SpecialOffer">
    <service-properties>
        <entry key="service.exported.interfaces" value="*"/>
        <entry key="service.exported.configs" value="org.osgi.sca"/>
        <entry key="org.osgi.sca.bindings" value="ForeignFood"/>
    </service-properties>

    <bean class="fancyfoods.department.foreign.ForeignFoodOffer">
        <property name="inventory" ref="inventory"/>
    </bean>
</service>
```

The extra SCA configuration file is exactly the same as that of the client-side bundle (listing 10.8), and is configured with a similar `SCA-Configuration:` reference in the bundle's manifest.

With the new `fancyfoods.department.foreign.sca` installed in the server-side framework, if you access http://localhost:8081/foreignfood?wsdl, you'll be able to see the generated WSDL description for the foreign food service.

10.6.4 *Interfaces and services*

The process of remoting services using SCA is similar to that of remoting them using CXF, although SCA does need some extra configuration files. But when you link up the remote service client to the remote services provider, an important difference between SCA and CXF becomes clear (see figure 10.24).

Remember that in section 10.2, we mentioned that distribution providers are only required to support distributed invocations with simple parameter types. Although CXF allowed you to use interfaces with much more complex parameters, such as `Food`, Tuscany's WSDL binding doesn't. This means the `SpecialOffer` interface can't easily be used for Tuscany remote services.

Remoting complex types is often handled by writing an `XMLAdapter` class to convert between complex and simpler types, and annotating method declarations or classes with the `@XmlJavaTypeAdapter` annotation. In the case of Fancy Foods, you'd add an annotation to the `SpecialOffer` class, as follows:

```
@XmlJavaTypeAdapter(value=fancyfoods.FoodAdapter.class,
   type=fancyfoods.foods.Food.class)
```

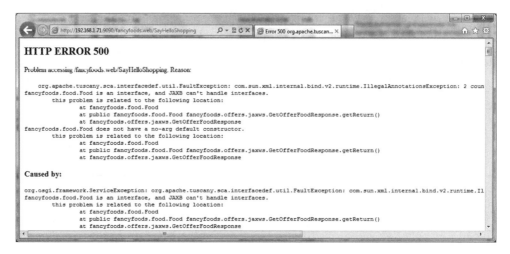

Figure 10.24   As this server error demonstrates, SCA's WSDL binding only works well for services whose interfaces are restricted to using primitive types.

The difficulty comes when you try to implement a `FoodAdapter`. By necessity, it will depend on a `FoodImpl` implementation class, which leaves the `SpecialOffer` interface with a dependency on an implementation class. If you're getting into the OSGi spirit of things, this should leave you feeling like you haven't brushed your teeth in a week.

A much more OSGi-centric solution to the problem is to wrapper the complex `SpecialOffer` service with a simpler `PrimitiveOffer` service for the purpose of distribution. A Blueprint reference listener can be used to track `PrimitiveOffer` services. The listener would automatically detect and consume each bound `PrimitiveOffer` service, and use it to generate and register a wrapper `SpecialOffer` service. But this significantly increases the complexity of using SCA for service remoting.

Does this mean you shouldn't use SCA for remoting your OSGi services? Not necessarily. Although we haven't provided a detailed example, SCA does provide support for distributed transactions, which may be critical to your application. Furthermore, as you'll see in chapter 11, SCA offers a lot more than remote services. You may find SCA remote services fit neatly into a broader SCA-based architecture. If your application server includes SCA, you can bypass the hand-assembly of your stack that we described earlier. And if your service interfaces are already based around primitives and Strings, you won't need to worry about rewriting services to avoid the use of complex types.

10.7   *Summary*

Remoting is generally considered to be one of the more difficult parts of enterprise programming. We hope that you can now see how the intrinsic dynamism and modularity of an OSGi framework dramatically simplifies this situation. Not only does OSGi lend itself to a remote model, but it also provides simple, easily reusable remoting specifications. Conveniently, several open source implementations of this specification are available.

With a small amount of effort, and no changes to your core application at all, you've seen that you can successfully add a remote service to your application. At no point in this chapter did you have to deviate from a standard, and the only piece of customization you did was to specify CXF and SCA configuration types in your endpoint definitions.

Although the Remote Services Specification is a straightforward way of remoting OSGi services, its scope is restricted to relatively homogeneous OSGi-only systems. In our experience, heterogeneous environments, with a mix of new and old components, and OSGi components and non-OSGi components, are more common. Although it works as a remote services implementation, one of SCA's real strengths is the flexibility of its bindings and component types, which allow a wide range of different types of systems to be knit together into a harmonious unified architecture. We'll discuss strategies for integrating heterogeneous systems, as well as how to migrate legacy applications to an OSGi-based platform, in the next chapter.

Migration and integration

In this book, we've been looking at how to write OSGi applications from scratch. This is fun, and also useful to know how to do, but it isn't usually the case that you can begin a brand new project with no existing code. Normally, you'll have application code to bring with you, either code that needs to be migrated into OSGi as part of your project, or external services that you need to be able to use from within the OSGi framework. Having to bring these sorts of things with you often results in a sinking feeling, particularly if the code has to keep working in more than one environment.

We're happy to tell you that migrating to OSGi is almost certainly not as hard as you think, and that there are a number of helpful OSGi tools and specifications that make these sorts of requirements possible.

When writing any enterprise application that's going to be put into production, one of the main tasks is usually to integrate with an existing system or service. It's unlikely that this service is OSGi-based, and there's a decent chance that it isn't even using Java. Regardless of how the backend service is implemented, there are techniques you can use.

270

11.1 Managing heterogeneous applications

We introduced you to SCA as a remoting technology for OSGi in section 10.6, but SCA is capable of much more than connecting two OSGi frameworks. Connecting one OSGi service to another is only a fraction of what SCA can do.

In an ideal world, your entire enterprise architecture would be based on a single technology, and that technology would—naturally—be OSGi-based. You would use remote services to hook together the disconnected parts of your system. In practice, we've never seen such an architecture, or at least not in an organization that had more than a few developers, or one or two years of history. Although technologies continue to evolve, old applications and systems based on old technologies can be stubborn in refusing to go away. One truly impressive example we've seen of this had a COBOL program providing information to a Python script, spanning *nearly 50 years* of application development! Even applications developed at the same time by different teams may be based on wildly varying technologies because of different development styles or skill sets within the teams.

It's worse than that, though—even applications developed at the same time within the same team may need to pick and choose capabilities from various technologies. Although it pains us to admit it in a book on enterprise OSGi, no single programming model can handle all requirements. Being able to stitch together applications that exploit the best capabilities of multiple technologies is clearly desirable.

How can these heterogeneous applications be managed and integrated? Are they doomed to remain in technology-specific silos, or is there a way of breaching the technology boundaries and moving operations and data between systems and across programming models? Over the years, there have been a number of attempts at integration technologies, but in recent years efforts have focused on service-oriented architecture (SOA) and the Service Component Architecture (SCA) technology. A different but related approach uses an Enterprise Service Bus (ESB) as an integration container to manage communication between disparate system components.

11.1.1 Using SCA to integrate heterogeneous systems

In section 10.6, we showed how to use web services bindings to connect two OSGi components together. SCA offers a range of bindings, so why web services? Part of the reason is that web services is a popular way to integrate distributed or heterogeneous applications. More pragmatically, web services is one of the few SCA bindings that are easy to get up and running on your little stack; Apache Aries isn't intended to be an application server, and the little sample assemblies don't include Java EE functionality like EJBs, CORBA, or JMS runtimes.

Assuming you're running with more application server support, what other bindings are available, and what else can SCA do for you in a heterogeneous environment?

At a high level, an SCA system consists of components and bindings. Components are functional elements; bindings allow components to communicate with one another. In general, components and bindings are mix-and-match, allowing business logic to be neatly separated from communication protocols (see figure 11.1).

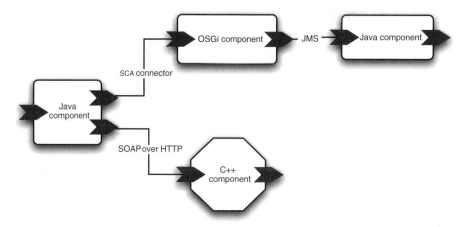

Figure 11.1 SCA systems consist of components connected by bindings.

SCA allows a range of component types and bindings. We've already seen the OSGi component type in section 10.6 (where it was cunningly disguised as an implementation of the Remote Services Specification). Other component types include the SCA Java component type, whose components resemble normal Java classes with some SCA-specific annotations, the BPEL component type, a Spring component type, and even C++ and Python component types. These components can be bound together using web services, JMS, EJB protocols, Comet, ATOM, JSON-RPC, or a default SCA communication binding (see figure 11.2).

Most of the SCA bindings, like web services, aren't SCA-specific, and this allows SCA-based applications to communicate with external applications that haven't even heard

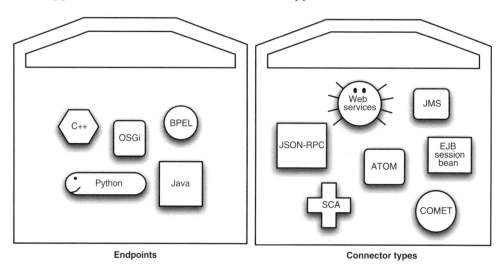

Figure 11.2 SCA provides a toolkit of component types and a toolkit of connectors that can be mixed and matched to bind endpoints together. The component types and bindings we show here aren't an exhaustive list, not least because SCA is extensible.

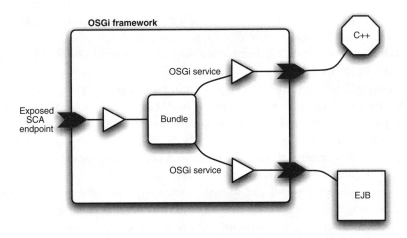

Figure 11.3 SCA bindings are exposed to OSGi applications as services, which means non-SCA-aware OSGi applications can communicate with non-SCA-aware applications of other types by consuming normal OSGi services.

of SCA. For example, anything that can drive a web service can communicate with an SCA component that exposes a web services binding. They also allow an SCA component—such as an OSGi service—to communicate transparently with external services with no awareness either of OSGi or of SCA (see figure 11.3).

INTEGRATING WITH AN EJB

SCA allows OSGi services to interact with EJBs. Although EJBs might seem like a component type, they're a binding. One way of thinking of this is that EJBs have a *language* (or communication protocol) and the SCA EJB binding provides a translation layer that allows things that aren't EJBs to communicate with EJBs.

Hooking an OSGi service up to an EJB is therefore as simple as replacing the web services binding in the food-config.xml configuration file (listing 10.8) with an equivalent EJB binding, as shown in the following code:

```
<sca:binding.ejb
    name="ForeignFood"
    uri="corbaname:iiop@localhost:4201#ForeignFoodFacadeBeanRemote" />
```

Assuming you have an EJB with the right name listening on the configured port, it will be accessible as an OSGi service inside the OSGi framework.

INTEGRATING WITH JMS

Accessing an external JMS queue is similarly transparent. The binding for a JMS queue called (for example) FoodQueue is as follows:

```
<sca:binding.jms
    uri="jms:FoodQueue" />
```

By default, a method called `onMessage` is called on the bound component, but if the component only has one method, then that will be called instead. Properties specifying the method to call can also be added to incoming messages.

Although it's another binding, in practice the JMS binding has some different characteristics from the web services and EJB bindings, and you may end up thinking about the asynchronous nature of the JMS binding when you're designing your component. For example, you may want to specify callbacks in your component definition to allow two-way communication. If you're connecting to an external queue, you may need to adjust the message format used by SCA to align with what's already in place. You can specify the wire format, extra headers, and operation properties. You can also use message selectors to filter incoming messages.

SCA is an extremely powerful and versatile technology for enterprise OSGi integration. After reading this section and section 10.6, you may be reeling slightly at how versatile SCA is and how many possibilities there are. It's a big topic, so we can only skim the surface of it here. If you're interested in learning more, we recommend *Tuscany SCA in Action* by Simon Laws, Mark Combellack, Raymond Feng, Haleh Mahbod, and Simon Nash (Manning, 2011).

But wait—there are even more possibilities to consider. Not only is there more than one way of integrating your application using SCA, there's a range of technologies beyond SCA that can be used for integration. Apache CXF, which worked so well as a remote services implementation in section 10.4, is intended to be a more general integration platform. Like SCA, it supports a range of component implementations and standardized communications protocols, such as web services, and JMS. CXF itself is a product supporting a range of standards, rather than a standard supported by a number of products, as SCA is. The primary orientation of CXF is web services, so it supports fewer languages and communication protocols than SCA.

11.1.2 *Integrating using an ESB*

A range of other integration technologies is available that falls into the general category of Enterprise Service Buses, or ESBs. As the name suggests, ESBs are intended to provide an adaptable asynchronous communications channel between loosely coupled enterprise components. Mediations allow conversions between a range of message formats and wire protocols (see figure 11.4).

ESBs and SCA

ESBs and SCA are designed to address similar problems—how can a technologically diverse set of applications be knit together into a functioning system without lots of hand-cranking and manual gluing? Importantly, though, an ESB is an architectural pattern, rather than a specific standard like SCA. As a technology, ESBs predate SCA, and many established ESBs started making use of SCA in some form or another after its introduction. Some ESBs are based on SCA, whereas others support SCA components as another type of deployable artifact.

(continued)
Whether you choose to use an ESB or SCA will probably be determined by what technologies you're already using. SCA usually has a lower initial cost for connecting together two specific things, but an ESB may have lower long-term costs because it's a more general-purpose solution to an infrastructure problem.

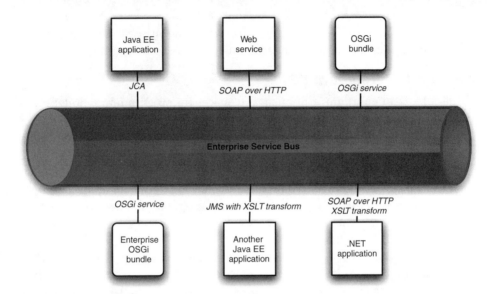

Figure 11.4 **An ESB acts as a common transport channel loosely connecting diverse endpoints. Communications may be mediated with XSLT transforms or other adjustments to the content.**

A number of ESB providers use OSGi for their internal architecture. But fewer of these ESBs include support for user's OSGi bundles, and fewer still include enterprise OSGi support in their runtime. But you do have some choices if you want to use your enterprise OSGi application with an ESB.

APACHE SERVICEMIX
The most comprehensive enterprise OSGi support is arguably provided by Apache ServiceMix. ServiceMix provides native hosting for your OSGi bundles and built-in Blueprint support, based on Apache Aries. Some nice extensions mean Blueprint can even be used to configure the message routing.

FUSE ESB
Closely related to ServiceMix is Fuse ESB, a productized offering of ServiceMix. Fuse ESB is still open source, but commercial support subscriptions are available.

APACHE KARAF PLUS APACHE CAMEL
ServiceMix is based on a combination of Apache Karaf and Apache Camel, with features to handle security, registries, and extra configuration. Some users find they don't

need this extra function, and the lighter combination of Karaf and Camel works well for them. You've already seen Karaf as a testing environment in section 8.3.4, and we'll be coming back to it as a production environment in section 13.2. Camel is a router. Karaf on its own certainly isn't an ESB, and Camel on its own doesn't offer OSGi support, but in combination they make a nice little integration platform. Camel provides Karaf with features that allow it to be easily installed into a Karaf instance, although you may need to adjust the JRE properties and OSGi boot delegation in some cases.

This completes our tour of SCA and ESBs. Talking to external services isn't the only problem you face when trying to start using enterprise OSGi. What do you do with existing Java EE artifacts if you want to use them in your application?

11.2   *Migrating from Java EE*

Java EE is an enormously popular and successful programming model for enterprise applications. If you picked up this book as someone with Java EE experience, you might have skipped ahead to this section. If so, we recommend cooling your jets and taking a step back to some of the earlier content in this book. Migrating Java EE applications to OSGi can be surprisingly easy, but it helps to have a good understanding of OSGi fundamentals before you start. If you try to migrate an application without that understanding, then things may seem confusing, but for those of you who *have* read chapters 2 and 3, you may find that this section reinforces what you thought already.

Java EE offers a huge range of support and integration points for many different enterprise technologies, so huge that there are few applications that use it all. Most applications stick to a small subset of the Java EE programming model. Recognizing this, in Java EE 6 the Java Community decided to allow the Java EE specifications to be grouped into *profiles* offering a reduced set of functions. The first profile introduced is known as the *Web profile* and unsurprisingly focuses on Java EE web applications (WARs) and the technologies most commonly used with them.

Having identified WARs as the most commonly used Java EE module type, it makes sense to start by looking at how you can migrate a Java EE WAR file into the OSGi container.

11.2.1   *Moving from WARs to WABs*

Unless you've skipped the majority of this book, you'll certainly have been introduced to the concept of the OSGi WAB. A WAB, or Web Application Bundle, is defined by the Web Applications Specification from the OSGi Enterprise Expert Group and is, by design, a close partner of the Java EE WAR. One of the key requirements for OSGi's Web Applications Specification was that it must be possible to write any WAB such that it's also a valid WAR file.

The wonderful thing about this requirement is that it not only dramatically simplifies the description of a WAB file, but that it also makes it trivial to migrate most Java EE WARs. Structurally, there's no real difference between a WAB and a WAR file. Both expect the web deployment descriptor (web.xml to you and me) to be located in WEB-INF and to be called web.xml, and expect to find servlet classes on the internal classpath of the web application. As a result, you don't need to change your WAR's internal structure at all!

The only important detail that separates a WAB from a WAR is that it has OSGi metadata in its manifest that makes it an OSGi bundle. By including this metadata, most standalone WARs can be converted into working WABs with no other changes at all!

CREATING OSGI METADATA FOR A WAR

All Java manifest files must declare the version of the manifest syntax that they use. To make a valid OSGi bundle, there are two more required headers, a `Bundle-Manifest-Version` with a value of 2, and a `Bundle-SymbolicName` that defines the bundle's name. Because a WAB is a bundle, it also needs these two headers, but it must also add a third that identifies it as a WAB. This is the `Web-ContextPath` header, which not only identifies the bundle as a WAB, but also defines a default context root (base URL) from which the web application should be served. Although versioning your bundle isn't strictly required, we would never build a bundle without versioning it properly, and would urge you not to either (for more information about why, see section 5.1.1).

The result of this is that the smallest possible WAB manifest looks something like the following listing.

Listing 11.1 A minimal WAB manifest

```
Manifest-Version: 1
Bundle-ManifestVersion: 2
Bundle-SymbolicName: my.simple.wab
Bundle-Version: 1.0.0
Web-ContextPath: /contextRoot
```

COPING WITH THE WAR CLASSPATH

It's clearly easy to provide enough metadata to get OSGi to recognize a WAR file as an OSGi WAB, but this isn't enough to make the WAR file work as a WAB. One of the most critical differences is surprisingly easy to overlook: the internal structure of the WAR file itself!

Changing the extension of a Java EE module from .jar to .war has a much more extensive effect on the module than changing its name. WAR files have an internal classpath that's different from normal JAR files. In a WAR, the servlet classes are supposed to live in WEB-INF/classes, *not* the root of the WAR (which is used for noncode resources). Furthermore, library JARs can be included inside a WAR file; any file with a .jar extension in the WEB-INF/lib folder of your WAR is implicitly added to the internal classpath (see figure 11.5).

One of the best things you can do to help turn your WAR into a WAB is to remember that the internal classpath of an OSGi bundle is (by default) like a normal JAR. This means that you have some work to do to allow OSGi to find your classes! You have two options: you can either adjust the structure of your WAR to match a standard JAR layout, or you can adjust the classpath of your OSGi bundle to match the layout of your WAR. The latter approach has several advantages: it's less invasive, less error-prone,

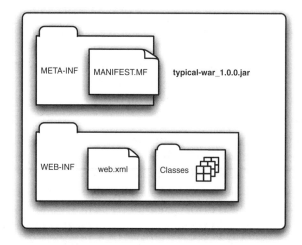

Figure 11.5 A typical WAR layout

more easily understandable for WAR developers, and, most critically, it allows the WAR to continue being used as a WAR and as a WAB!

Changing the default internal classpath of an OSGi bundle can be easily achieved using the `Bundle-ClassPath` header. This takes a comma-separated list of classpath locations, which can either be folders or JAR files, that are specified relative to the root of the bundle. If you were trying to make the WAR from figure 11.5 work in OSGi, then you would need to set the classpath as follows:

```
Bundle-ClassPath: WEB-INF/classes, WEB-INF/lib/myLib.jar,
  WEB-INF/lib/secondLib.jar
```

When your WAR has correctly specified its internal OSGi classpath, then you're much closer to being able to get it running. In the majority of cases, you still won't be able to load any of your classes. The internal classpath of a bundle is only a small part of the story.

FINISHING OFF YOUR OSGI METADATA

The key piece of information missing from your WAR is the most fundamental part of making your WAR into an OSGi bundle; it's the modularity statement, the set of packages that you want to import. Some of the packages that need to be imported are obvious; for example, we would wager that your WAR needs to import `javax.servlet` and `javax.servlet.http`.

> **Supported versions**
>
> Over the life of the Java EE specifications, there have been a number of versions of the Servlet Specification. The OSGi Web Applications Specification defines support for version 2.5 of the Servlet Specification. As a result, you shouldn't rely on being able to migrate Servlet 3.0 applications to an arbitrary OSGi web container. On the other hand, the OSGi Web Applications Specification does allow for implementations to support Servlet 3.0 applications. If you do need to use Servlet 3.0 in your application, then make sure that your container supports it, and also remember that the correct semantic version for the Servlet 3.0 package is 2.6.

Working out what other imports your WAR needs can be simple, or it can be difficult; it depends completely on how complex your WAR file is. You may need to add imports for packages used in your servlets, but it's also possible that you may not, if the code is supplied by a JAR in WEB-INF/lib. There may even be some dependencies needed by the library JARs in WEB-INF/lib! If your dependencies are nontrivial, then you can use trial and error to find out what packages you need, but there are also tools that offer smarter ways to approach this. Because most portable WARs have few dependencies (other than on the servlet API), we'll leave discussing these tools in detail until section 12.1.3.

The `webbundle` URL scheme

Another approach you can use to get WAR files running in an OSGi framework is the `webbundle` URL scheme. The OSGi Web Applications Specification defines a URL handler for URLs that start with `webbundle:`. If you install a bundle using this URL, then the WAR file it points at will be automatically converted into a WAB. The `webbundle` URL scheme is a compound URL, so the first thing after the `webbundle:` is the real URL to the WAR. After this part of the URL, you can add one or more parameters using URL query syntax. These parameters can be used to configure manifest headers for things like the WAB context root, as in the following example:

```
webbundle:file://myFolder/myWarFile.war?Web-ContextPath=myContextRoot
```

Although the `webbundle` URL scheme might seem like an easy option for using a WAB in OSGi, we wouldn't recommend it as a primary option. The reason for this is simple. You never get an OSGi bundle! Having installed your WAR using the `webbundle` URL scheme, you never get access to the generated WAB. This makes the WAB hard to debug and hard to reuse.

EVOLVING BETTER MODULARITY

You may remember that back in section 5.3.1 we recommended avoiding library JARs in OSGi WABs. The main reason for this is that it reduces the degree to which you can share classes and bundles in the runtime. If you're bringing a WAR into OSGi, then you're likely to have libraries inside it. We don't think it's reasonable to ask you to completely remove all of these library JARs immediately, which is why we added them to the bundle classpath. If the WAR file is going to be *really* modular, then you shouldn't be packaging JARs inside it.

What you can do is to break out the library JARs one at a time. Removing a library from the WAB will require you to add some more package imports to the WAB (unless the JAR wasn't being used), but it will allow other bundles to share the same library instance, reducing the memory footprint. In some cases, you may find that the library you're using isn't available as an OSGi bundle. In this case, you can either leave the library in your WAB or use the information in section 12.1 to help you obtain an OSGi-bundled version.

Following these guidelines should allow you to migrate any WAR file to OSGi, but WAR files are only one part of the Java EE specification. What do you do with some of the other types of modules?

11.2.2 *Using persistence bundles*

JPA is a popular persistence model, and is the Java EE standard for Object-Relational Mapping. As a result, JPA is tightly integrated with other Java EE specifications. Although JPA does fit nicely with other Java EE technologies, it's also possible to use it in Java SE, as this is a common pattern, even inside enterprise web applications. Let's start by looking at how to get a standard JPA bundle working in OSGi.

PACKAGING PERSISTENCE UNITS

As you saw in chapter 3, it's easy to make use of JPA in OSGi, but there are some important differences. In Java SE you can package a persistence descriptor called persistence.xml in the META-INF folder of a JAR to define persistence units. This descriptor can then be located on the classpath by a JPA provider and used to build the required object models, table descriptions, and database connections. In OSGi, things have to be a little different. The persistence descriptor and the JPA provider shouldn't be part of the same bundle, but if they aren't then the JPA provider won't be able to see persistence descriptors that are hidden away in other bundles. This is a specific example of a more general problem that affects Java SE programs in OSGi, one that we'll cover more in section 12.2.1.

To get around this issue, OSGi persistence bundles add one important piece of information to their manifests. This is the `Meta-Persistence` header. This header is used to identify and advertise the locations of the JPA persistence descriptors in the bundle, and has a default value of META-INF/persistence.xml, like Java SE. Unlike Java SE, the header can also point to persistence descriptors in other parts of the bundle, even ones that aren't named persistence.xml. A big advantage of this header is that it can be used to provide different persistence descriptors in Java SE and OSGi. Java SE will always use META-INF/persistence.xml, but OSGi can be told to use a different descriptor, potentially with different properties, that's better suited to the OSGi environment.

In JPA the persistence descriptor isn't the only important resource; there are also the *managed classes*, which are the classes that can be mapped into the database by the JPA provider. These are sometimes called the *entity classes*, but strictly speaking that term only refers to a subset of persistent classes. Because these classes are so closely related to the persistence descriptor, it's important that they get packaged into the same bundle (which is almost always the case in Java SE JARs).

OTHER TYPES OF PERSISTENCE BUNDLE

We're focusing on Java SE JPA usage, but it's worth briefly mentioning that Java EE defines persistence behavior for both EJB JARs and WAR files. If a bundle is an EJB JAR or WAR, then it's automatically searched for persistence descriptors and managed classes. To help developers working with these module types in OSGi, the Aries JPA container has semantic understanding of the headers that define both WABs and EJB bundles. As a result, you don't need to specify a `Meta-Persistence` header as well as a `Web-ContextPath` header, unless you wish to override the default WAB search locations of WEB-INF/classes/META-INF/persistence.xml and WEB-INF/lib/<library.jar>!/META-INF/persistence.xml. Like WABs, EJB bundles will also be searched automatically, although their default is the same as for normal bundles, META-INF/persistence.xml.

CREATING A PERSISTENCE BUNDLE MANIFEST

In addition to specifying the `Meta-Persistence` header, persistence bundles have to define all of the other OSGi metadata you would expect for an OSGi bundle. Unlike the web bundles you migrated in section 11.2.1, persistence bundles are unlikely to need to specify an internal classpath, because the default is nearly always correct. This means that persistence bundle manifests are usually simpler to author than web bundle manifests. Importantly, you still need to make sure that the persistence bundle imports the right packages; for example, `javax.persistence` is almost always needed. An example persistence bundle manifest is shown in the following listing.

Listing 11.2 Specifying a custom location for the persistence descriptor

```
Manifest-Version: 1
Bundle-ManifestVersion: 2
Bundle-SymbolicName: basic.persistence.bundle
Bundle-Version: 1.0.0
Meta-Persistence: persistence/descriptor.xml
Import-Package: javax.persistence
```

If your entity classes are complex, or your persistence bundle contains data access code as well as the managed classes, you may find that your imports are too complex to manage by hand. If this is the case, then, as for web applications, we suggest looking at some of the tooling options described in section 12.1.3.

MISSING IMPORTS FOR JAVAX.PERSISTENCE AND OTHER PACKAGES

If your persistence bundle contains a persistence descriptor and managed classes, but no code that persists them or retrieves them, then it's likely that you'll only use the `javax.persistence` package to access annotations. Because of the way annotations work, it's possible to load a class even if the annotations it uses aren't on the classpath. In this case, the annotations won't be visible to the runtime. This means that it's possible for your persistence bundle not to import `javax.persistence`, and for your managed classes to still be loadable!

This may seem innocuous, or even helpful, but it can lead to some extremely nasty problems—many of which are horrendous to debug. What's worse is that some of the problems can be subtle, or even implementation dependent, and easily missed until they cause a huge production failure costing thousands, or even millions, of dollars. What exactly is this problem, and how does it cause such awkward problems?

Annotations are used by a large number of enterprise technologies, such as JPA, EJBs, servlets, and Spring, to provide configuration and mapping information. This information is critical if the technology is to work correctly, and so its presence or absence results in huge behavior changes. The problem with a missing package import for annotations is that the annotations are still visible if you know where to look! Any annotation with a retention policy of class or runtime is compiled into the bytecode of the class (unlike source retained annotations). If the JPA container, JPA provider, EJB container, Spring, or anyone else, looks at the raw class bytes to determine which classes need to be managed, then the annotations can be found easily. This is a common way to locate annotated classes, and so most containers will locate your annotated classes, even if you don't import the annotation package. Up to this point there isn't a problem; annotated classes will be found correctly, the problem is with what happens next…

Having identified an annotated class for processing, it's common practice to load it, and then use the Java reflection API to find the rest of the annotations present on the class. There are two main reasons for this. First, it's much easier to use the reflection API than bytecode scanning to find all the annotations on a given class, and the annotations are returned in a more easily used form. Second, by loading the class it's much easier to find any annotations it has inherited from its type hierarchy. Those of you who are particularly on the ball may now have noticed the problem. If the type is loaded but the annotation package isn't available, then none of the annotations will be visible! If you're lucky, this will cause an immediate failure, but usually containers have sensible defaults for cases where there are no annotations. This can lead to part-configured objects being used by the container, almost always with spectacularly unpleasant results.

`javax.persistence` isn't the only package that can potentially cause this problem, and because some packages contain *only* annotations, it's entirely possible that you might run into this problem elsewhere. If you do use annotations, then consider using a manifest generation/validation tool like bnd to make sure that you don't accidentally end up in this situation.

JPA CLIENTS IN OSGI

Building a working manifest for a persistence bundle isn't a particularly difficult task, but this is only part of the story. The other difference between OSGi and Java SE is the way in which clients obtain an `EntityManagerFactory`. Unfortunately, this often requires changes to the client code. In Java SE, the API for obtaining an `EntityManagerFactory` is the `Persistence` bootstrap class, as follows:

```
Persistence.createEntityManagerFactory("myPUnit");
```

This model has a number of problems in OSGi. We've already mentioned the visibility of the persistence descriptor, but there are also general problems with static factories in OSGi that we'll discuss further in section 12.3.1. To avoid these problems in OSGi, the JPA runtime registers the `EntityManagerFactory` as a service in the Service Registry. After a client has looked up this service, it can use it in the same way that it did before. In the case where there are multiple persistence units defined in the system, then clients can filter on the persistence unit's name using the `osgi.unit.name` service property.

This code change may seem like a big problem, but it's almost never pervasive. Because `EntityManagerFactory` objects are designed to be created once and reused, there's almost always only one place in the code where they get created. This means that it's often easy to replace a call to the `Persistence` bootstrap class with a service lookup. Ideally, the code will already use a dependency injection model, or it can easily be changed to do so. You saw back in listing 3.5 how you could use a Blueprint namespace to easily inject JPA resources (in that case, it was a managed `EntityManager`). When using dependency injection, JPA resource access is a simple matter of configuring the dependency injection container to use the appropriate mechanism for the current platform. When accessing JPA in this way, client code can continue to work in OSGi and Java SE unchanged.

JAVA EE JPA CLIENTS

Java EE has a different model for JPA usage than Java SE, and luckily it's one that fits a little better with OSGi. Java EE modules are either injected with JPA resources or they look them up in JNDI. As a result, some OSGi-aware containers are able to transparently request these objects from the Service Registry. This support isn't available from all containers, and if it isn't, it's a trivial exercise to use the `osgi:service` JNDI scheme to locate the resource instead. (We discussed `osgi:service` lookups in sections 2.4 and 3.2.1).

Now that you've seen how WAR and JPA modules can be migrated, it's time to look at another common Java EE module type, the EJB JAR.

11.2.3 EJBs in OSGi

WARs and JPA persistence archives both have related OSGi standards. As a result, our advice so far has been portable across multiple environments. Unfortunately, there's no such specification support for EJBs in OSGi. The EJB project in Apache Aries is one of the newest, and at the time of writing Apache Aries EJB is still preparing for its first release.

Despite the comparative lack of support for EJBs in OSGi, there are still multiple supporting platforms. Oracle's GlassFish Server supports EJB JARs that use OSGi metadata and classloading. Apache Aries approaches this from the other direction (OSGi bundles that contain EJBs), but there has been a significant effort to meet in the middle. As a result both Apache Aries and GlassFish use the same metadata to describe EJBs within an OSGi bundle, meaning that although EJB bundles aren't strictly standard, they're reasonably easy to use across multiple platforms.

EJB BUNDLE PACKAGING AND METADATA

An EJB JAR has a simple structure. It has a normal JAR classpath, and it contains EJB classes. These classes can be identified using annotations, XML, or a mixture of both. If XML is used, then the XML file is called ejb-jar.xml and it lives in the META-INF directory of the JAR. Just like WABs do with WARs, EJB bundles follow exactly the same structure as EJB JARs (although as bundles they can choose to have a nonstandard internal classpath). The advantages of this approach are clear: it makes it easier to author an EJB bundle with existing tooling and skills, and it allows a module to be a valid EJB JAR and EJB bundle at the same time. The key difference between an EJB JAR and an EJB bundle is rather unsurprising: an EJB bundle must declare OSGi metadata in its manifest.

EJB bundles have to define standard OSGi metadata in exactly the same way that WABs, persistence bundles, and normal OSGi bundles do. We imagine that you're comfortable with symbolic names, versions, and package imports by now, so we'll skip the boring example and suggest that your import package statement is likely to need to contain an import for `javax.ejb` at version `[3,4)` or `[3.1,4)` depending on which version of the EJB specification you're using.

The important piece of information that distinguishes a bundle as an EJB bundle is the `Export-EJB` header. The presence of this header allows the bundle to be recognized and loaded by an OSGi-aware EJB runtime. In many ways, this header behaves like `Web-ContextPath` does for WABs, but its value does something rather different. We'll discuss exactly how the `Export-EJB` header can be used shortly, but it's useful to know that your EJBs will be loaded and run, even if the header has no corresponding value.

EJBs in WAR files

Starting with EJB 3.1, it's possible to define EJBs in a web module. This can be extremely useful if the EJB contains relatively little code, or if it's only used by the WAR file. With WARs and WABs so similar, the EJB support in Apache Aries also allows EJBs to be defined in WABs. You don't have to do anything special to make use of this function—the EJB runtime automatically scans any WABs for EJBs. The WABs don't even need to specify the `Export-EJB` header, although if they do, then it will be processed.

One important thing to note about defining EJBs in WABs is that the ejb-jar.xml descriptor must be placed in WEB-INF, *not* META-INF. This is the same location used by the EJB specification when EJBs are defined in WAR files.

INTEGRATING EJBS AND OSGI

At the time of writing, the EJB integration in Apache Aries provides support for versions up to and including the latest release, EJB 3.1. Combined with the reasonably simple structure of an EJB JAR, this means that it's usually easy to convert an existing EJB JAR into an EJB bundle. When running in an OSGi framework, however, accessing the EJBs might not feel particularly natural. Normally, EJBs are accessed through JNDI, and although this is still possible in Aries, it isn't how OSGi bundles normally do things. Where possible, OSGi bundles use the OSGi Service Registry to integrate, and this is exactly what you can do with certain types of EJBs.

A number of different types of EJBs exist, but the most commonly used are Session Beans. Session Beans have a further set of distinct types; of these, the Stateless and Singleton Session Bean types behave a lot like OSGi services. They're looked up, potentially by multiple clients, used for a period, and possibly cached in the meantime. It would be ideal if this usage pattern could integrate easily with other OSGi technologies such as Blueprint, and the Service Registry is an excellent place to do that. As a result, the Apache Aries runtime can be configured to register OSGi services for any Singleton or Stateless Session Beans inside an EJB Bundle.

SELECTING EJBS TO EXPOSE IN THE SERVICE REGISTRY

Getting the Aries EJB runtime to expose your EJBs as OSGi services is remarkably easy, and it relates to the value of the `Export-EJB` header. The value of this header defines a comma-separated list of EJB names. This list is a simple whitelist that's used to select the EJBs that should be exposed as OSGi services. As we mentioned earlier, this header can only cause Singleton and Stateless Session EJBs to be registered, but because these are the most commonly used types of Session EJBs (and you shouldn't be trying to call a Message Driven Bean directly), this covers the majority of EJB applications.

You might wonder why the `Export-EJB` header works differently from some of the other Java EE integration headers that you've seen, and also why it's a whitelist rather than a blacklist. This is an interesting discussion, and bears a little thought. In many ways, EJBs are similar to Blueprint beans or other managed objects. They can be wired together using dependency injection, and they can be exposed externally. We hope that we've convinced you by now that one of the most important aspects of a well-architected OSGi bundle is that it hides as much as possible. This is equally true of managed objects inside the bundles. You wouldn't normally expose every bean in a Blueprint file as a service; some are used internally by the other beans. Exactly the same is true of EJBs. You should be making a decision to expose the beans, not hoping that nobody starts calling them. This is why, by default, no EJB services get exported. To help in those times that you do want to export everything, or when you want to be extra explicit that nothing should be registered, there are two special values that you can associate with the `Export-EJB` header. These are `ALL` and `NONE`, and their behavior is self-explanatory.

When an EJB has been exposed as a service, the Aries EJB container will register one OSGi service per client view of the EJB. This can be a local interface, a remote interface, or the no-interface view of the EJB. The services will be registered with some special properties: `ejb.name` gives the name of the EJB, and `ejb.type` gives the type of the EJB (either Singleton or Stateless). These services can then be used like any other OSGi service; they can be easily consumed using Blueprint, or the OSGi API, or in any other way that you fancy.

Remote EJBs and remote services

The EJB programming model includes comprehensive support for incoming requests from remote clients. This is supported through the use of remote EJB interfaces. Back in section 10.2, we showed that OSGi services can support remote call semantics as well. Given that remote EJB interfaces are designed to be remotely accessible, it's only natural that they should be easy to expose as remote OSGi services. The Aries EJB container works to help you out here. All EJB services that correspond to remote interfaces have the `service.exported.interfaces` property set automatically by the Aries EJB container. This means that remote EJB services automatically integrate with a Remote Services Distribution Provider.

In addition to Java EE technologies, there's one framework that's widely used throughout enterprise programming: the Spring dependency injection framework.

11.2.4 *Moving to Blueprint from the Spring Framework*

The Spring Framework is a large ecosystem of projects, and there are books covering the wide variety of features available. Although there are powerful aspect-oriented programming tools and Web MVC helpers, the majority of Spring applications make significant use of Spring's dependency injection, but are much less reliant on the other Spring projects. A typical Spring application might contain configuration similar to the following listing.

Listing 11.3 A simple Spring application definition

```
<beans xmlns="http://www.springframework.org/schema/beans"
  xmlns:jee="http://www.springframework.org/schema/jee"
  xmlns:xsi="http://www.w3.org/2001/XMLSchema-instance"
  xsi:schemaLocation="http://www.springframework.org/schema/beans
   http://www.springframework.org/schema/beans/spring-beans-2.5.xsd
   http://www.springframework.org/schema/jee
   http://www.springframework.org/schema/jee/spring-jee-2.5.xsd">

  <jee:jndi-lookup id="dataSourceFromJNDI"              ◁── Find datasource
                 jndi-name="jdbc/MyDataSource"              in JNDI
                 cache="true"
                 lookup-on-startup="false"
                 proxy-interface="javax.sql.DataSource"/>

  <bean id="myBusinessBean" class="fancyfoods.business.SpringBean">
    <property name="datasource">                        ◁── Inject beans into
      <ref bean="dataSourceFromJNDI" />                      business logic
    </property>
  </bean>
</beans>
```

The Spring XML in listing 11.3 is simple, but it demonstrates an important point. Because of Blueprint's heritage, it's extremely easy to turn Spring XML into valid Blueprint XML. This can often be accomplished with few changes. If you were to write a roughly equivalent Blueprint version of the Spring example, it would look something like the following listing.

Listing 11.4 A simple Blueprint application definition

```
<?xml version="1.0" encoding="UTF-8"?>
<blueprint xmlns="http://www.osgi.org/xmlns/blueprint/v1.0.0">    Use Service
                                                                  Registry, not JNDI
  <reference id="dataSourceFromJNDI"              ◁──
          filter="(osgi.jndi.service.name=jdbc/MyDataSource)"
          interface="javax.sql.DataSource"/>

  <bean id="myBusinessBean" class="fancyfoods.business.SpringBean">
    <property name="datasource">                        ◁── Injecting beans
      <ref bean="dataSourceFromJNDI" />                      is the same
```

```
      </property>
    </bean>
</blueprint>
```

The Blueprint version of the application descriptor is slightly different, in that it uses the OSGi Service Registry to find the `DataSource`, but functionally it's doing exactly the same job, and it looks remarkably similar. We haven't picked a particularly special example here; most of Spring's XML syntax can be directly used in Blueprint with few, or sometimes no, changes. These parallels are explicitly listed in the documentation for Eclipse Gemini (the reference implementation for the Blueprint container service), which was contributed to Eclipse by SpringSource. This documentation is available at http://www.eclipse.org/gemini/blueprint/documentation/reference/1.0.1.RELEASE/html/blueprint.html#blueprint:differences. Most usefully, this page includes a table indicating the different names used by Spring and Blueprint for the same logical structures. A subset of this table is visible in table 11.1.

Table 11.1 A comparison of Spring and Blueprint XML syntax

Element/Attribute meaning	Spring syntax	Blueprint syntax
Namespace declaration	http://www.springframework.org/schema/beans or http://www.springframework.org/schema/osgi	http://www.osgi.org/xmlns/blueprint/v1.0.0
Root element	\<beans>	\<blueprint>
Default bean activation policy	default-lazy	default-activation
Bean ID	id	id
Bean class	class	class
Bean scope	scope	scope
Built-in scopes	singleton, prototype, request, session, bundle	singleton, prototype
Default bean activation policy	lazy-init=true/false	activation=lazy/eager
Explicit dependencies	depends-on	depends-on
Initialization method	init-method	init-method
Destruction method	destroy-method	destroy-method
Bean static/Instance factory method	factory-method	factory-method
Instance factory bean	factory-bean	factory-ref
Instantiation argument	\<constructor-arg>	\<argument>
Injection property	\<property>	\<property>
Injecting bean references	ref	ref
Injection value	\<value>	\<value>

Table 11.1 A comparison of Spring and Blueprint XML syntax (continued)

Element/Attribute meaning	Spring syntax	Blueprint syntax
Exposing a service	<service>	<service>
Consuming a single service	<reference>	<reference>
Consuming multiple services	<list>	<reference-list>

SPRING TRANSACTIONS

In addition to its dependency injection model, Spring offers declarative transaction support to beans using aspect-oriented programming. This can be a little complicated to configure, but typically you would use one of Spring's predefined transaction aspects with a Spring transaction manager. A simple example might look like the XML in the following listing.

Listing 11.5 Controlling transactions with Spring

```xml
<?xml version="1.0" encoding="UTF-8"?>
<beans xmlns="http://www.springframework.org/schema/beans"
  xmlns:xsi="http://www.w3.org/2001/XMLSchema-instance"
  xmlns:aop="http://www.springframework.org/schema/aop"
  xmlns:tx="http://www.springframework.org/schema/tx"
  xsi:schemaLocation="
  http://www.springframework.org/schema/beans
  http://www.springframework.org/schema/beans/spring-beans-2.5.xsd
  http://www.springframework.org/schema/tx
  http://www.springframework.org/schema/tx/spring-tx-2.5.xsd
  http://www.springframework.org/schema/aop
  http://www.springframework.org/schema/aop/spring-aop-2.5.xsd">

  <aop:config>                                        ❶ Intercept all methods in
    <aop:pointcut id="requiredTxBeans"                  fancyfoods.persistence
      expression="execution(* fancyfoods.persistence.*.*(..))"/>

    <aop:advisor pointcut-ref="requiredTxBeans"
      advice-ref="requiredTxAdvice"/>
  </aop:config>

  <tx:advice id="requiredTxAdvice">
    <tx:attributes>                                   ❷ Require transaction
      <tx:method name="*" propagation="REQUIRED"/>      for all methods
    </tx:attributes>
  </tx:advice>
                                                      ❸ Bean will be
  <bean id="inventory"                                  transactional
    class="fancyfoods.persistence.InventoryImpl"/>

</beans>
```

The XML in listing 11.5 defines a number of things. In ❶ it defines the locations into which the transaction aspect should be injected. The aspect itself is defined at ❷, and declares that this injection point should create a transaction if none exists already. Finally, you can see the declaration of the bean itself at ❸.

> ### What's aspect-oriented programming?
>
> Aspect-oriented programming is a programming methodology that's rather different from the object-oriented programming most of us know and love. In object-oriented programming, you try to identify groups of data that represent state and encapsulate them within an object. In aspect-oriented programming, you try to identify common problems or functions (usually known as cross-cutting concerns) and encapsulate them within aspects. These aspects (sometimes known as *advice*) are then *woven* into the code at points defined by `pointcuts`.
>
> Aspect-oriented programming is a powerful mechanism for adding common code to objects, removing the need for them to declare it directly. This can significantly simplify the code within the object, and is particularly useful for things like logging and transactions, which are typically orthogonal to the main purpose of the running method.

You've already seen how to use the Aries transactions project to add declarative transactions to Blueprint beans in section 3.3.6, but it's worth looking at the following listing to see how Blueprint compares to Spring.

Listing 11.6 Controlling transactions with Blueprint

```xml
<?xml version="1.0" encoding="UTF-8"?>
<blueprint
    xmlns="http://www.osgi.org/xmlns/blueprint/v1.0.0"
    xmlns:jpa="http://aries.apache.org/xmlns/jpa/v1.0.0"
    xmlns:tx="http://aries.apache.org/xmlns/transactions/v1.0.0">

  <bean id="inventory" class="fancyfoods.persistence.InventoryImpl">
      <tx:transaction method="*" value="Required"/>          ⟵  All methods require
                                                                 transaction
  </bean>
</blueprint>
```

As you can see, it's easy to add transactionality to Blueprint beans using the Blueprint transactions namespace, as Spring beans can with the Spring transactions namespace. Because of their equivalent levels of function, it's entirely possible to move between Aries Blueprint and Spring's transaction syntax as necessary.

11.3 *Summary*

We've now covered a broad range of migration strategies for a variety of enterprise module types. We hope that you agree that moving enterprise applications to OSGi need not be an impossible, or even painful, process. The new standards introduced by the OSGi Enterprise Expert Group and the extensions provided in the Apache Aries project allow for many commonly used technologies to be migrated easily, often with no code changes.

In cases where migration *is* difficult, or where you don't wish to migrate away from the existing system but do want to use OSGi for other parts of the application, then

SCA can be used to link together the heterogeneous modules in a clean, implementation-independent way. All in all, life looks good for enterprise developers.

Given how easy migration can be, why does OSGi have such a reputation for being difficult to use? And why isn't it already the de facto platform? One common theme throughout this chapter has been that you've had control of the source code and packaging, allowing you to change the modules as necessary. For the libraries that you use in your applications, this isn't always the case! In chapter 12, you'll learn some approaches for making use of code that isn't OSGi-aware, and that, for whatever reason, you can't change.

12

Coping with the non-OSGi world

This chapter covers

- How to use existing third-party libraries with OSGi
- Patterns to avoid in OSGi where you can
- How to work around some common problems
- How to avoid doing more work than you need to

We've spent the majority of this book talking to you about how amazing OSGi is, and the fact that everybody should be using it. We believe this to be true, as do many others, but not everybody thinks of OSGi when writing their code. If they did, then there wouldn't be much need for this book! Even though so many people do now think of OSGi, there are plenty of excellent libraries that have been in use for years, long before OSGi was as widely used as it is now.

We don't expect enterprise OSGi developers to work in isolation from all of the non-OSGi code that exists. In fact, we would think you rather over-zealous if you tried to. Rather than having to give up all those useful libraries, or waiting for them to be packaged as OSGi bundles (which you should still ask for!), it's important to learn how to work with what's already out there.

When it comes to using existing code with OSGi, packaging isn't the only problem; there are a number of other issues.

The most common problem people encounter when trying to use enterprise OSGi for the first time is that they want to make use of their favorite libraries, but don't have a copy packaged as an OSGi bundle. On hitting this first hurdle, some give up, but there are a number of simple approaches that you can use to overcome this problem.

12.1 Turning normal JARs into OSGi bundles

As we've already mentioned, the Java ecosystem is large and contains a huge number of libraries providing all manner of functions. Some of these libraries are widely used; others are specific to certain fields and may only be useful to a handful of developers; but in all cases, they provide something that other people want to use, and don't want to have to write for themselves. Because these libraries are developed by such a big community, you can't rely on them always being provided as OSGi bundles. After all, not everyone has been using OSGi for the last decade!

> **Native libraries**
>
> Not all libraries are written in Java and packaged as JARs. Sometimes the right way to perform a particular operation, for example, encryption or vector calculus, is to communicate with some specialist hardware or to use some optimized assembly code. These situations are rare for most Java developers, particularly in the enterprise space.
>
> Thanks to its origins in embedded systems, OSGi has a well-designed integration point for calling native code libraries, but we consider this to be well beyond the scope of enterprise OSGi. If you're interested in getting native code or other low-level concepts running in OSGi, then we can recommend *OSGi in Action* (Hall et al., Manning Publications, 2011) as a useful book on the subject.

When your favorite library isn't packaged as an OSGi bundle, it can't be used in an OSGi framework, but some effort is usually enough to turn up an OSGi-packaged version.

12.1.1 Finding bundled libraries

It's always a good idea to reuse code in the form of libraries where you can; it saves effort and tends to reduce the number of bugs in your code. For exactly the same reason, it's a good idea to try to find a copy of your library that has already been turned into an OSGi bundle. If you do find a bundled copy of your library, then you should definitely use it. It saves time, and is typically much more reliable at producing well-formed bundles than other approaches.

You may think that being told to find a bundled copy of your library is a little silly; after all, the whole point of section 12.1 is that your library isn't an OSGi bundle. On the other hand, it's unlikely that you're the first person to want to use a given library in OSGi, and it's definitely worth taking advantage of any existing solutions if you can.

UPGRADING OR CHANGING YOUR LIBRARY

One of the most reliable, and most frequently overlooked, ways of obtaining your favorite library as an OSGi bundle is to go to the development site for the library and look. You may feel that this advice is rather useless, but most people are surprised by how many library developers have adopted OSGi packaging in the last couple of years. This is another clear sign of OSGi's increasing popularity throughout the Java community. Given that mature libraries are often released irregularly, it can be easy to miss a release that adds OSGi metadata to the library's packaging.

If you can find an officially released version of your library packaged as an OSGi bundle, it's by far and away your best option. Not only do you have a reasonable level of support, but you can also expect some thought to have been put into the packaging. Typically, the only downside that you encounter when moving to an official OSGi packaged version of your library is that you may have to take a newer version. This sometimes leads to API changes, but unless the library has changed beyond recognition, and would require you to significantly rewrite your application, it's the right way to go.

If you're already using the latest and greatest version of your library and you know there isn't an OSGi version you can use, then you should definitely raise a requirement with the library developers. It's possible that they're already thinking of adding OSGi packaging, and even if they aren't, they will be after you've asked for it. They may not know how to provide OSGi metadata, and so providing a patch with your suggested OSGi helpers can often speed things up. If you're using a library that's no longer actively maintained, or there's no chance of getting an OSGi-packaged release, then it's time to get a little more creative in your search.

Most libraries aren't created in a vacuum; there are few that are the *only* choice for providing a given function. Some libraries are much more popular than their competition, but that doesn't mean that the competition isn't worth considering. You may find that even though the library you want to use isn't available as an OSGi bundle, one of its competitors is. If it's possible to switch to another, OSGi-aware, library implementation with relatively little effort, then this is definitely worth considering. A less-invasive option is to take advantage of a number of repositories that repackage popular libraries as OSGi bundles.

LET SOMEONE ELSE DO THE WORK

The whole point of using software libraries is to reduce the amount of effort that you have to expend when writing your code. In that spirit, we recommend not moving on to more drastic bundling steps until you've exhausted the possibility that someone else has done the work for you. Even if the developers of your library have not yet offered an OSGi bundle distribution, or you absolutely need a particular version of the library for your application, that doesn't mean that there isn't an OSGi bundle for you.

The SpringSource Enterprise Bundle Repository

As is apparent from its name, this bundle repository is operated by SpringSource. The Enterprise Bundle Repository contains a large number of *bundlized* open source projects. These have their metadata generated automatically through bytecode analysis, then packaged in with the code. This means that the EBR is a good place to find commonly used libraries that don't offer an OSGi bundle distribution. The bundles provided by the EBR are available under a variety of different licenses, the same ones with which the original projects were made available.

Maven Central

Many popular libraries are available on Maven Central as OSGi bundles, even when the library authors haven't made a bundle packaging available. The JAR and bundle packaging can co-exist on Maven Central because they have different group IDs; usually, the group ID of the bundle is the ID of the project that repackaged it. This makes it harder to find individual bundles, but easier to browse the whole collection.

The Apache ServiceMix and Apache Geronimo projects have both pushed a large number of useful bundles to Maven Central. Therefore, the most common group IDs for repackaged bundles on Maven Central are `org/apache/servicemix/bundles/`, `org/apache/geronimo/bundles`, and `org/apache/geronimo/specs`.

If you're unlucky enough to find that the library you want to use isn't available from SpringSource, Apache, or anywhere you've managed to search on Google, then it's time to start thinking about taking matters into your own hands. A couple of options are open to you here, options broadly similar to those used by Apache and SpringSource.

12.1.2 *Building your own bundles*

When you've reached the point where you need to convert your library JAR into a bundle yourself, we're afraid that things get more difficult for you. Unfortunately, there's no magic wand to wave, but there's a little pixie dust we can introduce you to later. We'll start by looking at how to build your library bundle by hand. This isn't particularly easy, but it's important to know how it's done, even though later we'll show you some of the automated tools.

HAND-CRAFTING A MANIFEST

Although it may seem like a lot of effort, as long as you don't have more than a couple of simple libraries to convert, building OSGi manifests by hand isn't always a bad idea. You learn a lot about the library in the process. The first step for building an OSGi bundle from a JAR is simple: you need to extract the JAR's manifest file. This can be done using a zip utility, or by using the `jar` command, as follows:

```
jar xf jarfile.jar META-INF/MANIFEST.MF
```

Having extracted your manifest file, the first and most important things you need to add are `Bundle-ManifestVersion: 2` and a `Bundle-SymbolicName` for your bundle. While you're at it, you should also provide a version for your bundle using the `Bundle-Version` header. At this point you have, theoretically, added enough information to the manifest to turn your library into a valid OSGi bundle. If you remember back to the start of the book, you didn't even need to specify the bundle version for that, though hopefully you now know why you always *should* supply a version.

Although there's now enough metadata to install this bundle into an OSGi framework, it wouldn't be useful in its current state. To be able to use this library, you'll have to export some packages from it. Assuming the library is well documented (and at least vaguely well organized), it should be easy to identify its API packages. When these packages have been identified, you should add them to an `Export-Package` header in the manifest along with their version, which you may have to assume is the same as the version of the library.

If the library you're packaging is simple or low-level, and only has dependencies on core Java classes, then you're done at this point. Unfortunately, most libraries do have dependencies on other library code. Some more complex libraries have large numbers of dependencies. Depending on the quality of the documentation for your library, you may be able to find out what other libraries, and importantly what packages from those libraries, it depends on. Failing that, if you have access to the library source you can read through it to find out what packages are needed.

After you've added in any necessary `Import-Package` header entries to your bundle (complete with version ranges derived from the documentation or build dependencies), you're ready to repackage your manifest into the JAR. This is a trivial operation, but you should *not* use a standard zip tool to do it. The JAR specification requires that the manifest file is the first entry in a JAR, something that you can't guarantee unless you use a tool specifically for creating JARs. A good command-line tool to use is the `jar` command, as follows:

```
jar ufm jarfile.jar ./META-INF/MANIFEST.MF
```

If you prefer a build tool to the command line, then there are a variety of other options; for example, in an ANT build, as follows:

```
<jar destfile="jarfile.jar" manifest="META-INF/MANIFEST.MF"
    update="true">
```

Signed JARs

In some cases, the library JAR you wish to convert may be signed, or perhaps the license prevents you from modifying the JAR in any way, so that it isn't possible for you to update the JAR manifest. Don't worry, all isn't lost! In this case, you should create your OSGi manifest from scratch providing the same headers, but also adding the header `Bundle-ClassPath: jarfile.jar`. What you need to do then is to create a new JAR containing your OSGi manifest and also add the original library JAR to the root of the new bundle. Simple!

Note that creating bundles in this way does have one major disadvantage. The bundle can no longer be used as a normal JAR file because it has an internal classpath.

As you've seen, building manifests by hand is simple as long as the library JAR isn't too complex. Sadly, as the library JAR becomes larger and has more dependencies, that situation changes quickly. Identifying the dependencies for a library can be hard, particularly if the library isn't well modularized (which is likely, given that it isn't an OSGi bundle). This makes hand-writing manifests of limited practical use in many cases, which is why a number of tools have been developed to smooth the process.

12.1.3 *Generating bundles automatically*

As we've said before, it's a sad fact that there are many useful Java libraries that aren't yet available as OSGi bundles. You now know how to turn these JARs into bundles by hand by updating the manifest with the right headers, but it's not particularly easy. You might be able to work out which packages to export, based on a published API, but how do you know what to import? If it was easy to work out a bundle's dependencies by looking at it, setting a normal Java classpath wouldn't be such a nuisance! See figure 12.1.

Rather than suffer through the slow process of converting every library JAR by hand, a few OSGi developers turned their attention to automating the process. Reading through this section, you'll see that there are a few problems with automatic bundle conversion, but that for the most part it dramatically speeds up the process of building an OSGi bundle. A number of tools are available for you to use, too many for us to describe all of them in detail. We'll cover the most popular options.

USING BND

In section 8.2.1., we first introduced you to bnd as a useful build-time tool for packaging OSGi bundles. One of the most useful functions of bnd has nothing to do with building. Bnd can use the same logic it uses to generate manifests at compile time to generate manifests for existing JARs.

To demonstrate bnd, you'll need the command line version of bnd itself (http://www.aqute.biz/Bnd/Download) and a simple demonstration JAR. Rather than trying to use a real library, which would probably be too complicated, you'll use the Fancy Foods superstore chocolate department bundle from back in chapter 3. This may sound odd—after all, the chocolate department is already an OSGi bundle—but remember that a bundle is still, at its heart, a JAR file.

> #### How to run bnd
> Bnd is a multipurpose tool that integrates with lots of other build tools and runtimes. As a result, there are dozens of ways that you can use and launch bnd. To keep things simple, you'll use bnd from the command line, but there are plenty of other options described in bnd's documentation.

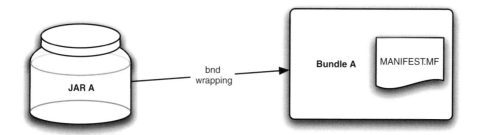

Figure 12.1 Tools can take a conventional Java JAR and produce sensible OSGi bundles more reliably than converting them by hand.

In the simplest case, you can wrap the chocolate department JAR by pointing bnd at it and invoking the `wrap` command, as follows:

```
java -jar biz.aQute.bnd.jar wrap
 fancyfoods.department.chocolate_1.0.0.jar
```

This will create an OSGi bundle called fancyfoods.department.chocolate_1.0.0.bar. If you forget the naming convention and look on your filesystem for a new JAR file, it may take you some time to find the wrapped JAR! When you've found the generated bundle, you should see that it contains a manifest that looks something like the following listing.

Listing 12.1 A bnd-generated default manifest

```
Manifest-Version: 1
Bnd-LastModified: 1309600295603
Bundle-Blueprint: OSGI-INF/blueprint/*.xml
Bundle-ManifestVersion: 2
Bundle-Name: fancyfoods.department.chocolate_1.0.0
Bundle-SymbolicName: fancyfoods.department.chocolate_1.0.0
Bundle-Version: 1.0.0
Created-By: 1.6.0 (IBM Corporation)
Export-Package: fancyfoods.chocolate;uses:="fancyfoods.food,fancyfoods.o
 ffers",OSGI-INF,OSGI-INF.blueprint
Import-Package: fancyfoods.food;resolution:=optional,fancyfoods.offers;r
 esolution:=optional
Tool: Bnd-1.44.0
```

If you inspect the manifest bnd has generated, you'll see that bnd has wrapped the chocolate department JAR into a bundle in the least restrictive way possible; every package in the JAR is freely exported, and every imported package is optional. If you look closely, you'll see that the bundle manifest is even less restrictive than you might have expected. The exports for the bundle are so loose that it even exports its OSGI-INF and OSGI-INF/blueprint folders!

Bnd has a good reason for being so unrestrictive. These defaults mean the generated bundle is guaranteed to start in any OSGi environment, but they don't guarantee that the bundle will work properly! The optional imports and generous exports give you an OSGi bundle with the character of a conventional JAR, where all classes are externally visible and missing dependencies won't be detected until classes fail to load at runtime.

As you know, you aren't using OSGi to make things work like they do with normal Java! It's at this point where hopefully you'll understand why we covered building OSGi bundles by hand in section 12.1.2, before looking at automated tools. Every tool needs some level of configuration to produce a sensible result, and that configuration needs to be built with at least a vague understanding of the bundling process.

Fortunately, you can easily refine the bundle bnd produces by using a bnd file in the wrapping process. As a starting point, you may want to set a sensible symbolic name and version; you'll notice that the default symbolic name for your bundle is particularly unpleasant! Next, because you know that neither of your imports is optional, you should make your imports compulsory by adding an `Import-Package` header. This doesn't require you to list the imports, because you can use `*` as a wildcard. As with build-time usage of bnd, any spurious imports can be individually removed using a `!<package name>` entry. Finally, you should tighten the package exports by overriding the default `Export-Package: *` used by bnd. In this case, you don't want to export anything, so leave the entry blank. It's also a good idea to let bnd know which packages in your bundle have private implementation using the `Private-Package` entry.

In the general case, you may find that you want to keep some package imports optional because they're associated with poorly modularized optional code paths. These can be explicitly added to the `Import-Package` section of the bnd file including the `resolution:=optional` directive.

When you've finished writing your bnd file, you should have something that looks like this:

```
Bundle-Name: Fancy Foods Chocolate Bundle
Bundle-SymbolicName: fancyfoods.department.chocolate
Bundle-Version: 1.0.0
Private-Package: fancyfoods.chocolate
Export-Package:
Import-Package: *
```

To use the bnd file, you need to add a `-properties <bndFile.bnd>` argument when you invoke bnd, as follows:

```
java -jar /biz.aQute.bnd.jar wrap -properties
   fancyfoods.department.chocolate.bnd
   fancyfoods.department.chocolate_1.0.0.jar
```

The manifest for the resulting bundle, shown in the following listing, should now look much more like the original, well-modularized manifest for the Fancy Foods chocolate department; the only missing bits of information are version ranges on the package imports.

Listing 12.2   A bnd manifest generated with configuration

```
Manifest-Version: 1
Bnd-LastModified: 1309602664432
Bundle-Blueprint: OSGI-INF/blueprint/*.xml
Bundle-ManifestVersion: 2
Bundle-Name: Fancy Foods Chocolate Bundle
Bundle-SymbolicName: fancyfoods.department.chocolate
Bundle-Version: 1.0.0
Created-By: 1.6.0 (IBM Corporation)
Import-Package: fancyfoods.food,fancyfoods.offers
Private-Package: fancyfoods.chocolate
Tool: Bnd-1.44.0
```

Given that the manifest still isn't entirely right, there's a small amount of tinkering still to do. Bnd does attempt to fill in the import version range for any package imports that it generates, but in the absence of any information about the exported version of the package, there's not a lot it can do! Fortunately, bnd does offer a way for you to provide this information by including one or more JARs on the classpath. Extend your command further to add the `fancyfoods` API JAR to the bnd classpath using the `-classpath` argument, as follows:

```
java -jar /biz.aQute.bnd.jar wrap -properties
 fancyfoods.department.chocolate.bnd
 -classpath fancyfoods.api_1.0.0.jar
 fancyfoods.department.chocolate_1.0.0.jar
```

The resulting manifest file is now nearly as good as it was to start with, as shown in the following listing.

Listing 12.3 A well-generated bnd manifest

```
Manifest-Version: 1
Bnd-LastModified: 1309685933015
Bundle-Blueprint: OSGI-INF/blueprint/*.xml
Bundle-ManifestVersion: 2
Bundle-Name: Fancy Foods Chocolate Bundle
Bundle-SymbolicName: fancyfoods.department.chocolate
Bundle-Version: 1.0.0
Created-By: 1.6.0 (IBM Corporation)
Import-Package: fancyfoods.food;version="[1.0,2)",fancyfoods.offers;vers
 ion="[1.0,2)"
Private-Package: fancyfoods.chocolate
Tool: Bnd-1.44.0
```

To the untrained eye the manifest is now done, but if you look more closely you'll see that the version ranges on the `Import-Package` statements aren't right. The code in your bundle doesn't only consume the packages it imports, it implements API from them as an API provider. This means that a minor version increment would still be considered a breaking change. Bnd doesn't cope well with this scenario because there isn't enough information in the Java class files to tell bnd whether the interfaces are implemented by the consumer or the provider. What you can do is alter your configuration file to let bnd know that you provide implementations for the packages you import by using the `provide` directive with a value of `true`, as follows:

```
Bundle-Name: Fancy Foods Chocolate Bundle
Bundle-SymbolicName: fancyfoods.department.chocolate
Bundle-Version: 1.0.0
Private-Package: fancyfoods.chocolate
Export-Package:
Import-Package: *; provide:=true
```

Running with this updated configuration, you finally get back a correctly modularized manifest, as in the following listing.

Listing 12.4 A completely configured bnd manifest

```
Manifest-Version: 1
Bnd-LastModified: 1309804592021
Bundle-Blueprint: OSGI-INF/blueprint/*.xml
```

```
Bundle-ManifestVersion: 2
Bundle-Name: Fancy Foods Chocolate Bundle
Bundle-SymbolicName: fancyfoods.department.chocolate
Bundle-Version: 1.0.0
Created-By: 1.6.0 (IBM Corporation)
Import-Package: fancyfoods.food;version="[1.0,1.1)",fancyfoods.offers;ve
  rsion="[1.0,1.1)"
Private-Package: fancyfoods.chocolate
Tool: Bnd-1.44.0
```

We hope that the advantages of a tool like bnd are now obvious; although it certainly isn't a zero-effort solution, it's considerably faster than building the manifest by hand. The other big advantage that you get from a tool like bnd is that you don't need to guess at the packages your bundle should import, or have to debug unpleasant `Class-NotFoundException` errors on rarely used code paths. Bnd isn't your only option for packaging JARs as OSGi bundles, so let's take a look at some of the competition.

USING BUNDLOR

Bundlor (http://www.springsource.org/bundlor) is an open source tool developed and maintained by SpringSource. Although Bundlor isn't as widely used in the community as bnd is, it's the tool used to generate OSGi bundles for open source JARs in the SpringSource Enterprise Bundle Repository. Bundlor is used for the same purposes as bnd, and it's able to wrap existing JAR files or create manifests for code at build time. As a result, it's equally good for this example.

Using Bundlor is remarkably similar to using bnd. It also has integration points for Apache Ant and Apache Maven builds, but for this example you'll continue to use the command line. Getting Bundlor to create a manifest is as simple as issuing the following command (there are Windows and Linux scripts available):

```
bundlor.bat -i <path to jar>
```

Issuing this command, you'll see that the behavior for Bundlor is different from bnd's (see figure 12.2).

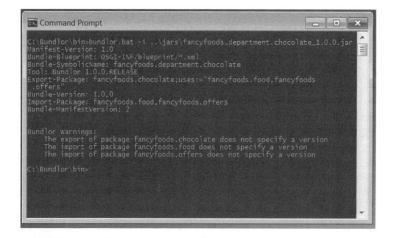

Figure 12.2   The output from Bundlor

As with bnd, Bundlor creates a manifest for the JAR file, but the default output is to `System.out`. This isn't the most useful location for wrapping bundles, but it's easy to get Bundlor to package the manifest back into a JAR file using the `-o` property to specify an output file, as follows:

```
bundlor.bat -i ..\jars\fancyfoods.department.chocolate_1.0.0.jar
 -o ..\out\fancyfoods.chocolate.bundled.jar
```

The manifest file in the bundle created by Bundlor is a little different from the one created by bnd, as shown next.

Listing 12.5   A default manifest from Bundlor

```
Manifest-Version: 1.0
Bundle-Blueprint: OSGI-INF/blueprint/*.xml
Bundle-SymbolicName: fancyfoods.department.chocolate
Tool: Bundlor 1.0.0.RELEASE
Export-Package: fancyfoods.chocolate;uses:="fancyfoods.food,fancyfoods
 .offers"
Bundle-Version: 1.0.0
Import-Package: fancyfoods.food,fancyfoods.offers
Bundle-ManifestVersion: 2
```

The default manifest that comes out of Bundlor is stricter than the one that came out of bnd. Note that none of the imports are optional, and that only the package containing code is exported. Other than this, though, there isn't much difference between the Bundlor output and the first bundle you generated with bnd. Neither has versioning, and neither has any concept of *private* implementation. Bundlor wouldn't be of much use if these generated manifests couldn't be refined in some way, and they can through the use of *template* manifests.

Template manifests in Bundlor are similar to bnd configuration files. Any headers specified in the template are copied into the generated manifest, and some special header values are used as processing instructions to guide generation. Given that Bundlor does a better job of defaulting the bundle's symbolic name and version, you can avoid specifying them (though, in general, specifying them is a good idea). What you do need to do is to tell Bundlor about your private packages and the versions of your imports.

In Bundlor, packages can be marked as private using the `Excluded-Exports` header in the template manifest; in this case you need to exclude the `fancy-foods.chocolate` package. Adding version ranges to your package imports also requires a modification to the template manifest. In this case, you need to add an `Import-Template` header. The `Import-Template` header allows you to provide attributes for selected package imports, using `*` as a wildcard if necessary. The resulting template manifest should end up looking something like the following listing.

Listing 12.6   A template manifest for use with Bundlor

```
Excluded-Exports: fancyfoods.chocolate
Import-Template: fancyfoods.*;version="[1.0,1.1)"
```

After you've created your template manifest, you can provide it to Bundlor using the -m option, as in the following command:

```
bundlor.bat -i ..\jars\fancyfoods.department.chocolate_1.0.0.jar
 -m ..\templates\bundlor.template.mf
 -o ..\out\fancyfoods.chocolate.bundled.jar
```

Now that you've provided configuration, the manifest generated for your JAR looks as good as it did before, as shown in the following listing.

Listing 12.7   A configured, generated manifest from Bundlor

```
Manifest-Version: 1.0
Bundle-Blueprint: OSGI-INF/blueprint/*.xml
Bundle-SymbolicName: fancyfoods.department.chocolate
Tool: Bundlor 1.0.0.RELEASE
Bundle-Version: 1.0.0
Import-Package: fancyfoods.food;version="[1.0,1.1)",fancyfoods.offers;
 version="[1.0,1.1)"
Bundle-ManifestVersion: 2
```

You may have noticed that we spent much less time describing and configuring Bundlor than we did bnd. We feel duty bound to tell you that this isn't a sign that Bundlor is much simpler than bnd. You may remember that you started out with a JAR that was an OSGi bundle. One of the things that Bundlor does is copy across any headers from the old JAR that aren't updated by the generation code. This means that other than the import and export headers all of the headers in your generated manifest are copied from the original bundle. This even includes the `Bundle-ManifestVersion` and `Bundle-SymbolicName`. If you'd started with an emptier JAR manifest, you would have found that rather more configuration was required to get Bundlor working as you want it to.

Having now seen how similar bnd and Bundlor are, it shouldn't be surprising to find out that other tools, such as Apache Felix's mangen, work in a similar way. Rather than covering these tools with further examples, we think that armed with the previous examples and relevant documentation, you should have no problem using any manifest generation tool you choose.

Now you know how a standard JAR can be converted into an OSGi bundle, overcoming the significant hurdles that put off many potential users of OSGi. But further issues are associated with using standard JARs and other Java technologies in OSGi. Even though your JAR is now an OSGi bundle, that doesn't mean that the things the code will try to do are OSGi-friendly!

12.2   *Common problems for OSGi-unaware libraries*

For many people, the problems with OSGi begin and end with correctly building a bundle manifest. As long as you're correctly able to identify your dependencies, then typically things *work*. This is a testament to the simplicity and resilience of the OSGi model. Unfortunately, there are a number of things that can cause huge problems.

These issues typically show up in libraries that use their own plug-in model or try to manage their own modularity. In normal Java, it's perfectly acceptable to do this sort of thing, but in OSGi it competes with the inherent modularity of the framework. This is the cause of many of the problems that libraries have when moved into OSGi for the first time.

Given that you've gone to so much trouble getting your library JAR packaged as an OSGi bundle, it would be rather silly not to use it because of the problems that you might encounter, but it would be good to know what some of the common problems are. One of the most common problems you encounter when moving to OSGi comes from the different classloading model that OSGi has, and how it interferes with reflection.

12.2.1 *Reflection in OSGi*

Reflection is a commonly used pattern in Java that aims to provide a degree of modularity in the code. You may remember that we introduced reflection as a poor modularity implementation all the way back in chapter 1! Given that it has been such a long time since we last covered reflection, it's worth a quick recap.

Generally the term *reflection* is used to describe the concept of a computer program *looking inside itself*, known as *introspection*, and modifying its behavior or operation as a result. In Java, this sort of reflection falls into two camps:

- Locating and calling methods on a known class dynamically
- Locating and loading classes that were not available at compilation time, or configuration files

When Java developers talk about reflection, they're usually referring to the first option, where methods can be located and invoked without a compilation dependency. The main reason for thinking of this type of reflection first is that the tools used to do it are in the `java.lang.reflect` package. Fortunately, in OSGi this sort of reflection works reasonably well. If you can get hold of an `Object` or `Class`, then all of the standard reflection APIs will work correctly because they come from the base runtime, which is shared by *all* bundles, regardless of version or modularity statements.

The big problem for method-level reflection comes at the point when you try to invoke the method or to find a particular method by specifying its arguments. If the method only refers to types from the base runtime—for example, it has an `int` return type and a `java.lang.String` argument—then there are no problems. If the method has more complex types in its signature, then class space compatibility becomes a factor. When invoking the method you must have the right view of all the arguments and return type (use types loaded by the right classloader) for things to work properly. If you get this wrong, you'll get a rather confusing `ClassCastException`, which often appears to be a failure converting a type into itself.

This problem sounds serious, but it isn't as bad as you might think. It's comparatively rare for bundles to be able to get hold of classes that they don't share a class space with, although you may occasionally find that some methods refer to types your bundle hasn't imported. It's the second kind of reflection that causes the majority of reflection-related problems in OSGi.

REFLECTIVE CLASSLOADING

When a Java program dynamically loads a class by name, rather than by referencing a type during normal execution, this is another form of reflection. The program is inspecting its classpath for a particular class that can then be loaded and used to affect its operation. In principle, there's no problem with this behavior in OSGi as long as you take into account the way OSGi classloading works. If a piece of code uses its own classloader to try to load another class, it will only be successful if that class exists inside the bundle or is imported from another bundle. If the class exists but is packaged somewhere else, then the class will fail to load.

This classloading model isn't dissimilar to the one from base Java, where any class on a classloader's classpath can happily be loaded by any other class. The hitch is that in OSGi the classpath is much smaller and more structured than the big, flat classpath in base Java. Problems therefore arise when one class expects to be able to see another, even though it's in a different bundle (see figure 12.3).

Because the class is loaded dynamically, there's no way to determine the dependency before runtime, and you can't know what to add to your manifest. Frequently, the class to be loaded is a private implementation class, and would not be exported anyway. Effectively, what you get is a break in the modularity of your system, which is why it's such a thorny problem to solve.

This sort of reflection problem isn't limited to classes. For example, library configuration files are usually packaged as part of applications, and then loaded reflectively

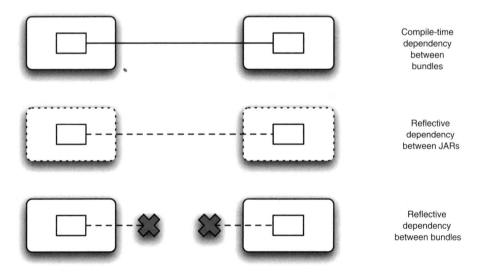

Figure 12.3   Unlike compile-time dependencies (solid lines), reflective dependencies (dashed lines) may not be explicitly declared in bundle manifests. This won't cause problems for JARs, which have little distinction between internals and externals, but it can cause runtime failures for bundles.

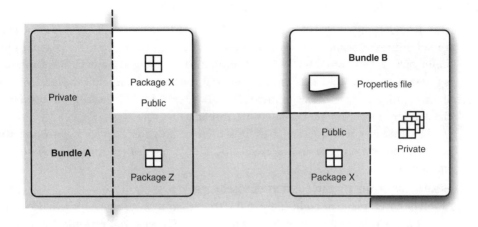

Figure 12.4 If the containing folder of a configuration file, or other resource, isn't explicitly exported as a package by Bundle B, it won't be visible in the class space of Bundle A.

by the library. If the classpath isn't flat, resources may not be visible, causing resource loading to fail (see figure 12.4).

Is everything doomed to failure when classes or resources are loaded by reflection? Not at all—all that's required to make it work is to follow the normal OSGi rules for classloading. Anything that is to be loaded must have its package exported by the owning bundle. This applies to Java code, unsurprisingly, and also to file resources, which may surprise you. For example, if a fancyfoods.config bundle wants to make a fancyfoods/config/properties/ff.properties file available to other bundles, fancyfoods.config must include the following in its manifest (even if `fancyfoods/config/ properties` doesn't have any Java classes in it!):

```
Export-Package: fancyfoods.config.properties
```

Similarly, bundles trying to load the ff.properties file must import the `fancyfoods .config.properties` pseudo-package. The same is true for any classes they want to load reflectively. What happens if the package isn't known at compile time? This is where `DynamicImport-Package` can be useful—more on that in section 12.3.3.

Even if you were extremely careful to export your configuration package from the application bundle and import it into the library, you could still only have one configuration file package wired at a time. If another provider of the package came along, then one or the other of you would end up using the wrong configuration!

Even in the absence of OSGi, these classloading problems are sometimes visible in Java, particularly in Java EE, where part of the runtime might need to load a class from the application. In these cases, Java makes use of something called the thread context ClassLoader.

12.2.2 *Using and abusing the thread context ClassLoader*

The thread context `ClassLoader` is used in Java EE as a *Get out of Jail Free* card. The thread context `ClassLoader` is set by various Java EE containers, such as an EJB container or a servlet container, before calling into a managed object. This `ClassLoader` is the same one used by the application, and the same delegation hierarchy. In a Java SE environment, the thread context `ClassLoader` is initialized to be the same as the classloader of the class that created the thread.

The thread context `ClassLoader` is used in Java for a specific purpose: when a piece of code on one classloader needs to act on classes or resources visible to another classloader.

PROPER USE OF THE THREAD CONTEXT CLASSLOADER

A well-behaved piece of code can use the thread context `ClassLoader` to access classes or resources only visible to another classloader. One example would be a library or component that lives inside a server runtime, or at EAR scope within a Java EE application. This library will be visible to any module inside the rest of the application, but crucially the module won't be visible to the library.

If one of the things the library needs to do when it's accessed is locate some configuration or instantiate one of the module's classes, then it's stuck. Because the classloader that loads the library is the parent of the classloader that can load the configuration, visibility is only one-way. To get around problems like this, libraries can use the thread context `ClassLoader` to find the necessary classes or resources. The thread context `ClassLoader` will have been set by the server immediately before the invocation of a servlet or EJB, making it available to any libraries called by the servlet or EJB.

This approach may seem a little haphazard, but it's part of a number of Java EE specifications. For example, if a JMS resource adapter receives an `ObjectMessage`, then it needs access to the class of the `Object` to instantiate it. As with a library loading a configuration file, this is problematic. The JMS resource adapter is almost always part of the Java EE server runtime, not part of the application. In this case the JMS resource adapter is required to use the thread context `ClassLoader` to find the application class stored in the `ObjectMessage`.

Although there are good reasons for using the thread context `ClassLoader`, there are also times when it's used somewhat inappropriately.

POOR USE OF THE THREAD CONTEXT CLASSLOADER

The thread context `ClassLoader` is extremely useful, but as we've mentioned before it's seen as something of a *Get out of Jail Free* card. This is a problem, because it means the thread context `ClassLoader` is extensively used in places that it wasn't originally intended for. This problem is exacerbated by the fact that most people using the thread context `ClassLoader` make assumptions about it that aren't guaranteed to be true, particularly if you have an OSGi classloading model.

The biggest assumption that most people make about the thread context `ClassLoader` is that it can load internal library and server implementation classes. This may

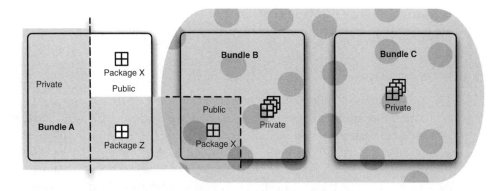

Figure 12.5 The thread context `ClassLoader` gives Java code in Bundle A visibility of classes that aren't normally in its class space (solid gray area). But in an OSGi environment, the class space of the thread context `ClassLoader` (dotted area) may exclude classes normally visible to Bundle A.

not seem like a big deal, but it leads to some sloppy coding. Libraries often end up using the thread context `ClassLoader` to load their own internal classes, even though it's only supposed to find classes from the application. For most Java EE environments this will never be a problem, but, as we know, OSGi is a little different (see figure 12.5).

OSGI AND THE THREAD CONTEXT CLASSLOADER
In OSGi, the thread context `ClassLoader` isn't defined. This immediately causes a significant problem for libraries that rely on it. For some libraries, the lack of a thread context `ClassLoader` is fatal, and others can only limp along in a less-than-desirable way.

Because the thread context `ClassLoader` isn't defined by OSGi, framework implementations are free to do as they see fit. This means that the situation for libraries isn't as bad as it might be. In Equinox, for example, if there's no thread context `ClassLoader` explicitly set, then the framework provides one for you. This avoids unpleasant `NullPointerExceptions`, and generally makes life a lot easier, but there's an important question. What classloader do you get?

In OSGi, the classloading model doesn't lend itself well to providing a thread context `ClassLoader`. Clearly it doesn't make much sense to rely on the Java SE model of a single thread context `ClassLoader` set when the thread is created. As threads pass through different bundles, it would be a huge violation of OSGi's modularity for them all to see the internals of the bundle that created the thread. The Java EE model makes more sense, in that the thread context `ClassLoader` is set differently at various points through the execution of the application. Unfortunately, core OSGi doesn't define things like servlets or EJBs, but it does define bundles. This means that the default thread context `ClassLoader` is the classloader for the bundle that loaded the currently executing class.

By setting the thread context `ClassLoader` in this way, Equinox prevents many libraries from completely collapsing, but it doesn't help them to get visibility to resources outside their bundle. The bundle also becomes nonportable. As with reflective classloading, using the thread context `ClassLoader` in OSGi is an attempt to break the modularity rules built into the system. As a result, the consequences for using it are typically bad.

12.2.3 *META-INF services*

The awkwardness of reflection and the trickiness of the thread context `ClassLoader` compound one another if you need to adapt a JAR that uses META-INF services to run in an OSGi environment. Many libraries use this pattern to supply implementations of an interface without tightly coupling consumers to the implementation class. The way it works is that a `ServiceLoader` searches all text files in META-INF/services folders. Files must be named after interfaces and contain the name of an implementation class. We discussed this factory system in section 1.2.4, and concluded it was limited compared to OSGi services. Nonetheless, it's a popular pattern, and chances are you'll have to handle JARs that use it.

Normally, the `ServiceLoader` searches the class space for resources in the META-INF/services folder. As you saw in section 12.2.1, any JAR wanting to expose this file must cheat and export a pseudo-package called `META-INF/services`. But the `ServiceLoader` can only be wired to one `META-INF/services` *package* at a time, so the cheat clearly won't scale well!

As if that wasn't enough of a hurdle, the `ServiceLoader` uses the thread context `ClassLoader` to look for and load resources. We've already seen that this classloader is undefined in OSGi. Even if one is available, it's unlikely to be able to see internal implementation classes, unless these classes are explicitly exported from the providing bundle. It goes without saying that exporting implementation packages is an OSGi anti-pattern, and completely subverts the encapsulation the META-INF services pattern was trying to achieve!

The good news is that enterprise OSGi has devised a way of making things work without requiring pseudo-packages and exported internals. The Service Loader Mediation Specification allows META-INF services to be made available through the Service Registry with relatively non-invasive manifest changes. All that's required is an indication to the OSGi service loader extender that META-INF services should be processed. For example, to expose a service for the `shop.Bananas` interface, the following should be added to a bundle manifest:

```
Require-Capability: osgi.extender;
 filter:="(osgi.extender=osgi.
serviceloader.registrar)"
Provide-Capability: osgi.serviceloader; osgi.serviceloader=shop.Bananas
```

JARs that use the `ServiceLoader.load()` API can opt to have those calls magically transformed into ones that will have the correct visibility of required implementations in OSGi by requesting processing with a manifest header, as follows:

```
Require-Capability: osgi.extender;
 filter:="(osgi.extender=osgi.
serviceloader.processor)"
```

If you're wondering what the requirements and capabilities are, they're the same ones we introduced in chapter 7. Although they look long-winded in the manifest, they're a robust way of ensuring that the necessary infrastructure is available, and also configuring that infrastructure at the same time.

Apache Aries has a project known as SPI Fly, which is one of the inspirations for the OSGi Service Loader Mediation Specification. SPI Fly uses a simpler mechanism to register services. For example, to process all META-INF/services files in a bundle, all that's needed is the following header:

```
SPI-Provider: *
```

A full discussion of SPI Fly and service loader mediation is beyond the scope of this book, but we hope this introduction will point you in the right direction if you do encounter this Java SE pattern. There's one more Java technology that can cause serious problems when moved into OSGi: Java serialization.

12.2.4 *Serialization and deserialization*

Most Java developers are at least vaguely familiar with Java's support for serialization. Serialization is the process by which live Java `Object`s can be persisted, or transported, in a standard interchangeable binary data format. Serialization is supported by the base Java runtime, and because of this you might expect things to work as easily in OSGi as they do elsewhere. To an extent this is true, but there are some potentially thorny issues.

SERIALIZATION IN OSGI

Serialization in OSGi is a relatively simple process, and does work more or less exactly like the serialization process in Java SE. A serializable `Object` can be passed to an `ObjectOutputStream`, at which point the entire `Object` graph connected to that one `Object` is also serialized. This is no different from Java SE.

Writing serializable objects in OSGi is a little more difficult than in normal Java, primarily because it's not possible to serialize objects like `BundleContexts` or OSGi services. The dynamic nature of these `Object`s means that they can't be relied upon to be recreated when `Object`s are later deserialized. On the whole this isn't too big an issue, particularly for libraries that weren't using OSGi services in the first place.

One of the biggest problems with serializing objects in OSGi is that the graph of connected `Object`s doesn't necessarily come from one bundle. There must be a consistent class space, but fields in one object may refer to private implementation types from other bundles. This doesn't cause a problem at the time of serialization; the serialization code in the virtual machine knows all of the implementation types and can easily handle the object graph.

Given that the object graph can be serialized, even when private implementation types are stored as fields, why is there a problem? The issue in an OSGi framework is at deserialization time. When a bundle tries to read an object from an `ObjectInput-Stream`, the underlying runtime needs to load all of the types in the object graph that were serialized. This is fine for classes that came from the bundle doing the deserialization, but not for ones that came from another bundle, which are almost certainly not exported. Unless the object graph is entirely contained within a single bundle, this will always be a problem.

You may think that things are alright as long as all the types in the object graph are visible through package imports, which is partly true. In cases where all types are either contained within a single bundle *or* visible to that bundle as package imports, you may find it helpful to write a custom serializer that accepts that bundle's classloader of the serialized class as a parameter, as shown in the following listing.

Listing 12.8   An `ObjectInputStream` that can handle restricted class visibility

```
public class SmartObjectInputStream extends ObjectInputStream {
    private ClassLoader loader;

    public SmartObjectInputStream(InputStream in, ClassLoader loader)
            throws IOException {
        super(in);                                          ◁─ Accept classloader
        this.loader = loader;                                   as parameter
    }

    protected Class resolveClass(ObjectStreamClass clazz)
            throws IOException, ClassNotFoundException {
        if (loader == null) {                               ◁─ Delegate to
            return super.resolveClass(clazz);                  superclass if needed
        } else {                                            ◁─ Use appropriate
            String name = clazz.getName();                     classloader
            return Class.forName(name, false, loader);
        }
    }
}
```

Even in the ideal case where all classes are visible to a nominated classloader, there's the potential for more subtle problems. If the bundle has been reresolved since it serialized the object, then it may have been resolved to different packages. To combat this, it's important to make sure serialization versioning is included in any declared package versions.

One commonly used type of library that demonstrates several of the *problem patterns* described in this section is the logging framework.

12.3   *An example library conversion—logging frameworks in OSGi*

A large number of logging frameworks are available, and it isn't our intent to name and shame any particular implementation, but to point out the common patterns they use, and why this is a problem in OSGi. We'll assume that you've already run the logging framework JAR(s) through a tool to convert them into OSGi bundles.

Logging frameworks are typically structured with an independent API. This is the part of the framework that applications code to, and typically has static factory methods for obtaining logger implementations. The applications then use the API to log out messages independently from the underlying logging implementation.

12.3.1 Common problems with loggers in OSGi

The structure of a logging framework sounds like a great, modular design that should be ideal for an OSGi environment. That would be the case if, for example, the application used the Service Registry to obtain a logging implementation. Using a static factory demonstrates the first big problem with logging frameworks.

LOADING THE LOGGING IMPLEMENTATION

The API for logging frameworks almost always contains the static factory for obtaining the logger. This means that the logging API has to load the logging implementation class. This isn't a problem if the implementation is in the same bundle, but many implementations have pluggable backends that are packaged separately. These pluggable implementation classes aren't API, but unless they're packaged inside the same bundle they have to be exported anyway.

If the logging API were to have a hard dependency on each possible implementation, then it would mean that you needed all of the possible implementations to be installed into the OSGi framework for your logger to even resolve. Clearly this is a bad idea, meaning that the dependencies must be optional. But this still means that all of the potential implementations must be known in advance to be loadable!

Another problem introduced by the static factory is that it divorces the client (in this case, the class doing the logging) from the lifecycle of the logging implementation. If the implementation is stopped, or even uninstalled, then the client has no way of knowing that their logger needs to be thrown away.

The separation of the logging API from the implementation isn't only an issue when trying to load the logging internals; it also causes problems when trying to load configuration files and customizations.

CLIENT-PROVIDED RESOURCES

One of the common concerns for libraries is how they can be configured. For some libraries, the amount of configuration is sufficiently small that it can be provided in some sort of registration call, or even be passed in whenever the library is called. For most libraries, this solution is insufficient; as the amount of configuration grows, it becomes increasingly unmanageable in code. Furthermore, it's unpleasant to require users to recompile their code to change their configuration.

Normally this sort of issue is solved by using an XML file or properties file, either in a fixed, library-specific location within the client JAR, or in a client-specified location. This is the most common way to configure a logging framework. As we're sure you'll remember from section 12.2.3, the way that the logging framework loads resources provided by the client is by using the thread context `ClassLoader`. For all the reasons we covered then, this doesn't always work in OSGi. By the time the library code is invoked, the thread context `ClassLoader` can no longer see the content of the OSGi bundle.

Unfortunately, it's not only configuration files that cause an issue. Logging frameworks, like many other types of libraries, often allow clients to configure customized plug-in classes using configuration. Clearly the logging framework uses the thread context `ClassLoader` to load these plug-in classes as well as the configuration, creating yet another problem.

Given the unpleasant problems we see, you might expect existing logging frameworks to be a lost cause in OSGi. Clearly, their Java EE behavior doesn't stand much chance of working properly in OSGi. There are some things you can do to improve matters.

12.3.2 *Avoiding problems in OSGi*

You can improve the situation for logging frameworks in OSGi in a number of ways; some are more invasive to the code than others, but they do demonstrate useful ways to work around some of the problems that afflict Java libraries in OSGi. Many of these workarounds aren't normally recommended, but it's important to understand where rules can be bent.

CAREFUL PACKAGING

One of the big problems we noted with logging frameworks is the fact that although the API and implementation are notionally separate, from a modularity perspective they're tightly coupled. This is because the API needs to be able to load the implementation classes.

One of the things you can do to avoid the lifecycle and classloading problems associated with this packaging is to package the logging API and logging implementations as a single bundle. Clearly, there are advantages and disadvantages to this approach. One of the big advantages is that by including the API and implementation in the same bundle, you're always guaranteed to be able to load the implementation. Another big advantage of packaging the API and implementation together is that it's impossible for the implementation to be changed independently of the API, leaving clients in an inconsistent state.

Given the advantages of this packaging, you might expect it to be the default, but there are some negative side effects. First, you have to package any logging implementation with the API, which dramatically bloats the bundle. Given that different clients may want different implementations, this can be a significant problem. It also only helps for logging implementations that you know you need ahead of time.

Given that packaging the logging API and implementation together solves problems, you might expect that packaging the logging library with the client would be even better. To an extent this is true. If you package the logging library with the client, then it will gain visibility of any configuration files and plug-ins; on the other hand, you'll have to bloat every single client, wasting runtime resources. Effectively, by doing this you're creating an even worse version of the Java classpath!

Our recommendation is to avoid packaging the logging library with the client code, unless there's only one client bundle. Even then you should think twice. What you can do is to package commonly used logging implementations along with the API. This will reduce some of the optional package import spaghetti, prevent some of the logging internals from having to be exported, and also avoid lifecycle problems.

Embedding JARs instead of converting them

The trick of embedding a plain Java library into an existing OSGi bundle, rather than converting it into its own bundle, works for more than loggers—it can be an effective workaround for all sorts of troublesome libraries. Because the embedded JAR shares a classloader with the consuming bundle, almost all class visibility issues vanish. But this convenience comes at the expense of reduced modularity and increased bloat. We recommend embedding JARs as an absolute last resort.

An alternative approach, used, for example, by SLF4J, is to package the implementation bundles as fragments of the API bundle. This neatly solves the implementation visibility issues. But fragments have a number of idiosyncratic behaviors, and not everyone likes using them, which is why this approach hasn't been universally adopted.

Repackaging the logging API and implementation is only one of the ways in which the bundles can be altered to improve your situation. Another option is to try to make sure that the thread context `ClassLoader` has the correct view.

CHANGING THE THREAD CONTEXT CLASSLOADER

We've talked about how the thread context `ClassLoader` is the source of many issues for Java libraries in an OSGi framework. One of the more obvious things to do, therefore, is to set the context classloader to one that can load the resources you need it to.

Setting the thread context `ClassLoader` is an invasive thing to do. It absolutely requires that you change your code and recompile; it's also not something that you would ever normally come across when writing Java code. For those of you who run with Java 2 Security enabled, you'll also find that changing the thread context `ClassLoader` is a privileged operation.

Setting the thread context `ClassLoader` is as simple as in the following listing, but it's also something that you must be careful about doing, particularly when it comes to setting it back afterward.

Listing 12.9 Setting the thread context `ClassLoader`

```
Thread current = Thread.currentThread();
ClassLoader original = current.getContextClassLoader();
try {
  current.setContextClassLoader(clToUse);

  //Make a call out to your library here

} finally {
  current.setContextClassLoader(original);
}
```

Given that setting the thread context `ClassLoader` is easy to do, it's a good way of ensuring temporary visibility of classes and resources. But there are some significant drawbacks. As we mentioned earlier, you have to change your code. This is invasive and potentially risky. Not all libraries even use the thread context `ClassLoader`, instead assuming the resource will be on their classpath.

In order for the code change to be effective, you have to get hold of a class-loader that can load the resources you need it to. If you can identify a class with visibility of the resources, then the classloader of the owning bundle is a good bet. Bundles don't directly expose their classloader, but a call like `ClassThatCanSee-Resources.class.getClassLoader()` will return a suitable classloader. If you have a bundle but no class, you can write a facade classloader that delegates to the `bundle.loadClass()` and `bundle.loadResource()` methods. As long as the bundle contains some classes, you can instead use `bundle.getEntries()` to introspect the bundle contents and find an arbitrary class name, and then use `bundle.loadClass().getClassLoader()` to get the classloader. Both of these methods are fragile and require caution.

The biggest problem with setting the thread context `ClassLoader` is that you can't always be sure it will stay set. When you call out to third-party code, it's entirely possible that the first thing it does is to change, or unset, the thread context `ClassLoader`. If it does, then you're a little stuck! All we can suggest is that if you're having thread context `ClassLoader` issues, then this is something to try.

If setting the thread context `ClassLoader` is too invasive for your taste, you don't have the source, aren't allowed to change the source by its license, or it doesn't work, then all isn't lost. Another, somewhat specialized, manifest header can come to the rescue. Given that this is the case, you may wonder why we haven't been extolling its virtues throughout this chapter. The answer is simple: this header comes with a price.

12.3.3 *DynamicImport-Package—a saving grace?*

We've spent a lot of time throughout this book discussing the use of package imports to achieve modularity. By correctly describing your dependencies, you gain a powerful understanding of your application and a lot of flexibility. There has been one consistent message, which is that until all of your dependencies are available, your bundle can't be used. This statement is weakened somewhat when using the `optional` directive, which allows your bundle to start in the absence of some packages. Importantly, the `optional` directive is an all-or-nothing deal: either your package will be wired when your bundle resolves, or it *never* will (unless the bundle is reresolved).

`DynamicImport-Package` operates like an optional import in that it won't stop your bundle from resolving. If that was all `DynamicImport-Package` did it would be useless, but there's an important difference. Whereas an optional import is either *wired* or *not wired*, you can think of `DynamicImport-Package` as imports that aren't wired *yet*.

Dynamic package imports indicate to the OSGi framework that it should attempt to wire the package when the bundle first attempts to load something from it. If the wiring fails, then so does the attempt to load the resource. Critically, when a dynamic import has been successfully wired, it's wired for good. At this point, a dynamic import is no different from a normal one.

Another key difference between dynamic imports and normal imports is that dynamic imports can be defined using wildcards, as follows. This allows a bundle to import a package that's unknown when the bundle manifest is created. This is one of the most useful features of the DynamicImport-Package header:

```
DynamicImport-Package: fancyfoods.*
```

In the above example, see how you can import any package that starts with fancy-foods. into your bundle. You could be even more general and import *any* package using * with no prefix. As with normal package imports, you can add version ranges and attributes to your imports.

DYNAMICIMPORT-PACKAGE AND LOGGING

You can use dynamic imports to help you with your logging library. If you think back to the problems we discussed, many of them were related to class and resource loading. If you add a DynamicImport-Package: * header to your logging API, then you no longer need to worry about all of the unpleasant imports for various logging implementations. In this case, the implementations can be wired dynamically as they're loaded.

Dynamic imports can also help you with configuration and custom implementations. As long as the package containing the configuration file or custom class is exported, then there will be no problem loading that either. Dynamic imports seem to be the wonder solution to your logging problems! Unfortunately, this isn't the case. There are a number of significant problems.

THE PROBLEMS WITH DYNAMIC IMPORTS

Dynamic imports are extremely powerful, but are also over-used. It may be hard to imagine how dynamic imports could be a problem at first, but there's one example that clearly shows how DynamicImport-Package is a poor way to load resources.

Assume that your logging library expects to find configuration in the file META-INF/logging-config.xml. In this case, you would need to export META-INF as a package from the client bundle and dynamically import it using either Dynamic-Import-Package: * or DynamicImport-Package: META-INF. Let's start by considering DynamicImport-Package: *. Although it's fun to use, because it requires little thought on the part of the person writing the bundle, the performance and modularity implications are bad. Any time a resource is loaded, OSGi's nicely structured classpath is turned into a big, slow, flat classpath. Searching this classpath is *slow*. Furthermore, the resource could end up being loaded from *anywhere*—you've bypassed all of OSGi's explicit dependency management. DynamicImport-Package: META-INF is a little bit nicer, but it still doesn't scale well to multiple client bundles. Which META-INF will you wire to? How do you version it sensibly? When the package is wired, either you'll get a random configuration file, which would be disastrous, or, if you select the right bundle using attributes, your logging implementation is tied to exactly one client! Even in the case where you don't have to export META-INF, you still end up in a situation where you can only wire to one bundle for the package, something that's never going to cope with multiple versions of the same bundle in the runtime.

The problems with dynamic imports don't stop there. Because dynamic imports behave like optional imports at resolution time, there's no guarantee that the package will be available to the running bundle. This means that your library must cope with the possibility that one, some, or *all* of its dynamic imports won't be available at runtime!

Effectively, dynamic imports are a means of circumventing the modularity of your bundle. If used properly, they're an invaluable tool, but for the most part they're best avoided.

12.3.4   *Other problems that are more difficult to fix*

The problems we've discussed so far have all had to do with modularization. Effectively, the libraries rely on the relatively poor modularity of Java SE and suffer problems when packaged as OSGi bundles. These sorts of problems can often (but not always) be fixed, if only in a limited way, by careful packaging. A different class of problems are altogether more unpleasant, though fortunately they're also much rarer. These are problems to do with bundle lifecycle and the structure of the framework itself.

URLS FOR CLASSPATH SCANNING

Some libraries attempt to do clever things by finding resources on the application's classpath. Typically, they look for resources using a pattern, but crucially they don't know the name of the resource before they find it. One example of this is if you wish to find and run all classes that have a name ending in Test. To do this, the library typically looks for the root of the classpath by asking the classloader for the resource corresponding to "/". Clearly, there are modularity problems here, but even if the library found the correct root URL, there's another, bigger problem waiting.

When the framework has a root URL, it typically identifies it as either being a file: or a jar: URL. After it has done this, it locates the directory or JAR on the filesystem, and starts to list its contents, looking for matching files. The issue here is that OSGi doesn't require the framework to have a fixed layout on the filesystem, or even be on disk at all! The OSGi specification expects the framework to return URLs in a custom namespace. This completely breaks any scanning performed by non-OSGi-aware libraries.

The only way around this sort of problem is to rewrite the library (or plug into it, if you can) to be OSGi-aware when it's scanning. The only safe ways to scan bundles are by using findEntries() on a Bundle or listResources() on a BundleWiring (the latter is only available on OSGi 4.3–compatible frameworks).

RESOURCE AND THREAD MANAGEMENT

If the library you're using creates its own threads or manages resources, for example database connections, then it needs to correctly terminate or close them to prevent erratic behavior and leaks. Given that many libraries are unaware of the OSGi lifecycle, it's likely that the library won't respond to either being stopped, or uninstalled, correctly, and will probably leave orphaned threads or resources.

This sort of problem can also be demonstrated if clients are stopped, uninstalled, or refreshed. Without proper resource management, the library can begin leaking memory, or worse, hanging on to things related to bundles that no longer exist.

These problems can be extremely difficult to fix, but in some cases it can be enough to add an `Activator` class to your bundle (see appendix A) and manifest. If this class is used to perform necessary cleanup when the library is stopped, then it can prevent the leakage that would otherwise occur.

12.4 Summary

In this chapter, we've taken an extensive look at how libraries developed for standard Java can be used in OSGi. We don't intend this chapter to be a cautionary tale, although most of the difficulties we describe here are used as reasons why OSGi is *too hard* or *broken*. For the most part, libraries converted to run in OSGi can be used without any intervention or special effort; it's merely unfortunate that some commonly used libraries suffer from the majority of the problems.

We hope that, having read this chapter, you understand how easy it is to take a JAR and package it as an OSGi bundle, preferably using a combination of tooling and hand-finishing. Although this isn't always the end of the story, for many libraries this is all you need to do.

If you're unlucky enough to come across problems after converting your library, we hope that you also feel confident enough to work through them. Some of the class-loading problems that appear can be hairy, but most can be avoided or fixed with a little intelligence and some judiciously applied packaging changes.

Now that you've seen how to pull libraries into OSGi, even when they weren't originally written to use it, you've reached an advanced level of knowledge. You've reached the point where your OSGi knowledge is sufficient for you to start building your own runtimes. In the next chapter, we'll look at doing exactly that: comparing the features offered by a range of prepackaged runtimes with those that you can piece together yourselves.

13

Choosing a stack

This chapter covers

- Your options for running enterprise OSGi applications
- An overview of popular enterprise OSGi platforms

This book is a book about enterprise OSGi, rather than any particular implementation or server. Nonetheless, no one's going to get far with enterprise OSGi without some sort of implementation to play with! In the examples, you've been using a little toy assembly to get you going on the important stuff without getting bogged down in the details of any particular application server.

Now that you've got the hang of enterprise OSGi, you're probably thinking about going into production. We definitely don't recommend your toy stack for this—as we've said several times, Apache Aries on its own isn't an application server! Working through the examples in this book, you've hit several limitations that disappear when you move to a more full-featured application server. What *should* you be using to run your real applications, when you've moved beyond your simple sample stack?

You probably won't be surprised to hear that the answer is "it depends." After all, if everyone was running enterprise OSGi applications the same way, we would have shown you that, rather than using the Aries assembly! More and more application server vendors and communities are adding support for OSGi applications to their products. You can go for a minimal runtime, like Apache Karaf, or an enterprise-strength server like WebSphere Application Server, or anything in between. How you choose will depend on how much server you want and also how much enterprise OSGi you want, because some products provide more of the programming model than others.

Let's start with a high-level view of which servers have the enterprise OSGi features we've discussed in this book.

13.1 What's in what server?

The OSGi function in these servers has different levels of maturity. Some haven't completed implementing the enterprise OSGi specification yet, whereas others provide the specification and innovations on top of it. Implementations that aren't complete at the time of writing will continue to improve over time and may be fully mature by the time you're choosing your stack. It may also be that your application doesn't require the whole enterprise OSGi programming model, in which case you can choose your server based on other criteria. All of the servers we'll look at allow you to run OSGi bundles as web applications, and connect bundles together using some form of dependency injection of OSGi services.

Table 13.1 summarizes the features available in the various servers. You should only take this table as a rough guide; some servers might not have had a feature at the time of writing, but it might have been added by the time you're using the server. Other features might be available in principle, but require configuration to get working in your application!

Table 13.1 Feature comparison of enterprise OSGi servers

Server	Apache Karaf	Apache Geronimo	IBM WebSphere	Eclipse Virgo	GlassFish	JBoss	Paremus Nimble
Blueprint	✔	✔	✔	✔		✔	*
Declarative Services		✔		✔	✔	✔	*
JPA	J	✔	✔	✔	✔	On roadmap	*
JTA	✔	✔	✔	✔	✔	✔	*
JNDI	✔	✔	✔	✔	✔	✔	*
Aggregate applications	Features, `.eba` archives	`.eba` archives	`.eba`, and composite bundles	Plan, `.par` files			
EJBs	T				✔		
GUI console	✔	✔	✔	✔	Separate plug-in	✔	

Table 13.1　Feature comparison of enterprise OSGi servers *(continued)*

Server	Apache Karaf	Apache Geronimo	IBM WebSphere	Eclipse Virgo	GlassFish	JBoss	Paremus Nimble
Application isolation			✔	✔			✔
JEE container		✔	✔	JEE, Spring	✔	✔	*
SCA			✔				

Key
　X—Support available in released version
　T—Support available in Aries trunk
　*—Provisioning support available, but third-party implementations must be installed
　J—Feature files for Aries JPA, but no feature files for JPA engine

Because enterprise OSGi is an open standard, you should find that your applications are generally portable between servers as long as you stick to features that are covered by the specification (and implemented in the server you're switching to). For maximum portability you might want to avoid aggregate applications and EJB integration, because these aren't included in the first version of the enterprise specification.

> **WARNING: WATCH OUT FOR WONKY VERSIONS** At the time of writing, several of the servers we'll discuss ship with incorrectly versioned `javax.servlet` and `javax.persistence` packages. Although the OSGi Enterprise Specification specifies versions for these packages, these semantic versions aren't the same as the marketing versions, which caused a few implementation hiccups. If you migrate an application from the little Aries assembly to an affected server, you may find some bundles no longer resolve. If this happens, we're afraid you'll have to grit your teeth, forgo semantic versioning temporarily, and import a broad version range for `javax.servlet` and `javax.persistence`.

A table can only tell part of the story, so let's discuss each of these servers in more detail.

13.2　Apache Karaf

One of the lightest-weight options for running OSGi applications, Apache Karaf is halfway between an OSGi runtime and an application server. Karaf is proving increasingly popular both as an OSGi platform in its own right and as a foundation for other products such as Geronimo and ServiceMix. Several other projects don't ship with Karaf by default, but do provide Karaf features so they can be installed into a Karaf instance.

Karaf and ServiceMix

Although it's technically correct to say ServiceMix is built on Karaf, it doesn't tell the whole story; it's also true to say Karaf is based on ServiceMix. Karaf began life as the ServiceMix kernel, and was spun off into its own project when it became apparent how generally useful it would be.

13.2.1 Karaf features

One of Karaf's headline functions is known as *Karaf features*. A Karaf feature is an XML file that describes a set of bundles that can be installed into a Karaf runtime. (You may recall seeing Karaf features before, in section 8.3.4.) Karaf ships preconfigured with a repository with many useful feature definitions, and new feature repositories can easily be added.

The features feature

Confused about the features feature, and how Karaf features relate to other Karaf features? Is features a feature, or is it a function? Karaf features illustrate the perils of overloading common words when naming product, er, features. We haven't yet found a good way of disambiguating between Karaf features (canned chunks of third-party function that can easily be provisioned into a Karaf runtime), Karaf features (Karaf's support for provisioning said third-party function), and Karaf features (all the other bits of Karaf function that make it such a handy runtime). We're afraid you'll have to rely on the context and hope for the best!

To see the available features, use the `features:list` command (see figure 13.1).

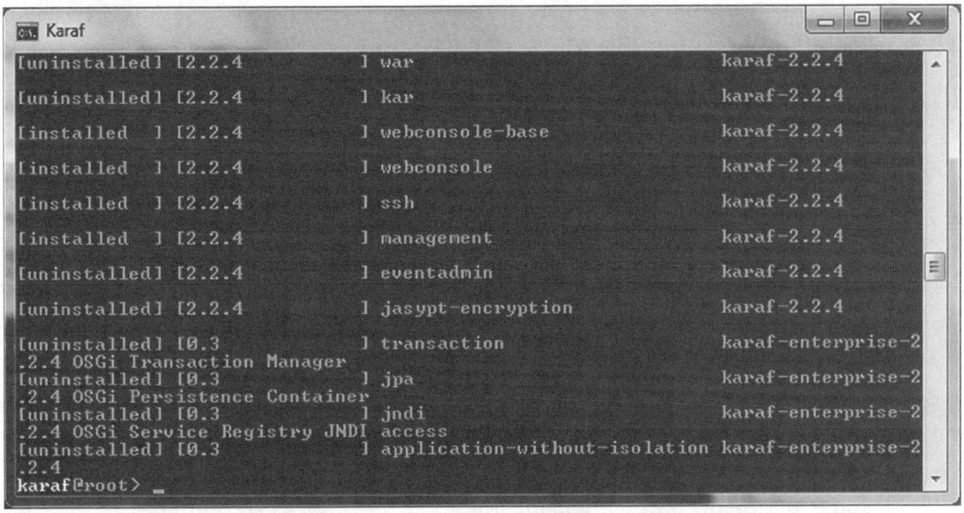

Figure 13.1 To see the features Karaf can install, use the `features:list` command.

As a bonus, Maven URLs are supported. This makes installing feature-compliant products and applications as easy as typing (for example) the following:

```
features:addurl mvn:fancyfoods/fancyfoods.karaf/1.0.0/xml/features
features:install fancyfoods
```

Maven URLs were used for convenience here, but file and http URLs also work. The feature definition file for the Fancy Foods application would be as follows:

```
<features xmlns="http://karaf.apache.org/xmlns/features/v1.0.0">
 <feature name="fancyfoods" version="1.0.0">
   <bundle>mvn:fancyfoods/fancyfoods.api/1.0.0</bundle>
   <bundle>mvn:fancyfoods/fancyfoods.web/1.0.0</bundle>
   <bundle>mvn:fancyfoods/fancyfoods.business/1.0.0</bundle>
   <bundle>mvn:fancyfoods/fancyfoods.datasource/1.0.0</bundle>
   <bundle>mvn:fancyfoods/fancyfoods.persistence/1.0.0</bundle>
   <bundle>mvn:fancyfoods/fancyfoods.department.chocolate/1.0.0</bundle>
   <bundle>mvn:fancyfoods/fancyfoods.department.cheese/1.0.0</bundle>
 </feature>
</features>
```

It's used here because the content is familiar, but the Fancy Foods application perhaps isn't the best example of how to use Karaf features. A similar effect can be achieved by packaging all of the Fancy Foods bundles up into a .eba file, as we did in chapter 4. Features are more useful for distributing centrally—or remotely—managed infrastructure bundles. For example, many Apache projects provide Karaf feature files to allow them to be installed into Karaf without any initial download.

If you try to install it, you'll discover that the Fancy Foods application won't install correctly on a basic Karaf installation because its dependencies are missing; current releases of Karaf don't have any ability to provision features based on bundle dependencies. Don't worry, we'll show you how to configure Karaf with the right features in a moment.

13.2.2 *Installing Aries into Karaf*

Despite being a relatively lightweight runtime, Karaf has awareness of, and support for, Aries. Base Karaf ships with the Aries Blueprint implementation. Although not installed by default, the Karaf enterprise repository includes feature definitions for most Aries components. The feature definitions are maintained by the Karaf team and so versions may lag slightly behind the latest Aries releases (see figure 13.2).

> **WARNING: BUT WHERE IS THE ARIES FEATURE?**   None of the Karaf feature definitions for the Aries bundles includes *aries* in the name, so they're easy to miss if you're looking for a feature called `aries`.

Unfortunately, although there are Karaf feature files for the Aries JPA component, which provides integrations for JPA in an OSGi environment, at the time of writing there are none for the OpenJPA engine itself. You'll need to install OpenJPA into Karaf manually, either by using the `bundles:install` command or by writing your

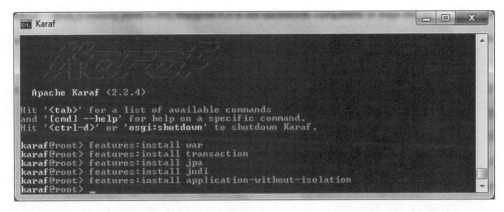

Figure 13.2 **To install Aries into Karaf, you'll need to install the** `war`, `transaction`, `jpa`, `jndi`, **and** `application-without-isolation` **features.**

own feature for OpenJPA. Because OpenJPA has its own nontrivial dependencies, a feature is probably easier. An example feature definition is as follows:

```
<features xmlns="http://karaf.apache.org/xmlns/features/v1.0.0">
    <feature
        name="persistence"
        version="1.0.0">
        <bundle>mvn:commons-collections/
            commons-collections/3.2.1/</bundle>
        <bundle>mvn:commons-lang/commons-lang/2.4</bundle>
        <bundle>mvn:commons-pool/commons-pool/1.5</bundle>
        <bundle>mvn:org.apache.derby/derby/10.8.1.2</bundle>
        <bundle>mvn:org.apache.servicemix.bundles/
            org.apache.servicemix.bundles.serp/1.13.1_2/</bundle>
        <bundle>mvn:org.apache.openjpa/openjpa/2.0.1</bundle>
    </feature>
</features>
```

> **WARNING: EXECUTION ENVIRONMENTS** Some versions of Karaf don't have the execution environments configured correctly, which means installation of the `fancyfoods` feature fails. To correct the problem, add the `JavaSE-1.6` environment to the list of supported environments in Karaf's etc/config.properties file.

After the Aries and OpenJPA bundles are installed, your `fancyfoods` feature should install. Alternatively, because you've had practice with features by now, you could take advantage of Karaf's hot deploy feature and copy your Fancy Foods .eba file into the deploy folder in your Karaf installation. The Fancy Foods application will be accessible on http://localhost:8181/fancyfoods.web/SayHelloShopping.

> **WARNING: CHEESE OFFER MISSING?** The Fancy Foods application has been written to take advantage of some features that were introduced in the 0.4 release of the Aries JPA bundle, and the 0.3.1 release of the transaction wrappers bundle. If you're using earlier versions of this bundle, you'll see that the chocolate offer is present, but the cheese offer is missing. To get the cheese offer

working, you'll need to adjust the persistence.xml to use the more verbose JNDI names for the datasources, for example: `OSGi:service/javax.sql.Data-Source/ (OSGi.jndi.service.name=jdbc/xafancyfoodsdb)`. You'll also need to manually enhance your JPA entities.

Depending on what you're trying to do, you may need to install other bundles into your Karaf runtime. As you've seen, the ability to group bundles into features and the support for Maven URLs make this pretty easy. Karaf has another handy protocol handler that simplifies installing normal JARs.

13.2.3 *Handling non-OSGi bundles*

Karaf ships the Pax Wrap URL handler. This convenient utility allows you to install normal bundles into the Karaf runtime by converting them into OSGi bundles on the fly. Bnd is used to do the generation of the bundles. For example, to install a legacy bundle, the following command could be used (or the URL could be added to a feature definition file):

```
bundle:install wrap:mvn:company/my.legacy/1.0.0
```

So far, we've shown you two Karaf commands: `features:install` and `bundle:install`. These are only scratching the surface of the capabilities of the Karaf shell.

13.2.4 *Blueprint-aware console*

Karaf has a slick text console based on the Felix Gogo shell, but with lots of improvements and extensions. The Karaf shell allows you to do all the things you could do in a normal OSGi console, like starting, stopping, and querying bundles, but with the welcome benefit of content assist and command history. Importantly for products built on top of Karaf, the console can be dynamically extended with new commands and rebranded. From an enterprise OSGi perspective, though, the most interesting feature of the Karaf console is its Blueprint support. Not only is the console aware of Blueprint, Blueprint is a first-class citizen; the default bundle listing shows the Blueprint status of every bundle (figure 13.3).

> **The Karaf web console**
>
> If you prefer to use a GUI console, you can install the optional web console into Karaf using the command `features:install webconsole`. Because of OSGi's dynamism, as soon as the console feature is installed, the web console will be available. If you miss the command line, the web console even embeds a version of the shell. Sadly, the one thing absent from the web console is the shell's Blueprint status list.

Karaf is a nice integration framework, with many handy extensions to what you get if you run a plain OSGi framework like Felix or Equinox. We like the console and the integrated Blueprint support. But Karaf isn't an application server; even if you add in lots of Karaf features, it won't do all the things an application server does.

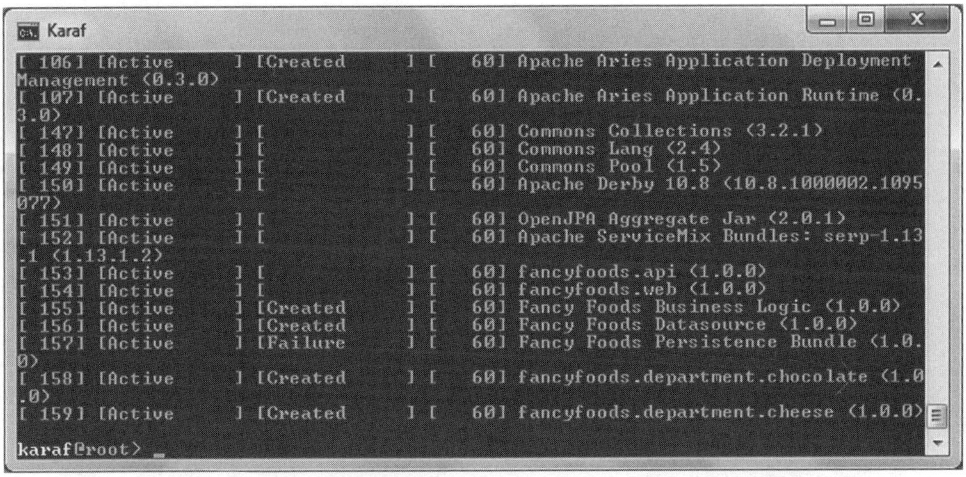

Figure 13.3 Out of the box, Karaf shows the Blueprint status when listing bundles. In this case, the datasource JNDI name in the persistence.xml is incorrect, so Blueprint can't inject an `EntityManager` into the inventory bean, and reports a failure.

13.3 *Apache Geronimo*

If Karaf is too low-level for you, you'll find many of the same characteristics in Karaf's bigger cousin, the Apache Geronimo application server. From version 3.0 onwards, Apache Geronimo supports the enterprise OSGi programming model. Geronimo provides a feature-complete and well-integrated enterprise OSGi runtime, based on Apache Aries. As with Karaf, the version of Aries embedded in Geronimo will usually lag slightly behind the leading edge release of Aries itself.

Geronimo itself is built on top of Karaf, so it retains many of Karaf's excellent features, such as the Blueprint-aware console. But unlike Karaf, Geronimo is a full-fledged Java EE–certified application server. This means many features that have to be manually installed or hand-cranked in Karaf work out of the box in Geronimo. (The corollary of this is that Karaf is a lot faster than Geronimo—or almost anything else—to start!) Geronimo ships with a built-in Derby database, EJB container, JMS container, and transaction manager. If you plan to combine Java EE and OSGi components, you'll be grateful for this extra function. Even if you're doing a strictly OSGi application, you may find Geronimo's management and debugging facilities handy. Geronimo's OSGi application management is more well-integrated and sophisticated than Karaf's. For example, Geronimo's console displays the web context root of installed WABs (see figure 13.4).

The Geronimo web console also provides more general management of installed OSGi bundles. Graphical views of a bundle's wired bundles, imported and exported services, and manifest are provided by the console (see figure 13.5).

Geronimo is one of the most straightforward ways to use Apache Aries; Geronimo contains most of the Apache Aries components you've been using through this

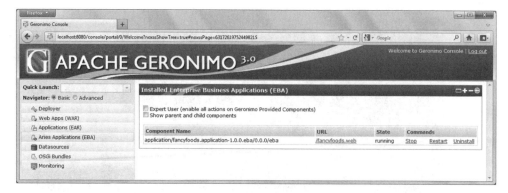

Figure 13.4 Geronimo lists all installed EBAs and allows you to start, stop, and uninstall them. Conveniently, it also shows the web context root.

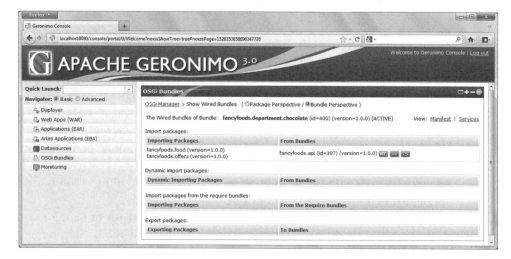

Figure 13.5 The Geronimo console includes a nice graphical bundle viewer that shows a bundle's package and service dependencies.

book, but it wraps them in a proper application server environment, with administration, databases, datasources, JPA entity enhancement, security, and other application-server goodies.

13.4 *WebSphere Application Server*

An even higher level of application server support is available with WebSphere Application Server. Like Geronimo, WebSphere incorporates and integrates the Apache Aries components. It also provides nice extensions and enhancements to enterprise OSGi support beyond what's available in Aries. WebSphere support for OSGi applications has been available since WebSphere Application Server version 7. In version 7, the support was shipped as a separate feature pack, whereas in version 8, OSGi application support was included in the base server.

Full disclosure

Both authors have helped develop WebSphere Application Server, and are Apache Aries committers, so we're more familiar with this stack than some of the others.

13.4.1 Provisioning and bundle repositories

WebSphere provides good support for application provisioning by shipping with an OBR bundle repository implementation, and allowing users to configure third-party repositories.

BUILT-IN BUNDLE REPOSITORY

WebSphere includes an integral bundle repository with the application server (see figure 13.6). This allows common utility bundles to be provisioned without having to set up a third-party bundle repository. Provisioning bundles, rather than packaging them with applications, reduces application footprint and makes rolling out new versions of common bundles easier.

CONFIGURABLE EXTERNAL BUNDLE REPOSITORY

WebSphere can provision bundles from any bundle repository that complies with the draft RFC112 (OBR) specification (discussed in chapter 7). All that's required is to configure a name and URL for the external repository.

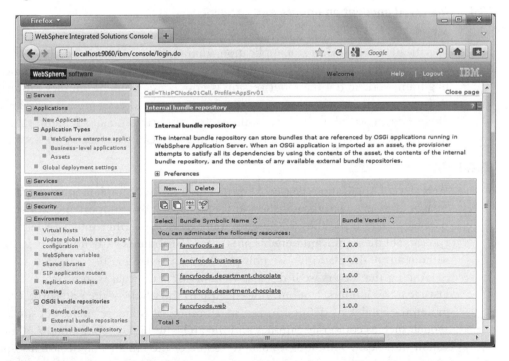

Figure 13.6   The Fancy Foods bundles installed in the WebSphere bundle repository. This allows them to be automatically provisioned and shared between several applications.

13.4.2 *Module granularity*

As well as providing a complete implementation of the enterprise OSGi programming model, WebSphere provides some useful extensions, particularly in the area of module granularity. To some extent, these extensions anticipate developments in the next release of the OSGi Enterprise Specification.

APPLICATION ISOLATION

When running in the WebSphere server, OSGi applications don't have visibility of bundles belonging to other applications. This ensures applications don't interfere with each other. Each application runs in its own OSGi framework, instead of all application bundles running in a single flat framework (the normal pattern for OSGi frameworks). This is similar to the normal mode of operation for Java EE applications, where only JARs within the same EAR are on the classpath. Sharing bundles is often convenient, so your applications can include a mix of private content and shared content.

COMPOSITE BUNDLES

WebSphere supports the notion of a *composite bundle*. A composite bundle is composed of several constituent bundles, but it appears as a single bundle to the outside world. This extra level of granularity makes it easier to distribute coherent collections of bundles and also allows packages to be shared within a composite bundle, but hidden from the outside world.

13.4.3 *Managed application update and extension*

Another area where WebSphere adds value beyond what's in the OSGi Enterprise Specification is in the area of application administration. One of the beauties of OSGi is that all OSGi applications are updateable; multiple versions of a bundle can co-exist in a framework, and if the older version is stopped, dependent bundles will rewire to the new version (or the other way around, if you want to downgrade a bundle). WebSphere provides administrative support for application management that allows upgrades to be staged, and then rolled out in a managed way (see figure 13.7).

13.4.4 *SCA*

WebSphere Application Server also includes an SCA implementation, based on Apache Tuscany. Having both SCA and enterprise OSGi support precanned in one package makes using the two programming models together much easier; it means you can get the significant benefits of SCA for distributed OSGi and legacy integration without any of the platform assembly pain we hit in chapter 10.

Among the servers we'll discuss, WebSphere is unusual in how many enterprise OSGi features it offers. Not only does it support the whole of the enterprise OSGi programming model, as defined in the specification, it offers several extensions to the model, such as composite bundles and the ability to update components of an application with near-continuous availability. Some of the enhancements are also present in the Apache Aries codebase, but some are unique to WebSphere.

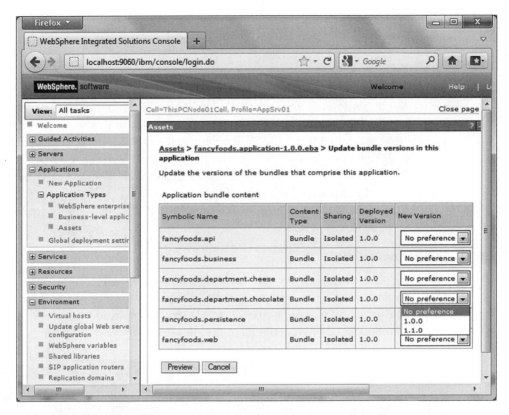

Figure 13.7   WebSphere Application Server provides management support for updating individual bundles in an EBA. For example, the `fancyfoods.department.chocolate` bundle may be updated from version 1.0.0 to 1.1.0 after the initial deployment when a new version of the chocolate bundle becomes available.

13.5   *Eclipse Virgo and Gemini*

We've discussed Apache Aries extensively throughout this book, but it's not the only enterprise OSGi implementation in town. One of the great things about standards-based technologies is that there *are* multiple implementations; as a user, you're free to pick and choose the one that suits you best. Eclipse Gemini is an Eclipse project with a mission similar to Apache Aries; it provides independently consumable components that implement various sections of the enterprise OSGi specification. Gemini provides the reference implementations for the web application container and Blueprint service parts of enterprise OSGi. Like Apache Aries, the Gemini components are intended to be incorporated into an application server.

The primary consumer of the Gemini components is the Eclipse Virgo application server. Virgo is based on an initial donation from SpringSource of the Spring dm Server. Because of its rich Spring support (it even packages Spring 3), Virgo will appeal to you if you develop for Spring. Virgo's JPA implementation is written with EclipseLink in mind, rather than OpenJPA, so if you're using EclipseLink, Virgo may also be a convenient choice—although, in principle, any implementation of the JPA service specification should work with any provider.

13.5.1   Debug support

One of Virgo's nice features is the ability to collect and view dumps of the system state when OSGi resolution failures occur. This can make debugging missing dependencies easier. Bundles in a plan file are installed transactionally, so if one fails to resolve, any bundles that were already installed will be uninstalled so that the system state remains unchanged. For example, if you try to install the `fancyfoods.department.chocolate` bundle without first installing the `fancyfoods.api` bundle, a dump is generated that can be browsed in the dump inspector (see figure 13.8).

Clicking on an unresolved bundle in a snapshotted OSGi state shows the resolution failure message shown in figure 13.9.

13.5.2   Application isolation

Like WebSphere, Virgo allows applications to be isolated from the main server runtime. Applications run in a user region that's insulated from the Virgo kernel. Some parts of the server, such as the web console, also run as applications in the user region. Application bundles do have visibility of bundles from other applications.

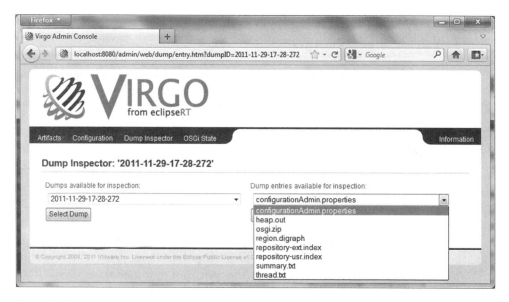

Figure 13.8   A dump will be automatically generated for a variety of failures, including OSGi resolution failures. The dump records active threads, the current configuration, repository contents, and a snapshot of the OSGi state of the server.

Figure 13.9 If you install the `fancyfoods.department.chocolate` bundle before the `fancyfoods.api` bundle, the chocolate bundle can't be resolved. Exploring the snapshotted OSGi state shows the reason for the resolution failure.

13.6 GlassFish

Although Virgo is a well-established alternative to Apache Aries, there are several other independent enterprise OSGi implementations. Since version 3, GlassFish ships with enterprise OSGi support. The support available in version 3 was mostly limited to web applications, but much more complete support, including JPA, JTA, and EJB integration, shipped in version 3.1. GlassFish has coined the term *hybrid applications* to describe applications that combine the modularity of OSGi with the ability to take advantage of Java EE infrastructure. The hybrid application programming model is the enterprise OSGi programming model, but we think the phrase nicely captures the ideas behind enterprise OSGi.

13.6.1 Dependency injection

Uniquely among the servers in this chapter, GlassFish doesn't include a Blueprint implementation. The assumption is that users will use Java EE's CDI (Contexts and Dependency Injection) for inversion of control. In its base form, CDI has no awareness of OSGi, but GlassFish has extended it with an `@OSGiService` annotation that allows services to be injected. This approach has the advantage of being annotation-based, which allows dependencies to be injected concisely. It will also feel natural if you're already used to using CDI. But because it's not standards-based, applications written for the GlassFish CDI won't be portable to other application servers.

If you'd rather use Blueprint, you can install the bundles of a Blueprint implementation (such as Aries) into GlassFish. The set of Aries bundles shipped with Karaf is a good minimal set to get Blueprint working in GlassFish. This is a popular approach.

13.6.2 EJBs

Another area where the GlassFish enterprise OSGi support isn't entirely standard is its support for EJBs. We've already discussed how both Apache Aries and GlassFish can be used to run EJBs in an OSGi environment in section 11.2.3. EJB support is an important part of GlassFish's hybrid application approach, because it makes more of the normal Java EE programming model accessible from within an OSGi environment. The EJB support in Aries and GlassFish is unrelated, and so portability of OSGi EJBs between the two platforms is limited. If you're keen on EJBs, it's worth noting that the GlassFish support made it into a released version before the Aries version, and that it may take a while for the Aries implementation to trickle into releases of consuming servers such as Karaf and Geronimo.

13.6.3 Administration

By default, the GlassFish web console doesn't have views for OSGi administration, but a console plug-in based on the Felix web console is available as a separate download. GlassFish also ships the Felix Gogo console (see figure 13.10).

Although it has an open source license, a commercial edition of GlassFish is available, known as Oracle GlassFish Server. This edition includes support and bug fixes.

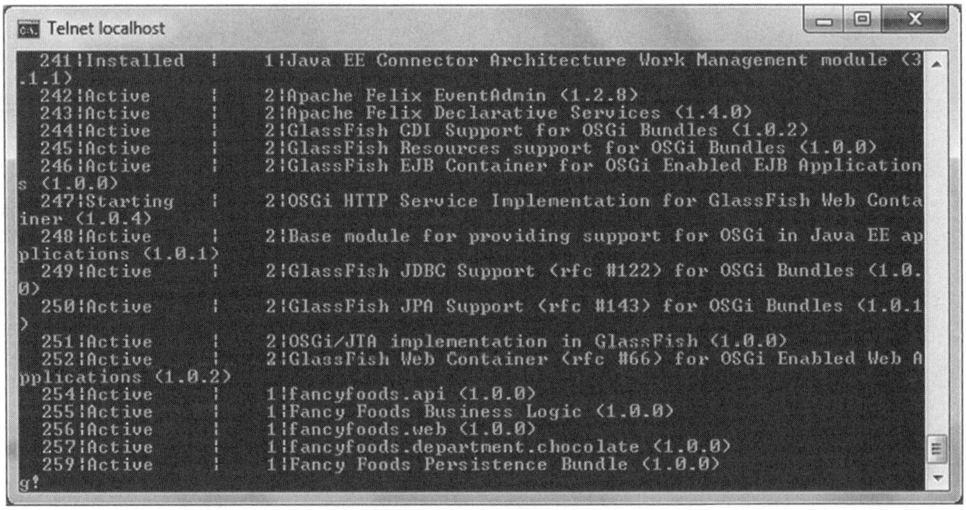

Figure 13.10 The Felix Gogo shell, as it appears in GlassFish

13.7   JBoss

Another well-established application server that has introduced support for OSGi applications in recent editions is JBoss. Like GlassFish, JBoss is open source, but paid support is available. JBoss OSGi is a new feature in JBoss Application Server 7 that provides support for OSGi applications. JBoss provides a Blueprint implementation and WAB support, as well as other OSGi functions like Config Admin and Declarative Services.

In some other areas, JBoss doesn't include as many enterprise OSGi features as some of the other servers we've discussed. At the time of writing, JBoss doesn't support persistence bundles and has only limited JNDI function. Web application support is also limited, because OSGi web applications run on the Pax Web container rather than the default JBoss web container. Several useful features are missing from the Pax Web container, including integrated security, servlet 3 annotations, and JSP support.

Because of these constraints, the JBoss team currently recommends using Java EE for web applications, with JNDI bridges to OSGi bundles for the rest of the application. These hybrid applications are arguably less modular than pure-OSGi applications, but they allow applications to use JSPs and servlet annotations. Improved JNDI, persistence bundle support, and migration of the WAB support onto the JBoss web container are all on the medium term JBoss roadmap.

Interestingly, JBoss OSGi isn't based on an existing OSGi framework like Felix or Equinox; instead it leverages and extends existing modularity capabilities within the application server. One implication of this is that JBoss can't exploit normal OSGi consoles like the Equinox and Felix ones. The JBoss web console allows administration of the base OSGi framework properties and bundles (see figure 13.11). The server also

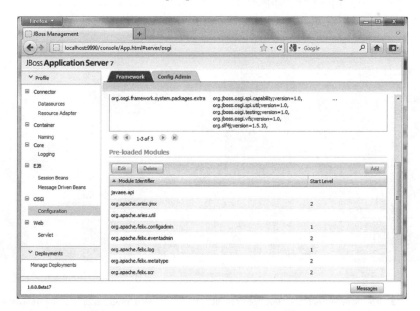

Figure 13.11   The JBoss administrative console has an OSGi section that allows you to view and configure the framework properties and server bundles.

includes a version of the Felix web console that allows more complete management of all the installed bundles, packages, and services, and application bundles can also be managed with a JMX client like JConsole.

OSGi support is relatively new in JBoss, and we're looking forward to seeing the support continue to develop. In contrast, the last two products we'll discuss, Paremus Nimble and Service Fabric, have OSGi support baked in.

13.8 *Paremus Nimble and Paremus Service Fabric*

With the possible exception of Apache Karaf, which is more of a platform than a server, all the products that we've discussed so far are relatively conventional Java EE application servers. The last product we'll discuss, Paremus Service Fabric, is rather different. The main feature of Service Fabric is its cloudiness—it provides a private cloud that can run Java EE, web, or OSGi applications. The Service Fabric cloud is built on an OSGi platform, Paremus Nimble. Nimble is in many ways analogous to Apache Karaf; it provides a layer on top of the basic OSGi runtime with significant improvements to the shell, logging, and deployment.

13.8.1 *Provisioning and deployment*

One difference between Karaf and Nimble is Nimble's provisioning support. One of the main focuses of the Service Fabric platform is sophisticated provisioning and deployment of applications, and this support is built into the Nimble kernel. When an application is deployed or fresh function is exercised, Nimble automatically downloads and installs appropriate runtimes and containers (see figure 13.12). For example, Service Fabric's Java EE support is based on the GlassFish Java EE container, but this container isn't loaded until a Java EE application is deployed. When the application is undeployed, GlassFish is unloaded.

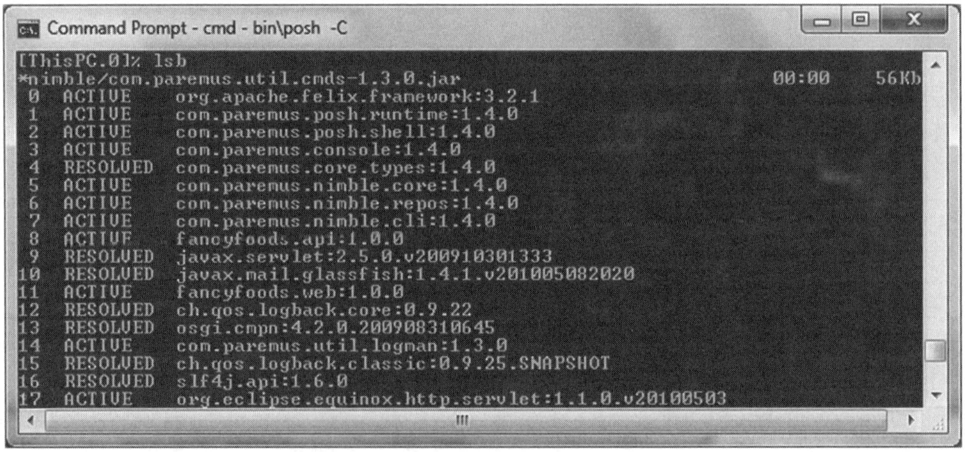

Figure 13.12   The bundle IDs show that the core Nimble distribution includes only a handful of bundles. When the `fancyfoods.api` **and** `fancyfoods.web` **bundles are installed, more bundles are provisioned, including the jetty web container and a few GlassFish bundles.**

Nimble can provision a wide range of stacks—as well as web and Java EE containers, it can handle all the dependency injection frameworks we covered in chapter 6: Blueprint, Declarative Services, iPojo, Peaberry, and Guice. Nimble can even provision runtimes for non-Java JVM–based languages such as Scala and Groovy. If a requirement can be satisfied in more than one way (for example, a web application could be run using either Tomcat or Jetty), the Nimble resolver can be configured with a policy for choosing between the two.

> **WARNING: GETTING REPOSITORY INDEXES RIGHT** Not all versions of Nimble automatically check for requirements like Blueprint in the indexes. This is presumably a performance optimization, because finding and parsing Blueprint files does have a cost. But this can catch you out if you're not careful, because it's not well documented, and a Blueprint implementation won't be installed unless Nimble spots bundles that need it. The same goes for JTA, JPA, and JNDI providers. To ensure enterprise OSGi requirements are indexed, add the `--enable-ee-spotters` flag to your indexing command.

This kind of resolution is more comprehensive than the OBR-based resolution of OSGi dependencies we discussed in chapter 7. We definitely didn't cover Scala in chapter 7! The power of Nimble provisioning demonstrates the flexibility of OBR resolution; it can handle OSGi applications, steamed puddings, and Scala. Although the Nimble resolver is OBR-based, Nimble repositories do include extra metadata not found in most public OBR repositories. Nimble can convert a normal OBR repository to a Nimble one by re-indexing it. Nimble also hosts handy re-indexed versions of popular OBR repositories (see figure 13.13).

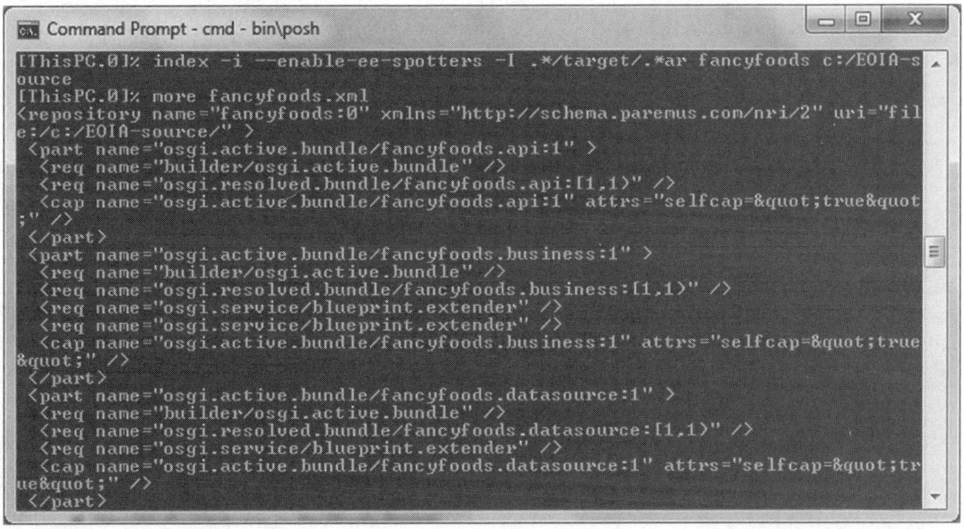

Figure 13.13   A repository that contains the Fancy Foods application can be generated by indexing a built copy of the source tree. If the `--enable-ee-spotters` flag is added, the resulting OBR index will include extra requirements for enterprise OSGi function. The index can be viewed from within the Posh shell using the `more` command.

As with the other platforms we've discussed, Nimble resolution can be controlled by specifying what repositories are used. You'll probably need to add a few repositories to the default repositories to install and provision your application.

13.8.2 *Remote services*

Nimble includes an implementation of the OSGi Remote Services Specification (chapter 10). If you're interested in remote services, you may find it convenient to use a runtime with integrated support, particularly because the Nimble implementation is stable and well respected.

13.8.3 *Console*

One of the nicest features of Nimble is its shell, the Paremus OSGi shell, or Posh. It's built on the Felix Gogo shell, but the Felix foundation is pretty unrecognizable! The inspiration for the Posh shell is Unix's bash, and Posh includes some commands more usually associated with Unix shells than OSGi consoles, such as pwd, more, and grep. It also includes command completion and history, as you'd expect, and the ability to run scripts with loops and conditions, which you might not expect.

The Posh shell is extensible, so that new commands can be added. The backing bundles for new commands can even be automatically provisioned. As you run commands, you can see new bundles being installed into the runtime, which gives a good feel for what's going on under the hood.

13.8.4 *Installing Aries*

Like Karaf, Nimble requires third-party implementations of enterprise programming models such as JPA and JTA. Unlike Karaf, it also requires an external Blueprint implementation. Nimble knows about Blueprint to the extent that it can recognize bundles that require Blueprint, but none of the built-in repositories include a Blueprint implementation.

Either Aries or Gemini components can be installed into Nimble. You can build an enterprise OSGi repository by indexing Aries bundles (for example, from your Maven repository). You'll also need to hand-crank some extra repository rules that declare that the Aries bundles provide JTA, JPA, JNDI, and Blueprint implementations. The Nimble OBR indexer can identify enterprise OSGi requirements, but not enterprise OSGi capabilities. This isn't too surprising, because spotting an implementation is much harder than spotting a consumer!

Because you'll need to generate your own Aries repositories and rules, you may find getting enterprise OSGi working in Nimble is more effort than it is in Karaf or the higher-level application servers. Java EE support is also provisioned into the server as a distinct component, and so you may find that Java EE isn't as thoroughly integrated as it is in servers that are built as Java EE servers.

Another difference between Nimble and many of the other servers we've discussed is the licensing. In common with WebSphere Application Server, Nimble is a commercial product, with no open source license. This has some—obvious—costs and also some advantages. Both Nimble and WebSphere Application Server are free to use for evaluation and development, so you'll only need to buy a license when you move into production. Because of their commercial nature, both Nimble and Web-Sphere Application Server come with professional support. Two of the other servers we discussed, GlassFish and JBoss, have the option of paid support with premium editions. And Karaf, Geronimo, and Virgo have active mailing lists and helpful development communities.

13.9 Summary

With so many products to choose from, how on earth do you choose one? It may be your choice is already made for you because you're working in an Apache shop, or a JBoss shop, or a WebSphere shop. The good news is that with so many products supporting enterprise OSGi, you've got a good chance of having a platform on which you can write modular applications, even if the decision about what application server to use has already been settled.

If you're starting from scratch, there are a few factors to consider. Do you want an open source license, an open source license with paid support, or a commercial license? Are you willing to get under the hood and bolt bits together, or do you want something that works out of the box? Do you want a super-light OSGi platform, or a full-featured server? Do you need the whole enterprise OSGi programming model, or will web applications or dependency injection do? Ultimately, how much server do you need? Table 13.2 shows how the various stacks compare to each other in terms of cost and scale.

Table 13.2 Feature comparison of enterprise OSGi servers

Server	Apache Karaf	Apache Geronimo	IBM WebSphere	Eclipse Virgo	GlassFish	JBoss	Paremus Nimble
Vendor	Apache Software Foundation	Apache Software Foundation	IBM	Eclipse	Oracle	Red Hat	Paremus
License	Apache license	Apache license	Proprietary license (free restricted license for developers)	Eclipse Public License	Dual license: Common Development and Distribution License (CDDL) and GNU General Public License (GPL)	GNU Lesser General Public License (LGPL)	Proprietary license (Nimble only available with a free restricted license for developers)

Table 13.2   Feature comparison of enterprise OSGi servers *(continued)*

Server	Apache Karaf	Apache Geronimo	IBM WebSphere	Eclipse Virgo	GlassFish	JBoss	Paremus Nimble
Support	Community	Community	Included with license	Community	Commercial support available	Commercial support available	Included with license
Type	Provisionable framework	Application server	Application server	Application server	Application server	Application server	Provisionable framework
Enterprise OSGi technology	Aries	Aries	Aries	Gemini	In-house	In-house	Unspecified

Some of the platforms we've discussed have rich enterprise OSGi support, whereas others are rolling out the basics. What excites us about all of these servers is the general recognition that building modular applications is great. The industry is investing in enterprise OSGi and the range of options available to you, as an enterprise OSGi developer, is getting bigger and better.

appendix A
OSGi—the basics

OSGi is a big subject, and we're not going to attempt to cover all of it in a single appendix. Instead, we'll be going over the basics of OSGi at a high level. We'll also delve into greater detail into some aspects of OSGi that may not be familiar to most readers, but that are important to understand when writing enterprise OSGi applications. For a more comprehensive introduction to OSGi and OSGi reference, have a look at *OSGi in Action* by Richard Hall, Karl Pauls, Stuart McCulloch, and David Savage (Manning, 2011).

A.1 Where did OSGi come from, and where is it going?

One of the stories of software engineering has been that of increasing abstraction and resulting improvements in modularity. The earliest programs were written in assembly language, which mapped directly to the instruction set of the machine executing the program, or coded directly as machine instructions. There was no higher-level structure above the individual machine codes, little abstraction, and limited scope for sharing and reusing programs. Because there was so little abstraction between the code and the hardware it ran on, even slight hardware changes could mean that the application had to be extensively rewritten. Higher-level languages introduced subroutines, allowing code to be grouped into named functions and reused. The abstraction away from raw machine instructions also meant that code could be recompiled rather than rewritten for new hardware. Next came libraries, large groupings of code with a separate interface and implementation. This abstraction allowed different pieces of code to be changed independently from one another without rebuilding entire applications; these libraries are therefore modular code. Finally, object orientation provided finer-grained modularity by grouping data and behavior together into encapsulated objects. This abstraction substantially improved the level to which changes in a program could be isolated from the rest of the program, and the level to which code could be reused, marking a dramatic improvement in modularity.

Although object orientation provided good modularity, it didn't provide *enough* modularity, particularly for embedded systems. A nonprofit industry consortium known as the OSGi Alliance set out to design a system that enabled greater modularity in Java. In addition to Sun, IBM, and Oracle, its original members were, for the most part, mobile phone manufacturers like Motorola and Ericsson, and networking companies like Lucent and Nortel. There were also energy companies involved, such as Electricité de France and the late Enron Communications. OSGi is used in a surprising range of systems, from cars and locomotives to set-top boxes and application servers.

Because of the small physical size of an embedded device, the Java classpath for each software component had to be well-defined and compact. Devices might be physically appearing and disappearing off the network at any time as users plugged them in, so the coupling model had to be loose and fully dynamic. Modern application servers have a lot of disk space accessible to them, but they still have classpath problems. Because they're trying to do so much, their classpath will bloat uncontrollably unless there's some sort of dependency-management scheme in place. Similarly, the enormous span of the system means that the abilities to keep couplings loose and dynamically register and unregister components are essential.

OSGi came to the attention of the mainstream Java community in 2003, when Eclipse made the technical shift to OSGi. Eclipse was already using a home-rolled modularity system to power its plug-in architecture, so it made a lot of sense to switch to a more standardized solution. After Eclipse made the leap, application server vendors then started to base their servers on OSGi. IBM WebSphere, Oracle WebLogic, Apache Geronimo, GlassFish, and JBoss are now all built out of OSGi bundles. OSGi is firmly in place in middleware implementations, and most middleware vendors are members of the OSGi Alliance.

A.2   Versions

We discuss OSGi versioning in sections 1.2.1 and 5.1.1. But versioning is important enough that it's worth revisiting to re-emphasize the basics and cover some of the subtler points before we continue with our OSGi refresher.

Bundles, exported packages, and imported packages may all have versions. Bundles and package exports specify an exact version, but package imports use a version range. Although versions are optional, being disciplined about specifying versions is a good practice and can avert a range of compatibility problems as development progresses.

Version ranges are defined using the standard mathematical convention for intervals. Square brackets represent an *inclusive* range, and round parentheses an *exclusive* range.

A.2.1   The semantic versioning scheme

Versioning is a way of communicating about what's changing (or not changing) in software, and so the language used must be shared. Consumers of a class must be able to distinguish between changes that will break them by changing an API, and changes that are internal only.

The OSGi Alliance recommends a scheme called semantic versioning. It's simple, but it carries much more information about what's changing than normal versions. Every version consists of four parts: major, minor, micro, and qualifier (M.m.µ.q). A change to the major part of a version number—for example, changing 2.5.0 to 3.0.0—indicates that the code change isn't backward compatible. Removing a method or changing its argument types are examples of this kind of breaking change. A change to the minor part indicates a change that is backwards compatible for a consumer of an API, but not implementation providers. For example, the minor version should be incremented if a method is added to an interface. If a change doesn't affect the externals, it should be indicated by a change to the micro version. Such a change could be a bug fix, or a performance improvement, or even the removal of methods from classes that are internal to a bundle. Having a strong division between bundle internals and bundle externals means the internals can be changed dramatically without anything other than the micro version needing to change. Finally, the qualifier is used to add extra information like a build date.

A.2.2 *Guarantees of compatibility*

One of the benefits provided by the semantic versioning scheme is a guarantee of compatibility. A module will be bytecode compatible with any versions of its dependencies where only the minor or micro version has changed.

Backward compatibility is no guarantee of forward compatibility, and so modules should not try to run with dependencies with minor versions lower than the ones they were compiled against.

A.2.3 *Coexistence of implementations*

The other major benefit provided by versioning is that it allows different versions of a module to coexist in the same system. If the modules weren't versioned, there would be no way of tagging them as different and isolating them from one another. With versioned modules, OSGi classloading allows each module to use the version of its dependencies that is most appropriate (see figure A.1).

When importing a package, it's always a good idea to add version constraints. Usually, the minimum is the version currently being used, and the maximum is the next major increment (non-inclusive). It's not sensible to accept the next major increment, because you know (because of semantic versioning) that this version will have breaking changes in it. Minor version increments can be safely accepted, and they may bring bug fixes or other improvements. The following import statement will resolve against any version of the food.nice package above or equal to 1.4.3, but less than 2.0.0 (which would contain a breaking change):

```
Import-Package: food.nice;version="[1.4.3, 2.0.0)"
```

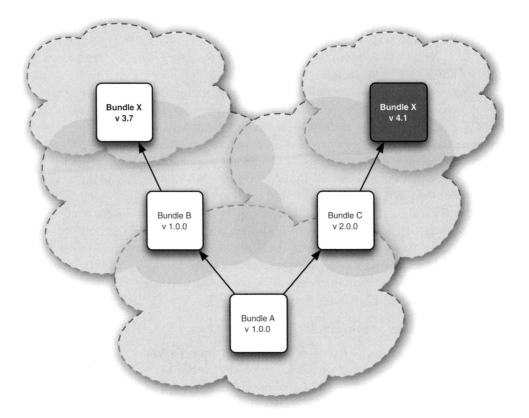

Figure A.1 **The transitive dependencies of a module (the dependencies of its dependencies) may have incompatible versions. OSGi allows the implementations to coexist by isolating them from one another.**

A.2.4   *Why everything has a version*

Every exported package and bundle in OSGi has a version. Even if you don't specify an explicit version, you still have an implicit version of 0.0.0. This version may or may not be what you want. For example, let's assume you release a package without specifying a version (your version is 0.0.0):

```
Export-Package: food.experimental
```

Other bundles can import the package in several ways. If no version is specified as follows, any available version of the package will be imported:

```
Import-Package: food.experimental
```

This is equivalent to the following:

```
Import-Package: food.experimental;version="0.0.0"
```

> **WARNING: PRECISE VERSIONS AND VERSION RANGES** Package imports are always ranges. If only one version is specified on a package import, it's a *minimum* version, not an exact version. This isn't totally intuitive, so it's easy to forget, even for developers who've been using OSGi for years. To specify a

precise version of 1.0.0 on a package import, you would need to write ver-
sion="[1.0.0, 1.0.0]". Specifying version="1.0.0" means any version
greater than 1.0.0.

But this import is pretty vague. The importer risks being broken by changes to the
food.experimental that aren't backward compatible. To avoid this, the importer
should explicitly specify a minimum and maximum range as follows:

```
Import-Package: food.experimental;version="[0.0.0,1.0.0)"
```

But what's a sensible range? The rules of semantic versioning don't apply to versions
below 1.0.0. Some projects (including Apache Aries) treat all minor increments below
versions 1.0.0 as potentially breaking changes. One sensible upper range is
"[0.0.0,0.1.0)". On the other hand, when you release a new version of the
food.experimental package, you may decide to reform your nonversioning ways, and
start on a clean slate with a sensible version of 1.0.0. Neither an import of
"[0.0.0,1.0.0)" nor "[0.0.0,0.1.0)" would be satisfied by a food.experimental
package exported with version 1.0.0, even if nothing significant had changed. The net
effect of this ambiguity is uncertainty for importers of the package. They won't know
whether a change from 0.0.0 to 1.0.0 is a breaking change or a trivial change to move
to a versioned package. The easiest way to avoid all the confusion is to start off as you
mean to go on and give packages meaningful versions from the first release.

A.2.5 *Consumers and providers, not clients and implementors*

One of the most confusing things about semantic versioning is that it can't be boiled
down to, "I implement interface X, therefore I need a version range of [1,1.1]." This
is why we talk about API providers and consumers rather than any less generic terms.

A provider of an API isn't only the bundle that exports the package, but also any
bundle that provides a backing implementation for use by a consumer. A good example here would be the Servlet API and a Web Container implementation (for example,
Jetty). The Servlet API bundle is clearly a provider, but less obviously, so is Jetty. This is
because consumers of the Servlet API (web applications, to the developer) expect the
presence of a Web Container as well as the API classes.

It doesn't normally take much of an effort for people to understand that providers
may not export the API they use, they can still fall back on the mental model that if
they implement an interface then that makes them a provider. Unfortunately, this
isn't correct! Once again the Servlet API provides a good example. Clearly a web application is a consumer of the Servlet API, but web applications extensively implement
abstract classes and interfaces from the Servlet API. Try writing a functional servlet
without extending Servlet or HttpServlet. There are plenty more examples in the
Servlet API, but also in other APIs.

To truly understand semantic versioning, you need to have a clear division
between API interfaces that are implemented or extended by a provider (for example
HttpServletRequest), and ones that are implemented or extended by the consumer
(for example HttpServlet). If you add a method to an interface implemented by a

consumer, then this is a breaking change that needs a major version increment. After all, it would be pretty disastrous for most web applications if you were suddenly expected to implement a new doSuperGet() method on all your servlets!

A.2.6   *Semantic versions and marketing versions*

It's important to remember that semantic versions are different from marketing versions. Versioning is about communication, and it only works if everyone uses the same language. Because not everyone is using semantic versioning, marketing versions can go out of step with semantic versions. This can feel counterintuitive; for example, the Servlet 3 API is correctly versioned at 2.6. Similarly, JPA 2 packages should be versioned at 1.1. The OSGi Enterprise Specification specifies versions for these packages, but several of the servers we discussed in chapter 13 include bundles that were released into the wild with incorrect versions of the javax.servlet and javax.persistence packages. This can cause difficulties for consumers of these packages, which can't use the semantic versioning rules on the imports.

A.3   *Bundles*

Bundles are one of the most basic OSGi constructs. A bundle is a normal Java JAR, but with extra metadata in its manifest that identifies it as an OSGi bundle. Bundles have special dependency management and classloading behavior that allow much greater modularity. Unlike normal JARs, bundles also have a lifecycle.

A.3.1   *Manifest headers*

The most important OSGi manifest header is the bundle symbolic name, but there are many other possible headers. Table A.1 lists the defined OSGi manifest headers. We've included all of the core and enterprise OSGi headers; more are defined in the Compendium Specification. (Confused about which specification is which? Have a look at appendix B.)

Table A.1   OSGi manifest headers

Header	Attributes and directives	Comments
Bundle-ActivationPolicy	lazy blueprint.timeout	See section A.4.
Bundle-Activator		See section A.4.2.
Bundle-Blueprint		See section 2.3.3.
Bundle-Category		
Bundle-Classpath		Defaults to ".". Particularly useful for WABs, where WEB-INF/ classes is a sensible value.

Table A.1 OSGi manifest headers *(continued)*

Header	Attributes and directives	Comments
Bundle-ContactAddress		
Bundle-Copyright		
Bundle-Description		
Bundle-DocURL		
Bundle-Icon	size	
Bundle-License	description link	
Bundle-Localization		
Bundle-ManifestVersion		Should always be present and set to 2.
Bundle-Name		
Bundle-NativeCode	language osname osversion processor selection-filter	
Bundle-RequiredExecutionEnvironment		In common use until v4.3, but now deprecated.
Bundle-SymbolicName	singleton	Required.
Bundle-UpdateLocation		
Bundle-Vendor		
Bundle-Version		See section A.2.
DynamicImport-Package	bundle-version version	See section 12.3.3.
Export-Package	bundle-symbolic-name bundle-version exclude include specification-version uses version	See sections 5.1.2 and 7.2.1.
Export-Service		Deprecated.
Fragment-Host	bundle-version extension	See sections 2.2.4 and 7.1.2.

Table A.1   OSGi manifest headers (*continued*)

Header	Attributes and directives	Comments
Import-Package	bundle-symbolic-name bundle-version resolution specification-version version	See sections 5.1.2 and 7.2.1.
Import-Service		Deprecated.
InitialProvisioning-Entries		
Meta-Persistence		See chapter 3.
Provide-Capability	effective:1 uses	See chapter 7.
Remote-Service		See section 10.4.2 .
Require-Bundle	bundle-version resolution visibility	See section 5.1.2.
Require-Capability	effective:1 filter resolve	See chapter 7.
SCA-Configuration		See section 10.6.
Service-Component		Path to declarative services metadata files. Wildcards may be used. See section 6.2.3.
Web-ContextPath		See section 2.2.1.

A.3.2   *The bundle context*

Every active bundle has a bundle context. The bundle context acts as an intermediary between the bundle and the outside framework. The bundle context can be used to programmatically install new bundles and query the existing bundles. It can also be used for more advanced functions, such as requesting persistent storage areas, subscribing to events, registering services, and retrieving services.

A.3.3   *Dependency management*

One of the main functions of OSGi bundles is to allow dependencies to be explicitly declared and resolved. Resolving is an import concept, and we discussed it in depth in chapter 7. Resolving is the process by which the OSGi framework determines whether bundles have all of their required package imports, and which bundles should supply these package imports. (It's the absence of resolving in standard Java that results in the dreaded `ClassNotFoundExceptions` at runtime.) We say a bundle is wired to another bundle if it provides classes to that bundle.

Dependencies may be declared with `Import-Package:` or `Require-Bundle:` headers. As we explained in chapter 5, using `Import-Package:` is a best practice.

A.3.4 *Classloading*

OSGi's classloading uses a different model from conventional Java classloading. Instead of every class in the virtual machine being loaded by a single monolithic classloader, classloading responsibilities are divided among a number of classloaders (see figure A.2). Each bundle has an associated classloader that loads classes contained within the bundle itself. If a bundle is wired to a second bundle, its classloader will delegate to the other bundle's classloader for classes exported by the second bundle. In addition to the bundle classloaders, there are environment classloaders that handle core JVM classes.

Each classloader has well-defined responsibilities. If a classload request can't be satisfied, it will pass it up the delegation chain (see figure A.3).

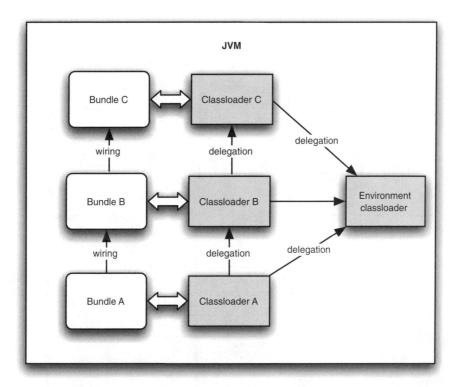

Figure A.2 The JVM contains many active classloaders in an OSGi environment. Each bundle has its own classloader. These classloaders delegate to the classloaders of other bundles for imported classes, and to the environment's classloader for core classes.

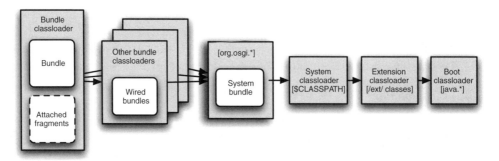

Figure A.3   The classloaders form a delegation chain. If a classloader can't load a given class, it passes the request to the next classloader in the chain.

SUBSTITUTABILITY

Somewhat surprisingly, being included in a bundle doesn't guarantee that a package will be wired to that bundle. This is a principle known as substitutability. It allows bundles to maintain a consistent class space between them by standardizing on one variant of a package, even when multiple variants are exported. Figure A.4 shows the class space for a bundle that exports a substitutable package.

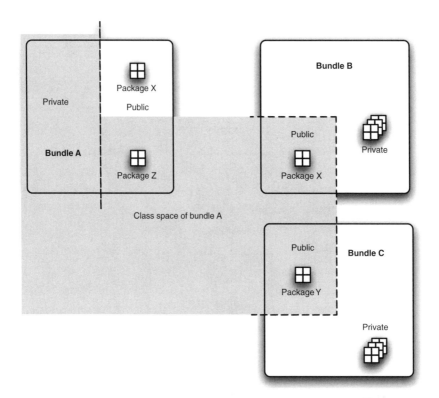

Figure A.4   The class space for a bundle includes all of its private classes, and the public classes of any bundle it's wired to. It doesn't necessarily include all of the bundle's public classes, because some might be imported from other packages instead.

Before version 4 of OSGi, substitutability was guaranteed; a bundle implicitly imported all the packages it exported. From version 4 onward, substitutability must be explicitly enabled by importing exported packages. This is an OSGi best practice. The following manifest exports a substitutable package:

```
Manifest-Version: 1.0
Bundle-ManifestVersion: 2
Bundle-SymbolicName: com.supermarket.core
Bundle-Version: 1.0.0
Export-Package: com.supermarket.api
Import-Package: com.supermarket.api, some.other.package
```

A.3.5 Fragments

Fragments are extensions to bundles. They attach to a host bundle and act in almost every way as if they were part of the host (see figure A.5). They allow bundles to be customized depending on their environment. For example, translated resource files can be packaged up by themselves into a fragment and only shipped if needed. Fragments can also be used to add platform-specific code to a generic host.

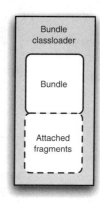

Some OSGi developers prefer to avoid bundle fragments. Although they have some useful behaviors, many of the normal rules for OSGi bundles don't apply to fragments, which can cause things to go awry in subtle ways. A colleague of ours describes fragments as *bundle flakes*!

Figure A.5 A bundle fragment attaches to its host and shares a classloader.

A.4 Bundle lifecycles

Unlike normal JARs, OSGi bundles have a lifecycle. They can be stopped and started on demand, with their classloaders and classes appearing and disappearing from the system in response. Figure A.6 shows the complete state machine for OSGi bundles.

A.4.1 Activation policies

A bundle has some control over when it moves between these states. After a bundle gets started, it may move immediately from the STARTING state to the ACTIVE state (eager activation), or it may wait until one of its classes is loaded (lazy activation). The default policy is eager activation; lazy activation may be enabled by adding the following to the manifest:

```
Bundle-ActivationPolicy: lazy
```

A.4.2 Bundle activators

Before moving into the ACTIVE state, a bundle will have a chance to perform some initialization. If a bundle declares an activator, its activator will be notified whenever

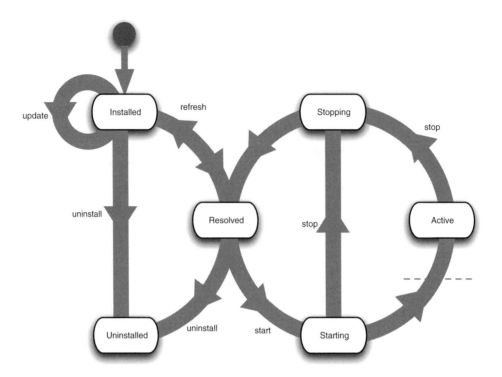

Figure A.6   Bundles may move between the installed, resolved, starting, active, and stopping states. A starting bundle can be lazily activated, and if so it won't move to the active state (crossing the dashed line) until it's needed by another bundle. A bundle is resolved if it's installed and all its dependencies are also resolved or started. When a bundle is uninstalled, it's no longer able to start, nor can it provide packages to any new bundles.

the bundle is started or stopped. The activator class is declared in the bundle manifest as follows:

```
Bundle-Activator: com.supermarket.Activator
```

Although they're widely used and handy in core OSGi, bundle activators aren't such a common pattern in enterprise OSGi. Chapter 6 demonstrates how Blueprint allows you to do everything you can do with an activator, but in a much more flexible and powerful way.

A.4.3   *Installation and resolution*

Installation is the process by which new bundles are added to an existing OSGi framework at runtime. This can be done in a number of framework-specific ways, but there's a commonly used, framework-independent mechanism for installing a bundle from any local or remote location.

The `BundleContext` can be used to install a bundle using a string URL that points to a bundle file somewhere in the ether, as follows:

```
org.osgi.framework.BundleContext.installBundle(String location)
```

After installation into a framework, an OSGi bundle is in the INSTALLED state, and is a pretty boring, inert object. An INSTALLED bundle doesn't have a classloader and can't provide code or packages to anyone. What happens to the bundle next is the real magic of OSGi, and is known as the resolution process. When all of a bundle's dependencies are available in the OSGi framework (there are exported packages available for all of its imports), then the framework resolver will attempt to *resolve* the bundle. This process creates fixed wires between package imports and exports, obeying the versioning criteria declared in the metadata. If a consistent set of wires can be created for a bundle, then that bundle is said to be RESOLVED. A RESOLVED bundle is much more interesting than an INSTALLED bundle—it has a classloader, and so classes and resources can be loaded from the moment the bundle resolves. The wires created by the resolver have a huge impact on how classes are loaded in OSGi, but also guarantee that dependencies are available at runtime and eliminate the risk of a `NoClassDefFoundError`.

A.4.4   *Starting and stopping bundles*

After a bundle has entered the RESOLVED state, it's eligible to be STARTED. Given that classes can be loaded from a bundle as soon as it's resolved, some people get confused as to what starting a bundle means. A few things happen when a bundle starts, such as the invocation of a bundle's `BundleActivator`, if it has one, and moving the bundle to the ACTIVE state.

The most important change on starting a bundle is that an active `BundleContext` is created for a bundle as it starts. The `BundleContext` can be used by a bundle to interact with the framework, influence the lifecycle of other bundles, and most importantly, access the OSGi Service Registry.

Stopping a bundle is, unsurprisingly, more or less the inverse of starting a bundle. The framework moves the bundle back into the RESOLVED state, it calls the `stop` method on the bundle's `BundleActivator`, and it ensures that any services registered by the bundle are unregistered from the Service Registry.

A.4.5   *Uninstalling and updating bundles*

When a bundle is no longer needed in a runtime it can be uninstalled. Contrary to what you might expect, uninstalling a bundle doesn't remove it from the runtime! Uninstalled bundles are marked so that they're no longer eligible to provide packages when the framework resolver attempts to resolve new bundles, but they continue to provide packages to existing bundles.

An uninstalled bundle that's still providing packages to other bundles (that aren't also uninstalled) can't be removed immediately; doing so would forcibly take the package away from the running bundles and result in a rather unpleasant mess. Uninstalled bundles are only able to be discarded by the framework when no other resolved bundle is wired to them. Typically, after a bundle is uninstalled, the framework is *refreshed* using `PackageAdmin.refreshPackages()` or `bundle.adapt(FrameworkWiring.class).refreshBundles()`. This causes the framework to reresolve any bundles that are using packages from an uninstalled bundle. This allows the framework to clear up the uninstalled bundles. An uninstalled bundle that's unable to be removed because it's still providing packages to another bundle is sometimes known as a *zombie bundle*.

Updating a bundle is an operation that isn't possible in standard Java. An update is like an atomic uninstall/reinstall operation that allows the content of a bundle to be changed. The full explanation of bundle update behavior is rather involved, and a complete description isn't in the scope of this book, but one of the more common side effects is as a direct result of the behavior for an uninstallation. If a bundle A_1 is being updated to A_2, and it provides packages to another bundle B, then the *old* version of the bundle A_1 can't be removed without breaking B. This situation doesn't stop the update from occurring, but it does mean that you end up with both A_1 *and* A_2 available at the same time! B will continue to use A_1 (until it's refreshed), but future resolutions will all wire to A_2. Similarly to uninstallation, refreshing the framework after an update allows the framework to clear up old versions of bundles and to generally sort everything out.

If you're confused by uninstallation and update, we don't blame you; they're conceptually the most difficult part of the bundle lifecycle (though writing an OSGi resolver would be a harder task if you were to implement a framework!). Probably the most important thing to take from this is that dynamic dependency management is hard, and sometimes you can end up in some pretty odd situations. Fortunately OSGi has solved these issues with well defined, if slightly interesting, consequences.

A.4.6   *Managing dependencies in a dynamic system*

Bundles may be stopped at any time. What happens to bundles that depend on the stopped bundle? In most cases, very little. When a bundle is stopped, it still has a `ClassLoader`, so its exported packages remain available to other bundles that are wired to it. One thing that does change is that the stopped bundle no longer has a `BundleContext`. This means that any services that the bundle registered while it was started are forcibly unregistered by the framework (assuming the bundle didn't tidy up after itself!). Obviously, bundles that depended on these services are no longer able to use them, but if the stopped bundle is started again, then things usually (in a well-designed system) return to their original state.

Uninstalling a bundle is a much more destructive operation than stopping it. An uninstalled bundle isn't able to provide packages in any resolution, and it definitely can't provide any services. The framework automatically removes uninstalled bundles, but sometimes this isn't possible. If the uninstalled bundle was providing packages to other bundles before it was uninstalled, then these wirings will keep the uninstalled bundle's `ClassLoader` alive. This is often called a *zombie* bundle; the bundle isn't alive anymore, and there's no way to bring it back, but somehow it's still walking around. The system can be reconciled by restarting the framework, by calling `refreshPackages` on the `PackageAdmin` service, or by calling `refreshBundles` on the `FrameworkWiring` service.

Any bundles that depended on the now-absent uninstalled bundle will be stopped and re-resolved. This may mean that they move all the way back to the INSTALLED state.

Stopping and uninstalling aren't the only actions that can impact dependent bundles. OSGi bundles can be dynamically updated, and an update may remove previously exported packages or introduce new package requirements. As with uninstalled bundles, the removed exports will remain available to existing users (from the old pre-update version of the bundle) until the framework is restarted or refreshed.

A.5 Services

Services are an extremely important part of OSGi. Services allow bundles to share object instances in a loosely coupled way.

Figure A.7 shows a simple OSGi service, represented by a triangle. The pointy end faces the provider, not the consumer. The reason is that the service can only have one provider, but it can have lots of consumers.

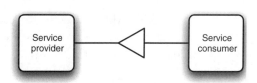

Figure A.7   A service that is provided by one bundle and used by another bundle. The triangle points toward the service provider.

A.5.1 The Service Registry

Management and discovery of services is handled by a shared Service Registry. Services are registered and retrieved using interface names and optional query parameters. (We'll come to service filters in section A.5.3.)

Services are registered on the bundle context. (If you're using Blueprint, this happens under the covers for you.) Services can only be provided by bundles that are STARTED. When a service is registered by a bundle, it provides one or more class names that mark the API of the service, and the service object itself. Optional properties can provide extra information about the service, and can be used to filter what services get returned when services are looked up. Service properties aren't intended for use by the service itself.

If Blueprint or Declarative Services aren't used, registration of a service can be done in a couple of lines of code as follows:

```
Hashtable<String, String> props = new Hashtable<String, String>();
props.put("check.type", "slow");
ctx.registerService(SpecialOffer.class.getName(), props);
```
Properties used to refine lookups

By using String interface names and simple property types, the OSGi Service Registry allows OSGi bundles to avoid worrying about their class spaces. If two versions of a service interface exist, then it's only possible to use an implementation that you share a view of the interface with. If you were to try to use a service that was in a different class space from your bundle, then you would generate a ClassCastException. This may seem odd, but in Java, a class is identified not only by its name, but by the classloader that loaded it.

A.5.2   *Accessing services*

In conventional OSGi, services are looked up using the bundle context. As you've seen, enterprise OSGi allows services to be accessed declaratively instead. This is almost always a best practice, because it's both easier and more robust. What are you missing out on by using Blueprint? The following example looks up a service, but without any error-handling code:

```
String interfaceName = SpecialOffer.class.getName();
ServiceReference ref = ctx.getServiceReference(interfaceName);
SpecialOffer lister = (SpecialOffer) ctx.getService(ref);
```

After you've added in code for error-handling, cleanup, and accounted for OSGi's dynamism, the code to cleanly look up a service is much longer. Almost every line needs a null check. This is why Blueprint is a best practice!

> ### Cleaning up afterwards
> When code is done with a service, it should call `ungetService` to release the service. Forgetting to unget services prevents the framework from being able to free up the resources associated with a service, and may prevent an application from operating properly.

When using the standard lookup method, the OSGi framework ensures that you only ever find services that share your class space for their declared API. This guarantees that you can always use any service that you find using that method, though it does sometimes lead to some confusing debugging when a lookup ignores a seemingly good service!

CONSUMING MULTIPLE SERVICES

What happens when multiple providers of the service have been registered? The service consumer has a choice between getting one, or getting a list containing all of them (see figure A.8). If the service is something like a credit card processing service, it's only necessary to take a payment once. In this situation, one service provider is sufficient, and it probably doesn't matter too much which provider is chosen. In the case of a logging service, on the other hand, logged messages should be sent to all the available loggers as follows, rather than one of them:

```
ServiceReference[] refs = ctx.getServiceReferences(Logger.class
        .getName());
if (refs != null) {
    for (ServiceReference ref : refs) {            Go through each
        Logger logger = (Logger) ctx.getService(ref);   service reference
        logger.doSomeLogging();
    }
}
```

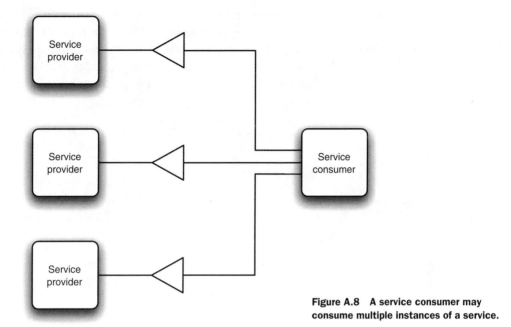

Figure A.8 A service consumer may consume multiple instances of a service.

SERVICE LIFECYCLES

Services are much more dynamic than you may be accustomed to. They may appear and disappear at any time. This allows for more interesting applications, but it also creates some challenges when handling services. Blueprint does a lot of this work for you, which is why it's preferable to the raw service APIs.

If a bundle is stopped, any services it registered are automatically unregistered. Users of those services need to be able to cope with the possibility of their services going away. For example, a logging service might be writing to a remote disk that is disconnected. Instead of the service staying available even though the disk it manages is gone, the entire service will be unregistered.

What happens to users of a service if the bundle hosting the service is stopped? The service is unregistered, but instances that have already been created won't magically vanish. But they'll be *stale*. The behavior of such services is undefined; they may continue to work fine, or they may throw exceptions. To avoid being left holding stale services, the use of ServiceTracker objects to detect when services are unregistered is a good practice in conventional OSGi. But it adds a lot to the volume of code required to use services. The enterprise OSGi technologies of Declarative Services and Blueprint both provide neater handling of the service dynamism.

USING SERVICETRACKERS

Although ServiceReferences are the most obvious way to access services programmatically, the API is pretty low-level and subject to several potential problems. Therefore, even developers who aren't using Declarative Services or Blueprint tend to prefer a higher-level API: the ServiceTracker. As the name suggests, ServiceTrackers allow you to track services as they're registered and unregistered, and take appropriate actions. But they also simplify normal service access by eliminating the need to unget services. For this reason, using service trackers instead of service references is considered a best practice. The following code gets a service using a `ServiceTracker`, but with the error handling code that was missing from the earlier `ServiceReference` example:

```
String name = SpecialOffer.class.getName();
ServiceTracker<SpecialOffer, SpecialOffer> tracker;
tracker = new ServiceTracker<SpecialOffer, SpecialOffer>(
        ctx, name, null);
tracker.open();
SpecialOffer offer = (SpecialOffer) tracker.getService();
if (offer == null) {
    throw new RuntimeException(
            "The SpecialOffer service is not available.");
}
tracker.close();
```

ServiceTrackers also allow you to access services in a way that's slightly insulated from startup order effects; because bundles may start in any order in an OSGi framework, services may be registered in any order. Code that expects services to always be present may work most of the time, but then drive you crazy with timing bugs. As with most things to do with service access, Blueprint eliminates this complexity. If you aren't using Blueprint, it would be a good idea to wait for a service as follows, rather than getting it and expecting it to be present:

```
SpecialOffer offer = (SpecialOffer) tracker.waitForService(TIMEOUT);
```

A.5.3 *Filters*

Filters are widely used in OSGi. They're sometimes used in bundle manifests, but their main use is in looking up services. The OSGi filter syntax will be familiar to those who write LDAP filters. Every filter expression has the following general format:

```
(
Attribute
        Operator
        Value
)
```

(There shouldn't be any whitespace between the elements in the filters.) `Attribute` is the name of the property to be selected for, `Operator` is a Boolean operator, and `Value` is the value to be matched. The `"="`, `"~="`,`"<="`, `">="`, and `"!"` operators are supported. The reserved characters `"\"`,`"*"`,`"("`, and `")"` must be escaped if they're contained in the value.

For example,

```
(aisle=fruit)
```

matches something whose aisle is fruit.

More complex constructions are also possible using *and* ("&") and *or* (" | ") in front of expressions surrounded by parentheses. For example,

```
(&(aisle=fruit)(colour=blue))
```

will match something whose aisle is fruit and whose color is blue (probably a blueberry!).

Substrings may be matched using the * operator; for example,

```
(colour=b*)
```

will match items whose color begins with "b"—"blue", for example, and also "brown."

Like many things, filters are created using the BundleContext, as follows:

```
Filter f = ctx.createFilter("(log.type=text)");
ServiceReference[] refs;
refs = ctx.getServiceReferences(Logger.class.getName(), f.toString());
```

So far we've been discussing what you can do in an OSGi application. Now let's consider how you run an OSGi application.

A.6 *OSGi frameworks*

These core elements of OSGi—bundles, lifecycle management, and service infrastructure—are supported by an environment known as an OSGi framework. It's useful to think of each element as a layer in an OSGi onion. (Like onions, OSGi has been known to make grown developers cry, but gives wonderful benefits.) Figure A.9 shows how the layers stack together. It's possible to use OSGi bundles without ever touching bundle lifecycles or services. To take advantage of OSGi services, on the other hand, an application must already be making use of bundles.

In addition to the layers we've already discussed, the OSGi platform includes a security layer that provides extensions to the Java 2 security architecture. The security

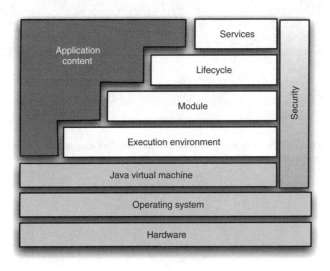

Figure A.9 The functionality of OSGi includes a number of layers. The white elements are provided by OSGi, the gray elements are prerequisites, and the black elements are user content. Applications will take advantage of the core OSGi framework by providing modules, possibly with sophisticated lifecycles. These modules may communicate with one another and the supporting platform using OSGi services. Security is provided across all layers.

layer cuts across the other layers. For a fuller discussion of OSGi security, see *OSGi in Action* (Hall et al., Manning, 2011).

A number of OSGi frameworks are in wide use today. The most popular are Eclipse Equinox, Apache Felix, Knopflerfish, and ProSyst. Equinox underpins the Eclipse IDE and Rich Client Platform, whereas Felix is at the heart of the Apache Tomcat application server. ProSyst is embedded in devices like routers and automotive GPS systems.

A.7   *The OSGi console*

The front-loading of dependency management in OSGi can take some getting used to. "Why can't my bundle start?" is a common worry for the new OSGi developer—and also for the experienced one. The most convenient way to control the lifecycle of a bundle, inspect bundle states, and diagnose bundles that refuse to start is by using an OSGi console. The OSGi console is also a good way of exploring an OSGi framework to see what packages and services are available. An OSGi console is a fairly low-level tool, particularly in an enterprise environment, and the command syntax of the textual consoles can be intimidating. But a console can help debug OSGi issues, so it's worth familiarizing yourself with one. Figure A.10 shows the Felix Gogo console, with the minimal set of bundles for the Felix framework and the Gogo console itself. (The Gogo console is an extension to the base Felix console, but one we recommend if you're not using Equinox or a higher-level console like Karaf.)

OSGi consoles do vary depending on the framework implementation. Figure A.11 shows the Equinox console. A number of third-party consoles are available, some of which have more inviting user interfaces. The essential capabilities are similar between implementations.

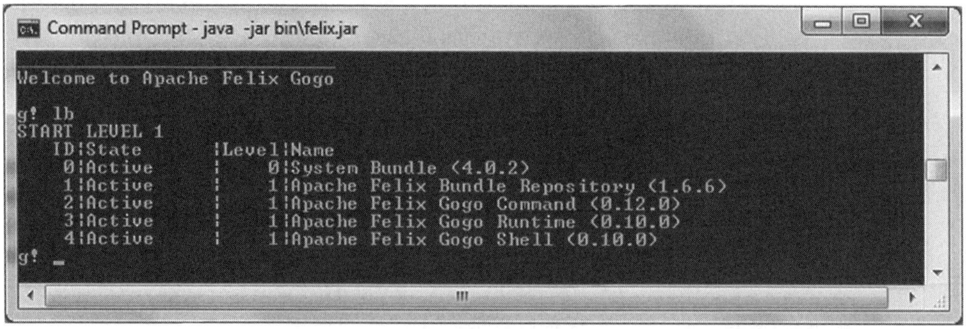

Figure A.10   The Felix OSGi console, in a minimal Felix installation. Bundles may be queried, installed, started, and stopped. Available bundles may be listed using the lb command.

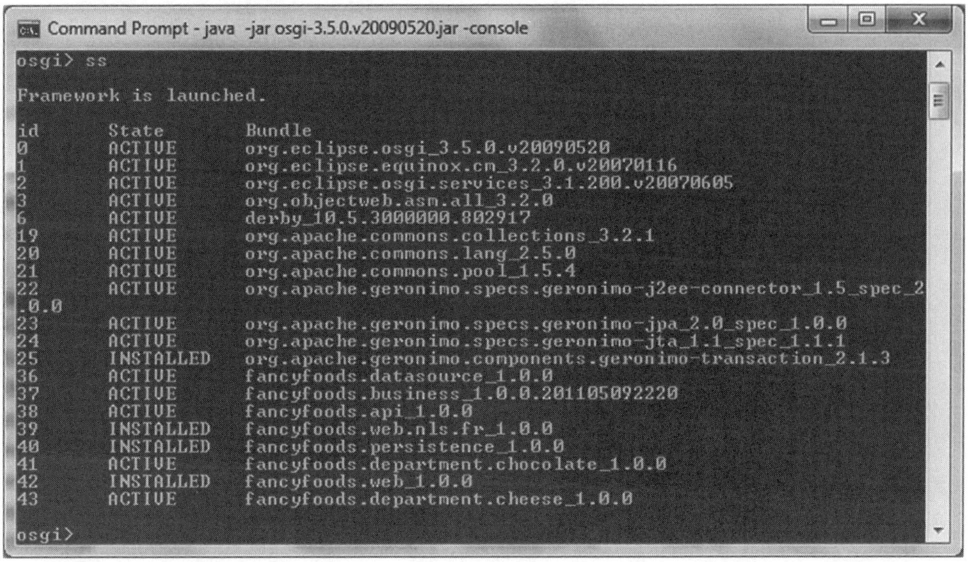

Figure A.11 The Equinox OSGi console. Available bundles may be listed using the `ss` command. In this case, the Fancy Foods application is installed, but many of its dependencies aren't, so most of the application bundles don't resolve (and are shown as INSTALLED only).

A.8 *Summary*

This appendix has been a relatively rapid introduction to OSGi. If you're new to OSGi, we hope it helps give you a grounding in the basics; if you're more experienced with OSGi, we hope it's shed light on some of the finer points of core OSGi that are important to getting the most out of enterprise OSGi. A full introduction to core OSGi is beyond the scope of the book, but many excellent resources are available if you're still keen to know more.

appendix B
The OSGi ecosystem

This appendix explains where OSGi came from, who owns it, and where it's going. It also gives an overview of the various OSGi specifications and how they relate to each other.

B.1 The OSGi Alliance

OSGi as a technology is *owned* by the OSGi Alliance, a nonprofit industry consortium funded by a large number of member companies. The OSGi Alliance is responsible for developing and releasing OSGi standards, as well as maintaining Compliance Test suites for the standards that they create. Importantly, the OSGi Alliance also ensures that reference implementations for the various standards are available under reasonably business-friendly software licenses, but typically it doesn't maintain them. The ongoing maintenance and development of OSGi specification implementations typically resides with the open source project or company that created them. Most OSGi standards have more than one implementation available.

The OSGi Alliance is organized into a number of different *Expert Groups*. An Expert Group consists of a number of OSGi experts from various OSGi Alliance member companies who are interested in particular applications of OSGi. These experts meet regularly to discuss bugs, new requirements, potential new specifications, and specification drafts. Of the several Expert Groups within the alliance, two are particularly relevant to enterprise OSGi developers. These are the Core Platform Expert Group (CPEG) and the Enterprise Expert Group (EEG).

THE CORE PLATFORM EXPERT GROUP

CPEG's purview is, unsurprisingly, the core OSGi platform. CPEG's role is to guide the growth of the OSGi framework, and it also provides a small level of oversight to the other Expert Groups. CPEG introduces comparatively few standards into the core, primarily because only broad use cases need support within the Core Specification, but also because there's a significant effort made to keep the core platform small.

Keeping the core platform small is important to OSGi because the core platform *must* be shared by all OSGi users, whether they're running an embedded system inside a car radio or on an enterprise production server with hundreds of gigabytes of memory.

THE ENTERPRISE EXPERT GROUP
The EEG is a comparatively new member of the OSGi Alliance, having only been set up in 2008, but as with most new standardization efforts, a lot happened quickly. Many of the technologies used in the examples in this book are OSGi Enterprise Specification standards, or are heavily based on them. EEG's focus is, as you would expect, enterprise-level technology. This means that EEG specifications typically focus on technologies that will be useful on hardware scales running from laptops to mainframes. Primary requirements for EEG specifications are typically qualities of service, data access, and remote communication. The Enterprise Expert Group also works toward making OSGi a more suitable container for large-scale applications.

B.2   OSGi specifications

Although we tend to talk about OSGi, there are several different OSGi specifications. Each one defines a range of services and technologies, although some chapters are duplicated across the various noncore specifications.

We've been discussing core OSGi, but OSGi is a big platform. In addition to the Core Specification, there are a number of other specifications, each defining a range of extra services and technologies. It's important to know about the various OSGi specifications to understand why there are lots of OSGi-related open source projects, each of which seems to provide a different set of features.

There are four OSGi specifications—the Core Specification, the Services Compendium, the Enterprise Specification, and the Mobile Specification. The relationship between the specifications is illustrated in figure B.1. The Compendium, Enterprise,

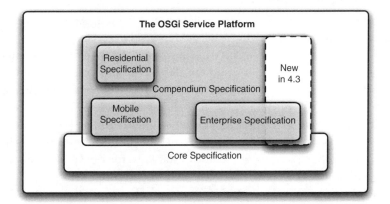

Figure B.1   The OSGI service platform includes a number of specifications. The Core Specification is the foundation on which the other specifications are built. The Compendium Specification defines a range of extra services. The Enterprise and Mobile Specifications are subsets of the standards defined in the Compendium Specification. Some elements of the Enterprise Specification were defined after the most recent version of the Compendium Specification and will be rolled back into the next version.

and Mobile Specifications all build on the Core Specification. These three specifications also have a lot of overlap in terms of their content.

B.2.1   *The Core Specification*

The Core Specification is the oldest and most important part of OSGi. The Core Specification defines the APIs for interacting with the framework, the structure of an OSGi bundle, and its manifest metadata. The module layer, lifecycle layer, service layer, and security layer are all defined by the OSGi core. Without these rules it would be impossible to build anything at all.

The Core Specification also defines a handful of value-added services. For example, there's a service that allows bundles to be started conditionally based on a *start level*, and a service that allows bundle wirings to be reflectively explored.

Because it's so fundamental, implementing the Core Specification is required for something to call itself an OSGi framework. It doesn't matter if you're running on a tiny embedded processor in a car entertainment system or on a gigantic supercomputer with terabytes of memory—if it's in there you have to do it to be compliant. As a result this means the Core Specification tends to change more slowly than some of the other specifications, and most importantly it has to stay small. New features are only added when it isn't possible to implement them any other way.

In this book, when we say that the framework does something, what we mean is "the OSGi Core Specification requires the framework to do *xxx*." This is likely to be the only interaction your application has with the Core Specification. Although in many senses the Core Specification is the most important of all the OSGi specifications, it isn't the main focus of this book. What we think is exciting is what you can do with the tools built on top of the Core Specification in the other specifications!

B.2.2   *The Compendium Specification*

The OSGi programming model is extremely service-oriented. Apart from the core framework, almost every OSGi feature is defined as a service. The Core Specification includes some particularly essential services, but there are many more services that would be useful. A large number of these are defined in the OSGi Service Compendium. The Compendium is an enormous document; at 732 pages, it's almost three times the size of the Core Specification. It includes services for almost everything, from preferences, to remote services, to configuration admin, to HTTP communication, to universal plug-and-play devices. It also includes some extensions to the OSGi programming model. For example, it includes a standard for Declarative Services, and an API for tracking services.

Unlike the Core Specification, which lays out a cohesive platform, the Compendium Specification is much more of an amalgamation of bits and pieces. It would be strange for an implementer to implement only part of the Core Specification, and there's a Technology Compatibility Kit (TCK) that verifies implementations comply with the entire Core Specification. Most implementations of the Core Specification (such as Equinox and Felix) also provide a JAR that includes Compendium interfaces. But not all of these interfaces have backing implementations. For example, the Log Service and HTTP Service are implemented by Felix and Equinox, and the Wire Admin Service is implemented by Equinox only. This can make understanding what's in the compendium and where to get implementations tricky.

We don't refer to the compendium too often in this book because it isn't within the scope of what we're discussing. This isn't to say that the compendium services aren't useful, but describing them is best left to books on core OSGi. Most of the things in the Compendium Specification that are useful to the enterprise are also reproduced in the Enterprise Specification.

B.2.3 *The Enterprise Specification*

Because it's so broad, the OSGi compendium doesn't stand on its own as a programming model. The Enterprise Specification was introduced to provide a much more coherent programming model for an enterprise audience. The Enterprise Specification is sometimes referred to as a profile, because it selects a subset of specifications. It also adds some new service definitions that aren't in the compendium to provide interoperability between Java EE standards and core OSGi.

Because the Enterprise Specification has a tighter focus than the compendium, it's much more natural for implementers to provide the whole of the specification. For example, Apache Aries and Eclipse Gemini are both specifically designed as enterprise OSGi implementations, and both implement almost the whole specification. But several of the other servers we described in chapter 13 only implement selected chapters of the Enterprise Specification.

Whereas the OSGi Enterprise Specification is based around enterprise grade services, the OSGi compendium focuses on tools, features, and containers that are useful for OSGi client runtimes. This does lead to some functional overlap between different services in the two specifications, such as the Http Service and Web Applications, or Declarative Services and Blueprint. The key point to remember is that the compendium is generally most useful for small-scale work, and the enterprise for large scale work. For example, the Http Service allows you to register servlets individually, but web applications can deploy hundreds or thousands of servlets at a time using metadata.

The main purpose of the Enterprise Specification is to provide application developers with access to enterprise services, the majority of which are already available in Java EE. One of the guiding rules of the OSGi Enterprise Specification is that where a enterprise service is already available in Java EE, the OSGi version of that service should be as similar as possible. This means that it should use the same API, have the same semantics, and be accessible in a similar way. This isn't always possible, but for the most part it is. In addition to maintaining the existing behavior of Java EE services, the Enterprise Specifications also try to make any enterprise service as OSGi-friendly as possible. One of the more common (and unsurprising) results of this is that OSGi-enabled enterprise services are usually available in the OSGi Service Registry, which allows them to be dynamically swapped at runtime.

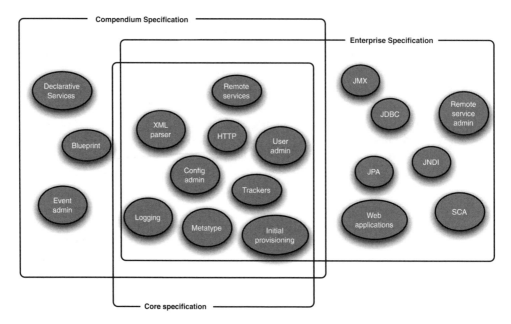

Figure B.2   How the OSGi Enterprise Specification overlaps with the Compendium and Core Specifications. Version 4.3 of the Compendium Specification should be a superset of version 4.2 of the Enterprise Specification.

Table B.1 and figure B.2 list the contents of the Enterprise Specification, and show the extent of the overlap with the Core and Compendium Specifications. At the time of writing, version 4.3 of the Core Specification, and versions 4.2 of the Compendium and Enterprise Specification were released. We expect version 4.3 of the Compendium Specification will also include all the new specifications introduced in version 4.2 of the Enterprise Specification. The focus of this book is these new specifications, rather than the entire contents of the Enterprise Specification.

Table B.1   The contents of the OSGi Enterprise Specification. Many of the capabilities of the Enterprise Specification are also included in the Compendium and Core Specifications. The first version of the Compendium Specification was version 4.0, and the first version of the Enterprise Specification was version 4.2.

Capability	Core Specification	Compendium Specification	Enterprise Specification	Chapter
Trackers	v2 and up	v4.1 and up	v4.2 and up	See *Osgi in Action*
Remote services	v4.3 and up	v4.2 and up	v4.2 and up	10
Remote service admin			v4.2 and up	10
Declarative Services		v4.2 and up	v4.2 and up	6
Blueprint container		v4.2 and up	v4.2 and up	2 and 6

Table B.1 The contents of the OSGi Enterprise Specification. Many of the capabilities of the Enterprise Specification are also included in the Compendium and Core Specifications. The first version of the Compendium Specification was version 4.0, and the first version of the Enterprise Specification was version 4.2. *(continued)*

Capability	Core Specification	Compendium Specification	Enterprise Specification	Chapter
HTTP service	v2 and up	v4.0 and up	v4.2 and up	See *Osgi in Action*
Web applications			v4.2 and up	2
JNDI service			v4.2 and up	2
JDBC service			v4.2 and up	3
JPA service			v4.2 and up	3
JTA transaction services			v4.2 and up	3
JMX management model			v4.2 and up	See *OSGi in Depth*
Log service	v2 and up	v4.0 and up	v4.2 and up	See *Osgi in Action*
Configuration admin	v2 and up	v4.0 and up	v4.2 and up	See *OSGi in Depth*
Metatype service	v2 and up	v4.0 and up	v4.2 and up	See *Osgi in Action*
User admin service	v3 and up	v4.0 and up	v4.2 and up	
Initial provisioning	v3 and up	v4.0 and up	v4.2 and up	
Event admin		v4.0 and up	v4.2 and up	See *OSGi in Depth*
SCA configuration type			v4.2 and up	10 and 11
XML parser service	v3 and up	v4.0 and up	v4.2 and up	

B.2.4 Other specifications

OSGi includes two other specifications, the Mobile Specification and the Residential Specification. Like the Enterprise Specification, the Mobile Specification is a convenient packaging of bits from the Compendium that are useful for mobile computing, along with some entirely new service definitions. The Mobile Specification on its own isn't useful for enterprise computing, and we don't cover it in this book. New in OSGi 4.3 is the Residential Specification, which is designed for devices like home stereo systems, thermostats, and washing machines.

B.3 OSGi—future frontiers

Where next for OSGi? After it makes its mark in the embedded world, the mobile world, and the enterprise, are there any industries left to conquer? Occasionally, discussions about using OSGi as a gaming platform can be heard, but it's not clear yet that the problems of the gaming industry line up so well with the solutions offered by OSGi. The bigger challenge for OSGi in the future might be its relationship to core Java.

B.3.1   *OSGi and Jigsaw*

OSGi has had a long relationship with the Java SE specification, but the relationship is slightly uneasy. The first flirtation with incorporating OSGi into Java SE goes all the way back to 1999, with JSR-8. This JSR was withdrawn and never made it into the Java specification. OSGi continued to gain popularity as an independent add-on to Java until the subject of Java modularity was re-introduced with JSR-277, "Java Module System." JSR-277 was followed by two more JSRs, JSR-291, "Dynamic Component Support for Java SE," and JSR-291, "Improved Modularity Support in the Java Programming Language." JSR-291 is based on the OSGi specification, and provides modularity as a layer that sits on top of core Java. JSR-277 and JSR-294, together known as Jigsaw, integrate modularity support into the architecture Java SE platform. The design of JSR-294 and JSR-277, and which release the implementation should be targeted for, has been subject to regular revision. After slipping from Java 7 to Java 8, it's currently slated for delivery with Java 9. The extent to which these new specifications should borrow ideas from OSGi or interoperate with OSGi is controversial. It does seem that neither Java 7's nor Java 8's baked-in modularity will be sufficient to satisfy the requirements currently satisfied by OSGi, and that OSGi won't be made obsolete by Jigsaw in the near future.

index

RELATED MANNING TITLES

OSGi in Action
Creating Modular Applications in Java
by Richard S. Hall, Karl Pauls, Stuart McCulloch,
    and David Savage

ISBN: 978-1-933988-91-7
576 pages, $49.99
April 2011

OSGi in Depth
by Alexandre de Castro Alves

ISBN: 978-1-935182-17-7
392 pages, $75.00
December 2011

Spring Dynamic Modules in Action
by Arnaud Cogoluègnes, Thierry Templier,
    and Andy Piper

ISBN: 978-1-935182-30-6
548 pages, $59.99
September 2010

Spring Integration in Action
by Mark Fisher, Jonas Partner, Marius Bogoevici,
    and Iwein Fuld

ISBN: 978-1-935182-43-6
368 pages, $49.99
September 2012

For ordering information go to www.manning.com

YOU MAY ALSO BE INTERESTED IN

Camel in Action
by Claus Ibsen and Jonathan Anstey

    ISBN: 978-1-935182-36-8
    552 pages, $49.99
    December 2010

Mule in Action
by David Dossot and John D'Emic

    ISBN: 978-1-933988-96-2
    432 pages, $44.99
    July 2009

RabbitMQ in Action
Distributed messaging for everyone
by Alvaro Videla and Jason J.W. Williams

    ISBN: 978-1-935182-97-9
    312 pages, $44.99
    April 2012

ActiveMQ in Action

by Bruce Snyder, Dejan Bosanac, and Rob Davies

    ISBN: 978-1-933988-94-8
    408 pages, $44.99
    March 2011